More praise for *Business and Society: A Critical Introduction*

'Goes beyond conventional accounts to critically expose the complex realities of the relationship between business and society. With clarity and originality, the authors illuminate the role of business for shaping society both in the past and present.'

Sara Gorgoni, University of Greenwich

'Offers a wide-ranging introductory interdisciplinary text for the study of the modern world. Rich in conceptual debate, it provides students with incisive analysis and criticism. This is the antidote to the anodyne business school textbook.'

Liam Campling, Queen Mary University of London

Business and society

A critical introduction

Kean Birch

and Mark Peacock, Richard Wellen, Caroline Shenaz Hossein,
Sonya Scott and Alberto Salazar

Zed Books
London

Business and Society: A critical introduction was first published in 2017
by Zed Books Ltd, The Foundry, 17 Oval Way, London SE11 5RR, UK.

www.zedbooks.net

Typeset in Arnhem and Kievit by Swales & Willis Ltd, Exeter, Devon
Index by Ed Emery
Cover design by Kika-Sroka Miller
Printed and bound by CPI Group (UK) Ltd, Croydon, CR0 4YY

A catalogue record for this book is available from the British Library.

ISBN 978-1-78360-449-4 hb
ISBN 978-1-78360-448-7 pb
ISBN 978-1-78360-450-0 pdf
ISBN 978-1-78360-451-7 epub
ISBN 978-1-78360-452-4 mobi

Contents

Tables and figures

Acknowledgements

We would like to thank a number of people. First, we would like to thank our colleagues and students, past and present, for their contributions and suggestions. We are especially thankful to our students over the years, who are the ones who inspired us to write this book in the first place. Second, we would like to thank Ken Barlow at Zed Books for his efforts over the last couple of years in keeping us on the straight and narrow. Third, we would like to thank the anonymous reviewers and reader for their suggestions and comments to improve the book; they have all contributed to its development. Finally, we thank our families for their forbearance and support during the writing of the book – without them, none of this would have been possible or worthwhile.

A note on authorship

Getting to the point of publication has been a complicated process for us, especially coordinating the work and input of six contributing authors to the book. Kean Birch coordinated the overall project and authored or co-authored a majority of the chapters, to which he has not added his name. The rest of the chapters were authored or co-authored by everyone else, and they have added their names to the relevant chapters. (In addition, J.J. McMurtry co-authored chapter 17 with Kean Birch.) Each chapter, however, has benefited from suggestions and written contributions by all of us on things like content, layout, case studies, definitions and so on. As such, this book has been a collaborative project to which we all contributed in a number of ways.

Kean Birch is an associate professor in the Business and Society programme at York University, Canada. His recent books include: *We Have Never Been Neoliberal* (2015); *The Handbook of Neoliberalism* (2016, co-edited with Simon Springer and Julie MacLeavy); and *Innovation, Regional Development and the Life Sciences: Beyond Clusters* (2016).

Caroline Shenaz Hossein is an assistant professor in the Business and Society programme in the Department of Social Science at York University, Canada. She is the author of *Politicized Microfinance: Money, Power and Violence in the Black Americas* (2016).

Mark Peacock is professor in the Business and Society programme at York University, Canada. His research interests include the philosophy of economics and the theory and origins of money. He recently published the book *Introducing Money* (2013).

Alberto Salazar is an assistant professor in the Department of Law and Legal Studies at Carleton University, Canada. His most recent publications appear in the *American Journal of Comparative Law* and *Osgoode Legal Studies Research Papers*.

Sonya Scott is a sessional assistant professor in the Business and Society programme at York University, Canada. She is the author of *Architectures of Economic Subjectivity: The Philosophical Foundations of the Subject in the History of Economic Thought* (2013).

Richard Wellen is an associate professor in the Business and Society programme at York University, Canada. His recent research deals with the political economy of higher education as well as transformations and alternatives in scholarly publishing markets. His books include *Making Policy in Turbulent Times: Challenges and Prospects for Higher Education* (2013, co-edited with Paul Axelrod, Theresa Shanahan and Roopa Deesai-Trilokekar).

Introduction: a critical introduction to business and society

Introduction

This book is about the relationship between **business** and **society**. As such it is concerned not only with how different business forms, practices and knowledges shape society *and* how different social forms, practices and knowledges shape business, but also with how this mutually constitutive relationship has changed over time. Contemporary capitalist societies, for example, are going through a profound shift in the way that businesses account for natural resource use and pollution (Jackson 2009). Specifically, capitalist societies have moved from treating the environment as a 'free' gift to incorporating pollution as an economic cost; this has happened alongside growing social awareness and action to address the implications of harmful environmental changes – we discuss this in more detail in Chapter 9. In this context, business and society cannot be isolated from one another in their treatment of environmental problems, since they are so entangled with one another that it makes no sense to posit a simple one-way causative relation (i.e. societal values forcing changes in business practice, or vice versa).

Definition: Business

The term business is a generic term we use to mean any organization that engages in for-profit activities, no matter how those profits are subsequently distributed. That means that business covers a range of organizations, including: public corporations (see below), private firms, partnerships, family firms, sole proprietorships, state-owned enterprises, worker co-operatives and consumer co-operatives.

Definition: Society

The term society is a generic term we use to mean a collective group of people who share a common set of social institutions (e.g. law, money, government, citizenship, language etc.), social norms (e.g. beliefs, conventions etc.) and geographical space (e.g. territory). We do not assume that societies are homogenous, static or consensual in that every society – every social group really – involves diversity, change and conflict.

Business plays a major role in our lives as many scholars have noted (e.g. Bakan 2004). Most of us are either employed by businesses or run our own businesses; most of us depend on businesses for the basic services and infra-structures we take for granted (e.g. phones, energy, mobility); almost all of us are reliant on businesses for our daily subsistence (e.g. food); and much besides. Many of us are excluded from the benefits of business (e.g. employ-ment, products and services etc.) as the result of societal prejudice and dis-crimination – an issue we address in Chapter 15. Outside of the economic sphere, businesses dominate public debate through lobbying and other influ-ences on politics (Birch 2007), discussed in Chapter 6; they dominate policy-making and regulation, discussed in Chapter 13; they dominate our cultural life through the production of art, film, music, games and so on (McChes-ney 2000); on top of this, the ubiquity of advertising, marketing and brand-ing means that business representations of themselves and of consumers no longer register on our consciousness (Ewen 1976).

It has got to a stage that business and society are largely inseparable; busi-ness is society, and society is business. It is hard to imagine a world in which private business does not exist, or does not dominate our lives in quite the same way it does today. And this domination has become a global issue, as we outline in Chapters 7, 8 and 9. However, a world without business as we currently know it did exist, so it is important to remember that private busi-ness and capitalism more generally are not 'natural' or even inevitable (see Chapters 1, 2 and 3). Moreover, there are alternatives, as we outline later in this book (see Chapters 16, 17 and 18).

In the rest of this introduction, we open with a discussion of the impor-tance of markets and of business to society reflecting a key debate in the social sciences – and elsewhere – on the rise of 'neoliberalism' (see below). We do so in order to raise a key question in the next section: why is business still impor-tant in society if markets supposedly reign supreme? We then finish by pre-senting our approach in this book to understanding the relationship between business and society.

The market triumphant?

Nowadays, it often seems like the 'free' market has won; it is presented as the solution to all sorts of social problems, from crime to climate change. We discuss the theoretical basis for these claims and the criticisms of them in Chapters 10, 11 and 12, especially the influential idea that **the market** leads to a social order that benefits everyone. Collective, political or social action, on the other hand, whether undertaken by governments or charities or inter-national organizations, has seemingly failed to deliver on the promises made to us of a better world. Instead, the market has become the *de facto* institu-tion for managing our societies. According to many critical scholars, activists and politicians, however, this has meant that our politics, societies and econo-mies are now dominated by something called neoliberalism, a concept they frequently use to describe a range of nefarious and egregious policies, ideas and behaviours ranging from corporate tax evasion through rising student debt to environmental deregulation. For an introduction to neoliberalism as a concept see the work of David Harvey (2005) and others (e.g. Crouch 2011; Mirowski 2013; Birch 2015a, 2015b).

Key concept: The market

Markets mean different things to different people. Mainstream economics textbooks, for example, frequently only provide a vague definition of markets (or 'the market') as a mechanism that brings together buyers and sellers who wish to exchange goods and services with one another. Generally speaking, these types of market are associated with the rise of capitalism from the fifteenth century onwards, although it is important to remember that every human society has had some form of market in order to exchange things. Modern capitalist markets, then, entail other characteristics, including: private property, contractual relations, competition between producers, prices determined by interactions between supply and demand, the use of money as the basis of exchange, and the compulsion people face to sell their labour for a wage in order to survive. Furthermore, the benefits of capitalist markets arise from their role as a determinant of prices, which often leads to the market being described as a price mechanism. Prices are supposed to provide people with information and incentives that promote the 'efficient' allocation and distribution of resources in society, especially by promoting specialization or the division of labour (e.g. each of us specializes in what we are good at and then trades with one another).

Source: Aldridge (2005)

In his book *A Brief History of Neoliberalism* the geographer David Harvey (2005) defines neoliberalism as the deliberate extension of markets as the main, if not only, institution to organize society and ourselves – see Chapter 10 for more on this view. Neoliberalism is based on an analytical perspective that emphasizes individual preferences, individual responsibility and individual choices – what many refer to as *homo economicus*, which we discuss in Chapter 11 – as the best and only way to understand human nature and human organization. This view of the world has become so dominant in countries like the USA, UK and Canada that it has become 'common sense'; for example, when we ask our students if humans are naturally or inherently selfish, most students say 'yes'. Instead, there is a need to unpack the role played by our personal relationships, our family lives, our cultural values, our religious or non-religious beliefs, our social institutions etc. because all these things complicate the notion of inherent self-interest or selfishness. It is important to remember that we can be selfish, we can be altruistic, we sacrifice for the greater good and so on, and often do so in complicated, inconsistent and often contradictory ways.

3

The triumph of the 'free' market – and we will explain those scare quotes around 'free' shortly – is manifested in many different ways. Here, we want to present the example of **free trade** treaties like the North American Free Trade Agreement (NAFTA) signed by the USA, Canada and Mexico, which came into force in 1994. More recent examples include the Trans-Pacific Partnership (TPP) and Transatlantic Trade and Investment Partnership (TTIP), which have yet to be implemented or negotiations finalized as of 2016 (see Sayer 2015). Supporters of these trade and investment agreements argue that they will promote trade by reducing trade tariffs (i.e. customs duty on imports and exports) and other non-tariff barriers to trade (e.g. country-specific product regulations), thereby promoting economic growth. However, critics point out that these outcomes are far from certain or likely to happen. One reason that these outcomes may not happen – and the reason we use scare quotes around 'free' – is that few people outside each country's negotiating team ever get to see copies of the draft agreements before they are formally signed. Consequently, it is difficult for citizens and subjects to review these sorts of treaty before they come into effect.

> **Definition: Free trade**
>
> Imports and exports can be taxed by national governments. Such tariffs, as they are called, can be imposed for different reasons. For example, tariffs have been used throughout history by various countries to support domestic producers against overseas competitors (e.g. the USA imposed tariffs on imports throughout the nineteenth century). Globalization advocates argue that tariffs restrict trade and, thereby, reduce economic efficiency by supporting inefficient producers; these advocates therefore argue that the world's economy would be better off without tariffs.

This lack of transparency is a problem because of the potential implications such treaties could have on things like access to medical and pharmaceutical treatments, a concern raised by organizations like Médecins sans Frontières (MSF).[1] In reference to the TPP agreement, for example, MSF has criticized changes to intellectual property rights (IPRs) – including patents, copyright etc. – which have been extended and strengthened, meaning that citizens will end up paying more for pharmaceutical drugs than before. Contradictorily, then, such 'free' trade agreements can actually reduce market competition as IPRs protect against competition (Sayer 2015). We return to these issues in Chapter 18. Since these agreements are made without public input or even review of the treaty process or its provisions, it is hard to see how markets are in and of themselves liberating, despite what some scholars have argued (e.g. Friedman 1962).

1 MSF Website: www.msf.ca/en/trans-pacific-partnership (accessed May 2016)

Whether or not the market is a liberating force is actually beside the point, however. If we examine the perspectives of market critics (e.g. Harvey 2005) or market supporters (e.g. Friedman 1962), both sides in this debate overlook, to a large extent, the place of business in our societies. While the market may represent an ideal to which many thinkers and politicians aspire, it is business that dominates everyday life – that is, it is an organizational entity and not the market mechanism that shapes our world. How we govern business, how we ensure that business is responsible and how we ensure that business does not dominate society are all important issues, and ones we address in this book – see Chapters 4, 5 and 6.

Why business and society?

Understanding the relationship between business and society is critical for understanding contemporary society. On the one hand, business is a major institution and organization in all our lives, although in different ways. Most people work for private businesses, frequently for large **(public) corporations**. According to Deakins and Freel (2012), for example, between 35 and 50 per cent of private employment in the USA, UK and Canada is in large enterprises, whether corporations or not. Moreover, across a number of countries in the Global North, small business represents a significant proportion of total private business entities and total private employment; such small enterprises are often individually-owned operations, family businesses and such like. Other people, fewer in number but growing, work for charitable, voluntary and community organizations, which often adopt private business practices and methods (e.g. accounting), or social economy organizations like co-operatives, mutual associations, credit unions and so on (Amin et al. 2002; Birch and Whittam 2012) – see Chapters 15 and 17. A final group of people work for the state, often in government bureaucracies (e.g. civil service) but also in state-owned business and arms-length corporations. Business is, in this sense, incredibly diverse, and it is too simplistic to equate business with a faceless, pathological corporation of popular opprobrium (e.g. Nace 2003; Bakan 2004).

On the other hand, business has had a rocky relationship with society throughout history; for example, business has been the frequent target of social critique and anti-business social movements for one reason or another. As the corporate revolution – which we discuss in Chapter 3 – matured in the USA, for example, the concentration of corporate holdings into larger and larger organizations led to significant resistance against monopolies like Standard Oil at the end of the nineteenth century. The political theorist Scott Bowman (1996) notes that this led to growing criticism of business corporations by scholars and thinkers of the time (e.g. Thorstein Veblen), as well as popular movements against corporate power. More recently, similar criticism has been directed at banks and other financial businesses after the 2007–2008

Key organization: The (public) corporation

In this book we use the term 'corporation' to mean a for-profit business that has a distinct ownership and governance structure. A corporation has shares – also called stocks – that are owned by investors (also called shareholders) who can trade those shares on a public stock market like the London Stock Exchange or New York Stock Exchange. These shares make up the equity investment in a corporation and provide investors with a claim on the value of the assets of the corporation and on the profits made by the corporation (called a dividend). The value of a share – or share price – is determined by the demand for it on the stock market; that is, the more demand there is for a share the higher the share price. Demand is usually driven by the expected future earning potential of a corporation, although there are numerous examples of share price bubbles throughout history. The total number of shares multiplied by individual share price equals the total market capitalization of a corporation, which is often used as a proxy for the total value of the corporation. Corporations are governed in particular ways as well, which we discuss in Chapter 4, and have particular legal and social responsibilities, which we cover in Chapter 5.

global financial crisis (van Staveren 2015), especially because many of these banks are deemed 'too-big-to-fail' (Birch 2015a) – for more on resistance and alternatives to corporate power, see Chapter 16.

In light of these issues, it is helpful to remember what institutional economists like Herbert Simon (1991) and Geoffrey Hodgson (2005) point out; namely, a significant proportion of economic activity takes place *within* business organizations and *not within* the market. So, whatever our attitude to business – whether positive or negative – we are still left with an important question: if markets are the dominant institution in society, how come business plays such an important, if not central, role in our societies and economies, both today and historically? According to many mainstream or orthodox economists, the existence of business simply reflects a situation in which economic activity is more efficiently organized collectively than through market transactions (e.g. Coase 1937; Jensen and Meckling 1976). However, returning to Hodgson (2005: 551), he points out that in order to understand business and the relationship between business and society we have to look at business as a 'historically specific entity that has arisen in a historically specific legal framework' – we cannot simply treat it as an analytical given – see Chapters 3. Capitalism, for example, has always involved some form of business organization, although this has often varied between countries (see Chapter 7); in fact, business organization, including the corporate form, actually emerged prior to capitalism in medieval societies (Barkan 2013). Consequently, it is more apt to argue that business underpins capitalism and capitalist markets, rather than reflects the failure of capitalist markets to function properly.

Our approach in this book

Throughout this book, we take a critical approach to the study of business. Our aim is to problematize the idea that business and business practices are wholly positive forces in society, in our lives. This approach and aim is underpinned by a commitment to political economy as a way to understand 'economic' life, although we do not think it is helpful to distinguish and separate the *political* from the *economic*, or both of these from the *social* for that matter. Our approach is framed by the view that economic, political and social matters are thoroughly entangled with one another, meaning that to understand business and the relationship between business and society entails understanding the economic, political *and* social aspects of that relationship. Consequently, it means (1) analysing the functioning of markets as a price mechanism (i.e. economic), as well as (2) analysing the historical origins and evolution of business forms and other institutions such as money (i.e. political) and (3) analysing the cultural and ethical values of people in different societies towards money and business, as well as the family, friendship, love etc.

Although our approach is framed by a concern with political economy, we do not come from one theoretical tradition or another; rather, we bring together a number of traditions in this book in order to present a range of alternatives to the mainstream, orthodox economic position that dominates much scholarly, political and social debate about business, the economy and society more generally. As such, we bring perspectives from critical political economy, institutional economics, human geography, sociology, political science, feminism, postcolonial studies and political ecology amongst others, all of which contributes to the pursuit of interdisciplinary social science. Despite our heterogeneity, though, our approach in this book is underpinned by several key analytical concepts. These can be summarized as follows:

- *Production and systems of value*: most social scientific traditions of political economy, outside of neoclassical economics at least, engage in one way or another with Karl Marx (1867 [1976]). While our perspective is not Marxist, it is strongly influenced by his critique of political economy and several key processes he highlighted. In this book, we take it as axiomatic that the economy is historically contingent, it is not 'natural' or 'inherent' – the market is not waiting for us to find it. Rather we organize it as we live it. Capitalism emerged as an economic system as the result of certain social processes, often violent and inhumane ones. In order to understand the relationship between business and society, then, we have to analyse how (economic) value is produced, how it is distributed, and how this production and distribution are legitimated as part of historically and geographically contingent *systems of value*. As such, this necessarily entails challenging dominant,

7

Western perspectives on the global development of capitalism and modernity (Amin 1977, 2013; Rodney 1982).

- *Politics, ethics and social values*: as we noted, the economy is not a distinct thing separate from the rest of our lives. All of our lives are bound up with the configuration of the economy, especially in the form of business, but also more broadly in seemingly non-economic activities. As many writers in the eighteenth-century Scottish Enlightenment noted, including Adam Smith (1759) in *The Theory of Moral Sentiments*, commerce and business are not neutral objects of enquiry; the same contention applies today as much as it did then. First, over the last half century a number of thinkers in the Global North have posited a transformation from industrial capitalism to a *knowledge-based* or *cognitive capitalism* (e.g. Boutang 2011). While these ideas have various bases in reality, they also represent visions of future society to which we can aspire. In this sense, the political, ethical and social values inherent in such visions function to legitimate certain policies and practices. Second, housework, childcare and other caring activities are ignored in many political-economic analyses because they are unwaged and, therefore, seen as uneconomic (Bezanson and Luxton 2006). Obviously, this does a massive disservice to the role women have (often) had in society. What these examples illustrate is that economies do not exist *outside* of human actions and decisions; instead, it is important to remember that we are the ones who *make* our economies and, hence, this is why they are so diverse (Roelvink et al. 2015).

- *Institutions and organizations*: perhaps the greatest conceptual influence on our book has come from the ideas of various institutional theorists, especially the work of Karl Polanyi (1944 [2001]). In particular, Polanyi's discussion of land, labour and money as *fictitious commodities* helps to ground our analyses of other social institutions (e.g. money, law, corporate governance etc.) as constituted by geographically-specific political, social and economic action and decisions – again, not natural givens. Aside from Polanyi, our perspective is also grounded in the work of thinkers on business organization; these include (old) institutional economists like Thorstein Veblen and more recent ones like Geoffrey Hodgson (2005), as well economic sociologists and others who work on organizational theory (e.g. Fligstein 1990; Simon 1991; Roy 1997). An important part of this is acknowledging and analysing the importance of non-conventional economic systems and organizations, including the *social economy* (Amin et al. 2002) and *informal economy* (Hann and Hart 2011).

- *Constitutive discourse*: a final conceptual angle is the notion that knowledge and knowledge claims (or *discourse*) are constitutive of the world, although this position is tempered by the need to relate discourse to the socio-material system. Drawing on work in postmodernism, anthropology, cultural

8

political economy, and science and technology studies (e.g. Gibson-Graham 1996; Callon 1998; Muniesa 2014), we stress the need to take ideas seriously, especially as they relate to claims about the economy. Neoclassical economics, for example, is powerful not because it *represents* the world accurately, but because it is *performed* by many powerful social actors.

As the discussion of these key concepts illustrates, how we analyse and represent the economy matters in an everyday context. A final example might help demonstrate what we mean here. As we mentioned previously, the idea that people are selfish is often treated as a 'common sense' assumption. However, the notion of individual ownership of private property as we currently understand it – which represents the pursuit of personal self-interest – is not inherent to our lives. Private property is not a natural desire born of selfishness, nor is it a natural right; rather, it is a cause and effect of the specific political-economic system in which we live, capitalism. If we take a critical look at ownership and property rights – which we do in Chapter 18 – we can identify (a) what types and forms dominate, (b) their relation to broader socio-political contexts, and (c) the underpinning ethical and moral discourses that legitimate their current structure – issues we address in Chapter 14. On the last point, for example, a number of radical thinkers, especially anarchists and socialists, have argued that private property is by definition the same thing as theft; or, more succinctly, **'property is theft'**. They make this claim based on the argument that any form of individual, private ownership of something – e.g. land, commodities, knowledge etc. – necessarily leads to the exclusion of others from its common use, thereby inhibiting any further adaption or changes except by the owners. Meanwhile, owners benefit from the collective investment in the property made over many generations. It is such questions that motivate our arguments in the rest of the book.

Key concept: 'Property is theft'

There is a famous aphorism coined by Pierre-Joseph Proudhon, an anarchist from the early nineteenth century, in which he stated that 'property is theft'. What he meant by this was that all things in all societies are, inherently, the products of that whole society, all of its peoples, throughout its history, in its socio-economic context etc., and *not* the products of individual people working alone. Consequently, any claims to private property by an individual are claims to expropriate (i.e. take) the something that is the product of everyone's work, now and in the past. In that sense, private property is a theft.

Source: Frase (2013)

Bibliography

Aldridge, A. (2005) *The Market*, Cambridge, Polity Press.

Amin, A., Cameron, A. and Hudson, R. (2002) *Placing the Social Economy*, London, Routledge.

Amin, S. (1977) *Imperialism and Unequal Development*, New York, Monthly Review Press.

Amin, S. (2013) *The Implosion of Capitalism*, New York, Monthly Review Press.

Bakan, J. (2004) *The Corporation*, London, Random House.

Barkan, J. (2013) *Corporate Sovereignty*, Minneapolis, University of Minnesota Press.

Bezanson, K. and Luxton, M. (2006) *Social Reproduction: Feminist Political Economy Challenges Neo-Liberalism*, Montreal, McGill-Queen's University Press.

Birch, K. (2007) 'The totalitarian corporation?', *Totalitarian Movements and Political Religions*, Vol.8, pp.153–161.

Birch, K. (2015a) *We Have Never Been Neoliberal: A Manifesto for a Doomed Youth*, Winchester, Zero Books.

Birch, K. (2015b) 'Neoliberalism: The whys and wherefores ... and future directions', *Sociology Compass*, Vol.9, pp.571–584.

Birch, K. and Whittam, G. (2012) 'Social entrepreneurship', in D. Deakins and M. Freel, *Entrepreneurship and Small Firms* (6th Edition), London, McGraw Hill, pp.105–123.

Boutang, J.-M. (2011) *Cognitive Capitalism*, Cambridge, Polity Press.

Bowman, S. (1996) *The Modern Corporation and American Political Thought*, College Park, Pennsylvania State University Press.

Callon, M. (ed.) (1998) *The Laws on the Markets*, Oxford, Blackwell Publishers.

Coase, R. (1937) 'The nature of the firm', *Economica*, Vol.4, pp.386–405.

Crouch, C. (2011) *The Strange Non-death of Neoliberalism*, Cambridge, Polity Press.

Deakins, D. and Freel, M. (2012) *Entrepreneurship and Small Firms* (6th Edition), London, McGraw Hill.

Ewen, S. (1976) *Captains of Consciousness*, New York, Basic Books.

Fligstein, N. (1990) *The Transformation of Corporate Control*, Cambridge MA, Harvard University Press.

Frase, P. (2013) 'Property and theft', *Jacobin* (September): www.jacobinmag.com/2013/09/property-and-theft/ (accessed May 2015).

Friedman, M. (1962) *Capitalism and Freedom*, Chicago, University of Chicago Press.

Gibson-Graham, J.K. (1996) *The End of Capitalism (As We Knew It): A Feminist Critique of Political Economy*, Oxford, Blackwell Publishers.

Hann, C. and Hart, K. (eds) (2011) *Markets and Society: The Great Transformation Today*, Cambridge, Cambridge University Press.

Harvey, D. (2005) *A Brief History of Neoliberalism*, Oxford, Oxford University Press.

Hodgson, G. (2005) 'Knowledge at work: Some neoliberal anachronisms', *Review of Social Economy*, Vol.63, pp.547–565.

Jackson, T. (2009) *Prosperity without Growth*, London, Earthscan.

Jensen M. and Meckling, W. (1976) 'Theory of the firm: Managerial behavior, agency costs and ownership structure', *Journal of Financial Economics*, Vol.3, pp.305–360.

McChesney, R. (2000) *Rich Media, Poor Democracy*, New York, The New Press.

Marx, K. (1867 [1976]) *Capital: Volume 1*, London, Penguin.

Mirowski, P. (2013) *Never Let a Serious Crisis Go to Waste*, London, Verso.

Muniesa, F. (2014) *The Provoked Economy*, London, Routledge.

Nace, T. (2003) *Gangs of America*, San Francisco, Berrett-Koehler.

Polanyi, K. (1944 [2001]) *The Great Transformation*, Boston, Beacon Press.

Rodney, W. (1982) *How Europe Underdeveloped Africa*, Washington DC, Howard University Press.

Roelvink, G., St. Martin, K. and Gibson-Graham, J.-K. (eds) (2015) *Making Other Worlds Possible*, Minneapolis, University of Minnesota Press.

Roy, W. (1997) *Socializing Capital*, Princeton, Princeton University Press.

Sayer, A. (2015) *Why We Can't Afford the Rich*, Bristol, Policy Press.

Simon, H. (1991) 'Organizations and markets', *Journal of Economic Perspectives*, Vol.5, pp.25–44.

Smith, A. (1759 [1976]) *The Theory of Moral Sentiments*, Oxford, Oxford University Press.

Van Staveren, I. (2015) *Economics after the Crisis*, London, Routledge.

1 | The emergence of capitalism in Western Europe

Mark Peacock

Introduction

Today our lives are dominated by capitalism as the economic organizing system for our societies and the global economy. However, capitalism has not always existed, which raises the questions of how, where and why capitalism emerged.

There are many approaches to explaining the development of capitalism. Mainstream approaches see the evolution of capitalism as a 'natural' process, whereby the apparently natural desire of human beings for wealth and money is allowed to flourish freely, something which results in the creation of capitalist markets as the main mechanism of economic exchange (see Wood 2002 for a critical analysis of these mainstream claims).

In the eighteenth century, **Adam Smith** (1776 [1976]: I.ii.1) wrote of a 'propensity in human nature ... to truck, barter, and exchange one thing for another', by which he meant that, if left unhindered, humans would instinctively enter into market exchanges with one another. This has led some historians, like Henri Pirenne (1956), to look for the origins of capitalism in urban centres of trade in medieval Europe, in cities such as Florence, Venice and Milan. Mainstream approaches account for the absence of capitalism through the existence of restrictions or restraints on commerce imposed by rulers. Without these restrictions, according to mainstream approaches, capitalism would have developed earlier, but restrictions on commerce prevented its emergence.

Key thinker: Adam Smith

Adam Smith (1723–1790) was Professor of Moral Philosophy at the University of Glasgow. His most famous work, *The Wealth of Nations* (1776), is often used as a defence of capitalism which was emerging in Britain in the eighteenth century. The book includes the key notion that humans are, by nature, selfish, an idea which has had a lasting impact on economics as a discipline (see Chapter 11 of this volume). In his *The Theory of Moral Sentiments* (1759), however, Smith developed a more nuanced and sophisticated view of human nature and of the moral concerns which occupy human beings. In this book, Smith expressed the idea that humans are not merely selfish but are capable of sentiments such as sympathy of justice.

Mainstream approaches leave important questions unanswered which are addressed by alternative accounts of the development of capitalism. This chapter presents two such alternative accounts: one is a Marxist perspective, the other a Weberian one. They are non-mainstream because neither sees anything natural, let alone, inevitable, about the development of capitalism. Instead, both theories see capitalism unfolding only after major social upheavals.

Key discussion questions

- What is feudalism?
- What were the enclosures?
- In capitalist society, workers are propertyless. What does this mean and what are the implications for workers' freedom?
- What significance does Protestant religious doctrine have in Max Weber's accounts of the origins of modern capitalism?
- What does Weber mean by economic traditionalism?
- Name a key difference in Marx's and Weber's approaches to explain historical change.

Marxist approaches

Marxist perspectives draw on the work of the nineteenth-century thinker **Karl Marx**. They are characterized by the contention that *social classes* are the key agents of historical change because different social classes have conflicting or antagonistic interests. The conflict between classes gives rise to *class struggle* as a driving force in historical change. To understand the emergence of capitalism from a Marxist perspective, we must first understand **feudalism** in England, the country in which capitalism first developed. It is important to note that feudalism varied greatly at different times and places in Europe. What follows is a generalized account of feudalism in England which does not necessarily apply to other parts of Europe.

Key thinker: Karl Marx

Karl Marx (1818–1883) was a German activist and one of the most influential thinkers of the modern world. He spent much of his life in British exile, having been expelled from his native Germany, and his ideas were fundamental to the formation of the international communist movement. His three-volume work *Das Kapital* provides a monumental diagnosis of the capitalist mode of production.

In feudal society, the majority of the population were peasants who lived on a lord's manor. The lord possessed the title to land and peasants were required to work for the lord. The land cultivated for the lord's use was called the *demesne* which could be one continuous tract of land or be divided into fields (strips). Peasants lived in cottages located in a hamlet or village located on the demesne. They, too, had access to land, in the form of strips – fewer in number and perhaps of lesser quality than the lord's – which they cultivated for their subsistence needs. Most peasants were unfree (*villeins* or *serfs*); their serf status came with various obligations to the lord which we associate with *serfdom*. Serfdom defines the relationship between the two central classes in feudal society: landlords and peasants.

Serfs had to work on the lord's land for a certain number of days per week. The number of days varied from manor to manor and was fixed by custom. These labour services were sometimes commuted into money payments, but whichever form they took, these obligations were a source of enrichment for the lord. Lords appropriated wealth from serfs, with as much as half the value of a peasant family's annual harvest going to the lord (Postan 1971: 603). Although they were subject to the lord's impositions, peasants did enjoy *customary rights*, for example, they could use common land to graze their animals (Neeson 1993).

Not all peasants were serfs. Some were *free*: like serfs, free peasants possessed land but were not subject to the levies of the lord. Whether free or serfs, peasants who did not own sufficient land to subsist on their own produce worked as wage labourers either on the lord's demesne or for wealthier peasants, who themselves had holdings of land. Perhaps half of peasants had to supplement their own cultivation through wage labour, especially when feudal obligations were commuted from labour services to money payments, for monetary payments to lords presupposed that peasants acquired money, either through selling their agricultural produce or their labour time in exchange for cash (Postan 1971).

The contentious relationship between lords and peasants gave rise to class conflict about the appropriation of the peasants' product – who got how much. Those peasants who possessed enough land could attain a high degree of *self-sufficiency*; they were neither dependent on their lord for survival, nor did they have to work for wages because they produced most of the goods (mainly food) that they consumed. Lords were parasitic; their exactions contributed nothing to agricultural output. Lords' interventions in peasants' lives were thinly disguised attempts to appropriate as much as they could from peasants. Some peasants fled from one lord to seek tenancy with another, although such attempts were not technically legal because they were not legally free to relocate. Unsurprisingly, medieval history is punctuated by episodes of peasant resistance or full-scale 'revolt' against landlords, e.g. the Peasants' Revolt of 1381.

Now that we have an idea of feudal society, let us trace some English history from the fourteenth to the eighteenth centuries. After the Black Death of 1348, which, in England, claimed one-third to a half of the population, lords acquired vacant lands. Serfs could not bequeath land to their heirs without the lord's permission, so, upon the death of a serf, the lord could claim the land. Lords rented their newly acquired lands to those able to pay what the market would bear; and as population increased, demand for land and rents rose. Renting land became a lucrative option for lords who rented larger parcels of land to each tenant, thus increasing the size of farms (Brenner 1976, 1985). The development of a market for land meant that peasant tenants had to compete for land at the market rate. This led to measures which raised the productivity of farming; for those tenant farmers who were the most productive could afford to pay the highest rents (Brenner 1985: 301). As agricultural efficiency rose, the need for agricultural labourers declined. These developments provided the context of a process known as *enclosure*, to which we now turn (see Marx 1867: Chapters 26–28).

Enclosure involved the privatization of manorial land. It refers to the *enclosing* of land by landlords who erected fences around land previously accessible to peasants. This spelled the beginning of the end of the so-called 'open field system' of agriculture, as peasants were denied access to their farming strips and to common land. Peasants' means of survival was thus under threat as their customary rights were removed. Enclosure was an attempt to dispossess peasants of land, and it did not go uncontested – see Chapter 16. But by the end of the seventeenth century, England's lords had laid claim to three-quarters of the country's agricultural land (Brenner 1976).

The lords' aim in enclosing land was often to convert it to pasture, usually sheep farming. Supporters of enclosure argued that enclosure would end the independence peasants enjoyed by virtue of possessing land (Neeson 1993: 34). Without access to land, peasants became less self-sufficient and increasingly reliant on wage labour which was needed for commercial farming. Enclosure is therefore associated with the creation of a class of people whose survival depends on their ability to find work. But the transition from a country of peasants, who were relatively independent of the need to work for a wage, to a country of workers, who had no option but to seek wage labour if they were to survive, was not smooth. The immediate effect of enclosure was the creation of a mass of people who possessed no land. These people were faced with a choice between working for a wage or dying. Two opportunities for earning wages presented themselves: (1) labouring on farms in the countryside or (2) working in craft or manufacturing in urban centres. But dispossessed peasants were not free to choose between these options. In England, legislation restricted peasants' freedom and hindered the creation of a labour market.

Before we review this legislation, note that enclosure engendered a law and order problem. First, peasants resisted enclosure, for many saw their survival under attack. Peasant 'enclosure riots' became common from the sixteenth century, despite being outlawed (Manning 1988). Peasants who were unsuccessful in stopping the enclosure of land and who did not find work as farm labourers were left with the option of finding work in towns and cities. This caused a second threat to law and order, to which we now turn.

Unable to find sufficient work, migrants who left the countryside for towns resorted to begging or thievery. Such people were known as 'masterless men' because they were without employment and thus without oversight by a lord or master who might keep them in order. Legislators reacted to the hoard of masterless men with 'vagrancy laws' (a 'vagrant' being a person without dwelling or job). These laws varied 'from the savage to the merely repressive' (Manning 1988: 159): whipping, branding, mutilation and hanging were amongst the punishments for vagrants (Marx 1867: chapter 28). Vagrancy made legislators aware of a more encompassing problem: the poor. The problem of the poor concerned not only their swelling numbers but also the question of what to do with them. *Poor Laws* were conceived to address this problem. A poor person ('pauper') was assigned to the parish in which he or she was born and would become part of the 'sedentary poor' and thus a recipient of poor relief financed by local taxes. Vagrants received no relief. If they did not work or could find none, they were considered criminals, but being 'able bodied', they were expected to work (Beier 1985: 9). Indeed, they could be forced to work under Elizabethan legislation known as the *Statute of Artificers* of 1563.

The *Statute of Artificers* regulated the employment of labour. Under the Statute, the unemployed could be compelled to work in certain trades or in farming at wages set by local magistrates. It was an offence under the *Statute of Artificers* to quit one's job and leave the place in which one lived without permission of the local authorities (Beier 2008; Tawney 1914). The Statute thus hindered the development of a national labour market in England because it denied three freedoms:

- freedom to decide where to work
- freedom to quit one's job
- freedom of employers and employees to negotiate wages.

16

This was an era of wage-labour without a labour market (Beier 2008), and the absence of the above three freedoms slowed the development of capitalism. It was not until the 1830s that these restrictions to the formation of a labour market were removed (Polanyi 1944 [2001]).

The above account of the rise of capitalism is a Marxist account because it focuses on social classes and their struggles as factors driving historical change. Note that the class which Marx associates most strongly with capitalism – the capitalist class or 'bourgeoisie' – was not the driving force in the creation of capitalism. Though there existed a merchant or commercial class, particularly in English urban centres like London, the transition to capitalism was initiated in the countryside and its main driver was the class of landlords. Some of these lords became capitalist farmers in the process, just as some peasants became tenants of those lords and ran their increasingly large plots of land as commercial farms. It was through the clash of lords' and peasants' interests that capitalism and the classes of capitalists and workers came into existence. Table 1.1 summarizes the key features of feudalism and capitalism according to Marxist perspectives.

TABLE 1.1 Comparison of feudalism and capitalism

	Feudalism	Capitalism
'Ruling' class	Landlords	Capitalists
Subordinate class	Peasants	Workers
Status of subordinate class	Unfree (serfs)	Free and (legally) equal
Relationship of subordinate class to means of production	Customary, direct access to land	Propertyless (no ownership of means of production)

The class divide in feudal society is between peasants and lords. In capitalist society, it is between capitalists (those who own the means of production) and workers. In order better to understand the class dynamic involved, it is helpful to contrast the two subordinate classes – serfs in feudalism, workers in capitalism. Feudal serfs were unfree; they were not allowed simply to throw off their obligations to lords; insubordination from peasants could be answered by lords using military or legal power. On the other hand, peasants had direct access to the means of production – they could use land through which they could provide themselves with the means of subsistence; in theory, they could survive independently of lords. For workers in capitalist society, it is the other way around. Workers are free: they may choose which job to pursue and may quit their job if they wish. Unlike feudal serfs who, by their very status as serfs had obligations towards the ruling class of lords, workers have no obligations to the ruling class of capitalists by virtue of being a worker. Therein lies workers' freedom. The only way workers can acquire obligations toward a capitalist is by accepting a job – the capitalist cannot compel the worker to work without the worker's consent. On the other hand, workers in capitalist society are propertyless; they have no access to means of production with which to produce the means of subsistence. Only capitalists own the means of production, and workers are dependent on them for work. Unlike feudal serfs who possessed land, workers in capitalist society cannot produce anything unless they are given access to the means of production by a capitalist.

This sheds a different light onto workers' freedom. In the previous paragraph, it appeared that workers were advantaged *vis-à-vis* feudal serfs because they are free. Only if they want to work, do workers have to work; they are free to choose whether or not to work. Feudal serfs had no such freedom to choose whether to work for a lord. But for workers in capitalist society, the choice between working and not working is really a choice between earning the means to survive and starving, for if a worker does not work, she cannot produce anything from which to live by virtue of being propertyless. For this reason, the capitalist does not have to force or coerce workers into accepting a job; workers who do not work for a capitalist will simply die. It is therefore from *economic necessity* that workers sell themselves on the labour market; and it is their lack of ownership of the means of production which compels them to work for a capitalist.

Marx (1867: 874) expressed this point by noting that workers in capitalist societies are 'free' in a 'double sense': (1) workers in capitalist society are free to seek whatever work they wish and they owe nobody anything by virtue of their status; only by entering a work contract of their own free will can workers oblige themselves to work for a capitalist, and workers are even free not to work if they choose not to do so; (2) workers are also free in a second sense, free, that is, from ownership of 'any means of production of their own'; workers, that is, are 'unencumbered' by means of production; they own nothing except themselves. This 'unencumberedness' makes the freedom in the first sense hollow: workers are formally free in the sense that nobody can compel them to work. But in reality, the choice whether or not to work is a choice between staying alive and dying – not much of a choice at all.

The history of the transition from feudalism to capitalism in England which we have traced in this chapter is the history of the expropriation of the 'immediate producers' (Marx 1867: 875). The immediate producers began this transition as peasants who lived off the land and had access to the means of production. They ended it as propertyless workers with one survival option – wage labour. This history, Marx writes, 'is written in the annals of mankind in letters of blood and fire'. This was not a history many peasants would have chosen, had they known what lay at the end of it, yet it is a history that has determined the fate of most of the world's population who became property-less workers.

Max Weber and the Protestant ethic

We now turn to a contrasting perspective on the emergence of capitalism, one associated with the German economist and sociologist **Max Weber**. According to Weber, *modern* capitalism, as we know it and as Weber knew it in the early twentieth century, has not always existed. Throughout history, Weber argued, in epochs which pre-date modern capitalism, types of behaviour also found in the modern capitalist world are not uncommon. These types of behaviour include profiteering, greed, acquisition (Weber 1920: 20–21). Such behaviour, be it amongst Chinese mandarins or Roman aristocrats, is bound by a 'frame of mind' alien to modern capitalism. Weber calls this pre-capitalist frame of mind 'economic traditionalism' (p.22). He illustrates this frame of mind by examining 'traditionalist' attitudes amongst labourers and business people.

Key thinker: Max Weber

Max Weber (1864–1920) was a German scholar whose ideas are often presented in contrast with those of Marx. He is known for his pessimistic diagnosis of modern life in which, he thought, individuals were trapped in a dull, impersonal and bureaucratized existence which stultified human freedom. His *Protestant Ethic and the Spirit of Capitalism* (first published 1904–1905) is still widely debated.

First, consider agricultural labourers who are paid 'piece rates', i.e. a wage rate for each unit of crop harvested. At harvest, if landowners wish to increase the productivity of labourers in order to get crops harvested promptly, they could increase labourers' wage rate. Landowners would do this in the hope that labourers would increase their hours of work rather than reduce them. Instead of working the usual 20 hours at $20 per hour (and earning $400 per month), labourers could work 60 hours and, at the increased wage rate of $40, they would each earn $2400 – as much as they would usually earn in six months. However, workers who have a traditionalist frame of mind, Weber tells us, will work less when the wage-rate increases. Why? Instead of asking: 'If I produce as much as possible [at the higher wage], how much money will I earn each day?', the traditionalist labourer asks: 'How long must I work in order to earn the [same] amount ... I have earned until now and that has fulfilled my *traditional* economic needs?' (pp.22–23).

Traditionalist workers are uninterested in increasing their income and improving their standard of living because they have become accustomed to a given standard of living. They see no need to increase this standard, especially if they have to exert themselves to do so. Weber thus concludes that '[p]eople do not wish "by nature" to earn more and more money' (p.23); they are not naturally acquisitive.

A traditionalist frame of mind also affects the way in which businesspeople conduct their affairs. Weber recalls a time when business owners had an 'easygoing' life, working 'perhaps five or six hours a day and occasionally considerably less' (p.28). Competition existed amongst businesses but was not fierce. 'There was time for long daily visits to the taverns, early evening drinks, and long talks with a circle of friends. A comfortable tempo of life was the order of the day' (p.28). This is a far cry from the more ruthless form of business we know today. So how did we get from the world of economic traditionalism to modern capitalism? Something 'upset' the 'ease and comfort' of traditionalist business life.

Those with a traditionalist frame of mind lack the '*spirit of* (modern) *capitalism*' (p.27). To exemplify this 'spirit', Weber (pp.14–15) quotes the American politician, inventor and entrepreneur, Benjamin Franklin (1706–1790) who issues advice on the acquisition of money. Franklin extols the virtues of thriftiness and industriousness and instructs people to save, for squandering money not only represents a loss of the principal but also of the interest one could have earned by saving money one spends. Buying on credit is bad, for one pays interest on loans and thus loses this amount. Wasting time is also bad, for idleness represents a loss of money one could have earned had one not been idle.

Franklin, argued Weber, proposes that the increase of personal wealth is a *duty*. Franklin was not describing what one should do if one happens to have a taste for becoming rich and living an extravagant lifestyle; rather, acquiring money is an 'end in itself' (pp.16–17). In fact, Franklin advised his readers to *reduce* expenditure on goods at any opportunity and to save instead. Striving to make money and yet more money becomes a moral duty to be carried out through the single-minded pursuit of a task – as a worker or a business owner – which Weber called a (vocational) 'calling'. This is the spirit of modern capitalism and it has, Weber contends, not existed prior to the modern epoch.

The spirit of modern capitalism is a frame of mind 'that strives systematically and rationally *in a calling* for legitimate profit' (p.27). Three features of this characterization are noteworthy. First, striving for profit is 'systematic' and 'rational'; it becomes the central organizing principle in one's life, and it is a rational pursuit, which one plans and calculates meticulously. Second, profit is pursued in a calling, a single economic activity towards which one directs one's efforts methodically. Third, one strives for legitimate profit; making money is to be done in an honest way. Who was responsible for introducing this frame of mind to business?

Weber gives us hints about the source of this spirit both in the title of his book and with the religiously connoted word calling. A calling is one's

God-given task, or one's place in the social division of labour (i.e. whether one is a carpenter, tanner, sheep farmer etc.) (pp.39, 107). Calling is a biblical concept, but the idea of one's calling becomes especially significant during the Reformation in Europe, in which Protestant reformers, such as Martin Luther (1483–1546), criticized Catholicism and paved the way for Protestantism. For Luther, the pursuit of one's calling was 'the highest expression that moral activity could assume' (p.39). Prior to this, pursuit of work was deemed ungodly; Christianity in its pre-Protestant forms is exemplified by monks who withdraw from the world and shun what Weber called 'this-worldly work', i.e. work as an activity in the world outside of a religious institution like a monastery (p.40). With Protestantism, one's profession or job acquired religious significance (p.41). This doctrine was radicalized by John Calvin (1509–1564).

Calvin preached the doctrine of predestination, which teaches that, prior to one's birth, God determines each individual's fate in the afterlife: we are either destined for salvation in heaven or doomed to eternal death in hell. God's decision about our fate is unalterable. Worse still, nobody knows whether she belongs to the chosen few destined for heaven of whether she will be damned (pp.55–59). This leads, Weber tells us, to an *Angst*-ridden life for Protestants, who constantly ask themselves whether they have been 'elected' by God to go to heaven after their death (p.64). To assuage their fear, Protestants were advised by religious leaders to work tirelessly in a calling, for this was 'the best possible means to *acquire* the self-confidence that one belonged among the elect' (p.66). Success in one's worldly calling was not a means of *acquiring* salvation but it was an *indication* that one stood in God's favour. The pursuit of one's calling had a second role, for it was through this pursuit that people achieved 'good works' which increased the glory of God on earth. God, as Calvin understood Him, did not require merely sporadic good works but continual striving after such works; the only way to honour God was through the systematic pursuit of one's calling (pp.70–71).

Success in one's calling led to the amassing of wealth, and it was also a much-wanted sign of God's blessing. This posed a problem for Protestants, for their religion forbade the consumption of luxuries and frowned on a life of comfort and extravagance. Hence, the Protestant was expected to strive methodically in his calling, and, if successful, he would become wealthy, but he was not allowed to consume this wealth; his life was to be *ascetic* (pp.115–116). Instead of consuming their wealth, they reinvested it in their business in the hope that they would meet with further business success which would strengthen the sign of their posthumous salvation.

Protestantism therefore ushered in a new attitude to making and using money. Previously, Christianity had frowned on wealth because it led to a life of luxury which was anathema to honouring God. The ascetic monk had been the highest symbol of piety prior to Protestantism. Protestantism, however, 'shatter[ed] the bonds restricting all striving for gain' and conferred legitimacy on the accumulation of wealth (as long as it was done honestly). It simultaneously proscribed the use of wealth for the purpose of living luxuriously (p.115). The result of the duty to accumulate wealth in one's calling and the prohibition of consuming one's wealth on luxuries led to '*the formation of capital* through *asceticism's compulsive saving*' (pp.117, 29). This is precisely the behaviour one requires of a capitalist whose business is to thrive and persist. There thus arose a new business ethic amongst Protestants: the businessperson felt empowered to pursue economic gain in their calling, whilst Protestant workers 'attached themselves to their work' with a zeal which removed the hindrances to increased labour productivity once posed by economic traditionalism (p.120).

The changes which Protestantism brought about date to the sixteenth century, but what does it have to do with our lives today? We do not associate success in business with people who are deeply religious. Weber notes that, at the start of the twentieth century, businesspeople were already 'indifferent, if not openly hostile, to religion' (p.31). So if his thesis about Protestant influence on the development of capitalism is correct, Weber must explain a transition from an early phase of modern capitalism, in which the growth of enterprise was driven by Protestants for religious reasons, to a subsequent stage, in which religion plays little or no part in the motives of businesspeople.

To understand this transition, consider a small town in which a few Protestants, imbued with the capitalist spirit, had set up business. Other businesspeople still adopted the easygoing rhythms of economic traditionalism. Which businesses survived market competition? Obviously, Protestant-run businesses that employed Protestant workers had an advantage because of their rigorous work ethic. Other businesspeople would have had a choice between keeping up with the Protestant businesses (by adopting a similar work ethic) or going out of business (p.29). In this way, a new business ethic spread to non-Protestant communities. To compete with Protestant businesses, non-Protestants had to adopt an ethic of hard work and single-minded dedication. With regard to contemporary businesspeople, Weber writes the Protestant '*wanted* to be a person with a vocational calling; today we *are forced* to be' (p.123). Today, if one wishes to pursue business, one has to adopt an ethic like that of Weber's early Protestants if one is to succeed. Similarly, if one seeks a job, one must adopt an ethic of hard work, reliability, loyalty to one's employer etc., for if one lacks this ethic, one will be fired. Few of us nowadays adopt this ethic for religious reasons; rather we have no choice but to adopt the ethic of hard work from necessity. The alternative is bankruptcy or unemployment.

Contemporary society, having become secularized, has also shed its disapproval of luxury and consumption. Today, few frown on those who amass fortunes and spend them on holiday homes, yachts and private jets. Consumerism has triumphed over asceticism, and over 100 years ago, when Weber

22

(p.124) was writing, the acquisition of material goods was no longer frowned upon. Modern capitalism thus survives without the religious undergirding of Protestantism which called it into life; and it also survives without the asceticism which was essential to its early development.

Conclusion: Marx, Weber and historical materialism

Marx and Weber are often seen as opposed in their accounts of the development of capitalism. There are, however, some similarities in their work. First, both saw capitalism as something radically new in history, neither a mere extension of what went before, nor as something which would inevitably come about if certain obstacles to the development of capitalism were removed. Second, both agreed that capitalism, in its earliest form, was not associated with either the rich commercial class in cities or with industrialism. For Marx, the site of early capitalist relations of production was the countryside, and the main agents of change were landlords. For Weber, small-scale Protestant businesspeople first carried the seeds of the capitalist spirit. One much-discussed difference between Marx and Weber concerns their approaches to historical change. This is a *methodological* difference, one which pertains to the difference in their approaches and methods to human history, to which we turn in closing this chapter.

Weber alluded to 'naive' **historical materialism**, the view that ideas, including religious beliefs, are a 'reflection' of the economic structure of society (1920: 19). Some form of this view, which Weber rejected, is supported by Marxists who believe that social change stems from economic factors and that ideas adjust themselves to economic factors but are not the driving force of historical change.

Key methodological issue: Historical materialism

In the 'Preface' to *A Contribution to the Critique of Political Economy* (1859: 211) Marx wrote:

> In the social production of their existence, men inevitably enter into definite relations, which are independent of their will, namely relations of production appropriate to a given stage in the development of their material forces of production. The totality of these relations of production constitutes the economic structure of society, the real foundation, on which arises a legal and political superstructure and to which correspond definite forms of social consciousness. The mode of production of material life conditions the general process of social, political and intellectual life. It is not the consciousness of men that determines their existence, but their social existence that determines their consciousness. This is a statement of historical materialism, the view that the dominant feature of a society is its economic structure which conditions other aspects of society.

Weber's remarks on historical materialism can be interpreted as a reaction to the 'vulgar' forms of Marxism of the late nineteenth century which interpreted Marx's writings in a rigidly 'economistic' sense (Giddens 1971: 193). Beliefs and ideas (like Protestantism), according to 'vulgar' Marxists, are secondary phenomena with no causal impact on the development of history. Few Marxists today see this as an adequate representation of Marx's ideas, and it is not fruitful to conceive Marx and Weber in an opposition according to which the former sees the key to historical change lying in the economic sphere whilst the latter sees it in the sphere of ideas. Weber's study of the development of capitalism illustrates how ideas can be causal forces in historical development (1920: 48), but he did not hold that ideas are the only or main driving force of historical change; nor did he think that, without the Protestant Reformation, modern capitalism could not have evolved.

Suggested readings

- Ch. 26–28, Marx, K. (1867 [1976]) *Capital: Volume 1*, London, Penguin.
- Ch. II and V, Weber, M. (1920 [2002]) *The Protestant Ethic and the Spirit of Capitalism* (2nd Edition), Los Angeles, Roxbury.
- Ch. 1 and 5, Wood, E.M. (2002) *The Origins of Capitalism: A Longer View*, London, Verso.

Bibliography

Beier, A. (1985) *Masterless Men: The Vagrancy Problem in England, 1560–1640*, London, Methuen.

Beier, A. (2008) '"A new serfdom": Labour laws, vagrancy statutes, and labour discipline in England, 1350–1800', in A. Beier and P. Ocobock (eds), *Cast Out: Vagrancy and Homelessness in Global and Historical Perspective*, Athens, Ohio University Press, pp.35–63.

Brenner, R. (1976 [1985]) 'Agrarian class structure and the development of capitalism', in T. Ashton and C. Philpin (eds), *The Brenner Debate*, Cambridge, Cambridge University Press, pp.10–63.

Brenner, R. (1985) 'The agrarian roots of European capitalism', in T. Ashton and C. Philpin (eds), *The Brenner Debate*, Cambridge, Cambridge University Press, pp.213–327.

Giddens, A. (1971) *Capitalism and Modern Social Theory*, Cambridge, Cambridge University Press.

Manning, R. (1988) *Village Revolts: Social Protest and Popular Disturbances in England, 1509–1640*, Oxford, Clarendon.

Marx, K. (1859 [1994]) 'Preface', trans. S. Ryazanskaya, in L. Simon (ed.), *Karl Marx: Selected Writings*, Indianapolis, Hackett, pp.209–213.

Marx, K. (1867 [1976]) *Capital: Volume 1*, London, Penguin.

Neeson, J. (1993) *Commoners: Common Right, Enclosure and Social Change in England, 1700–1820*, Cambridge, Cambridge University Press.

Pirenne, H. (1956) *Medieval Cities: Their Origins and the Revival of Trade*, New York, Doubleday.

Polanyi, K. (1944 [2001]) *The Great Transformation: The Political and Economic Origins of Our Time*, Boston, Beacon Press.

Postan, M. (1971) 'Medieval agrarian society in its prime: England', in M. Postan (ed.), *The Cambridge Economic History of Europe*, volume 1, Cambridge, Cambridge University Press, pp.548–632.

Smith, A. (1759 [1976]) *The Theory of Moral Sentiments*, Oxford, Oxford University Press.

Smith, A. (1776 [1976]) *An Inquiry into the Nature and Causes of the Wealth of Nations*, volume 1, Oxford, Oxford University Press.

Tawney, R. (1914 [1972]) 'The assessment of wages in England by justices of the peace', in W. Minchinton (ed.), *Wage Regulation in Pre-Industrial England*, New York, Barnes & Noble, pp.38–91.

Weber, M. (1920 [2002]) *The Protestant Ethic and the Spirit of Capitalism* (2nd Edition), Los Angeles, Roxbury.

Wood, E.M. (2002) *The Origins of Capitalism: A Longer View*, London, Verso.

2 | The spread of capitalism

Co-authored with Caroline Shenaz Hossein

Introduction

Early capitalist proponents like Adam Smith – who we introduced in Chapter 1 – thought that capitalism originated in cities and the urban, civilized and modern life they represented. Capitalism appeared as a bulwark against the *ancien regime* of feudalism; it challenged and eroded irrational and narrow beliefs, stultifying hierarchies and the limits of tradition and parentage. From this perspective, capitalism stimulated the Enlightenment and Scientific Revolutions which brought us new insights and technologies; it also promoted democratic and liberation movements, enabling people to break free from absolutism and tyranny (Slater and Tonkiss 2001). Consequently, the emergence of capitalism from the fifteenth and sixteenth centuries onwards – as outlined in the previous chapter – totally transformed European societies and economies, and continues to transform other countries around the globe. Today many argue that capitalism's subsequent diffusion has led us into the modern age in which the expansion of wealth and well-being go hand-in-hand. For example, the work of journalist Thomas Friedman (1999, 2005) lauds the promise of development offered by capitalism – we come back to this in Chapter 7 – while the historian Niall Ferguson (2011) puts Europe's ascendancy down to 'six killer apps', including competition. While some of this may reflect historical changes, it is far from the total picture; in particular, these claims hide a *dark side* to capitalism.

Capitalism has a dirty history, not only in the poetic terms evoked by William Blake's image of the 'dark Satanic mills' of industrialization, but in the dust, blood and tears of millions of people trampled, enslaved and massacred as a result of its spread around the world. The idea that capitalism emerges in one place (e.g. Europe) and then spreads around the world misses the point; capitalism only emerged in Europe *because* the rest of the world was forced – through war, slavery and colonialism – into a subservient position. Large parts of the world were turned into European colonies and dependencies, shipping their raw materials to the capitalist heartlands in return for goods and services they were no longer allowed to produce. What this illustrates is the fact that capitalism was a worldwide transformation; it was not limited to one country or one continent. As a result, all parts of the world are now entangled with capitalism, whether people like it or not. The view that capitalism is a world-wide system has a long history. For example, early Marxists like Rudolf

Hilferding, Michael Bukharin and Vladimir Lenin argued that imperialism was another stage in capitalist development (Brewer 1990). Their ideas influenced later thinkers and theories; these include people like Immanuel Wallerstein (1979b) who coined the concept of *world-system theory*. We will return to these ideas below.

The starting point for this chapter is the idea that capitalism cannot be explained as a simple, progressive story of modernity being spread around the world by enlightened European explorers, travellers and merchants. This is what we call the *linear story* of capitalism in which it is assumed that countries move from under-developed backwaters to modern, advanced capitalist economies through a number of intervening steps as they adopt capitalism. We problematize this notion by presenting a *non-linear* or *circular* story of capitalism's worldwide spread; it is a story told by a number of scholars including those mentioned above (e.g. Wallerstein) as well as other thinkers like Giovanni Arrighi (1994 [2010]), Samir Amin (1977, 2013) and Walter Rodney (1982). First we outline the linear narrative of European progress and exploration; that is, the idea of Europe bringing modernity to the rest of the world. Second, we challenge this linear story by discussing how European capitalism was and is based on the under-development of other countries around the world.

> **Key discussion questions**
>
> - What is development?
> - What is wrong with the linear story of capitalism?
> - In what ways did capitalism have violent roots in colonialism and slavery?
> - Why is dependency theory helpful in explaining the spread of capitalism?
> - Is capitalism a world-wide system?
> - How are joint-stock companies related to the spread of capitalism?

Mainstream perspectives

The linear story of capitalism Histories of the spread of capitalism often follow a linear format. It goes something like this. Prior to the emergence of capitalism the world economy was not integrated. Aside from a few long-distant and time-consuming merchant voyages or trips – for example, Marco Polo's travels from Europe to China in the thirteenth century – trade was mostly limited to neighbouring or nearby countries. For Europeans, the long trade routes to East Asia and the wealth it held were risky because of the threat from countries like the Ottoman Empire to European traders. In this climate, and up until the fifteenth century, Europe was a relative backwater in global terms; this claim contrasts somewhat with the history most of us in

Anglo-American and European countries learn at school. China and India had much larger economies as a result of the size of their populations (Dicken 2011: 15), and were more technologically advanced in many ways (Scott 2011). In contrast, until the emergence of capitalism only a few European cities were centres of wealth and technology, especially the independent Italian city-states like Milan, Florence, Genoa and Venice. These cities were major centres of population, banking, industry and trade – relative to the rest of Europe, at least – dominated by a merchant class, rather than the aristocracy.

All this changed, however, in the fifteenth century when European monarchs started to finance explorations of the rest of the world, the most famous being Christopher Columbus and the 'discovery' of the Americas in 1492. The rationale behind these journeys was to find alternative routes to China and India that would bypass the hostile Ottoman Empire, which had captured Constantinople in 1453. This so-called **Age of 'Discovery'** was dominated by a small number of European countries: it started with Portugal in the early fifteenth century; followed by Spain in the fifteenth and sixteenth centuries; and then the Netherlands, England and France from the sixteenth onwards (Slater 2005). Each of these countries sought to dominate particular spheres of the world and world trade, through direct means – like conquest, subjugation of indigenous populations, slavery and colonization – and indirect means – like control over trade routes. The expansion of trade and conquest brought an enormous amount of the world's wealth (literally gold and silver) flowing into Europe where it helped stimulate economic, scientific, technological, cultural and political revolutions. As exploration turned to colonization from the seventeenth century onwards, other parts of the world were brought into the orbit of Europe's early capitalist system, leading to the integration of the world economy and the gradual development and modernization of non-European countries.

Key concept: Age of 'Discovery'

Starting in the fifteenth century, a number of European countries sought to find alternative routes to East Asia that bypassed the Ottoman Empire. Some countries, like Portugal, sought to find sea routes around Africa, while others, like Spain, sought sea routes directly West over the Atlantic. The search for trade routes resulted in Europeans travelling to the Americas and other parts of the world with which they had had no (or only limited) previous links. Following exploration, European countries sought to invade, conquer and/or colonize the Americas, Africa, Asia and Oceania, driven by religious fervour (e.g. spreading Christianity), mercantilist capitalism (e.g. extracting wealth) and territorial ambitions (e.g. building empires). Over several centuries, millions of people around the world were subjugated, enslaved or killed as the result of war, famine and disease.

Source: Slater (2005)

The global expansion of Europe led to frequent conflicts between European countries, both in Europe and in other parts of the world, especially as they started to establish colonies from the seventeenth and eighteenth centuries. This resulted from disagreements about control over land and trade, and was driven by a particular way of thinking about trade and trading relations called *mercantilism*. The assumption underpinning mercantilism was that trade is a zero-sum activity in which one country's gain led to another country's loss; for example, if one country won control over trade to East Asia then it would benefit from all the wealth coming from that trade to the exclusion of all other countries (Marx 1867 [1976]). For most European countries then, mercantilism was an extension of territorial ambitions and inter-state competition; that is, increasing your wealth at the expense of another country gave you a major bonus when waging war. Mercantilism led many European countries to establish large trading companies with exclusive trading rights to different parts of the world – we return to this issue below when we discuss the English/British East India Company (Robins 2006). However, mercantilism did not last. In 1776 Adam Smith criticized the mercantilist form of capitalism in his book *The Wealth of Nations*. He argued that competition and trade could lead to a gain for both parties through the benefits of a division of labour; this theory was based on the notion that it was more productive to specialize and trade with others than to try and do everything yourself. Eventually, Smith's and other **classical political economy** theories came to dominate the policies of European countries and their governments, especially Britain, in the nineteenth century (Hobsbawm 1997).

Key thinkers: Classical political economy

Stretching from Adam Smith to Karl Marx, classical political economy covers all those eighteenth- and nineteenth-century thinkers who based their theories of capitalism on the labour theory of value. The labour theory of value is based on the idea that the value of a commodity is derived from the labour needed to produce that commodity. Classical political economy went into decline with the 'marginal revolution' in the late nineteenth century and is no longer a mainstream theory of capitalism. This is discussed in more detail in Chapter 12.

Modernization theory and the Western project In the twentieth century, this view of the spread of capitalism was increasingly associated with other concepts, like modernization, which emerged in 'Western' countries – today it is exemplified by people like Thomas Friedman (1999, 2005) and Niall Ferguson (2011). From this 'modern' perspective, Western values, practices and knowledges are characterized as universal examples of social and economic development. Earlier modernization theorists believed they had the prescriptions to 'develop' poor, non-Western countries by forcing them to imitate Western countries' experience with capitalism. According to political scientist Samuel Huntington (1971), for example, modern science and technology gave humans greater control over the natural and social environment whereas traditional or communal knowledge led to inferior standards of living. These ideas led Western elites to define people in the so-called 'Third World' as primitive and in need of saving. For example, David Apter's (1965) *The Politics of Modernization* begins with the claim that modernization theory represented a 'special kind of hope'. For many modernizers, the project of colonialism itself can be seen as a modern exercise in 'we know best'. The modernist assumptions were that the Western concepts of nation, state, civil society and representative government could be easily transplanted across the rest of the world.

Modernization was conceived as a top-down, global, lengthy, phased, homogenizing, irreversible, progressive, complex and revolutionary process that included industrialization, urbanization, social mobilization, secularization and democracy. The best known argument for modernization was put forth by the American economist W.W. Rostow (1960) in *Stages of Economic Growth: A Non-Communist Manifesto* where he argued that the transition from underdevelopment to modern development came through five successive stages influenced by economic development: transition society, preconditions for take-off, take-off, maturity and, finally, mass-consumption. Rostow's ideas reflected the broader geopolitical context in which he was writing. In the 1950s, and after the Second World War, the capitalist USA emerged as a global superpower opposed by the socialist USSR.

Modern capitalist development, as espoused by the likes of Rostow, was based on certain assumptions. Specifically, Rostow's (1960 [1991]) theory was built on the analysis of the British Industrial (and capitalist) Revolution, which led him to assert that all societies pass through this single, linear path where each stage is a prerequisite for the next.

However, many Western countries took quite different developmental pathways than those outlined by modernization theorists like Rostow; as we discuss in Chapter 7, there is more than one form of capitalism. Although modernization theory initially contributed to a problematic understanding of the Global South, revisionist modernizers have also attempted to consider the issues that occur within countries in order to understand the diverse and varied modernities that can result from diverse historical, political, social and cultural experiences.

To conclude this section, it is possible to summarize the linear story as premised on certain assumptions about the spread and evolution of capitalism around the world (see Chang 2008). These can be simplified as three basic ideas:

- *Exploration*: capitalism originates in Europe and then spreads outward from there as European countries explore and colonize the rest of the world, exporting capitalism as they extend European influence. As more countries are dominated by European countries they become integrated into a widening global economy which ties together colonial homelands (in Europe) with overseas colonies (in other parts of the world).
- *Development*: the spread of capitalism outwards from Europe was built on the back of new production processes (e.g. factories), new industries (e.g. cotton), new technologies (e.g. railways) and new ideas (e.g. science), all of which have subsequently contributed to the economic and social development of other places and their peoples around the world.
- *Modernization*: European countries modernized and developed as a result of capitalism, leading to rising living standards and other benefits (e.g. higher life expectancy). Other countries that followed the European example did and will benefit from the same outcomes.

In what follows we problematize this linear narrative, its underlying assumptions and the assumed benefits of capitalism and modernization.

Critical perspectives

There is a non-linear view of the spread of capitalism. It emphasizes the need to think about the interdependent relationships between different parts of the world; that is, to think of capitalism as a global economic system, rather than individual countries trading with one another. It is particularly important to think about how different parts of the world were integrated into a global economy as a consequence of colonialism and imperialism. To do this requires us to understand the international division of labour and international patterns of production and consumption. While Adam Smith – see Introduction – analysed specialization in individual factories and how this leads to productivity gains, similar arguments can be made about specialization between different countries in a global economic system like capitalism (e.g. Frobel et al. 1980). Usually this type of thinking is based on the idea of comparative advantage developed by the nineteenth-century political economist **David Ricardo**. His ideas justify claims about the benefits of free trade, supporting the view that unrestricted trade between countries will benefit everyone because each country can focus on what it is best at producing and then trade for everything else it needs (Krugman 1996). However, there are other, more critical, ways to understand global capitalism, and we examine some of these next.

The non-linear, or circular, story of capitalism Modernization theory was and is clearly limited by its Western lens. Although its perspective of the Global South was shrouded with ahistorical, homogenizing, linear, apolitical, ethnocentric and simplistic understandings of very diverse people, it was premised on improving the conditions of those who were faced with severe poverty, inequality, violence and instability. However, modernization theorists omitted several important elements in the development story; namely, the historical experiences of slavery, imperialism and colonialism. Modernization was not just about building roads, educating people, providing electricity and expanding trade, it was about the expansion of geopolitical power. Examining the world 'simply as it was' according to Western assumptions meant that modernization theory did nothing to challenge prevailing power relationships as well as institutions through which power was organized to sustain the *status quo*.

Modernization theory was criticized on these grounds by a number of 'dependency theorists'. Dependency theory critiques dominant ideas about the linear story of capitalist development (Isbister 2006). It arose largely out of the Global South, principally from Latin American and Caribbean scholars as an alternative explanation of underdevelopment and the spread of capitalism. Whereas modernization theorists argue that underdevelopment is a *condition*, dependency theorists argue that it is an ongoing *process*. According to dependency theory, underdevelopment is not simply a failure to develop; it is also an active process of impoverishment. In *How Europe Underdeveloped Africa*, for example, Walter Rodney (1982) argued that imperialist capitalism involved European extraction of riches and engagement in the slave trade in Africa and the Americas in order to finance Europe's industrial development – in this sense it had nothing to do with modernity or promoting modernization. Consequently, it makes no sense to talk of developed countries as being 'underdeveloped' in the past, although they may have been 'undeveloped' at one point. Another notable and prolific thinker from the dependency school is the Egyptian-born and Senegal-based Samir Amin (1977) who has critiqued the bias embedded in modernization theory. According to Amin, the root

32

cause of poverty and underdevelopment in the South is the result of capitalist development. In other words, countries of the Global South found themselves in positions of underdevelopment because of the operation of capitalism (Amin 2013).

Generally, dependency theory makes four claims: (1) underdevelopment is a process, not a condition; (2) poverty in the Global South (e.g. in former European colonies) is a result of Europe's industrial prosperity; (3) international and historical factors are key to understanding underdevelopment; and (4) a global capitalist system undermines economic development in the Global South. The impoverishment of the Global South did not result from so-called 'primitivism', but rather from the colonial and imperial activities of European countries which fuelled their economic growth at the expense of their colonial possessions (Amin 2013; Williams 1944 [2004]). As such, the process of under-development of the Global South was deliberate (Brohman 1995).

Dependency theory is distinct from modernization theory because it focuses on the *global* capitalist system. Unlike modernization perspectives, dependency theory seeks to examine the relations between core/metropole countries and periphery/satellite countries. As such it is based on the idea that capitalism involves core countries (e.g. European colonizers) extracting raw materials from peripheral countries (e.g. European colonies). This global capitalist system is conceived as decidedly non-linear. In particular, Immanuel Wallerstein (1979a) characterizes capitalism as a 'world system' in which even the farthest reaches of the globe are bound to an international system involving a chain of production and consumption relationships between cores and peripheries.

Rather than a linear process of economic development under capitalism then, it is more accurate to conceptualize the spread of capitalism around the

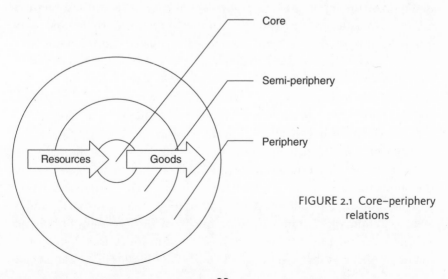

FIGURE 2.1 Core–periphery relations

world as a circular process in which countries were drawn into capitalism as a world system, especially through slavery, colonialism and empire. This process of uneven and unequal development goes back to at least the sixteenth century with the emergence of capitalist world economy in which the colonial powers (i.e. the core) were able to industrialize based on the agricultural and mineral primary goods extracted from the colonies (i.e. periphery) (Isbister 2006). Consequently, the present underdevelopment of the Global South is better thought of as the result of its centuries-long position in global capitalism, especially its experience with slavery, colonial exploitation and imperial conquest.

Capitalism, slavery and colonization We now want to examine the dark side of capitalism; this is most evident in the relationship between capitalism and slavery. The slave trade was started by Europeans in Africa and can be dated to the Portuguese explorations in the fifteenth century. In the Americas, the major colonies receiving slaves were Brazil and the Caribbean. According to the *Voyages* project (see Figure 2.2), for example, most of the 35,000 slave voyages from Africa went to these places (Eltis and Richardson 2010). These countries formed part of the so-called 'Triangular Trade' which linked Europe, Africa and the Americas in an international flow of enslaved people, raw materials and manufactured goods.

A key player in this triangular trade was the British Empire. It gained direct control of a number of Caribbean islands and territories in South America. Moreover, the 1713 Treaty of Utrecht granted enormous power to the British Empire under the *Asiento* contract in which Britain became the authorized slave distributor for the Atlantic (Black 1965) – the British government gave this contract to the South Sea Company, a joint-stock company (see below). The *Asiento* was a contract that the Spanish crown had established in 1595 giving a monopoly on the supply of slaves to Spanish colonies in Central and Southern America. When the *Asiento* was given to Britain in 1713, white indentured servants at the time, such as the Portuguese and Irish, moved into plantation management as African slaves were sold to plantations in British colonies as well. Even after it lost the *Asiento* in the mid-1700s, the British continued to support the plantation system in its own colonies of Barbados, Jamaica, Grenada and Trinidad because the earnings were so lucrative (Williams 1944 [2004]).

Millions of Africans lost their lives as the result of slavery. Slavery meant that African people were considered and treated as legal property (Olusoga 2015); enslaved people were brutalized, tortured and raped without recrimination. The profits made from the slavery of African people to the Americas financed Britain's Industrial Revolution. As such, it is possible to argue that the Industrial Revolution, which transformed the quality of life of so many British people through economic development, was rooted in the immoral, inhumane and racist practices that resulted in the deaths of millions of African people.

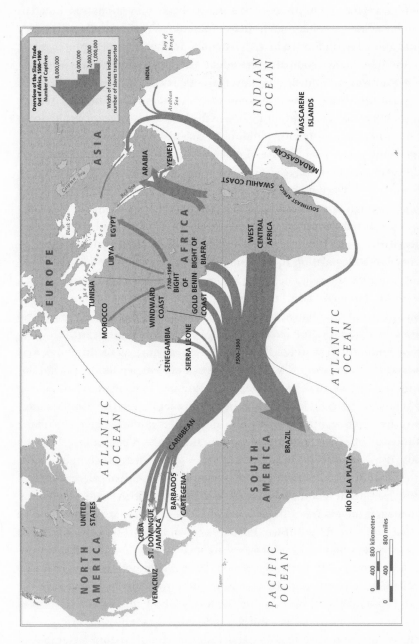

FIGURE 2.2 Map of transatlantic slave trade *Source:* Eltis and Richardson (2010),
The Trans-Atlantic Slave Trade Database: Voyages

European countries, like Britain, became rich through extracting resources with the enslaved labour of Africans in colonies. Even though slavery began to be abolished by European countries from the end of the eighteenth century, Eric Williams (1944 [2004]) argued that the abolition movement was rooted in economic decisions rather than humanitarian ones. The institution of slavery was first abolished in France in 1794; it ended in the British Empire in 1833; and in the USA in 1865 soon after President Abraham Lincoln's *Emancipation Proclamation* was enacted. Ending slavery was resisted by slave owners because of the great profits generated; in some cases, owners were compensated for losing their 'property', representing one of the largest transfers of wealth from the government to private individuals in British history (Olusoga 2015).[1]

Slavery illustrates that the use of enslaved African labour in the Americas and the extraction of resources from the Global South were not a free exchange of goods and services among partners, but rather goods and people were obtained through brutality and violence. After abolition, colonial plantations were not sustainable without forced labour and neither were plantations economical with the constant insurrections by the slaves. In response, the British Empire enacted legislation to carry out an expansive indentured worker system in a number of its colonies such as Guyana, Trinidad, Mauritius and, to a lesser extent, Jamaica. With subsidies from the British state, for example, the British East India Company transported thousands of poor (often low-caste) Indians from Calcutta, India to the British West Indies (Caribbean).

These indentured workers lived in the exact same slave dwellings and undertook the same work that African slaves once carried out under similar conditions. The Guyanese academic Walter Rodney (1982) made a compelling point that slavery, as an institution, did not in fact end in the colonies until the early twentieth century because the indentured worker system of Indians and Indo-Caribbean people continued into the 1900s. A plantation economy controlled by the British continued for many years after official emancipation in these Caribbean colonies. Colonization under British direct rule had a lasting and detrimental effect on the Caribbean. British male administrators managed the affairs of the colonies and local people were organized in ways that best suited the Crown. Resources such as bauxite, gold, silver and diamonds were pilfered; local people were given a Western Christian education; and all things African were banned. Of the local population those who were mixed-race (white and African) were somewhat privileged because the colonizers would cherry-pick among the locals who had access to resources under a strategic plan of 'divide and conquer'. Mixed-race persons often inherited the wealth of the white colonizers (Thomas 1988). Within a number of Caribbean societies, a class structure tied to race emerged in which mixed-

1 Legacies of British Slave-ownership project: www.ucl.ac.uk/lbs/ (accessed May 2016).

race persons had the right to vote and dark-skinned persons of African heritage did not (Rodney 1996).

Today, the richest families in the Caribbean can easily be traced to the colonization period. Those with a white lineage clearly benefited economically from this historical legacy. Colonies that experienced enslavement and colonization have local elites (born out of the colonizing project of miscegenation) and they have (mis)used their financial resources to sustain unequal structures in the Caribbean society, a legacy that continues today.

Case study

Reparations for slavery

A contemporary and collective movement of the African diaspora has started to agitate for dialogue on the slave trade, slavery and colonization by slave trading countries in Europe and to make a case for compensation for the pain, suffering and losses endured by the descendants of African slaves in the Americas.

Slavery and colonization have had dire repercussions for the development of African countries and their diaspora. It is not that African countries and their diaspora cannot 'modernize' but that persons of African-descent have been subject to centuries of gross human indignities and intense exploitation by racist colonizers – a part of the story that is often conveniently overlooked. The shameful past of slavery has been largely ignored by Europe. The socio-economic oppression encountered by millions of persons of the African diaspora is rooted in the experience of enslavement and colonialism. The underdevelopment of the Caribbean (and Africa) is the direct effect of the slave trade, indentured servitude and colonization.

Caribbean states, academics and civil society organizations in the region and the diaspora have started to mobilize a reparations movement. For example, a University of West Indies professor, Hilary Beckles, leads a task force for reparations from former European slave-trading nations such as Britain, France and Spain. The reparations movement seeks recognition from colonizer countries that they owe their industrial development to the wealth accumulated from the slave trade, slavery and colonization. As highlighted earlier, the minority whites in the Caribbean own most of the riches because they amassed huge fortunes from plantation slavery and also received compensation by the British state for the loss of their 'property'. No black person was ever compensated for the violence perpetrated against them as a people under enslavement (or colonization).

Empirical example: the British Empire

The British Empire dominated the world capitalist system for over a century (Arrighi 1994 [2010]). On the one hand, the Empire was based on colonialism, slavery and indentured servitude in the Caribbean and North America, as we have outlined above; on the other hand, it was based on international trading routes and large, semi-private trading companies in India and the Far East.

Aside from direct colonial control, large parts of the British Empire emerged from trading networks centred on **joint-stock companies** (JSC) like the East India Company (EIC), Royal Africa Company and South Sea Company. These JSCs were a form of business organization chartered by the Crowns of various European countries, including England/Britain, the Netherlands and France (Micklethwait and Woodridge 2005; Robins 2006). Their purpose was to undertake long and dangerous voyages to other parts of the world in order to engage in trade, especially the spice trade. In order to share the risks of these journeys, JSCs were structured so that many people shared ownership (i.e. shareholding). In general, JSCs were characterized by the following aspects:

- Created by a charter from by Crown for certain period of time (e.g. 21 years); this could be renewed at the end of each charter period. The charter gave the JSC monopoly privileges on trade with particular parts of the world; for example, the EIC had monopoly rights to trade with 'East India' – that is, India, Indonesia, Malaysia and so on. Consequently, no other English/British JSC could trade with East India.
- Independence from the Crown, in that the monarch and their government did not direct the actions of the JSC or own the JSC. Instead, the JSC was owned by many shareholders who could trade their shares in share markets; this was in order to spread the risk of failure amongst many investors.
- JSCs had separate a legal identity from their shareholders, so that a JSC's existence did not depend on the lifespan of its investors. Shareholders were given limited liability protection, which meant that investors were not responsible for the actions of the JSC.
- JSCs were given sovereign rights to wage war, print money and make treaties, since they operated in parts of the world many months away from their home countries.

Despite these JSCs being semi-private, independent entities, they were deeply implicated in English/British colonialism, although their activities were driven more by the commercial goals of private business (i.e. profit).

Key organization: Joint-stock company

The main examples from England and Britain include: Muscovy Company (est. 1555), East India Company (est. 1600), Hudson's Bay Company (est. 1670) and South Sea Company (est. 1711). Other countries also had similar JSCs; for example, the Netherlands (est.1602), Denmark (est. 1616), Portugal (est. 1628), France (est. 1664) and Sweden (est. 1731) all had East India Companies with monopolies of trade to East Asia. Of these, the two most important were the Dutch and English/British EICs.

The English / British EIC had a long history of operations, lasting from 1600 until 1874, and played an important role in establishing the British Empire in the Indian subcontinent. According to Robins (2006), who has written a history of the EIC, it was established at the end of 1600 by Queen Elizabeth I and was originally chartered to engage in the lucrative spice trade with places like Indonesia. However, by 1667 it was driven out of the spice trade by the Dutch EIC and shifted its attention to Bengal, in the Indian subcontinent. The EIC initially traded gold and silver bullion in exchange for textiles, since Bengal was a major textile manufacturing hub; for example, India had a 25 per cent share of world textile manufacturing in 1750 (Robins 2006). In 1757 the EIC waged war on the local Bengali rulers and was subsequently granted rights to collect taxes by the Mughal emperor in Bengal. This led to the EIC assuming a direct governing role which it used to destroy the Bengali textile industry.

The EIC slowly declined in importance during the nineteenth century as it lost trading rights and as the British state took over responsibility for the running of India as a colony. However, in the century and half that it dominated the Indian subcontinent it managed to do significant social and economic damage. This included the destruction of the textile industry; turning India into a primary commodity exporter (e.g. cotton); causing huge famines through speculating on food prices – for example, 10 million people died in Bengal as a result of the 1772 famine caused by artificial food shortages (Robins 2006); and exporting opium to China. The EIC gained such a bad reputation that even people like Adam Smith criticized its monopoly privileges and the speculation of its employees and lack of remedy for these abuses. For example, one 1773 British Parliamentary Committee concluded:

> In the East, the laws of society, the laws of nature have been enormously
> violated. Oppression in every shape has ground the faces of the poor
> defenceless natives; and tyranny in her bloodless form has stalked abroad.
> (Quoted in Robins 2006)

Conclusion

In this chapter we sought to do a number of things. First, we presented the dominant and linear narrative of world history taught in the Global North about the spread of capitalism and civilization after the European 'discovery' of the world in the fifteenth century. Second, we presented theories of dependency and a world system to problematize the linear story of capitalism. These theories show how the world economy is an integrated system in which the position of some countries at the core of capitalism has meant other countries are relegated to the periphery. This is not the natural or automatic outcome of capitalist forces and pressures like competition and innovation, but instead results from the violent domination of world markets, trade and production by European countries through conquest, slavery, colonialism and imperialism. We sought to present this dark side of capitalism so that there are no illusions about its impacts, and that the countries upholding capitalism used violence against human beings to do business. Third, we discussed this dark side as a necessary underpinning of world capitalism in that it drove the expansion and spread of capitalism, rather than simply being a by-product. Fourth, we illustrated our claims with the example of the British Empire and its leading role in the Atlantic slave trade and in the destruction of India's manufacturing capacity and its people through famine. Overall, our aim has been to show how capitalism is not a natural force spreading around the world producing benefits wherever it goes; rather, it is driven by the decisions and goals of different peoples, countries, businesses and governments.

Suggested readings

- Ch.5, Scott, B. (2011) *Capitalism*, New York, Springer
- Slater, T. (2005) 'The rise and spread of capitalism', in P. Daniels, M. Bradshaw, D. Shaw and J. Sidaway (eds), *Introduction to Human Geography* (2nd Edition), Essex, Pearson, pp.36–61.
- Ch.5, Rodney, W. (1982) *How Europe Underdeveloped Africa*, Washington DC, Howard University Press.
- *The Trans-Atlantic Slave Trade Database: Voyages*. www.slavevoyages.org/ (accessed June 2016).
- *Legacies of British Slave-ownership project*. www.ucl.ac.uk/lbs/ (accessed May 2016).

Bibliography

Amin, S. (1977) *Imperialism and Unequal Development*, New York, Monthly Review Press.

Amin, S. (2013) *The Implosion of Capitalism*, New York, Monthly Review Press.

Apter, D. (1965) *The Politics of Modernization*, Chicago, University of Chicago Press.

Arrighi, G. (1994 [2010]) *The Long Twentieth Century*, London, Verso.

Black, C.V. de Brosse (1965) *Story of Jamaica: From Prehistory to the Present* (revised edition), London, Collins.

Brewer, A. (1990) *Marxist Theories of Imperialism*, Florence KY, Routledge.

Brohman, J. (1995) 'Universalism, Eurocentrism, and ideological bias in development studies: From modernisation to neoliberalism', *Third World Quarterly*, Vol.16, pp.121–140.

Chang, H.-J. (2008) *Bad Samaritans*, London, Bloomsbury.

Dicken, P. (2011) *Global Shift* (6th Edition), New York, Guildford.

Eltis, D. and Richardson, D. (2010) *Atlas of the Transatlantic Slave Trade*, New Haven, Yale University Press.

Ferguson, N. (2011) *Civilization: The West and the Rest*, London, Penguin.

Friedman, T. (1999) *The Lexus and the Olive Tree*, New York, Farrar Straus Giroux.

Friedman, T. (2005) *The World Is Flat*, New York, Farrar Straus Giroux.

Frobel, F., Heinrichs, J. and Kreye, O. (1980) *The New International Division of Labour*, Cambridge, Cambridge University Press.

Hobsbawm, E. (1997) *The Age of Capital: 1848–1875*, London, Abacus.

Huntington. S. (1971) 'The change to change: Modernization, development and politics', *Comparative Politics*, Vol.3, pp.283–322.

Isbister, J. (2006) *Promises Not Kept: Poverty and the Betrayal of Third World Development* (7th Edition), West Hartford CT, Kumarian Press.

Krugman, P. (1996) *Pop Internationalism*, Cambridge MA, MIT Press.

Marx, K. (1867 [1976]) *Capital: Volume 1*, London, Penguin.

Micklethwait, J. and Wooldridge, A. (2005) *The Company*, New York, Modern Library Chronicles Book.

Olusoga, D. (2015) 'The history of British slave ownership has been buried', *The Observer* (12 July): www.theguardian.com/world/2015/jul/12/british-history-slavery-buried-scale-revealed (accessed August 2015).

Ricardo, D. (1817 [2001]) *On the Principles of Political Economy and Taxation*, Kitchener, Batoche Books.

Robins, N. (2006) *The Corporation That Changed the World*, London, Pluto Press.

Rodney, W. (1982) *How Europe Underdeveloped Africa*, Washington DC, Howard University Press.

Rostow, W.W. (1960 [1991]) *The Stages of Economic Growth: A Non-Communist Manifesto*, Cambridge, Cambridge University Press.

Scott, B. (2011) *Capitalism*, New York, Springer.

Slater, D. and Tonkiss, F. (2001) *Market Society*, Cambridge, Polity Press.

Slater, T. (2005) 'The rise and spread of capitalism', in P. Daniels, M. Bradshaw, D. Shaw and J. Sidaway (eds), *Introduction to Human Geography* (2nd Edition), Essex, Pearson, pp.36–61.

Thomas, C. (1988) *The Poor and the Powerless: Economic Policy and Change in the Caribbean*, New York, Monthly Review Press.

Wallerstein, I. (1979a) 'The rise and future demise of the world capitalist system', in I. Wallerstein (ed.), *The Capitalist World Economy*, Cambridge, Cambridge University Press, pp.1–36.

Wallerstein, I. (ed.) (1979b) *The Capitalist World Economy*, Cambridge, Cambridge University Press.

Williams, E. (1944 [2004]) *Capitalism and Slavery*, Chapel Hill, University of North Carolina Press.

3 | The corporate revolution

Introduction

As the last chapter should have shown, the spread of capitalism is bound up with the actions and activities of the state *and* of business, and not one *or* the other. The spread of capitalism is also embedded in a series of so-called revolutions in the organization of ownership, work, production and consumption – these stretch from the Agricultural Revolution discussed in Chapter 1, through the Industrial Revolution mentioned in Chapter 2, to the corporate revolution we focus on in this chapter. It is interesting to note that these revolutions, although related, did not necessarily follow on from one another geographically or historically; for example, although the Agricultural and Industrial Revolutions are most often associated with Britain, the corporate revolution happened, primarily, in the USA at the end of the nineteenth century (Cheffins 2008). The corporate revolution heralded the rise to dominance of corporations as the key business organization in capitalist countries, a trend which has lasted over a century and is still with us today. It has led to a range of debates about the responsibilities and roles of corporations in society (see Chapters 5 and 15), the expansion of corporate power (see Chapters 6 and 16) and the ethics of corporate decision-making (see Chapter 14).

The corporate revolution has its own particular and peculiar origins and characteristics; we briefly outline them here, but we want to emphasize that different people have very different perspectives about these as well. Generally, most scholars and social commentators agree that the modern corporation has its origins in the joint-stock companies (JSC) that helped fuel the spread of capitalism – see Chapter 2. However, in countries like Britain and the USA the laws and regulations governing JSCs changed quite significantly during the nineteenth century, leading to the corporate revolution at the end of the 1800s. A number of thinkers, especially in economics and management studies (e.g. Chandler 1977), saw this evolution of the corporation as a part of a trend towards rising efficiency over time in the organization of business resulting from competitive market pressures. Others, especially in fields like sociology and law, have argued otherwise (e.g. Whitley 1999). We want to emphasize that it is important to avoid taking an economically determinist perspective when discussing capitalism; that is, we need to avoid assuming that there are economic imperatives or market forces (e.g. competition) beyond human control that direct our actions, decisions and behaviours. Rather, a critical approach to understanding the relationship between business and society necessitates an examination of the social actors involved, their rationales, their institutional context and the processes they constitute.

In this chapter we provide a brief outline of the corporate revolution from a more orthodox perspective and from more critical perspectives. We do this in order to challenge the assumption that capitalism necessarily drives our economies towards rising efficiency through market competition. We start with a brief history of the corporation and how the corporate revolution can be understood from an economically determinist perspective. We then present the critical perspectives that challenge this economic determinism, especially in relation to the legal, institutional and normative evolution of the corporation as a business organization. We finish with an example of the changes that happened in the UK and USA during the nineteenth century which led to the corporate revolution at the end of that century.

Key discussion questions

- What is a corporation?
- What was the corporate revolution?
- Are corporations the most efficient form of business organization?
- How have corporations changed over the nineteenth and twentieth centuries?
- What are the different legal conceptions of the corporation?
- Was the corporate revolution a revolution in efficiency or institutions?

Mainstream perspectives

A brief history of business and the corporation Some people, like Micklethwait and Wooldridge (2005: 4–5), trace the historical origins of the modern corporation as far back as ancient Rome. They argue that Romans created organizational entities with separate and distinct legal identities from their individual, human members – companies and guilds, in particular. From a modern perspective we may find it perfectly normal to consider an organization (e.g. corporation) to have an identity that is separate from its members (e.g. managers, workers, investors), but this notion of **legal personhood** has a complex legal history when it comes to corporations – see our discussion below for more. Broadly speaking, people have been creating (technically) non-business collective entities and organizations to carry out collective activities for hundreds of years, if not thousands. Examples would include things like: religious communities, towns and cities, universities and so on. Legal personhood provides a number of benefits for undertaking these collective activities, including: independence from the state or crown; long-life so the entity can survive the death of its founders; collective identity so individual members are not held responsible for collective decisions and actions; and the capacity to undertake major tasks in the public interest, which individual people cannot do by themselves (Cheffins 2008).

Definition: Legal personhood

Not every human person is treated equally before the law; for example, children are usually treated differently from adults. Moreover, the law also allows people to establish organizations with a separate legal identity from themselves, like a corporation. This does not mean that an organization is a 'person', just that they are treated like one when it comes to the law (e.g. they can sue and be sued, they can own property, they can hire workers etc.).

When it comes to the history of the corporation, the key organizations – in a European medieval context at least – were the guilds and regulated merchant companies, according to Micklethwait and Wooldridge (2005). Regulated companies represented groups of merchants who were **granted a charter** by the Crown that gave them exclusive rights – known as a monopoly – to overseas trade routes with specific parts of the world. For example, the Russia Company was established in England in 1553 to trade with Russia, meaning that no other English company could trade with Russia (Cheffins 2008). The Russia Company was also the first joint-stock company (JSC) chartered by the English Crown, meaning that it was the first company owned by 'stockholders' and not those who managed the business – see Chapter 2 for more on JSCs and the rise of capitalism. Basically, people could buy shares (or stocks) in a JSC and benefit from any profit the JSC made from their trade voyages to far-off places without being liable for any debts incurred. Since these voyages were very risky (e.g. ships sank or were captured by pirates) it made sense to pool the risk amongst a number of investors and over several voyages (Micklethwait and Wooldridge 2005). The popularity of these JSCs waxed and waned in England (and then Britain) over the following century or so, until the late seventeenth and early eighteenth centuries when there was a rise in parliamentary charters leading to a stock market bubble and major stock market crash in 1720 – this was called the South Sea Bubble. After the South Sea Bubble, JSCs were largely banned in Britain until the 1800s; this ban was in spite of the massive growth of manufacturing and trade resulting from the Industrial Revolution during the same period (Handlin and Handlin 1945). Instead of the JSC, the Industrial Revolution was dominated by partnerships as a business structure; this was a very different business structure compared with the JSC, as outlined in Table 3.1.

Key concept: Grant theory of the corporation

Before the mid-1800s, joint-stock companies (JSC) could only be established in England/Britain through the granting of a charter from the Crown or Parliament. This meant that JSCs – the forerunner of modern corporations – and other corporate entities (e.g. towns) could not be set up by anyone whenever they wanted, they required the political consent of the state. The charter laid out what the JSC could do, what privileges it had and for how long. For example, charters gave corporate entities the right to hold property, to sue and be sued, to an existence independent from its members, and to control and discipline the actions of their members (e.g. workers). JSCs were distinct from other corporate entities because they also had exclusive rights to specific trade routes, exploration and even territory. A corporate charter had to be renewed every so often (e.g. every 21 years), which meant that the state could take back their grant if they were unhappy with the actions of the corporation.

Source: Barkan (2013)

TABLE 3.1 Joint-stock company vs. partnership

Characteristic	Joint-stock company	Partnership
Established	By grant from the state	As contract between individual partners
Ownership	Owned by shareholders	Owned by partners
Life-span	Renewed every few years; potentially forever	As long as lifespan of partners; dissolved when one dies
Liability	Shareholders not liable for debts of JSC	Partners liable for debts of partnership
Management	Shareholders elected directors who appointed overseas governors	Partners
Rights	Legal independent identity, own property, sue and be sued, etc.	Same as partners' individual rights

The corporate revolution: evolution towards efficiency? At the end of the nineteenth century Britain was the dominant world economy, attracting a significant proportion of global investment and producing a significant proportion of the world's manufacturing output. This reflected the advantage provided by the Agricultural and Industrial Revolutions that started in England and Britain. However, Britain's global economic dominance gradually shifted towards other countries after 1870, especially to the USA and Germany where new forms of business organization enabled these countries to expand investment in manufacturing. This gave rise to what scholars have called the *corporate revolution* and *managerial capitalism* (Whitley 1999).

According to sociologist William Roy (1997), the corporate revolution resulted from the marriage between finance and manufacturing which provided corporations with greater access to investment capital through an expansion and distribution of the shareholder base. This was done by enabling more people to buy and trade shares, which meant that shareholding was no longer limited to wealthy individuals. As a result, the ownership of shares became increasingly widespread and distributed, and corporations were able to grow much larger than previously with this influx of capital. This capital enabled corporations to integrate vertically so that their operations ran from resource extraction through manufacturing to final sales. All of this happened at the end of the nineteenth century, but led to a number of subsequent changes in the following century or so.

The phrase managerial capitalism is used to describe the period following the corporate revolution. According to Whitley (1999: 8), managerial capitalism was 'dominated by large vertically integrated, and often horizontally diversified, firms run by salaried managers organized into authority hierarchies'. Managerial capitalism is characterized by the separation of ownership and control, and is closely associated with the corporate revolution. At the start of the twentieth century, legal theorists like Berle and Means (1932 [1967]) argued that the corporate revolution had ushered in a clear separation between owners of and managers of corporations, which helped to transform the structure and strategies of corporations. This separation was the main way to distinguish business in the twentieth century from earlier business organizations. For example, business partnerships were popular before the corporate revolution, especially in the UK. In a partnership the owners (i.e. partners) also manage the business to ensure that it is successful. With a (public) corporation, however, the owners (i.e. shareholders) do not (usually) manage the business; instead, they leave it to professional managers trained in management techniques at business schools (Khurana 2007).

A number of scholars have argued that the corporate revolution and managerial capitalism result primarily from economic forces that reward economic efficiencies. First, the economist Ronald Coase (1937) argued that the firm (a less specific term than corporation) represented an important alternative to the market coordination of economic activity. Markets exist wherever agents or organizations involved in production buy inputs or services from outsiders or 'arms-length' suppliers rather than using a mechanism like a formal organization to hire and assign regular employees to make those inputs and services internally. By contrast, firms exist when it is more rational for an agent or organization to use its own resources and regular employees to 'make' rather than 'buy' from outsiders. Coase argued that the decision whether to 'make or buy' depended on what he famously called *transaction costs*. Although orthodox economic theory assumed that markets – conceived as transacting between independent agents who are free to set their own prices – are the most efficient way of coordinating production, it could not explain why so much production took place within organizations (i.e. not in markets). Coase's answer was that all market transactions involve some form of cost to them, including the cost of finding information, negotiating contracts, enforcing contracts etc. In this context, there are many risks and information deficiencies that people encounter when dealing with arm's-length suppliers or employees. For example, hiring and training workers for daily production runs can be very inefficient compared to hiring employees on long-term contracts. This is why it is often more efficient for production to be coordinated within firms and why Coase's theory could be used by so many later theorists as a model for explaining what the 'optimal' size of firms would be under certain conditions or in certain industries. .

Along similar lines to Coase, the well-known management expert Alfred Chandler (1977) argued that the organizational coordination of economic activities provided significant benefits from economies of scale within businesses, as opposed to the market coordination of those same activities. Chandler argued that the former, internal coordination by management, represented the '**visible hand**' of capitalism, as opposed to the 'invisible hand' of the market posited by Adam Smith in the late eighteenth century – see Chapter 10. Chandler argued that this internal coordination by management was more efficient than market coordination and, consequently, this explained why large corporations came to dominate American society – and then the rest of the world. Managers were able, for example, to take advantage of the size of corporations in their planning of economic activities, such as making long-term investment in corporate research and development departments which promised new products and services in the future. These sorts of investment were unlikely to happen if left to the market because market coordination is driven by short-term profit horizons.

Key concept: Invisible hand vs. visible hand?

The metaphor of the invisible hand comes from Adam Smith in *The Wealth of Nations* (1776). According to Smith, in capitalism no individual seeks to promote the public interest (or, the overall wealth of a country), nor could they know whether their actions did promote the public interest. However, this is not a problem because the competitive dynamic of market forces under capitalism is sufficient to ensure that resources are allocated in the most efficient manner. Capitalism is an economic system which is self-regulating, in which even if an individual 'intends only his [sic] own gain, and he is in this, as in many other cases, led by an *invisible hand* to promote an end which was no part of his intention'. In contrast, Alfred Chandler argued that managerial capitalism, in which managers planned and directed the administrative apparatus of large corporations, was based on the *visible hand* of management. The economic and professional leadership of the managerial class under capitalism – not the unguided play of market forces in Smith's model – is what allows the complex problems of the modern business system to be managed for the good of society.

Source: Chandler (1977)

From this brief discussion it is possible to highlight at least three ways that mainstream theories adopt an economically determinist view of the corporate revolution. This relates to assumptions about the following:

- *Legal structure*: they tend to assume that the legal structure of businesses and corporations necessarily follows economic pressures like market competition, transaction costs and economies of scale.
- *Organizational structure*: they tend to assume that there is one best way to organize business, and this reflects economic goals (e.g. profit). This assumption means that organizational structure is treated as the outcome of rational, self-interested action and decisions, which evolve towards more efficient structures over time.
- *Social structure*: they tend to assume that humans are individualistic and self-interested beings, which means that other considerations (e.g. ethics, social relations etc.) do not need explanation or taking into account.

We take a critical look at these three issues in the following section as we problematize the notion that business organization necessarily evolves towards more economically efficient structures as the result of economic pressures.

Critical perspectives

From a critical perspective the corporate revolution should not be read as a story of evolution towards economic progress and efficiency – that is, in economic determinist terms. The mainstream views we presented above imply that there was a gradual evolution of business organization from medieval JSCs to modern corporations with the assumption that the modern corporation, as the seeming endpoint of this evolution, is the most efficient way to organize business and, consequently, the best way to run the economy. This story of progress towards efficiency is inaccurate at best, as many scholars have stressed (e.g. Fligstein 1990; Roy 1997; Guinnane et al. 2007; Ireland 2010), and seriously misleading at worst. We want to highlight several aspects of the development of the corporation that need closer inspection in order to demonstrate how this notion of progress towards economic efficiency is deeply problematic on a number of levels.

- *Legally* corporations have evolved in relation to a range of forces, many of which have included political and social pressures and expectations as to the roles and responsibilities of large business organizations in society. Specifically, corporate structure and corporate personhood have evolved over time in response to these non-economic forces.

- *Empirically* corporations cannot be defined simply as business organizations responding to market signals and imperatives; they are social institutions that operate within broader social, legal and political contexts.
- *Normatively* the expansion of corporations has led to a number of problematic consequences which we briefly touch on here and come back to in later chapters.

We discuss each of these points in turn in this section, starting with the legal evolution of the corporation from the early nineteenth century onwards, focusing specifically on the United States. In running through these arguments we want to stress that any form of economic determinism – i.e. assuming economic imperatives (e.g. profit) shape society – needs questioning wherever it appears.

Legal evolution of corporate structure and personhood One of the critical things to bear in mind when discussing the corporate revolution is that legal concepts of the corporation have changed quite considerably over time, especially from the early nineteenth century to today – see Case Study. During this period of time, as the modern corporation emerged and rose to dominance, there have been at least four theories of the corporation that reflect a slow transformation of our understanding of corporate personhood and corporate governance. Here we draw on the legal work of William Bratton (1989) whose discussion largely focuses on the legal context in the UK and USA (see also Dewey 1926; Gindis 2009; Weinstein 2012).

- *Artificial entity and concession* (up to early nineteenth century): before **general incorporation** was introduced corporations were considered to be legal fictions created as a result of a concession (or charter) from the state. A (joint-stock) corporation was an artificial entity, created by the state, which provided its shareholders with **limited liability**.
- *Aggregate entity and contract* (late nineteenth century): as the UK and USA introduced general incorporation laws during the nineteenth century, the perception of the corporation shifted. Corporations were no longer seen as a concession or grant from the state – because the state no longer gave out charters – but as a contract between those people who owned shares in a corporation. Corporations were, therefore, seen as an aggregate entity representing all their individual members.
- *Natural or real entity* (post-1900 until 1970s): following the corporate revolution, the ownership and control of corporations was separated between shareholders and management respectively. The concept of a corporation in this period was dominated by the idea corporations are real entities with

their own identity that are run by managers in pursuit of the corporation's interests, rather than shareholders. Shareholders can buy or sell shares in a corporation as they desire, but do not represent the corporation and do not control its assets. This view is based on the reality that there are no permanent owners (e.g. shareholders trade their shares constantly) and owners have become passive rather than active (e.g. shareholders do not get involved in day-to-day management).

- *Nexus of contracts* (post-1970s): the most recent legal conception of the corporation comes out of financial economics by economists like Jensen and Meckling (1976), who built on the earlier work of Ronald Coase (see above). It is primarily based on the idea that a corporation is only a nexus (i.e. central connection point) of various contracting individuals (e.g. managers, shareholders, workers etc.); in this sense, a corporation is merely another kind of market. This perspective stresses that shareholders are owners and need to be able to control managers, who are characterized as the agents of the owners. This means creating incentives for managers to only make decisions that increase shareholder value (and nothing else).

Definition: General incorporation

This term refers to laws that enable people to establish businesses, especially corporations. What this means is that anyone can set up a business by submitting the relevant legal documents and does not need to request a charter from the government anymore. These laws were gradually introduced during the nineteenth century in the UK, USA and elsewhere.

Definition: Limited liability

This term refers to laws limiting the responsibilities of shareholders only to their monetary investment in a corporation. This means that shareholders are not responsibility for the actions of corporations, including any debts incurred as part of their operations. Consequently, shareholders do not have to think about or oversee their investments to ensure that they are being used in a financially *and* socially responsible manner. It enables the separation of shareholding and management.

What these legal definitions of the corporation illustrate is that the law's treatment of the corporation is not consistent over time; it changes as a result of legal debate and disagreement. While the legal concept of a corporation may seem like an esoteric topic, it is important because these legal concepts

Case study

Company law changes in the nineteenth century

Britain

Bubble Act repealed (1825):
- The 1720 *Bubble Act* limited the creation of new JSCs for fear that new JSCs were being created for purely speculative purposes. The *Bubble Act* was only repealed in 1825, which opened the way for the granting of new JSCs by Parliament. However, the establishment of a JSC was still a difficult process because it required parliamentary consent.

Companies Acts (1844, 1856, 1862):
- The three *Companies Acts* progressively extended limited liability and general incorporation.
- The 1844 Act enabled general incorporation of companies; the 1856 Act extended general incorporation and limited liability to most businesses, excluding banks and insurance companies; and the 1862 Act extended general incorporation and limited liability to banks and insurance companies.

United States

State law:
- US company law was made at the state level.
- In 1811 New York state extended general incorporation to some corporations, and then to all corporations in 1846.
- By the end of the 1800s, almost all US states had some form of general incorporation law.

Key legal decisions:
- A lot of US company law reflects key legal decisions.
- In the 1818 *Dartmouth College vs. Madison* decision, the judge ruled that corporations should be understood as private contracts and not government charters.
- In the 1886 *Santa Clara vs. Southern Pacific* decision, the judge ruled that corporations have rights normally limited to people, including rights to due process and equal protection before the law.

Sources: Nace (2003); Stout (2012)

---

impact the arguments and decisions that get made in court rooms, which then have implications subsequently for what corporations, shareholders, managers and others can do. Here we highlight one example of these impacts relating to managerial decision-making. The nexus of contract (NOC) definition of the corporation has become very influential since the 1970s, which has meant that most corporations are now run in specific ways (see Stout 2012). NOC is based on the idea that managers need clear incentives to ensure they *only* increase shareholder value, and not their own personal goals. One way to do this is to link managerial salaries to share prices, so that rising share prices lead to rewards for managers. This has involved giving senior managers (e.g. chief executive officers, or CEOs) share options that they can cash in when share prices rise; while this might sound sensible, a number of academics and others have pointed out several problems with this form of managerial remuneration. For example, it leads to managers focusing on short-term goals at the expense of long-term performance (Bratton 1989; Dobbin and Jung 2010; Stout 2012).

Corporation as social institution A second critical issue to bear in mind when it comes to the corporate revolution is that changes in business organization evolve as a consequence of the broader institutional context and not simply because of economic pressures. This is illustrated in the work of economic sociologists who analyse the corporate revolution and subsequent evolution of corporations in the USA, as well as the wider world (e.g. Fligstein 1990; Roy 1997; Whitley 1999). What this research shows is that there is limited empirical support for the idea that the corporate revolution happened as a result of business organization evolving towards more efficient organizational structures. There have been several significant shifts in business organization and strategies, especially of corporations, in the last two hundred years of US history.

The changes in business organization before, during and after the corporate revolution are documented by William Roy (1997) in his book *Socializing Capital*. Roy argues that understanding the corporate revolution necessitates understanding corporations as social institutions and not just as business organizations – the difference between **organizations and institutions** is an important one to understand in the social sciences. The point Roy is making is that business structures and strategies are not independent of their social and institutional context. This wider context includes things like: legal property rights and obligations, the changing social dimensions of those rights and obligations, and the role of the state when it comes to property (Roy 1997). In this sense, if we want to understand the corporate revolution and the subsequent rise of corporations, we have to understand more than economic forces and pressures. We also have to understand law, society, government and so on. Another scholar who makes similar claims is Neil Fligstein (1990). He stresses that the historical evolution of corporate strategies results from different 'conceptions of control' and not economic determinism – that is, each conception of control emerges from the last, being dependent on previous strategies and structures rather than on an independent drivers like economic efficiency. There are, for example, other drivers of change including the role and actions of the state (e.g. introducing new laws), changing managerial practices (e.g. avoiding competition) and so on (Fligstein 1990).

> **Key methodological issue: Organization vs. institution?**
>
> Social scientists make choices about what they study all the time. Studying the relationship between business and society necessitates choices over whether to focus on specific entities (e.g. one business) or broader socio-political trends and patterns (e.g. a range of businesses). Social scientists make an important distinction between organizations and institutions in this regard. Organizations are generally defined as individual entities which have a specific collective purpose, structure and strategies; in contrast, institutions are generally defined as broader and less clear-cut social structures that influence people's behaviour. Institutions can be formal and include things like *the* family as a social arrangement, *the* state as a governmental arrangement, *the* corporation as an economic arrangement etc. They can also be informal and include things like social customs, habits, trust etc. For the purposes of this book, it is important to remember that an institution is more than an individual entity.

In order to illustrate our argument here, we draw on Fligstein's (1990) work in his book *The Transformation of Corporate Control*. He argues that corporations have moved through a range of different structures and strategies since the nineteenth century, each period building on the last. First, the USA's post-Civil War era, at least until 1890, was dominated by the rise of monopolistic strategies, especially through the formation of cartels and trusts according to Fligstein (1990). Cartels and trusts are formal and informal agreements between businesses to collude with one another in order to limit competition – as such it was a *direct* form of control in a socio-legal context which lacked rules and regulations on business practice. Examples include businesses like Standard Oil. The direct control evident in the late nineteenth century was supplanted by a new conception according to Fligstein, which was driven by new legal limits on monopolies, those resulting from the 1890 *Sherman Antitrust Act*.

Second, from the late 1800s corporations adopted new organizational structures like the vertical integration of production; this meant incorporating all aspects of production from resource extraction through manufacturing to sales into one organizational structure. Examples here included businesses like General Electric that sold everything from electricity to electric products. Third, this evolved again in the 1920s as these large integrated corporations sought new avenues for growth through the introduction of things like marketing, branding and advertising. This change shifted focus from the production process to the product itself through an emphasis on brands and branding, leading many corporations to diversify into multiple product lines. Examples of these businesses included consumer product companies like Proctor and Gamble.

Fourth, in the 1950s these diversified corporations ended up as giant conglomerates with multiple product lines, competing in multiple markets. They were structured around a central headquarters and subsidiaries in different economic sectors and different countries. Examples here included most corporations in the post-Second World War era (until the 1980s at least). A final shift in corporate strategies has occurred relatively recently, since the 1980s, as financial accounting and finance departments in corporations have come to dominate corporate strategies. This has led to a focus on shareholder value and an emphasis on core competencies; hence, it has meant that many corporations have split up and sold off several of their divisions.

Critique of the rise of corporations Whether we take the corporate revolution to mean an increase in economic efficiency or not, it is important to question the outcomes and effects of the revolution more generally. We return to a critique of corporate power in Chapter 6, so limit ourselves to three observations here.

First, the ambiguity of corporate personhood and identity has meant that there have been and still are a number of problems with the way corporations operate and what they can get away with. For example, Veldman and Parker (2012) argue that this ambiguity has meant that corporations are able to claim human rights like the right to speech, even though they are not human. Claims to these sorts of human rights are problematic because corporations are not like humans in important ways; for example, they have a perpetual lifespan and enormous societal influence.

Second, the corporate revolution only happened because of specific changes in laws and regulations affecting corporations during the nineteenth and twentieth century, especially the extension of limited liability to a growing number of business organizations, not just corporations. Paddy Ireland (2010) highlights a key contradiction that comes with this shift. While the responsibilities of shareholders have been separated from the responsibilities of corporations, there have been contradictory pressures to ensure that corporations are run in the interests of shareholders. Consequently, shareholders benefit from the current situation without suffering the negative impacts from the actions of corporations.

Finally, the rise of managerial capitalism is associated with the expansion of the power of corporations. As corporations have become larger and larger, their influence over society (through advertising, employment etc.), politics (through lobbying, donations etc.) and the economy (through size, market power etc.) has also grown (Bakan 2004). We come back to this discussion of corporate power in Chapter 6, but suffice to say here that the corporate revolution gave rise to growing concerns about the role of corporations in society.

Conclusion

In this chapter we sought to question the notion that the organization of business, including corporations, is determined by economic and market pressures or forces – that is, that business naturally evolves towards greater efficiency over time. First, we outlined the history of the corporate revolution and how corporations are understood from an economically determinist perspective. Second, we problematize economic determinism by outlining the legal, empirical and normative dimensions of the corporate revolution. In particular, we highlighted the evolution of the legal and organizational understandings of corporations. Third, we finished by outlining some of the normative issues with the corporate revolution, which we return to in subsequent chapters. Throughout we have sought to show that corporations have evolved historically in a number of ways that cannot be explained by one perspective.

Suggested readings

- Ch. 2–4, Berle, A. and Means, G. (1932 [1967]) *The Modern Corporation and Private Property*, New York, World Inc.
- Conclusion, Chandler, A. (1977 [1993]) *The Visible Hand*, Cambridge MA, Belknap Press.
- Ch. 1, Fligstein, N. (1990) *The Transformation of Corporate Control*, Cambridge MA, Harvard University Press.
- Ch. 7, Nace, T. (2003) *Gangs of America*, Oakland CA, Berrett-Koehler.
- Ch. 1, Roy, W. (1997) *Socializing Capital*, Princeton, Princeton University Press.

Bibliography

Bakan, J. (2004) *The Corporation*, London, Random House.

Barkan, J. (2013) *Corporate Sovereignty*, Minneapolis, Minnesota University Press.

Berle, A. and Means, G. (1932 [1967]) *The Modern Corporation and Private Property*, New York, World Inc.

Bratton, W. (1989) 'The new economic theory of the firm: Critical perspectives from history', *Stanford Law Review*, Vol.41, pp.1471–1527.

Chandler, A. (1977 [1993]) *The Visible Hand*, Cambridge MA, Belknap Press.

Cheffins, B. (2008) *Corporate Ownership and Control*, Oxford, Oxford University Press.

Coase, R. (1937) 'The nature of the firm', *Economica*, Vol.4, pp.386–405.

Dewey, J. (1926) 'The historic background of corporate legal personality', *Yale Law Journal*, Vol.35, pp.655–673.

Dobbin, F. and Jung, J. (2010) 'The misapplication of Mr. Michael Jensen: How agency theory brought down the economy and why it might again', in M. Loundsbury and P. Hirsch (eds), *Markets on Trial: The Economic Sociology of the U.S. Financial Crisis (Part B)*, Bingley, Emerald, pp.29–64.

Fligstein, N. (1990) *The Transformation of Corporate Control*, Cambridge MA, Harvard University Press.

Gindis, D. (2009) 'From fictions and aggregates to real entities in the theory of the firm', *Journal of Institutional Economics*, Vol.5, pp.25–46.

Guinnane, T., Harris, R., Lamoreaux, N. and Rosenthal, J.-L. (2007) 'Putting the corporation in its place', *Enterprise and Society*, Vol.8, pp.687–729.

Handlin, O. and Handlin, M. (1945) 'Origins of the American business corporation', *The Journal of Economic History*, Vol.5, pp.1–23.

Ireland, P. (2010) 'Limited liability, shareholder rights and the problem of corporate irresponsibility', *Cambridge Journal of Economics*, Vol.34, pp.837–856.

Jensen, M. and Meckling, W. (1976) 'Theory of the firm: Managerial behavior, agency costs and ownership structure', *Journal of Financial Economics*, Vol.3, pp.305–360.

Khurana, R. (2007) *From Higher Aims to Hired Hands*, Princeton, Princeton University Press.

Micklethwait, J. and Wooldridge, A. (2005) *The Company*, New York, Modern Library Chronicles Book.

Nace, T. (2003) *Gangs of America*, San Francisco, Berrett-Koehler.

Roy, W. (1997) *Socializing Capital*, Princeton, Princeton University Press.

Stout, L. (2012) *The Shareholder Value Myth*, San Francisco, Berrett-Koehler.

Veldman, J. and Parker, M. (2012) 'Specters, Inc.: The elusive basis of the corporation', *Business and Society Review*, Vol.117, pp.413–441.

Weinstein, O. (2012) 'Firm, property and governance: From Berle and Means to the agency theory, and beyond', *Accounting, Economics, and Law*, Vol.2, pp.1–55.

Whitley, R. (1999) *Divergent Capitalisms*, Oxford, Oxford University Press.

4 | Corporate governance

Alberto Salazar

Introduction

In this chapter we critically review the models for governing for-profit corporations in modern capitalist societies. Governance generally refers to the mechanisms that control and direct the behaviour of individuals, groups or organizations. Corporate governance can be defined as the systems and processes that control and direct the conduct of corporations. It may involve legal and non-legal mechanisms that are used to govern corporations, their activities and the competing interests of shareholders, executives, managers, creditors, employees, consumers, suppliers, local communities, governments and society at large. The study of corporate governance is important because it helps us understand how and why corporations are regulated, the competing purposes of corporations, the extent to which the conflicting interests of corporate participants are balanced and whether the activities of the corporations have a positive or negative impact on the economy and society at large.

The current and dominant corporate governance model in countries like the USA, UK and Canada is called the 'shareholder primacy' (SHP) model. The SHP model relies on markets and legal and non-legal mechanisms to maximize shareholder interests, measured by short-term share value and firm profitability. SHP is based on agency theory and nexus of contracts approaches in neoclassical economics, and can be considered the mainstream agenda for corporate governance. In particular, the SHP model focuses on aligning the interests of executives and managers (or 'agents') with shareholders (or 'principals'). In this chapter, we argue that the SHP model is in crisis, not only because of the increasing abuses of executives and managers, but also because of the disregard it engenders in the interests of workers, citizen-consumers, local communities, small businesses, creditors and society at large (i.e. non-shareholder stakeholders).

We would argue that the future of the corporation lies in finding effective and creative ways of integrating the interests of non-shareholder stakeholders, while moderating the ideological commitment to profit-maximization, short-termism and elite wealth concentration without sacrificing growth. In fact, there are forces that are increasingly driving corporate governance systems around the world towards stakeholders' interest, long-term sustainability and the public interest while maintaining diverging corporate governance structures. This puts into question the validity of the arguments for convergence towards a SHP model and sheds light on the process of modern divergence among corporate governance systems.

After reviewing the contradictions of the SHP model, we critically examine the alternative, stakeholder-oriented models of corporate governance in liberal and coordinated market economies. First, we analyse the strengths and weaknesses of the team production theory along with fiduciary duty paradigms in liberal market economies. Second, we discuss the advantages of long-standing stakeholder models of corporate governance in coordinated market economies, especially in Germany and Japan. We then conclude the chapter with an example looking at low executive pay in Japanese corporations in order to illustrate modern departures from the SHP model.

Key discussion questions

- What is corporate governance?
- What is the shareholder primacy model of corporate governance?
- What is the stakeholder-oriented model of corporate governance?
- Why is the shareholder model of corporate governance problematic?
- Does the stakeholder model of corporate governance offer a superior form of governance capable of resolving the challenges of governing modern corporations today?

The shareholder primacy model

Shareholder primacy and the agency problem The shareholder primacy (SHP) model is the dominant approach to corporate practices in many parts of the world. It is based on the idea that prioritizing shareholders' interest should take priority because they bear the highest risk because their investment is unsecured (i.e. they are the 'residual claimant'). Macey (1989: 175) argued that 'shareholders retain plenary authority to guide the fate of a corporate enterprise because, at the margin, they have the greatest stake in the outcome of corporate decision-making and not because they hold certain ill-defined property rights'. Whereas employees, creditors, consumers and managers enter into explicit contracts with fixed payments, shareholders rely on implicit contracts that entitle them to whatever remains after the firm has met its explicit obligations and paid its fixed claims (Easterbrook and Fischel 1991). Shareholders are thus described as 'sole residual claimants' to a firm's value or 'sole residual risk bearers' (Clark 1986: 17–18; Macey 1989: 186; Easterbrook and Fischel 1991).

SHP is underpinned by two concepts: (1) nexus of contracts and (2) agency theory (Verret 2010). According to the nexus of contract concept, all participants are linked to the corporation through private contracts and organized under a single business plan. According to Jensen and Meckling (1976: 310–311), two key economists in these debates, the firm is considered a legal fiction which serves 'as a nexus for a set of contracting relationships' and 'as a focus for a complex process in which the conflicting objectives of individuals . . . are brought into equilibrium within a framework of contractual relations'. Moreover, the contractual relationship between shareholders and managers is also conceived as an 'agency problem'.

The notion of an agency problem originates in the separation of ownership and control in public corporations, and represents a key issue facing shareholders in the SHP model. Some of the earliest theorists in this area were Berle and Means (1932) who suggested that the separation of ownership and control resulting from the corporate revolution (see Chapter 3) facilitates opportunistic behaviour (i.e. mismanagement) by executives and managers. They observed in the 1920s that the equity ownership of the largest firms had dispersed among numerous shareholders who often owned a small fraction of shares and, as a result, had little incentive to pay close attention to the internal affairs of their firms. These dispersed shareholders were rationally apathetic and were dependent on the recommendations made by executives and managers. According to Berle and Means (1932), control of public firms shifted from dispersed shareholders to executives and managers by default. Although the agency problem concerned Berle and Means, they also recognized that executives and managers should run the corporation not just to serve the interest of shareholders but also employees, consumers and the community.

Later in the twentieth century, Jensen and Meckling (1976) characterized the relationship between shareholders and executives and managers as an agency problem and cost. They based their arguments on the notion that public corporations represent a contract between principals (i.e. shareholders) and agents (i.e. executives and managers); this usually involves the delegation of control to agents in the performance of a service for the principal. Jensen and Meckling (1976: 308) argued that '[i]f both parties to the relationship are utility maximizers, there is good reason to believe that the agent will not always act in the best interests of the principal'. This agency cost problem accompanied the growing 'rational apathy' of dispersed shareholders that flowed from the logic of free-riding and a lack of skills and incentives (Clark 1986). In such a context, executives and managers become very powerful as they increasingly control corporate decisions and critical information thereby further facilitating (a) the misalignment of their interests with the interests of shareholders and (b) managerial misconduct.

Minimizing agency costs and monitoring agents in particular became a central agenda for SHP approaches. Jensen and Meckling (1976) suggested that incentives for the agents to align their interest with the interests of principals (stockholders) can be established through contracts, law and other organizational forms. However, monitoring agents is costly, as is devising incentives to align the interests of executives and managers with shareholders. Some of the incentives suggested in agency theory include using executive pay, corporate control transactions, managerial job competition and bankruptcy, combined with corporate law rules (e.g. fiduciary duties of executives and managers, strengthening shareholders rights etc.), in order to align executives and managers' conduct with shareholder interests (Marks 2000). Moreover, corporate self-regulatory practices such as codes of conduct, disciplinary action by business associations and institutional shareholder activism have supplemented existent monitoring mechanisms.

Contradictions of the shareholder primacy model Despite the arguments above used to support the SHP model, it is not accurate to claim that shareholders are residual claimants. The only time that shareholders may be residual claimants is when a corporation goes bankrupt. When a corporation is operating normally, shareholders are not necessarily entitled to whatever is left after the firm has met its explicit contractual obligations with employees, creditors, managers or consumers (Stout 2002). For example, Stout (2002) points out that the board of directors has considerable control over corporate earnings or profits and decides when and how profits should be distributed among shareholders. Moreover, other stakeholders can be described as residual claimants or residual risk bearers themselves, because they may also enjoy benefits or endure burdens beyond those that are provided in their explicit contracts (Stout 2002). For example, employees may receive a pay increase, bonus, longer job security benefits, or suffer early lay-offs or reduced working hours.

Another issue is that the problem of agency cost remains largely unresolved. The many mechanisms developed to control the conduct of executives and managers, and align their behaviour with the interest of shareholders, are largely ineffective. Executives and managers engage in many forms of mismanagement, including financial fraud, or work in the interests of majority shareholders at the expense of minority shareholders and other stakeholders. For example, Oracle's Larry Ellison was the highest-paid CEO in the USA in 2012; he received $96.2 million that year, a 24 per cent increase, despite his company's share price falling 23 per cent (Fairchild 2013). More revealing, in the past 20 years nearly 40 per cent of the highest-paid CEOs in the USA have been bailed out, fired or arrested for illegal activities (Anderson et al. 2013).

Furthermore, new agency costs have arisen with the shift in share ownership from dispersed individual owners to concentrated institutional investors or intermediaries such as pension, mutual and insurance funds (Gilson and Gordon 2014). For example, and as outlined in Table 4.1, 'investment intermediaries now own over 70 percent of the stock of the largest 1000 US public

TABLE 4.1 Institutional ownership of largest US corporations, 2009

Corporations ranked by size	Average institutional holdings (%)
Top 50	63.7
Top 100	66.9
Top 250	69.3
Top 500	72.8
Top 1000	73.0

Sources: Tonello and Rabimov (2010: 27 tbl.13); Gilson and Gordon (2013: 875)

corporations, and in many corporations the ownership position of as few as two dozen institutional investors is large enough for substantial influence, if not effective control' (Gilson and Gordon 2014: 6–7); this change has been described as 'agency capitalism' (p.7). These ownership changes have produced a new agency costs; that is to say, 'institutional intermediaries engage in own-goal pursuit at the expense of ultimate beneficiaries' (p.7). Institutional investors or intermediaries lack strong incentives to engage in shareholder activism and instead tend to be reactive.

Finally, according to some people the SHP model has resulted in a focus on short-term share value and profitability over other considerations (Sayer 2015). According to this view, the SHP model has damaged the long-term sustainability of corporations, caused financial crises and widened the gap between executive pay and worker wages and society's inequality more generally (Sayer 2015). The gap between the rich and poor is growing faster and only the rich are likely to invest in the capital market and become shareholders, leading to further concentration of wealth. In this sense, wealthy investors still benefit from the SHP model, even with agency costs. Thus prioritizing and maximizing shareholder value in practice means organizing the corporation and even the economy to serve the capital accumulation plans of a rich shareholder class in society (Ireland 2005).

Stakeholder models of corporate governance

The belief that corporations should focus on maximizing shareholder value has been questioned by various scholars, activists, journalists and others. Several people suggest that there are better corporate governance models, especially ones that protect the interests of all stakeholders. In the Anglo-American world, this debate began in the 1930s between Adolf Berle and Merrick Dodd. On the one hand, Berle (1931: 1049) supported the SHP model, arguing that 'all powers granted to a corporation or to the management of a corporation, or to any group within the corporation . . . [are] at all times exercisable only for the ratable benefit of all the shareholders as their interest appears'. On the other hand, Merrick Dodd (1932) supported the idea that the purpose of a corporation was not confined to making profits for shareholders. In his view, a corporation also has a social service function and should provide secure jobs for employees, better quality products for consumers and contribute to the community.

More recently, the growing dissatisfaction with the SHP model has focused attention on stakeholder models of corporate governance, which are often associated with coordinated market economies (Hall and Soskice 2001). We review the alternatives to the SHP model in this section.

Stakeholder models in liberal market economies One influential stakeholder approach in Anglo-American, or liberal market economies (Hall and Soskice 2001), is team production theory. Margaret Blair and Lynn Stout (1999) developed this theory as an alternative to the SHP model. They recognize that employees, creditors, managers and governments contribute to the success of a corporation. They note that SHP may actually discourage non-shareholder constituents from making the types of firm-specific investments that are critical to a company's success (Blair and Stout 1999; Stout 2002). From this point of view, executives and managers should acknowledge and reward such contributions and should balance the multiple interests of shareholders, employees, creditors, suppliers, consumers and governments. As a result, the board of directors is vested with significant discretion to conduct the balancing act. The need to balance multiple interests is partially justified by the recognition that private contracting does not necessarily protect the interests and expectations of all corporate constituencies because of the difficulties in drafting complete contracts under conditions of complexity and uncertainty, contrary to the predictions of the nexus of contract approach (Blair and Stout 1999; Stout 2002).

Another recent development is fiduciary duty paradigms in corporate law. The fiduciary duty of executives and managers has been increasingly broadened to cover the interests of creditors, employees, consumers, local communities, the environments and governments. Furthermore, executives and managers are increasingly required to promote long-term sustainability and the public interest and avoid an excessive focus on short-termism and shareholder value.

These broader fiduciary duties have become extremely important in light of the growth of institutional investors. Such institutional investors have become very influential in corporate governance because of their role in administering huge amounts of capital. They are now asked to also consider the interest of non-shareholder stakeholders and the public interest. For example, in Canada pension funds are gradually required to look beyond the immediate imperatives of the market and beneficiaries' short-term returns as fiduciary duties are being broadened (Waitzer and Sarro 2012, 2014). Pension funds are increasingly charged with public responsibilities and are expected to consider longer-term, systemic concerns such as intergenerational equity and sustainable development (Waitzer and Sarro 2012, 2014).

However, these changes aside, the team production and fiduciary duty approaches have significant limitations. The balancing act required from executives and managers can be extremely problematic and unfeasible in the real world of corporate decision-making. In addition to the problem of persuading courts or legislators to make a law requiring executives and managers to exercise their duties with the goal of protecting multiple stakeholders' interests, directors will need to have the commitment to advance that goal. However, executives and managers may still serve their own interest by circumventing or breaching their fiduciary duties. Stout (2002) recognizes that problem and admits that executives and managers in a team production context can also face significant agency cost problems.

Controlling shareholders may actually hinder the attempts by executives and managers to maximize the interests of employees, creditors, suppliers, consumers and the community. Controlling or majority shareholders can put significant pressures on executives and managers to prioritize their interests with the possibility of even capturing the board to the detriment of non-shareholder stakeholders' interest (Coates 1999; Gold 2012; Millon 2000). This problem is further complicated by the fact that executives and managers are often shareholders of the corporations they run and thus may not necessarily be interested in sacrificing shareholder value in order to protect the interest of non-shareholder constituencies.

Ultimately, the limitations of the team production and fiduciary duty approaches in liberal market economies reveal that relying solely on the good will, skills and discretion of executives and managers to build a stakeholder-friendly corporation is extremely difficult and insufficient. It appears that the weaknesses of the team production theory render it unfeasible and might demonstrate that the SHP model, despite its problems, can be a second-best governance system as it provides an easily observed metric for executives' and managers' accountability, thereby better minimizing agency cost (Stout 2002).

Nevertheless, team production mechanisms and multi-stakeholder fiduciary duties could create incentives for stakeholder activism, which can in turn put pressure on executives and managers, shareholders and the corporation itself to protect non-shareholder stakeholders' interests. Such activism by, for example, workers may also help correct the problems of agency cost, excessive managerial discretion and controlling shareholder power. It may also encourage the adoption of some form of coordination or informal co-determination practices that are likely to be responsive to stakeholders' interests, long-term sustainability and the public interest. Such informal coordination or co-determination is partially facilitated by the institutional incentives created by stakeholder-oriented fiduciary duties and often takes the form of power struggles inside and outside boardrooms and courtrooms and beyond corporate law. From this perspective, the team production theory may still be a valuable and feasible alternative to the SHP model.

Stakeholder models in coordinated market economies Important alternatives to the SHP model are the stakeholder models of corporate governance prevalent in coordinated market economies; namely Germany and Japan. These stakeholder models do not rely on the ability of executives and managers to integrate the interests of multiple stakeholders as suggested by team production and fiduciary duty approaches. Instead, they grant decision-making power to multiple stakeholders, notably creditors and workers, and encourage strong forms of co-determination in which shareholders and executives and managers are not the sole decision-makers, but rather they coordinate their interests with the interests of creditors, workers, consumers and governments.

In Germany, corporate governance has been described as an insider-controlled and a stakeholder-oriented system (Franks and Mayer 2001; Schmidt 2004). It has two striking characteristics, namely, mandatory co-determination and a strong role for banks. Co-determination involves employee representation through a two-tier board system, a management board ('Vorstand') and a supervisory board ('Aufsichtsrat'). The management board manages and represents the company and the supervisory board appoints and oversees the management board of the company (Tungler 2000). Employee representatives sit on supervisory boards and often provide effective and highly informed monitoring of the management board (Fauver and Fuerst 2006). In addition to sitting on supervisory boards, employees also participate in the governance of German firms through Work Councils (Fauver and Fuerst 2006). These Councils represent employees' interest outside corporate boards and provide advice and are to be consulted on general working conditions.

Traditionally, banks have played a central role in corporate governance in Germany, along with family investors and the labour force (Bessler et al. 2013). Banks have been long-term lenders and have owned large equity stakes in German firms (Bessler et al. 2013). Their equity stakes have enabled banks to sit on supervisory boards and to act on behalf of investors through voting proxies, thereby often controlling the majority of voting rights in German firms (Bessler et al. 2013; Jackson 2005; Baums and von Randow 1995). As a result, banks have exerted substantial long-term-oriented influence over corporate governance decisions, which is reflected in a modest market for corporate control and little shareholder activism (Bessler et al. 2013).

Despite recent changes to the traditional dominant role of banks (e.g. integration of German capital markets into European and global financial markets, reduced monitoring role, tax incentives to reduce shareholding etc.), the German corporate governance system has been able to preserve its strong commitment to stakeholders' interest and long-term sustainability. Banks still hold a significant number of board seats in many German firms despite large sell-offs of their equity holdings; family investors continue to hold controlling stakes in a large number of listed small- and mid-sized firms; and workers and unions are still influential in corporate decisions due to mandatory co-determination and continue to present significant challenges to hedge fund activism inside and outside supervisory boards (Bessler et al. 2013).

In Japan, corporate governance departs from the SHP models and is another example of a stakeholder model. Generally, the Japanese corporate governance model is characterized by main bank capital markets, *keiretsu* cross-holdings and insider boards of directors (Higgins 2004; Basu et al. 2007). The *keiretsu* is an industrial group whose member firms are bound by long-term cross-shareholdings and maintain strong business and financial ties (Higgins 2004; Basu et al. 2007). The *keiretsu* system provides a strong monitoring mechanism, unlike the SHP model. By pooling voting rights, the *keiretsu* has control over member executives and managers, ensuring that none behave opportunistically (Basu et al. 2007). Firms that belong to the *keiretsu* are essentially bound together by a series of connected contracts which maintain the crucial business relationships. Japanese boards have a hierarchical structure and their composition depends on promotion from within the company with very little influence from 'outsiders' except for the main bank representatives (Higgins 2004). The extensive use of joint labour-management consultation allows employees to express their interests within Japanese corporate governance structures, unlike the more formal and legal participation of employees in German boards (Jackson 2005).

Banks were limited in their use of cross-shareholding after the deregulation of the financial systems and corporate governance reforms in Japan, and the Commercial Code in 2003 allowed Japanese firms to adopt a new board system with three committees (auditing, nomination and compensation) similar to the SHP systems and the majority of the committee members should be outside directors (Hoshi and Kashyap 2010; Sakawa et al. 2012; Gilson and Milhaupt 2005; Jackson and Milhaupt 2014). However, recent studies show that internationally exposed, more experienced and highly cross-held firms, with higher foreign ownership, are more likely to adopt the committee system (Chizema and Shinozawa 2012). On the other hand, firms with larger proportions of bank ownership are to some extent negatively associated with the adoption of the committee system. As a result, the traditional monitoring of firms by banks seems to be declining (Chizema and Shinozawa 2012). These corporate governance changes suggest that, for example, Japanese corporations may be making a slow transition from the traditional approval of self-proposed executive compensation at the annual shareholder meeting to compensation committee determination (Sakawa and Watanabel 2013).

Empirical example: executive pay in Japanese corporations

An important example of the difference between shareholder and stakeholder models of corporate governance is the difference in executive pay. Historically, for example, Japanese corporations developed a pattern of low executive pay and this exposes the excessive executive pay in liberal market economics (see Chapter 7). As data in Table 4.2 shows, Japan has had lower executive pay than the USA since at least the late 1980s.

The disparities between executive pay and worker wages further illustrate the extent to which Japan has diverged from liberal market economics on excessive executive compensation. Jackson (2005: 292) notes that 'CEO pay was 7.8 times higher in Japan than the average worker, and 25.8 times in the United States in 1991, and this figure rose 11 times higher in Japan and an astounding 35 times larger in the United States'. The CEO-worker pay disparity worsened in the United States in the following years and has reached alarming proportions particularly when compared to the Japanese ratio (see Table 4.3).

A central reason that explains lower executive pay in Japan is the governance measures protecting the interests of workers, which in turn informs executive pay decisions. The perception of corporate management as a

TABLE 4.2 International comparison of average executive pay (2001 US dollars)

Country	CEO pay (1988)	CEO pay (2001)	Percentage change 1988–2001	Ratio of CEO to worker pay, 2001	Foreign pay relative to US pay, 2001 US = 100	
					CEO	worker
Japan	$455,909	$508,106	11%	11.6	26%	93%
Canada	$383,999	$787,060	105%	23.2	41%	72%
USA	$730,606	$1,932,580	165%	153.7	100%	100%

Source: Mishel et al. (2003: 216)

TABLE 4.3 Ratio of CEO pay to average worker

Country	Ratio (CEO to worker pay)
Japan	67:1
Canada	206:1
United States	354:1

Source: Macleans (2014)

collective effort further encourages the need to relate CEO pay to worker salaries (Salacuse 2004). This is indicative of the central place that employee interests have in Japanese firms. This is also exemplified with Japanese corporations' traditional commitment to lifetime employment (Abe et al. 2005), although this has been declining in the last years (Kawaguchi and Ueno 2013) and has not been applied equally to male and female workers and the gender wage gap is still high (Nakamura and Rebein 2012). Nonetheless, the strong protection of worker interests is part of the larger commitment to promote industrial citizenship of labour in Japan (Jackson 2001).

Executive bonuses are also related to worker bonuses. If the latter is reduced in order to save labour cost and avoid massive lay-offs in tough economic times, executive bonuses are also expected to drop (Abe et al. 2005). These corporate practices may be partially explained by post-war ideas of equality that have prevailed in Japan, which is an important cultural constraint both to control excessive executive pay and reduce the gap between the executive and employee pay (Kono 2016). This practice of informally tying executive pay to the salary of workers helps both lower executive compensation and narrow the pay gap between CEOs and average Japanese workers down to some of the lowest in the world. This demonstrates the centrality of employee interests in Japan's stakeholder model of corporate governance.

Conclusion

In this chapter, we have critically examined the two dominant paradigms of corporate governance, namely the shareholder primacy (SHP) model and stakeholder models. We have reviewed the rationale for the SHP model and discussed its failures in light of evidence. We then discussed stakeholder-oriented models in liberal and coordinated market economies. The last section examined the advantages of long-standing stakeholder models of corporate governance in coordinated market economies focusing on Germany and Japan. The evidence indicated that despite the pressure from global capital markets such models remain committed to serve multiple stakeholders' interest. The pattern of low executive pay in Japan was used to illustrate a stakeholder model of governance and its strong relevance in the divergence–convergence debate.

This short review has also shown that there are growing forces that are increasingly driving corporate governance systems around the world towards the interests of a broad range of stakeholders and long-term sustainability while maintaining diverging corporate governance structures. Corporate governance in liberal market economies is under strong pressure to depart from the commitment to SHP and to consider stakeholder models, especially as the result of institutional shareholder activism and the expansion of fiduciary duties of managers and executives. A movement towards more stakeholder-friendly corporate governance systems is growing in the midst of power struggles inside and outside boardrooms and courtrooms – see Chapter 6 on corporate power. The activism of multiple local and global stakeholders, namely institutional investors, creditors, workers, suppliers, citizen-consumers, civil society organizations and governments, appears to be critical in pushing corporate governance systems towards stakeholders' interest, long-term sustainability and the public interest. These active stakeholders, however, need to be further legally, financially and politically empowered in order to foster a lasting stakeholder culture, build a facilitative institutional structure and sustain such a growing convergence towards stakeholder-friendly governance systems.

Suggested readings

- Bessler, W., Drobetz, W. and Holler, J. (2013) 'The returns to hedge fund activism in Germany', *European Financial Management*, Vol.21, pp.106–147.
- Blair, M. and Stout, L.A. (1999) 'A team production theory of corporate law', *Virginia Law Review*, Vol.85, pp.247–328.
- Jensen, M.C. and Meckling, W.H. (1976) 'Theory of the firm: Managerial behavior, agency costs and ownership structure', *Journal of Financial Economics*, Vol.3, pp.305–360.
- Stout, L.A. (2002) 'Bad and not-so-bad arguments for shareholder primacy', *Southern California Law Review*, Vol.75, pp.1189–1210.

Bibliography

Abe, N., Gaston N. and Kubo, K. (2005) 'Executive pay in Japan: The role of bank-appointed monitors and the main bank relationship', *Japan and the World Economy*, Vol.17, pp.371–394.

Anderson, S., Kingler, S. and Pizzigati, S. (2013) *Executive Access 2013: Bailed Out, Booted and Busted*, Washington DC, Institute for Policy Studies.

Basu, S., Hwang, L.-S., Mitsudome, T. and Weintrop, J. (2007) 'Corporate governance, top executive compensation and firm performance in Japan', *Pacific-Basin Finance Journal*, Vol.15, pp.56–79.

Baums, T. and von Randow, P. (1995) 'Der Markt für Stimmrechtsvertreter', *Die Aktiengesellschaft*, Vol.40.

Berle, A. (1931) 'Corporate powers as powers in trust', *Harvard Law Review*, Vol.44, pp.1049–1074.

Berle, A. and Means, G. (1932 [1967]) *The Modern Corporation and Private Property* (revised edition), New York, World Inc.

Bessler, W., Drobetz, W. and Holler, J. (2013) 'The returns to hedge fund activism in Germany', *European Financial Management*, Vol.21, pp.106–147.

Blair, M. and Stout, L.A. (1999) 'A team production theory of corporate law', *Virginia Law Review*, Vol.85, pp.247–328.

Chizema, A. and Shinozawa, Y. (2012) 'The 'company with committees': Change or continuity in Japanese corporate governance?', *Journal of Management Studies*, Vol.49, pp.77–101.

Clark, R. (1986) *Corporate Law*, Boston, LL Little Brown.

Coates IV, John C. (1999) 'Measuring the domain of mediating hierarchy: How contestable are U.S. public corporations?', *Journal of Corporation Law*, Vol.24, pp.837–867.

Dodd, M. (1932) 'For whom are corporate managers trustees?', *Harvard Law Review*, Vol.45, pp.1145–1163.

Easterbrook, F. and Fischel, D. (1991) *The Economic Structure of Corporate Law*, Cambridge, MA, Harvard University Press.

Fairchild, C. (2013) 'Sony CEO among 40 execs to give up bonuses as company struggles', *The Huffington Post*, 1 May.

Fauver, L. and Fuerst, M.E. (2006) 'Does good corporate governance include employee representation? Evidence from German boards', *Journal of Financial Economics*, Vol.82, pp.673–710.

Franks, J. and Mayer, C. (2001) 'Ownership and control of German corporations', *Review of Financial Studies*, Vol.14, pp.943–977.

Gilson, R.J. and Gordon, J.N. (2013) 'The agency costs of agency capitalism: Activist investors and the revaluation of governance rights', *Columbia Law Review*, Vol.113, pp.863–928.

Gilson, R.J. and Gordon, J.N. (2014) 'Agency capitalism: Further implications of equity intermediation', Working Paper No. 239, European Corporate Governance Institute.

Gilson, R. and Milhaupt, C. (2005) 'Choice as regulatory reform: The case of Japanese corporate governance', *American Journal of Comparative Law*, Vol.53, pp.343–377.

Gold, A.Gold, Andrew S. (2012) 'Dynamic fiduciary duties', *Cardozo Law Review*, Vol.34, pp.491–530.Gold, Andrew S.

Hall, P. and Soskice, D. (eds) (2001) *Varieties of Capitalism: The Institutional Foundations of Comparative Advantage*, Oxford, Oxford University Press.

Higgins, H. (2004) 'Corporate governance in Japan: The role of banks, keiretsu and Japanese traditions', in F.A. Gul and S.I. Tsui (eds), *The Governance of East Asian Corporations: Post Asian Financial Crisis*, London, Palgrave Macmillan, pp.95–116.

Hoshi, T. and Kashyap, A. (2010) 'Will the US bank recapitalization succeed? Eight lessons from Japan', *Journal of Financial Economics*, Vol.97, pp.398–417.

Ireland, P. (2005) 'Shareholder primacy and the distribution of wealth', *The Modern Law Review*, Vol.68, pp.49–81.

Jackson, G. (2001) 'The origins of non-liberal capitalism: Germany and Japan in comparison', in W. Streeck and K. Yamaura (eds), *The Origins of Nonliberal Capitalism*, Ithaca, Cornell University Press.

Jackson, G. (2005) 'Stakeholders under pressure: Corporate governance and labour management in Germany and Japan', *Corporate Governance: An International Review*, Vol.13, pp.419–428.

Jackson, R. and Milhaupt, C. (2014) 'Corporate governance and executive compensation: Evidence from Japan', *Columbia Business Law Review*, Vol.1, pp.111–171.

Jensen, M.C. and Meckling, W.H. (1976) 'Theory of the firm: Managerial behavior, agency costs and ownership structure', *Journal of Financial Economics*, Vol.3, pp.305–360.

Kawaguchi, D. and Ueno, Y. (2013) 'Declining long-term employment in Japan', *Journal of The Japanese and International Economies*, Vol.28, pp.19–36.

Kono, T. (2016) *Strategy and Structure of Japanese Enterprises*, Springer.

Macey, J.R. (1989) 'Externalities, firm specific capital investments and the legal treatment of fundamental corporate changes', *Duke Law Journal*, Vol.38, pp.173–201.

Macleans (2014) 'Who earns what: Global CEO-to-worker pay ratios', *Macleans*, 27 September: www.macleans.ca/economy/money-economy/global-ceo-to-worker-pay-ratios/ (accessed September 2016).

Marks, S.G. (2000) 'The separation of ownership and control', in B. Bouckaert and G. de Geest (eds), *Encyclopedia of Law and Economics: The Regulation of Contracts*, volume 3, Cheltenham, Edward Elgar, pp.692–710.

Millon, D. (2000) 'New game plan or business as usual? A critique of the team production model of corporate law', *Vanderlit Law Review*, Vol.86, pp.1001–1044.

Mishel, L., Bernstein J. and Boushery, H. (2003) *The State of Working America, 2002/2003*, New York, Business and Economics.

Nakamura, M. and Rebien, S. (2012) 'Corporate social responsibility and corporate governance: Japanese firms and selective adaptation', *University of British Columbia Law Review*, Vol.45, pp.723–778.

Sakawa, H., Moriyama, K. and Watanabel, N. (2012) 'Relations between top executive compensation structure and corporate governance: Evidence from Japanese public disclosed data', *Corporate Governance: An International Review*, Vol.20, pp.593–608.

Sakawa, H. and Watanabel, N. (2013) 'Executive compensation and firm performance in Japan: The role of keiretsu memberships and bank-appointed monitors', *Journal of Modern Accounting and Auditing*, Vol.9, pp.1119–1130.

Salacuse, J. (2004) 'Corporate governance in the new century', *Company Lawyer*, Vol.25, pp.69–83.

Sayer, A. (2015) *Why We Can't Afford the Rich*, Bristol, Policy Press.

Schmidt, R.H. (2004) 'Corporate governance in Germany: An economic perspective', in J.P. Krahnen and R.H. Schmidt (eds), *The German Financial System*, Oxford, Oxford University Press, pp.387–424.

Stout, L.A. (2002) 'Bad and not-so-bad arguments for shareholder primacy', *Southern California Law Review*, Vol.75, pp.1189–1210.

Tonello, M. and Rabimov, S. (2010) 'The 2010 institutional investment report: Trends in asset allocation and portfolio composition', *The Conference Board Research Report*, No. R-1468-10-RR.

Tungler, G. (2000) 'The Anglo-American board of directors and the German supervisory board: Marionettes in a puppet theatre of corporate governance or efficient controlling devices', *Bond Law Review*, Vol.12, pp.230–271.

Verret, J.W. (2010) 'Treasury Inc.: How the bailout reshapes corporate theory and practice', *Yale Journal on Regulation*, Vol.27, pp.283–350.

Waitzer, E.J. and Sarro, D. (2012) 'The public fiduciary: Emerging themes in Canadian fiduciary law for pension trustees', *Canadian Bar Review*, Vol.91, pp.163–209.

Waitzer, E.J. and Sarro, D. (2014) 'Fiduciary society unleashed: The road ahead for the financial sector', *Business Lawyer*, Vol.69, pp.1081–1116.

5 | Corporate responsibility

Introduction

In 2015 the car-maker Volkswagen (VW) admitted it had been bypassing US air pollution regulations by installing software that tricked regulators during official testing but otherwise did nothing to reduce nitrogen oxide emissions. It is rare that a business is caught so obviously in the act of cheating regulations designed to achieve some form of social and/or ecological objective, like the reduction of emissions, but that was clearly the case here. As such, it represents another example of corporate malfeasance to sit alongside a growing list of issues we highlight in this book and other authors highlight elsewhere (Bakan 2004). However, we want to emphasize that the VW case does not represent an example of deviant organizational wrongdoing; as Baxter (2015) notes, many other car-makers also seek to 'game' the regulatory system. Rather, it raises a major issue facing students of business today: what are the non-economic responsibilities of business to society and the environment?

A number of business scholars argue that integrating the idea of social and environmental responsibilities into corporate or business activities is vital for the survival and performance of the corporation or business, since businesses are dependent on their 'social licence' to operate (Gunningham et al. 2006). In the VW case, for example, the actions of executives and other employees at VW have had a major impact on the value of VW shares, largely due to the expectation that the company's actions will result in significant regulatory fines (Nieuwenhuis 2015). Consequently, the then CEO of VW, Martin Winterkorn, resigned. Scholars in management and business studies stress the need to take **corporate social responsibility** (CSR) seriously since it reflects an 'enlightened self-interest', in that businesses should act responsibly because it will benefit their bottom line, i.e. profit (see Carroll and Buchholtz 2015: 40). This notion is evident in the VW case where its actions led to damaging impacts on their share price, consumer and investor confidence, regulatory oversight and so on.

Although the fallout from the VW case is likely to lead to a range of regulatory changes, we would argue that it is actually unlikely to change the actions of corporations and businesses. Calls for corporate responsibility are not new, stretching back well over a century. The growth of CSR as a subject of study in business schools and elsewhere, the expansion of CSR activities by businesses, the development of global initiatives to promote CSR (e.g. the UN's Social Compact), and much else besides, has not stopped businesses from making socially- and environmentally-damaging decisions. As such, CSR has not necessarily made business practices more socially or environmentally responsible. For example, VW boasts of their 'tradition of global CSR engagement' on their website under the heading 'Sustainability and Responsibility',[1] none of which stopped the company from pursuing profit at the expense of the environmental consequences (see Chapter 8).

In this book, we want to problematize mainstream perspectives of CSR that are based on the notion profit and responsibility are compatible with one another, even virtuously self-reinforcing. Instead, we want to unpack the problems with CSR specifically and notions of corporate responsibility more generally. In particular, we argue that the integration of CSR – in its many forms – into management training and managerial practices does not provide an adequate means to address the damaging impacts that business can have on society, on the environment and on our lives. We start with a discussion of mainstream perspectives on CSR, its intellectual history and how it is manifested in society today. We then critique this perspective from a number of standpoints, before finishing with a discussion of forms of economic organization that provide better ways to integrate social concerns into business activity.

Mainstream perspectives on corporate responsibility

Changing attitudes to business Before asking what social responsibilities businesses have or should have, it is pertinent to wonder why this is an issue at

---

1 Volkswagen website: www.volkswagenag.com/content/vwcorp/content/en/sustainability_and_responsibility/CSR_worldwide.html (accessed May 2016).

all. As noted in the Introduction to this book, the relationship between business and society has often been fraught (Sexty 2008). In many countries, public attitudes towards and opinions of business have changed quite dramatically over the decades stretching back at least to the 1800s – see Table 5.1 for the USA. Moreover, these attitudes have often swung from positive to negative in a short space of time, as evident in the public reactions to the 2007–2008 global financial crisis. In our view, it is worth highlighting these changes in attitude in order to understand better the rise and embedding of CSR in business practices and decision-making, which we come back to below.

As Table 5.1 illustrates, public attitudes to business often reflect broader socio-economic circumstances. Primarily, negative attitudes to business

TABLE 5.1 Changing attitudes to business through US history

Time period	Attitude	Characteristics
Late 1800s and early 1900s	Negative	'Robber barons' – concentration of businesses in trusts and monopolies
1920s	Positive	'Roaring twenties' – stock market boom
1930s	Negative	Great Depression following Wall Street Crash
1950s and 1960s	Positive	'Golden Age of Capitalism' – full employment, rising wages and mass consumerism
1970s	Negative	Stagflation – rising unemployment and inflation
1980s	Positive	Government roll-back of regulations and rising stock markets
Early 1990s	Negative	Recession and business failures
Late 1990s	Positive	Dot.com boom and rising stock markets
Early 2000s	Negative	Dot.com crash in 2000 followed by major corporate scandals (e.g. Enron)
Mid 2000s	Positive	Growing emphasis on corporate social responsibility, 'green' business as well as rising house prices
Late 2000s to present	Negative	Global financial crisis of 2007–2008 and anger at banks

Source: adapted from Sexty (2008)

are associated with recessions, depressions and crises, while positive attitudes are associated with booms, growth and employment. At the end of the 1800s, for example, there was significant unrest in many countries as a result of the Long Depression starting in 1873 and in the USA in particular because of the increasing concentration of corporate power in the hands of a few so-called Robber Barons, which included people like John D. Rockefeller who owned Standard Oil (Trachtenberg 2007). The political theorist Scott Bowman (1996) notes the growing criticism of business corporations by scholars and thinkers of the time, including people like Thorstein Veblen (1899), and the rise of popular social movements against corporate power as well.

As a result of these social critiques and movements, the US government introduced laws like the 1890 *Sherman Anti-trust Act* to stop the formation of business monopolies and the pursuit of anti-competitive practices (Christophers 2016). As we discuss in greater detail in our discussion of business regulation in Chapter 13, the intention behind such laws, also enacted in other countries, was to break up the power of private business organizations so that they could not control markets and exploit consumers. Despite negative attitudes to business during this period, however, it is notable that public attitudes to business shifted quite dramatically in the early 1900s, becoming more positive. For example, during the Roaring Twenties more and more people in the USA invested in corporate shares and benefited from rising share prices, at least up until 29 October 1929 when the Wall Street Crash brought it all tumbling down again (Galbraith 2009 [1955]). More recent public attitudes towards banks and other financial businesses before and after the 2007–2008 global financial crisis reflect a similar situation (Birch 2015; van Staveren 2015).

Intellectual history of corporate social responsibility While we could write more on the history of public attitudes towards business, that is not our aim in this chapter. Rather, the brief outline above is meant to help us better understand the evolution of corporate social responsibility (CSR) as a concept and set of practices. According to Kemper and Martin (2010) and Barkan (2013), debates on the social responsibility of business first emerged in the 1930s at the time when the role of the corporation and corporate management was being hotly debated by American thinkers like Berle and Means (1932) – see Chapters 3 and 4 – during the Great Depression that followed the Wall Street Crash.

In the specific US context, corporate responsibility was associated with the growing influence of corporate managers and executives in society, especially as this related to managerial decision-making (Carroll 1999). Such managerial decisions could have major impacts on communities, especially when it came to the negative or positive impacts resulting from the building of new factories and facilities (e.g. unemployment versus employment). This influence of managers and executives on society has been defined as *managerial capitalism* or simply *managerialism* by some scholars (Whitley 1999; Locke and Spender 2011), and denotes the role of managers and executives in socio-economic change in contrast to other forms of economic coordination and organization (e.g. the state, the market).

In light of the influence of managerialism, the social responsibility of managers became an increasingly important issue in academic debates on the relationship between business and society. Archie Carroll (1999) provides a helpful overview of the evolution of these debates since the mid-twentieth century. For example, he splits the evolution of CSR into five time periods as follows:

- modern era begins in 1950s
- CSR formalized in 1960s
- definitions of CSR multiply in 1970s
- splintering of CSR concepts in 1980s
- alternative ideas developed in 1990s.

According to Carroll (1999), when it first emerged in the 1950s CSR was generally conceptualized in terms of the social responsibility of business managers, stressing the power they had over the rest of society. As scholars sought to define CSR more clearly in the 1960s, they argued that socially responsible business practices led to long-term benefits for businesses and that managers need to keep in mind the impact their businesses have on society. These ideas came under serious challenge in 1970 with the publication of a now famous article by Milton Friedman (1970) in the *New York Times Magazine*. This article, titled 'The Social Responsibility of Business Is to Increase Its Profits', was a direct attack on managerial notions of the social responsibility of business from the perspective of the Chicago School of Economics – sometimes defined as 'neoliberalism' – in which shareholder interests are presented as predominant. Some, like Kemper and Martin (2010), have even argued that academic debates on CSR since then have ended up as one response after another to this argument by Friedman.

Milton Friedman was a professor at the Chicago School of Economics, which was famous for its strongly pro-market position in academic and policy debates. Often characterized as a 'neoliberal' school of thought, the Chicago School of Economics has played and continues to play a major role in the direction of government, law and business (Birch 2015). In the 1970 article and his previous work, Friedman argued that the market provides the best way to coordinate economic activity, which contrasted with dominant perspectives at the time associated with managerialism and Keynesianism. In his *News York Times Magazine* article, Friedman (1970) basically argued that business only has one responsibility, namely the pursuit of profit for shareholders. While Friedman conflated business with public corporations in his argument, which is a point we return to below, his key claim was that shareholders *are* the owners of corporations and therefore the ones who *should* make decisions about where to spend their money. Managers, on the other hand, who assert the right to determine the social responsibility of the corporation are coercing shareholders (by taking their profits) and customers (by charging them higher prices) into undertaking actions they might not want if they had a choice. In fact, Friedman argued that the only time a business could pursue social responsibility was when these activities had instrumental and beneficial impact on the business itself (e.g. as a marketing ploy to endear it to customers and increase profits). Other than in such cases, it is both inaccurate and dangerous to conflate business pursuits and attempts to improve society.

In the 1970s and 1980s, and after Friedman, debates on CSR proliferated, leading to new concepts and ideas like corporate social responsiveness, corporate social performance, social contract theory, stakeholder theory etc. (Carroll 1999; Kemper and Martin 2010). During this period, several important concepts were developed by a number of scholars that are still influential today, and which we discuss below. Finally, in the 1990s and 2000s a range of new ideas around social responsibility emerged building on ideas of sustainability, sustainable development and sustainable business – see Chapter 9 for more on the roots of these ideas. This brief history cannot do more than hint at the diversity of ideas in debates about CSR, so we turn to some of the key theories next.

Some have observed that the degree and type of emphasis on CSR varies significantly between countries (Matten and Moon 2008). In countries with a relatively weak welfare state, where social goods like health care and economic security are not provided or guaranteed by the state, one can see more 'explicit' forms of CSR. For example, large US businesses like Exxon or Walmart make efforts to demonstrate their commitment to voluntary actions to curb pollution or monitor their overseas operations. In these liberal-market economies, CSR is called 'explicit' because it acts as a substitute for more institutionalized public provision of social benefits. In such contexts, explicit CSR allows corporations to be less threatening to social cohesion (Kang and Moon 2012). By contrast, CSR tends to be 'implicit' in other countries where the aims of social cohesion are achieved through state regulatory frameworks or strong normative constraints embedded within the business system and often internalized by its participants. One example of implicit CSR is the 'relational' system of corporate governance in Germany where workers' interests gain attention not by separate voluntary actions, but by ensuring employee representation into corporate governance bodies (see Chapter 4).

Major theories of corporate social responsibility While the history of CSR implies that there has been a proliferation of concepts and ideas about what constitutes corporate responsibility, it is possible to identify a few core theories from which modern CSR theories and practices emerged. Aside from Friedman's pro-market perspective (i.e. that business should only pursue profit), Kemper and Martin (2010) argue that current CSR debates centre on the following theoretical traditions: (1) the three-dimensional model, (2) the social contract model and (3) the stakeholder model.

First, the three-dimensional model, which has since been updated to four-dimensions, originates with the work of Archie Carroll in the late 1970s. Originally, he argued that business has three responsibilities: (1) an economic responsibility to make profit, (2) a legal responsibility to obey the laws of society and (3) an ethical responsibility to avoid harm and do good (Carroll 1979). Later, Carroll added a fourth dimension, a philanthropic responsibility to give back to society and be a good citizen (Carroll and Buchholtz 2015). Carroll emphasized that the economic and legal responsibilities are requirements, while the ethical and philanthropic responsibilities are desirable or expected. Each builds on the other, so ensuring a secure economic foundation for a business is necessary before anything else.

Second, the social contract model of CSR emerged in the 1980s with Thomas Donaldson's (1982) book *Corporations and Morality*. He sought to respond to Friedman's idea that the only responsibility of business is to make profit by stressing that the corporation was both a *moral environment* in itself and a *moral agent*. By this Donaldson meant that, on the one hand, corporations have an internal environment in which ethical questions need to be addressed, including issues like management and employee rights and obligations; on the other hand, as entities corporations have to engage with questions around their impact on other moral actors in society (e.g. customers, government, suppliers, investors etc.). According to Kemper and Martin (2010), these ideas have since influenced notions of corporate citizenship, drawing on the idea of a social contract between business and society.

Finally, the stakeholder model comes from the work of R. Edward Freeman (1984), especially a book called *Strategic Management: A Stakeholder Approach* – see also Chapter 4 on stakeholder models of corporate governance. In this book, Freeman argued that all businesses are impacted and in turn impact a range of external social actors (e.g. customers, suppliers, government, workers etc.), who he called *stakeholders* because they all have a stake in the success of the business. As such, this model is based on the notion that businesses, especially corporations, *should* address the impacts of their decisions on more than shareholders or owners; the reason being that many people *are* directly and indirectly impacted by these decisions. For example, employees have to invest in gaining specific skills to work in specific businesses, meaning that if that business simply moves its facilities elsewhere – for cost reasons – then its employees will have wasted their investment of time and energy in gaining skills that might not be transferable to another workplace. The stakeholder approach is based on the observation that the value of a business cannot be reduced to the financial profits it generates, at least not in the long run. In fact, businesses themselves can often gain by pursuing better and more constructive relationships to communities, governments, the environment and so on (Vilanova et al. 2009).

Examples of corporate social responsibility Our outline of these key CSR theories can only be, once again, a partial introduction to a complex topic, and one that has evolved considerably over time. Today, CSR and its close cousin business ethics – see Chapter 14 – are important fields of research and teaching in most business schools. They are also an increasingly important part of business practice in modern businesses and corporations. In fact, most corporations nowadays are keen to present and promote their CSR credentials as much as they can. It is, therefore, helpful to look at some examples of CSR practices in the contemporary business world. We consider two examples here but stress that there are many others.

First, most firms engage in different forms of reporting, organizing and other initiatives in pursuit of CSR activities. These activities stretch from sectoral and local organizations and groups, through to global networks, round-tables, and such like. For example, there are: global networks like the Business for Social Responsibility, which is a not-for-profit organization with a global membership of businesses that seeks to develop 'sustainable business strategies and solutions';[2] national fora like the Devonshire Initiative, which seeks to promote collaboration between NGOs and mining businesses around social issues and community development;[3] and reporting frameworks like the Global Reporting Initiative, which develops and promotes sustainability reporting by businesses.[4] These three examples are just a tiny selection of groups, organizations, networks, initiatives etc. that promote or support various forms of CSR activities, best practices, reporting and so on.

2 Business for Social Responsibility website: www.bsr.org/en/ (accessed May 2016).
3 Devonshire Initiative website: http://devonshireinitiative.org/ (accessed May 2016).
4 Global Reporting Initiative website: www.globalreporting.org/Pages/default.aspx (accessed May 2016).

Second, philanthrocapitalism refers to the idea that philanthropic giving by wealthy people and businesses can alleviate and ameliorate significant social problems, even major world problems. The term was coined by Matthew Bishop and Michael Green (2008) in their book originally titled *Philanthrocapitalism: How the Rich Can Save the World*. It is best exemplified by the work of the Bill & Melinda Gates Foundation, which funds a range of projects through grant-giving.[5] Described as a new and increasingly important phenomena, these philanthropic activities have been criticized by scholars like Linsey McGoey (2015). She argues that philanthrocapitalism is driven by the idea that social problems can be solved through the dynamism assumed to underpin capitalist business practices. Moreover, as a result of the growing influence of these wealthy philanthropists, their personal preferences and assumptions come to have an increasing influence on what social problems (e.g. disease) are deemed important and how they should be tackled. As a result, other social problems (e.g. inequality) end up side-lined or ignored.

Critical perspectives on corporate responsibility

While the different theories and forms of CSR we mention above may sound like they entail laudable intentions and practices, we want to critically unpack them in this section in order to understand better the problematic assumptions that underpin CSR thinking and the problematic implications that underlie CSR practices. In order to do this, we start this section with a discussion of responsibility as a concept, and then turn to specific issues arising from the key CSR theories we outline above.

What is responsibility? Any discussion of corporate responsibility is a discussion of ethical questions; that is, what should businesses do? And what should they not do? What are businesses responsible for? And what are they not responsible for? As we mention elsewhere in this book (see Chapter 14), these types of questions can conflate and confuse *descriptive* (or 'positive') issues with *ethical* (or 'normative') ones. For example, if a business is legally required to adhere to certain regulations – like Volkswagen was supposed to – does that mean it is ethically required to adhere to them as well? Answers to such questions are not easy to untangle without some thought.

In relation to the concept of *responsibility*, it is worth considering what this term means and how it relates to ethical decisions – see Jonathan Glover (1970) for a helpful philosophical introduction to responsibility. Responsibility can refer to two quite distinct things, especially when it is used in popular discourse. On the one hand, it can refer to an obligation or duty to do certain things in the future, which can be both legal and ethical (e.g. not

5 Bill & Melinda Gates Foundation: www.gatesfoundation.org/ (accessed May 2016).

to cheat environmental regulations). In this sense, responsibility involves intentional action rather than accidental effects, although this does not excuse deliberate and wilful negligence. On the other hand, responsibility can refer to blame for past actions or undertakings. In this sense, responsibility can be backward-looking to determine whether something should not have been done when it was. An example of such decisions would include things like the recent Canadian Truth and Reconciliation Commission that dealt with the horrific impacts of the residential schools system on First Nations.[6]

In the context of this chapter, these differences are important. Thinking about corporate responsibility necessitates thinking about how business organizations should act now and in the future *and* how they should have acted in the past. Since legal obligations frequently change, this means that normative (i.e. ethical) concerns might provide stronger direction and, therefore, continuity for the regulation and control of business. Consequently, normative issues are critical to coordinating and managing the relationship between business and society. Moreover, it is important to think about intentions when it comes to responsibilities since these establish the goals to which normative decisions are oriented; where these intentions are set by other considerations, such as profit, they limit the actions that business organizations can take. For example, the pursuit of profit means that businesses often seek to externalize their social and environmental responsibilities so they do not have to pay for them.

Problems with mainstream theories of corporate social responsibility It is important to consider the various CSR theories we discussed above in more depth so that we can unpack any problematic assumptions that might underpin them. We raise four problematic issues here relating to one or another CSR theory we discuss above.

First, it is important to note that Milton Friedman's (1970) arguments were considered radical at the time he wrote them; however, they have since become one of the dominant perspectives from which to view corporate responsibility. This is evidenced by things like the 2014 'shareholder spring' in the UK, which was driven by investors who were worried that the activities of corporate managers would impact shareholder value, i.e. share prices (Kollewe 2014). There are at least three problems with Friedman's position worth mentioning here. First, he conflated 'business' with 'corporation' assuming that the former is the same as the latter, ignoring the fact that they are not (i.e. corporations have shareholders, businesses need not) and assuming that they both have

6 Truth and Reconciliation Commission: www.trc.ca/websites/trcinstitution/index. php?p=3 (accessed May 2016).

the same fiduciary obligations (cf. Stout 2012). Second, he actually accepted that business has a responsibility to conform 'to their basic rules of society, both those embodied in law and those embodied in ethical custom' (Friedman 1970), which rather makes his argument moot. Finally, he conflated social responsibility with socialism by arguing that 'political mechanisms' to achieve those responsibilities are inherently socialist, even though his definition of politics is so broad as to include a range of political systems in its remit (Mulligan 1986).

Second, as business activities have globalized through the expansion of international trade and foreign direct investment – as we outline in Chapter 7 and 9 – they have engendered a growth in international regulations, codes, standards and such like (Braithewaite 2005). These rules of the game, as it were, are often favourable to multinational corporations (MNCs), even when they address concerns about social or environmental responsibilities. One example of this is the UN *Norms on the Responsibilities of Transnational Corporations and Other Business Enterprises with Regard to Human Rights* (2003). According to Barkan (2013), these Norms treated corporations as the same as nation-states, meaning that the UN largely accepts the extent and spread of corporate power and is merely trying to attach social goals to this power. See the next chapter for more on corporate power. Consequently, Barkan argues that these sorts of international rules merely consolidate the power of MNCs, rather than requiring them to meet their specific social and environmental responsibilities. As a result, the idea of a social contract between business and society misses the point that business can often be the more powerful actor in the relationship, especially if businesses operate globally, and therefore able to dictate the terms of the social contract.

Third, and related to the last point, the globalization of business activities has been accompanied by a growth in international campaigning, social movements, boycotts and law suits that are critical of business. While this might seem like it would enable more stakeholders to have a positive impact on business activities as businesses respond to these normative pressures, Shamir (2004) argues that the transnational activities of businesses are impossible to control because there is no comparable transnational government body capable of enforcing legal or ethical constraints. Instead, businesses are subject to a range of private or quasi-private governance entities and standards (e.g. UN Global Compact), each of which has its own distinct sense of corporate responsibility and issues with accessibility for non-business or non-state actors (e.g. workers, campaigners etc.). Moreover, most of these entities and standards are voluntary – meaning that a business can withdraw at any time with little practical consequence – or are co-opted by business involvement – meaning that they do not challenge business power. Consequently, Shamir argues that CSR has ended up as merely an issue of investor and consumer confidence in which branding and image management trump genuine commitment to social and environmental responsibilities (see also Beder 2006). This critical concern about the genuineness of CSR has caused some observers to assign the derogatory term 'greenwashing' to many types of CSR initiatives, especially where these initiatives seem to be designed primarily to boost the 'reputational capital' of business firms rather than bring about real change (Elving 2014). For example, Robert Reich (2007) argues that CSR is often simply a way for business to perpetuate the convenient belief that regulation of business by government is unnecessary; it thereby hides the fact that CSR is itself a substitute for potentially more effective approaches to challenging and reining in the power of business.

A final criticism is that CSR does little, if anything, to alleviate the actual problems engendered by capitalism, including poverty, alienation, dehumanization, inequality etc. The reason for this is that CSR does not challenge the organizational structure of capitalist business – that is, the pursuit of profit for the owners of capital. In contrast, the sociologist Charles Derber (2000) argues that challenging corporate power and capitalist business practices necessitates a wholesale transformation of business organization to make it more democratic and socially responsive. As such, it is important to think about how organizational form relates to social responsibilities; that is, are some organizations better suited to achieving social and environmental objectives than others? For example, Derber highlights a range of alternative business forms and governance like stakeholder models, employee ownership, workers cooperatives and so on – we come back to these in Chapters 16 and 17. The point of mentioning them here is that they represent ways to embed social or environmental objectives directly in the organization and governance of business, rather than relying on external CSR initiatives, reporting, collaborations etc.

Empirical example: investment banks and the global financial crisis

A useful empirical case to look at in reference to the problems with mainstream CSR is the role and actions of various financial businesses, especially investment banks, leading up to and during the 2007–2008 global financial crisis. The documentary *Inside Job* (2010, dir. Charles H. Ferguson) and the film *The Big Short* (2015, dir. Adam McKay) provide helpful introductions to these issues.[7] When it comes to CSR, at the heart of this case is the question of whether various investment banks acted responsibly – at least from the perspective of mainstream CSR theories.

---

7 *Inside Job*: www.sonyclassics.com/insidejob/ and *The Big Short*: www.thebigshort-movie.com/ (accessed May 2016).

Briefly, and therefore simplistically, in the lead up to the crisis various investment banks – including the now bankrupt Lehman Brothers – constructed a series of financial products (e.g. Collateralized Debt Obligations, or CDOs) that were based on bundling the income from mortgage interest payments from home 'owners'. Part of the bundling involved mixing together income from risky (e.g. subprime mortgages) and non-risky loans (e.g. prime mortgages). The ratings agencies then rated these CDOs as safe financial assets, which made them attractive to various investors (e.g. commercial banks, pension funds, mutual funds, insurance funds etc.). As the mortgage market started to turn in 2006, some of the investment banks – like Goldman Sachs – began to bet against the CDO market by buying Credit Default Swaps (CDSs) that would pay out if CDOs lost value, which they did (Cohan 2011).

According to the *Rolling Stone* journalist Matt Taibbi (2010), investment banks like Goldman Sachs knew that 'the mortgages it [Goldman Sachs] was selling were for chumps. The real money was in betting against those same mortgages'. Obviously, this raises some serious questions about the responsibility of investment banks to their customers who are buying the financial products they are then betting against. Taibbi describes Goldman Sachs, rather poetically, as 'a great vampire squid wrapped around the face of humanity, relentlessly jamming its blood funnel into anything that smells like money' (2010). In part, Taibbi characterizes Goldman Sachs this way because they were engaged in selling CDOs to investors with the knowledge that other investors were going to 'short' (i.e. bet against) those CDOs (see Cohan 2011: 508–510). In 2010, Goldman Sachs settled a case brought by the Securities and Exchange Commission (SEC) on fraud charges; it agreed to pay a fine of US$550 million but did not admit wrongdoing.[8]

We can look at the activities of these investment banks from a range of perspectives. First, if their only responsibility is profit (e.g. Friedman 1970), then the businesses that survived the crisis fulfilled their social responsibilities, it is only the ones that went bankrupt that did not. However, this means that the responsibility of business is simply to survive, at whatever cost. Consequently, it is likely that such crises will repeat themselves. Second, if the responsibility of financial businesses is to adhere to the law – no matter how ineffective it was – and to meet ethical expectations – no matter what these are – then it could be argued that they fulfilled their legal obligations, while whether they met their ethical expectations is muddied by the lack of moral opprobrium *before* the crisis. Again, responsibility is only raised as an issue after the fact, meaning that CSR simply does not stop the negative impacts of business, it

8 *New York Times*: http://dealbook.nytimes.com/2010/07/15/goldman-to-settle-with-s-e-c-for-550-million/ (accessed May 2016).

only addresses the aftermath. Finally, even if financial businesses increasingly promote and support CSR activities after the crisis, Kemper and Martin (2010) point out that the value of these activities to each individual company decreases as they can no longer charge customers a premium, since more and more businesses are doing it. At its heart, then, CSR entails at least two problems: first, it ends up being largely backward-looking, and does not deal with problems pre-emptively; and, second, there is a contradiction between the benefits CSR activities provide to other social actors (e.g. citizens) and to the businesses themselves, the more it benefits the former the less it benefits the latter.

Conclusion

Our goal in this chapter has been to provide a brief introduction to the issue of corporate responsibility, broadly conceived to include business more generally. We started by outlining the history of public attitudes to business and the intellectual history of mainstream CSR theories. We then provided a brief introduction to a number of key CSR theories. In the second part of the chapter we critically unpacked mainstream CSR theories and practices, drawing on the example of the global financial crisis to outline the limitations of these approaches. We want to finish by stressing that social and environmental responsibilities are intrinsically tied to the form and logics of business organization and governance; that is, it is not possible to separate out responsibility and treat it as a distinct normative issue from business practice.

Suggested readings

- Carroll, A. (1999) 'Corporate social responsibility: Evolution of a definitional construct', *Business & Society*, Vol.38, pp.268–295.
- Donaldson, T. and Preston, L.E. (1995) 'The stakeholder theory of the corporation: Concepts, evidence, and implications', *Academy of Management Review*, Vol.20, 65–91.
- Friedman, M. (1970) 'The social responsibility of business is to increase its profits', *The New York Magazine*, 13 September.
- Kemper, A. and Martin, R. (2010) 'After the fall: The global financial crisis as a test of corporate social responsibility theories', *European Management Review*, Vol.7, pp.229–239.
- Shamir, R. (2004) 'The de-radicalization of corporate social responsibility', *Critical Sociology*, Vol.30, pp.669–689.
- Taibbi, M. (2010) 'The great American bubble machine', *Rolling Stone*, 5 April: www.rollingstone.com/politics/news/the-great-american-bubble-machine-20100405 (accessed May 2016).

Bibliography

Bakan, J. (2004) *The Corporation*, London, Random House.

Barkan, J. (2013) *Corporate Sovereignty*, Minneapolis, University of Minnesota Press.

Baxter, L.F. (2015) 'VW is not alone: How metrics gaming is commonplace in companies', *The Conversation*, 15 October: https://theconversation.com/vw-is-not-alone-how-metrics-gaming-is-commonplace-in-companies-48393 (accessed May 2016).

Beder, S. (2006) *Suiting Themselves: How Corporations Drive the Global Agenda*, London, Earthscan.

Berle, A. and Means, G. (1932 [1967]) *The Modern Corporation and Private Property*, New York, World Inc.

Birch, K. (2015) *We Have Never Been Neoliberal*, Winchester, Zero Books.

Bishop, M. and Green, M. (2008) *Philanthrocapitalism: How the Rich Can Save the World*, London, Bloomsbury Press.

Bowman, S. (1996) *The Modern Corporation and American Political Thought*, Pennsylvania, Pennsylvania State University Press.

Braithwaite, J. (2005) 'Neoliberalism or regulatory capitalism', ANU: RegNet, Occasional Paper No. 5.

Carroll, A. (1979) 'A three-dimensional conceptual model of corporate social performance', *Academy of Management* Review, Vol.4, pp.497–505.

Carroll, A. (1999) 'Corporate social responsibility: Evolution of a definitional construct', *Business* & Society, Vol.38, pp.268–295.

Carroll, A. and Buchholtz, A. (2015) *Business and Society* (9th Edition), Stamford CT, CENGAGE Learning.

Christophers, B. (2016) *The Great Leveler: Capitalism and Competition in the Court of Law*, Cambridge MA, Harvard University Press.

Cohan, W. (2011) *Money and Power: How Goldman Sachs Came to Rule the World*, New York, Doubleday.

Derber, C. (2000) *Corporation Nation*, New York, St. Martin's Press.

Donaldson, T. (1982) *Corporations and Morality*, Englewood Cliffs NJ, Prentice-Hall.

Elving, W. (2014) 'Communicating corporate social responsibility in a skeptical world', in D. Türker, H. Toker and C. Altuntaş (eds) *Contemporary Issues in Corporate Social Responsibility*, Lanham MD, Lexington Books, pp.57–70.

Freeman, R. (1984) *Strategic Management: A Stakeholder Approach*, Boston, Pitman.

Friedman, M. (1970) 'The social responsibility of business is to increase its profits', *The New York Magazine*, September 13: www.colorado.edu/studentgroups/libertarians/issues/friedman-soc-resp-business.html (accessed May 2016).

Galbraith, J.K. (2009 [1955]) *The Great Crash, 1929*, London, Penguin.

Glover, J. (1970) *Responsibility*, New York, Humanities Press.

Gunningham, N., Kagan, R. and Thornton, D. (2006) 'Social license and environmental protection: Why businesses go beyond compliance', *Law & Social Inquiry*, Vol.29, pp.307–341.

Kang, N. and Moon, J. (2012) 'Institutional complementarity between corporate governance and Corporate Social Responsibility: A comparative institutional analysis of three capitalisms', *Socio-Economic Review*, Vol.7, pp.105–108.

Kemper, A. and Martin, R. (2010) 'After the fall: The global financial crisis as a test of corporate social responsibility theories', *European Management Review*, Vol.7, pp.229–239.

Kollewe, J. (2014) 'Shareholder revolts – timeline', *The Guardian*, 17 July: www.theguardian.com/business/2014/jul/17/shareholder-revolts-timeline (accessed May 2016).

Locke, R. and Spender, J.-C. (2011) *Confronting Managerialism*, London, Zed Books.

McGoey, L. (2015) *No Such Thing as a Free Gift: The Gates Foundation and the Price of Philanthropy*, London, Verso.

Matten, D. and Moon, J. (2008) '"Implicit" and "explicit" CSR: A conceptual framework for a comparative understanding of corporate social responsibility', *Academy of Management Review*, Vol.33, pp.404–424.

Mulligan, T. (1986) 'A critique of Milton Friedman's essay "The Social Responsibility of Business Is to Increase Its Profits"', *Journal of Business Ethics*, Vol.5, pp.265–269.

Nieuwenhuis, P. (2015) 'How Volkswagen got caught cheating emissions tests by a clean air NGO', *The Conversation*, 22 September: https://theconversation.com/how-volkswagen-got-caught-cheating-emissions-tests-by-a-clean-air-ngo-47951 (accessed May 2016).

Reich, R. (2007) *Supercapitalism: The Transformation of Business, Democracy and Everyday Life*, New York, Alfred Knopf.

Sexty, R. (2008) *Canadian Business and Society*, Toronto, McGraw-Hill.

Shamir, R. (2004) 'The de-radicalization of corporate social responsibility', *Critical Sociology*, Vol.30, pp.669–689.

Stout, L. (2012) *The Shareholder Value Myth*, San Francisco, Berrett-Koehler.

Taibbi, M. (2010) 'The great American bubble machine', *Rolling Stone*, 5 April: www.rollingstone.com/politics/news/the-great-american-bubble-machine-20100405 (accessed May 2016).

Trachtenberg, A. (2007) *The Incorporation of America: Culture and Society in the Gilded Age*, New York, Farrar, Straus and Giroux.

Van Staveren, I. (2015) *Economics after the Crisis*, London, Routledge.

Veblen, T. (1899 [1994]) *Theory of the Leisure Class*, New York, Penguin.

Vilanova, M. Lozano, J. and Arenas, D. (2009) 'Exploring the nature of the relationship between CSR and competitiveness', *Journal of Business Ethics*, Vol.87, pp.57–69.

Whitley, R. (1999) *Divergent Capitalism*, Oxford, Oxford University Press.

6 | Corporate power

Introduction

The concern that corporations and private business generally can have too much power has a long history. It stretches back at least to the time of Adam Smith (1723–1790), who himself criticized the joint-stock companies (JSC) we discussed in Chapters 2 and 3. The power of JSCs like the English/British East India Company (EIC) led directly to major world events like America's War of Independence starting in 1776. According to Bowman (1996: 5), for example, the USA's 'founding fathers' like Thomas Jefferson objected to the monopoly power held by JSCs because they were 'wary of the antidemocractic tendencies of concentrated power within the business corporation'. Adam Smith held similar views, as did many others at the time. These pre-modern corporations were seen as extensions of royal authority and power, since they were created by grants from the Crown and the grant itself represented the gift of special privileges by the Crown (e.g. monopolies on trade) (Korten 2001; Nace 2003).

Such negative attitudes towards corporations and business have not abated over the centuries, although they have waxed and waned over time. Following the corporate revolution at the end of the nineteenth century – see Chapter 3 – and the rise of managerial capitalism during the twentieth century, there was an accommodation, of sorts, between corporations and society – at least in countries like the USA (see Chapter 5). Generally speaking, during the middle of the twentieth century most people in countries like the USA and UK considered corporations to be contributing something useful to society through the creation of secure jobs, the provision of cheap products and services, and rising living standards (Sennett 2007). Corporate managers were even encouraged to think of themselves as socially responsible and as having a higher calling than simple profit (Khurana 2007). However, this changed in the 1970s and 1980s as greed made a comeback, epitomized by the character Gordon Gecko in the 1987 film *Wall Street* directed by Oliver Stone. These shifting currents eventually gave rise to the more recent chorus of journalists, commentators, academics and activists who criticize corporations and the expansion of **corporate power** (e.g. Monbiot 2000; Bakan 2004; Birch 2007; Wolin 2008).

Our aim in this chapter is to unpack and examine the concept of corporate power in order to provide it with analytical purchase alongside its wider normative dimension; that is, we want to do more than characterize corporate power as 'bad', we want to be able to identify it and examine how it is exercised

Key concept: Corporate power

Many people have written about the power of corporations and business; however, they do not all use the same terms, definitions or concepts. This means that concepts like 'corporate power' can be unclear or lack precision. For simplicity's sake, we use the term in this book to refer to two dimensions of corporate activity and governance: on the one hand, internal issues of control over corporations (e.g. who runs it, who owns it); and, on the other hand, external issues of influence in society (e.g. the capacity to shape regulation, public opinion, politics etc.). However, while this definition might provide a useful starting point for discussions of corporate power, it does not deal with the nature of that power and how it is exercised.

Source: Bowman (1996)

in society. We start the chapter by examining mainstream perspectives on corporate power, stretching back to Adam Smith, especially how it relates to the distortion of market efficiency. We then outline several critical takes on corporate power. In order to do this, however, we first discuss the concept of power and how it has been theorized in the social sciences. We then discuss several different aspects of corporate power: for example, its internal, structural and political dimensions. We then use one well-known corporate scandal to illustrate our arguments.

Key discussion questions

- What is power?
- What is corporate power?
- What are the internal and external dimensions of corporate power?
- How is corporate power exercised?
- Why is corporate power a societal problem?
- What are examples of corporate power?

Mainstream perspectives

Markets and efficiency According to Adam Smith markets are expected to produce the most efficient outcomes for society overall even if we all pursue our own selfish desires (see Chapter 11). Consequently, liberal thinkers since Smith – and especially orthodox economists – have promoted the extension of markets as the best way to secure social progress (Foley 2006). However, the corporate revolution we outlined in Chapter 3 problematizes this view since it illustrates the fact that business organizations can be as efficient as markets in the production, distribution and exchange of societal resources (Simon 1991).

Consequently, most economies and societies are now dominated by business enterprises, especially large corporations. As Lynn (2010) points out, one key reason for this situation is that no individual business wants to be forced to compete with other businesses, and so they seek to control their market rather than compete in it – this leads to the concentration of control in the hands of a few businesses as they buy up or merge with their competitors, or seek other means to put their competitors out of business.

The impact of business strategies on competition, by reducing it, is seen as a major problem from mainstream perspectives, especially because it leads to market inefficiencies (Keen 2001). Writing in the late eighteenth century Adam Smith, for example, argued that because managers of joint-stock companies (JSC) did not own the JSC, they would be negligent and wasteful in their decision-making – that is, they would be inefficient. This inefficiency would be compounded by the protection afforded to JSCs by their monopoly privileges granted by the Crown. Smith thought that JSCs would not use their resources efficiently in order to compete with other JSCs because they were protected from their competitors by their monopoly privileges. As a result, the *invisible hand* of the market, competition and self-interest would not be able to work their magic and promote the general social good. Today, many academics and others hold similar views about the workings of the invisible hand, especially the view that competition will ensure the efficient functioning of the economy (e.g. Friedman 1962).

Concerns about efficiency are based on continuing fears about the market power that comes from monopolies or oligopolies. These represent attempts by business to control whole areas or sectors of the economy – for example, the grocery sector, cellphone sector etc. As defined by Milton Friedman (1962: 120): 'Monopoly exists when a specific individual or enterprise has sufficient control over a particular product or service to determine significantly the terms on which other individuals shall have access to it'.

What this definition implies is that a monopoly does not mean *only* one individual or one business has control over 100 percent of a sector, which is a rare if non-existent phenomenon. Instead, a few people or businesses can have enough control to dominate the setting of prices, product conditions, terms of exchange etc. One example of a monopoly, in these terms, is Microsoft which dominates the software sector, especially when it comes to computer operating systems like Windows (Lynn 2010). According to Gardiner Means (1983), large businesses, and especially corporations, achieved this form of market power in the mid-twentieth century. They were, and still are, able to manage – or 'administer' in Gardiner's terms – prices and other aspects of their activities outside of market influence, meaning that the market has become a less important mechanism in the allocation and distribution of resources.

Balancing corporate power and corporate responsibility All of this creates a significant conceptual and moral tension in mainstream understandings of the economy, and one that often gets ignored in the media, academia and political debate. The dominance of business, individually and collectively, raises a number of questions about the role, power and legitimacy of these organizations in society – as we discuss in Chapter 5. This is why critics of business often use the term **corporate power** in their discussions of the capacities and actions of business organizations (see below). However, this term does not generally get used in mainstream discussions (e.g. Friedman 1962; Carroll and Buchholtz 2015), nor is it generally identified as an explanation for the various problems we face (e.g. unemployment, inflation, product quality etc.). Rather, the power of business is assumed to be a problem only when the capacity of an individual firm enables them to dominate or distort efficient markets, or to influence (disproportionately) the political system. Whichever view you take, it is important to understand how business depends on different forms of social legitimacy to function in society.

Key methodological issue: Measuring corporate power

Concepts like corporate power are not only difficult to define; they are also difficult to pin down methodologically. What we mean by this is that corporate power is difficult to measure, both quantitatively and qualitatively. Generally we could differentiate between corporate power in quantitative terms (e.g. influence over number of people) or qualitative terms (e.g. type and form of influence). More specifically, it is possible to identify corporate power in a number of different ways, as we outline in this chapter. A number of people use different indicators to represent this power, including: organizational size in terms of value of assets or income; size in terms of market capitalization; social influence in terms of number of employees; social influence in terms of brand recognition; political influence in terms of political lobbying and the 'revolving door' between business and government; market control in terms of monopoly position; and so on. Frequently, corporate power is represented in terms of (1) economic or (2) market power. Economic power reflects the power to control the labour process (e.g. work decisions), strategic decision-making (e.g. through ownership) and allocation of capital (e.g. lending and investing). Market power reflects the structural power engendered by the concentration of employment, investment, market capitalization, assets and so on in a small number of businesses.

Sources: Carroll (2010); Brennan (2014)

Even though many mainstream thinkers and commentators frequently miss what we think are crucial aspects of the relationship between business and society, they do highlight an important issue. For example, Carroll and Buchholtz (2015: 28) argue that business involves an implicit *social contract* with society. By this they mean that the views and attitudes of the public matter to business because business is dependent for its continuing existence on people working for them, buying from them, selling to them and so forth. Without the active and ongoing participation of the public in business, there would be no way to stay in business and no way to make a profit. Therefore, if public attitudes to business become so enraged that the public loses faith in the business world, as happened for many people during the recent (and ongoing) global financial crisis, the public – you and us – are likely to withdraw their support and find other ways to organize the allocation and distribution of resources in society – see Chapters 16 and 17 for examples of these alternatives. This helps to explain why there is a growing interest in the idea of corporate social responsibility (see Chapter 5).

We want to finish this section by noting that business has been naturalized as an inherent and normal part of our social fabric, something to be expected in our economies, societies and polities (Bakan 2004). For example, the prices we pay in stores and the wages we earn can appear to us as nothing more than reflections of our own decisions and choices, rather than those of businesses and their managers. Similarly, the impacts of businesses and their managers are frequently represented as the result of impersonal and inevitable market pressures, forcing businesses to make hard choices about investments, jobs and so on. While we would agree that there are certain *external logics* underpinning business activities – namely, the capitalist drive for profit and growth (see Introduction) – we also contend that these logics are very much embedded in the way business is organized (e.g. corporate structure and governance) and in the power of business and corporations to influence the economy as well as society and politics. This is largely ignored in mainstream perspectives, however.

Critical perspectives

The starting point for any critical engagement with the idea and reality of corporate power is to define what we mean by power. While we might want to say simply that 'we know it when we see it', this is an inadequate basis for discussions of contested and contentious topics like corporate power. To start with, we might want to define power as our capability or capacity to make someone else do something we want them to do; especially if it is something they do not want to do (e.g. we force students to write essays for us) – this is often referred to as 'relational' power (Strange 1988). However, this definition needs unpacking. On the one hand, this definition of power necessarily entails other features like jurisdiction and legal or quasi-legal authority; that is, we obey certain people and not others because one set of people can enforce their demands (e.g. police), while others cannot (e.g. a friend). On the other hand, this definition only relates to direct forms of coercion, which misses other forms of power (e.g. ideological influence). Consequently, the next thing we do here is highlight several ways to conceptualize power, before exploring the diversity of corporate power in society.

What is power? Scholars have wrestled with these sorts of questions about power over many years. Here we want to consider Lukes' (1974) conceptualization of power in detail, but refer to others like Michel Foucault, Robert Cox and Susan Strange as important theorists of power. In his book, *Power: A Radical View*, Lukes argued that there are three dimensions to or understandings of power. The *first dimension* is the view that power is distributed between diverse groups in society that pursue their own interests and possess different capacities to achieve their goals – this view is often called 'pluralism'. From this perspective power is possessed, visible and intentional. The *second dimension* is the view that power also entails the ability to control societal or institutional agendas so that some people's interests are ignored. Thus power can also involve 'non-decisions' – like the exclusion of certain people from collective decision-making (e.g. government) – although it is still intentional. The *third dimension* is a critique of the other two views; from this perspective, power can also involve the unintentional or unconscious repression of certain people's interests through the establishment of social structures, forms and institutions that embed and reinforce certain systemic and unconscious biases. For example, there is no natural or inherent reason why we work for a wage, but receiving a wage leads us to adopt, unconsciously, certain habits, behaviours and beliefs. In this way power involves the shaping of our identities, personalities and senses of self; moreover, we do not realize that this is happening and come to accept it as normal and even natural.

Others like Foucault (1980), Cox (1987) and Strange (1988) have also theorized power, although in different ways. On the one hand, Foucault (1980), who was an important French philosopher-historian, sought to uncover histories of the entanglement of knowledge and power in social institutions like the prison, hospital and state – although, interestingly, not business. What he sought to illustrate was that knowledge produced power, and vice versa. For example, as modern nation-states emerged just before and during the life of people like Adam Smith, there was a move towards collecting information about national populations (e.g. birth, death and morbidity rates, household sizes etc.), which enabled the state both to understand their populations and to control them. In this way, knowledge is always and necessarily complicit in the exercise of power, although Foucault also thought that should be thought of as productive and not just coercion. On the other hand, Cox (1987) and Strange (1988), who were influential political scientists, sought to define power in 'structural' terms as the power to set the rules of the game; more precisely, it means the power to determine both the rules that govern our relationships (e.g. regulations) and the social frameworks through which we can and do relate to one another (e.g. markets).

In light of this discussion of power and the mainstream perspectives, we think it is important to consider corporate power from a number of different angles, theoretically and empirically. We focus on the internal and external power of corporations in this section.

- *Internal*: who owns, runs and controls corporations is a key question that we need to consider.
- *External*: we also need to look at the forms, agents and sites of corporate power – individually and as an institution (see Chapter 3) – in order to understand their structural and ideological power. While corporations influence society and politics through various means (e.g. lobbying, 'revolving door' etc.), they also shape the political, economic and legal context in which they operate, especially and increasingly internationally (see Chapter 8). Corporations and private businesses dominate public debate and influence our behaviour in ways that we might not notice, or that might not be obvious. It is important to understand how they influence our ideas and behaviours without us being consciously aware of it.

Internal corporate power: who controls corporations? The starting point for most discussions of corporate power is the internal structures and dynamics of corporate control; that is, an examination of who runs and controls the actions of business entities themselves. Two important scholars in this area are Edward Herman (1981) and Scott Bowman (1996), and we draw on their work here. This issue of internal control stretches back to the separation of corporate ownership and control following the corporate revolution, which we discuss in Chapters 3 and 4. When it comes to this internal structure, it is important to consider who makes the strategic decisions about what a business does and how those decisions are carried out. Most private businesses are owned and run by the same people, for example, although this is not always the case. Where a private business is not owner-managed, the owner usually has significant control over managerial appointments and therefore influence over managers. Modern corporations, in contrast, have more complex governance arrangements, as we discuss in Chapters 3 and 4. Corporations are not *owned* by anyone *per se*, in that their assets are the property of the corporation itself, although they have shareholders who own shares (also called equity) in the corporation (Stout 2012). As we discuss in Chapter 4, the relationship between shareholders and management is complex and driven by different legal forms of corporate governance.

Generally, however, in Anglo-American countries internal control rests formally with the board of directors (BoD) that sits between shareholders and executive management, and represents shareholder interests – see Figure 6.1 for a simple depiction of the internal structures of control in a corporation. The BoD votes on key decisions, establishes executive's remuneration deals (e.g. pay and bonuses), and provides oversight of executive decisions, including through the formal auditing processes. As Herman (1981) points out, however, whether or not BoD's have formal control over a corporation, internal power still usually rests with the key executive officers like the CEO for several reasons. First, executives generally get to appoint a proportion of BoD members, which means they can stack it with their allies. Second, BoD members generally do not get involved in the day-to-day operations of a corporation, meaning that they often do not know what executives are doing and, therefore, cannot provide adequate oversight. Finally, BoD members and shareholders lack the inside knowledge that executives have about the corporation, which means they lack the ability to make informed decisions.

As Bowman (1996) highlights, it is important to appreciate that internal corporate governance structures – that is, how shareholders control the actions of management – have changed quite significantly over time; for example, moving from a more democratic structure (e.g. one vote per shareholder) to a more oligarchic structure (e.g. one vote per share) since the nineteenth century (Ireland 2010). Furthermore, nowadays different shareholders have different levels of control depending on things like: (1) the number of shares they own and (2) the types of shares they own, since some shares have voting rights and others do not. This means that it is not necessarily possible to identify the

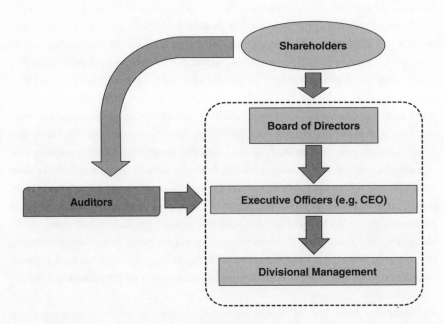

FIGURE 6.1 Internal corporate control

'best practice' for internal governance, or the most efficient way to ensure that shareholder interests are met by managers and executives. Moreover, these discussions of internal governance ignore a major element in the discussion of corporate power; namely, the power that managers have over their workers, whether or not there is shareholder oversight. As Ciepley (2013) points out, for example, corporations create their own laws internal to their organizations (e.g. dress code, work practice, wage regime etc.) to which workers are subject with little recourse to external legal jurisdiction, unless those rules contradict national laws (and even then it depends on the jurisdiction in which the corporation operates).

External corporate power: the corporate shaping of society Corporate power is not just an internal matter, limited to the actions and decisions that happen within a corporation. As people like Charles Derber (1998), Ted Nace (2003) and Joel Bakan (2004) note, the corporation now dominates many societies, especially places like the USA. Focusing on the internal workings of the corporation would miss the power they have to shape and influence their environment – that is, their structural and ideological power (Strange 1988). This power is not new either. Derber (1998) traces the rise of corporate power in the USA back to the corporate revolution; moreover, he argues that the problems associated with corporate power (e.g. concentration of wealth, inequality, excessive political influence etc.) have continued despite the emergence of countervailing forces in the shape of the central government, workers' movements or public citizenry. Today, as at the end of the nineteenth century, corporations are the dominant social institution; they are more powerful, in many ways, than governments, trade unions, professional organizations and even the law. For example, Bakan (2004: 5) claims that 'corporations dictate the decisions of their supposed overseers in government and control domains of society once embedded within the public sphere'.

While it is possible to criticize corporate power in general terms, it is also crucial to be able to understand and consider specific issues when discussing the relationship between society and corporate power. While we want to recognize that there are external controls on the actions of corporations (Herman 1981) in the form of government regulation, markets, societal attitudes, other businesses and so on, these are often as limited in the control they exert as the internal structures we discussed above. Consequently, we need to consider the structural and ideological power of business. In detailing this 'external' corporate power, we draw on the work of the Canadian sociologist William Carroll (2009, 2010), as well as other critics of corporate power who focus on the increasingly global nature of corporate power (e.g. Sklair 2002; Nace 2003; Beder 2006; Wolin 2008; Brennan 2014).

In his work, Carroll (2010) notes that corporate power has different forms, different agents and different sites. He argues that corporate power takes three forms: *operational*, *strategic* and *allocative*. Operational power relates to the decision-making of executives who determine the tasks, routines etc. of workers; strategic power relates to the capacity to determine the direction of a corporation, whether through shareholder or management control; and allocative power is about who controls the money corporations depend on for investment. All of these forms of power involve some form of internal and external control – although we are more interested in the latter here – and come to shape society in distinct ways. For example, operational power shapes the decisions of individual people in terms of employment choices (e.g. what jobs we can and cannot get); strategic power shapes the financial returns of different shareholders (e.g. small shareholders may lose out to larger ones who have more control); and allocative power shapes employment opportunities and levels of unemployment (e.g. through lack of investment).

Although the forms of corporate power help us to identify how it shapes society, it is important to identify who exercises this power and where it is centred. Building on earlier research, Carroll (2010) studies corporate elites (e.g. executives, directors, shareholders) and characterizes them as key agents of corporate power. He argues that corporate power has a class dimension to it in that corporate elites hold multiple and inter-locking positions across and within multiple corporations. As a result of these inter-locking relationships, corporate elites come to share the same identities, preferences and ideologies; this means that these elites are more likely to pursue their own class interests rather than the public interest. A number of academics have argued that this elite is increasingly global, representing an important element in what Sklair (2002) calls a *transnational capitalist class*. Importantly, corporate and political elites are increasingly blurred as individual members move from the private to public realm, and back again; a number of activists and academics have described this as a 'revolving door' between business and government because it has become so easy to move from one to the other (e.g. Prashad 2002; Rampton and Stauber 2004; Beder 2006).

The power of corporate elites is reinforced as a result of *where* corporate power is exercised outside of the corporation itself. There are many sites of corporate power outside the boardroom, according to Carroll (2009, 2010). These include: trade associations (e.g. Chambers of Commerce), policy planning groups (e.g. Trilateral Commission), think tanks (e.g. Fraser Institute, Heritage Foundation) and even government, state agencies and political parties. According to people like Nace (2003) and Beder (2006), these sites of corporate power are increasingly global and contribute to the structural and ideological power of corporations. However, it is important to note that corporate elites change and evolve; they do not stay the same. This is most obvious in the rise of financial corporate elites over the last few decades, especially new financial elites like hedge fund managers, investment bankers and so on. This means that corporate elites often come into conflict with one another, and do not always act in concert (Robinson 2010).

A lot of academics have written about the structural power of business and corporations when it comes to the global economy (see Chapter 7). Examples include Robert Cox (1987) and Susan Strange (1988) who both conceptualized structural power as the capacity to shape the global political-economic rules and structures. Closely linked to this structural power is the notion of ideological power, sometimes referred to as hegemony (see Chapter 8). Ideological power, or hegemony, reflects a broader, more social and cultural process of domination; it involves, according to Richard Peet (2007: 12), 'control and the production of consent by non-physically coercive means and institutions'. This form of power is tied to convincing people to accept a particular societal narrative or imaginary – for example, *business is good for society* – as a normal or natural state of affairs. As such, structural and ideological power closely map on to Steve Lukes' (1974) third dimension of power. Increasingly, business and especially multinational corporations are able to shape the rules they have to abide by, the framework in which they engage with each other, and how we understand and value those rules and framework. As Sharon Beder (2006) notes, for example, multinational corporations influence media discourse, regulation and national policy-making through their financing of academic research, their positions on international policy fora (e.g. World Economic Forum), lobbying of national governments, and the revolving door that enables corporate elites to move into and out of government with ease. As this implies, structural and ideological power often go hand in hand.

Empirical example: Enron and other corporate scandals

At the turn of the twenty-first century, there were a number of corporate scandals in the USA involving the collapse of large and often well-thought-of corporations. It started with Enron, an energy trader, which went bankrupt in 2001, and then spread to other corporations or businesses like WorldCom, Global Crossing and Parmalat, which all went into bankruptcy in 2002–2003. The reason for their collapse was because these corporations presented misleading financial statements to their shareholders and other investors that hid the fact they had high levels of corporate debt – in some cases (e.g. Enron) the auditors were also implicated in helping these corporations to present false financial statements. Other companies, like Tyco, were also the subject of scandals as their executives were accused of misleading shareholders in other ways.

These scandals can be understood differently from different perspectives. Through a mainstream lens, such as Carroll and Buchholtz (2015), these scandals are presented as a failure of corporate ethics, corporate social responsibility and corporate governance on the part of corporate executives. Simplistically, they can be seen as the consequence of individual greed. For example, we can understand the actions of Enron's Chairman Kenneth Lay and CEO Jeffrey Skilling as the deliberate misleading of shareholders, including their own employees, while these same executives protected their own interests by selling their own shares in Enron when they realized it was in financial trouble. At the same time, they presented a façade to everyone else that showed Enron was still performing strongly; consequently, when it went bankrupt all the other shareholders in Enron lost their investments. The film *Smartest Guys in the Room* (2005) provides a good introduction to what happened with Enron. In 2002, and in response to the Enron and other scandals, the US government introduced a new law called the Sarbanes-Oxley Act (SOX). It was designed to reinforce the interests of shareholders in corporate governance by strengthening financial reporting requirements.

From more critical perspectives, the emphasis on individual greed or individual corporate failure – the idea that these corporations represent 'bad apples' in an otherwise healthy economic system – ignores the structural and ideological roots of these scandals. First, if we adopt Carroll's (2010) approach, we might want to ask whether the whole system of financial auditing was compromised by the close relationships between corporate executives sitting on each other's boards. These friendly directors were less likely to provide rigorous oversight than more independent directors. Similarly, the revolving door between Enron and the US government documented by Prashad (2002) and Rampton and Stauber (2004) enabled Enron to lobby for energy deregulation and to avoid strict regulatory monitoring. Second, if we adopt the perspective of Cox (1987) and Strange (1988), we might question whether corporations like Enron sought to shape the structural framework in which they operated, and did so very successfully for a period of time before their actions caught up with them. Finally, from an ideological power perspective, we might suggest that Enron created a narrative of dynamic success that others sought to emulate, rather than critique, which was reinforced by the adoption of new and experimental forms of accounting. However we go about analysing these scandals, it is important to examine the *systemic* relationships rather than just treat them as the consequence of individual actions or decisions. To understand corporate power requires an understanding of more than the capacity of one or another corporation to change their environment as they wish.

Conclusion

In this chapter we have sought to introduce the notion of corporate power. As we note, it is difficult to clearly define and conceptualize. We presented the mainstream perspective that it can be understood as excessive economic or market power, distorting market prices so that competition no longer works efficiently. However, we also wanted to problematize this approach; in order to do that we discussed different ways to conceptualize power. In discussing corporate power from a more critical perspective, we outlined the internal and external dimensions to corporate power, and especially illustrated the different types of power we need to unpack in order to analyse corporate power. We finished the chapter by using the example of Enron to illustrate how corporate power can explain the corporate scandals that happened at the start of the twenty-first century.

Suggested readings

- Ch. 1, Bowman, S. (1996) *The Modern Corporation and American Political Thought*, Pennsylvania, Pennsylvania State University Press.
- Ch. 1, Carroll, W. (2010) *Corporate Power in a Globalizing World*, Oxford, Oxford University Press.
- Ch. 12, Carroll, A. and Buchholtz, A. (2015) *Business and Society* (9th Edition), Stamford CT, CENGAGE Learning.
- Ch. 1, Herman, E. (1981) *Corporate Control, Corporate Power*, Cambridge, Cambridge University Press.
- Ch. 2, Peet, R. (2007) *Geography of Power*, London, Zed Books.

Bibliography

Bakan, J. (2004) *The Corporation*, London, Random House.

Beder, S. (2006) *Suiting Themselves: How Corporations Drive the Global Agenda*, London, Earthscan.

Birch, K. (2007) 'The totalitarian corporation?', *Totalitarian Movements and Political Religions*, Vol.8, pp.153–161.

Bowman, S. (1996) *The Modern Corporation and American Political Thought*, Pennsylvania, Pennsylvania State University Press.

Brennan, J. (2014) 'The business of power: Canadian multinationals in the postwar era', PhD Thesis, York University.

Carroll, A. and Buchholtz, A. (2015) *Business and Society* (9th Edition), Stamford CT, CENGAGE Learning.

Carroll, W. (2009) 'Transnationalists and national networkers in the global corporate elite', *Global Networks*, Vol.9, pp.289–314.

Carroll, W. (2010) *Corporate Power in a Globalizing World*, Oxford, Oxford University Press.

Ciepley, D. (2013) 'Beyond public and private: Toward a political theory of the corporation', *American Political Science Review*, Vol.107, pp.139–158.

Cox, R. (1987) *Production, Power, and World Order*, New York, Columbia University Press.

Derber, C. (1998) *Corporation Nation*, New York, St. Martin's Griffin.

Foley, D. (2006) *Adam's Fallacy*, Cambridge MA, Belknap Press.

Foucault, M. (1980) *Power/Knowledge*, New York, Harvester Wheatsheaf.

Friedman, M. (1962) *Capitalism and Freedom*, Chicago, University of Chicago Press.

Herman, E. (1981) *Corporate Control, Corporate Power*, Cambridge, Cambridge University Press.

Ireland, P. (2010) 'Limited liability, shareholder rights and the problem of corporate irresponsibility', *Cambridge Journal of Economics*, Vol.34, pp.837–856.

Keen, S. (2001) *Debunking Economics*, London, Zed Books.

Khurana, R. (2007) *From Higher Aims to Hired Hands*, Princeton, Princeton University Press.

Korten, D. (2001) *When Corporations Rule the World*, San Francisco, Berrett-Koehler.

Lukes, S. (1974) *Power: A Radical View*, Basingstoke, Macmillan.

Lynn, B.C. (2010) *Cornered*, Hoboken NJ, John Wiley & Sons.

Means, G. (1983) 'Corporate power in the marketplace', *Journal of Law and Economics*, Vol.26, pp.467–485.

Monbiot, G. (2000) *Captive State*, Basingstoke, Macmillan.

Nace, T. (2003) *Gangs of America*, San Francisco, Berrett-Koehler.

Peet, R. (2007) *Geography of Power*, London, Zed Books.

Prashad, V. (2002) *Fat Cats and Running Dogs: The Enron Stage of Capitalism*, London, Zed Books.

Rampton, S. and Stauber, J. (2004) *Banana Republicans*, London, Robinson.

Robinson, W. (2010) 'Global capitalism theory and the emergence of transnational elites', UNU-WIDER, Working Paper No. 2010/02.

Sennett, R. (2007) *The Culture of the New Capitalism*, New Haven, Yale University Press.

Simon, H. (1991) 'Organizations and markets', *Journal of Economic Perspectives*, Vol.5, pp.25–44.

Sklair, L. (2002) *Globalization: Capitalism and Its Alternatives*, Oxford, Oxford University Press.

Smith, A. (1776) *The Wealth of Nations*: www.gutenberg.org/files/3300/3300-h/3300-h.htm (accessed January 2015).

Stout, L. (2012) *The Shareholder Value Myth*, San Francisco, Berrett-Koehler.

Strange, S. (1988) *States and Markets*, London, Continuum.

Wolin, S. (2008) *Democracy Inc.*, Princeton, Princeton University Press.

7 | Global economy and varieties of capitalism

Introduction

The world is getting smaller. Not in physical terms – Earth remains the same size – but rather in terms of distance and time. This shrinking of the world has been called **time-space compression** by the geographer David Harvey (1989) who links this shrinking of the world to the rise and spread of capitalism (see Chapter 2). We need to emphasize, however, that the world is getting smaller for *some* people, and not for everyone. What we mean by this is that some people – notably those living in the Global North – are now able to communicate across thousands of miles almost instantaneously using telephones, email, Facebook, Skype and other technologies. Moreover, the same people are now able to travel thousands of miles in a few hours by jet aeroplane, whereas only a hundred years ago it would have taken days if not weeks to travel the same distance by ship and train. It is important to remember, though, that for the vast majority of the world's population the world remains as large and difficult to traverse as ever.

> **Key concept: Time-space compression**
>
> This terms refers to the expansion of economic markets (space) and the increase in travel and communication speed (time) of goods, raw materials and money as they can be acquired from further afield and yet transported in a shorter period of time. This largely benefits large, multinational corporations which have operations or facilities in a number of countries around the world.
>
> *Source*: Harvey (1989)

This shrinking of distance and time is often presented as a process of *globalization* (Strange 1998; Brenner 2004; Dicken 2011). If we focus on the economy alone, as we do in this chapter, this process of globalization can be defined as the functional integration of different economic activities across territorial boundaries. As we outline later in this chapter, however, there is an enormous amount of debate about what globalization is, what its impacts are and whether it is actually happening or not. Despite this ongoing debate, however, there is general agreement that the last few decades have been witness to the growing interdependence of countries, peoples, cultures, economies and so on around the world. For example, what happens in China has a very real impact on what happens in Canada – and vice versa. Evidence of these impacts is visible in the aftermath of the 2007–2008 global financial crisis (GFC) when collapsing house prices, sub-prime mortgages and financial derivatives in the United States led to the so-called 2009 Great Recession around the world (Varoufakis 2013).

The reason that globalization is such an important process is because it has been promoted by numerous governments, **international financial institutions** (IFIs) and **multinational corporations or enterprises** as a means of economic development (Peet 2007). These various social actors frequently present globalization, or one particular form of *financial* globalization, as inevitable and irreversible, meaning that all countries need to restructure their economies to adapt to emerging global imperatives (Clark 1999), no matter their current situation or the impacts of this restructuring on their populations. Growing disquiet with this view of globalization emerged in the 1990s and continues today (see Chapters 5 and 16). Globalization has very real and frequently negative impacts on people in many different countries including: lost jobs through global outsourcing of work to countries with lower labour costs; financial volatility through free capital mobility as investors seek the highest returns on their investments; poverty and inequality as governments reduce their social welfare spending to accommodate the demands of IFIs, MNCs and other governments; and so on.

Definition: International financial institutions

IFIs are large non-governmental and non-business organizations which provide the framework for global governance and regulation. Examples include: World Bank, International Monetary Fund (IMF) and World Trade Organization (WTO). They have been criticized for promoting a particular form of globalization that limits economic development to 'free' trade and 'free' markets.

Key organization: Multinational corporations and multinational enterprises

An increasing number of businesses straddle the world in their activities. These businesses are commonly referred to as multinational corporations (MNC) or multinational enterprises (MNE). Both MNCs and MNEs are large businesses with operations, facilities and subsidiaries in a number of different countries, all of which are functionally integrated in the organization of production, trade or investment. As (public) corporations, MNCs are different from MNEs because they are owned by shareholders, even though their operations etc. may be located in very different countries from the country where they are listed on a stock exchange. Because of their size, several countries have developed specific rules about how MNCs and MNEs should operate globally (e.g. rules against bribery), as has the United Nations with its Global Compact, which is defined below. MNCs and MNEs are particularly associated with the so-called 'globalization' of the world economy.

In this chapter we go over the evidence of globalization as well as the mainstream and critical perspectives of it. We start by discussing the mainstream perspectives on the integration of the global economy, before briefly analysing the global economy as it stands today. We then turn to the critical perspectives, especially drawing on literature in economic geography, international political economy and sociology. We then discuss the case of the so-called BRICS and the transformation of their fortunes over the last decade or so to illustrate how mainstream perspectives ignore several important factors in explaining why some countries prosper while others do not in the global economy.

Key discussion questions

- Is there a global economy?
- What is globalization?
- In what ways has the world globalized? In what ways has it not?
- Who benefits from globalization? What are the problems with globalization?
- How powerful are multinational corporations?
- Is there one form of capitalism?

Mainstream perspectives

Hyper-globalists and their dreams of development A number of people, including journalists, academics, politicians and international policy-makers, have promoted the idea that *financial* globalization is good for everyone, no matter what country they live in and no matter the level of economic development in that country (Clark 1999). The idea that globalization is great is not restricted to a particular end of the political spectrum – left or right – but stretches from one end to the other. It is perhaps best exemplified in the academic literature by the Japanese management thinker Kenichi Ohmae (1990) in his book *Borderless World* and the American former-Secretary of Labor Robert Reich (1992) in *The Work of Nations*. Both authors, coming from different perspectives, arrived at similar conclusions in the early 1990s: namely, national economies face unprecedented pressure from global markets to change and adapt to new business networks, practices and demands. Furthermore, both agreed that these pressures cannot be avoided and, moreover, should not be avoided. Their perspective has been described as 'hyper-globalist' in light of their positive support for globalization (Held et al. 1999).

Ohmae and Reich define globalization as a process in which the expansion of global financial markets and global businesses (e.g. MNCs) has eroded the national organization of capitalism. As such, their theories imply an 'end of geography' as they argue that the national characteristics of each country no longer drive the success of businesses or national economies. Moreover, their conception of globalization places a particular emphasis on the benefits of reducing national government intervention in the economy (MacKinnon and Cumbers 2007). From this orthodox perspective, two things follow. First, globalization is meant to create a win-win situation in which countries around the world all benefit from the (expected) growth in trade and investment that free trade and capital mobility are expected to generate. According to another well-known exponent of this view, the journalist Thomas Friedman (2005), the world is now flat because there are no longer barriers to businesses integrating the design, production and retail of products and services across different national borders – and everyone benefits from their participation in this globalized world. Second, national governments must adopt business-friendly policies in order to benefit from globalization, anything less will simply result in stagnation and economic ruin. In an earlier book, *The Lexus and the Olive Tree*, Friedman (1999) argued that every country and their people needed to fit themselves into this 'golden straightjacket' to reap the benefits of globalization.

The 'golden straightjacket' reflects the demands of governments in the **developed world or Global North**, especially the USA, and IFIs like the World Bank – or what has been called the *Washington Consensus* (Williamson 1993) – see Chapter 8 for more on the issue of global governance. The straightjacket, or consensus, is based on two problematic assumptions: first, every national economy has developed the same way in the past, primarily through free trade and capital movement (Chang 2008); and second, it assumes that all national economies around the world have *and* should converge on one set of

Key methodological issue: Identifying world regions

There are different ways to describe different parts of the world. During the Cold War commentators and academics differentiated between First World (modern capitalist democracies), Second World (socialist states) and Third World (peripheral countries). However, since the end of the Cold War this terminology has become obsolete, and was viewed as disparaging anyway (e.g. 'Third World' implying bottom of the pack). Since then people have used terms like 'developed' and 'developing' countries to differentiate between modern capitalist countries and peripheral countries, but this terminology can also be criticized for its underlying assumptions (e.g. developing countries want to and should become 'developed' like Western Europe and North America – see Chapter 2). People increasingly use the terms Global North and Global South to represent differences between core capitalist economies like the USA and peripheral capitalist economies. It is important to note that these terms are fluid (e.g. a country can move from one category to another) and that they are not strictly geographical (e.g. Australia is in the Global North, yet also in the southern hemisphere).

government policies and one type of (free) market system (Clark 1999; Hay 2011). This has had the most impact on developing countries in the Global South which have been forced to adopt stringent fiscal and government spending measures – known as structural adjustment – as conditions for receiving international loans from the IMF or World Bank (Peet 2007, 2009). The measures promoted by the Washington Consensus in the developing world include some of the following: low public spending, low inflation, low trade and investment barriers, low wage protection, limited regulation of business, limited social welfare, limited taxation and limited government involvement in the economy (van Waeyenberge 2010). These policies, however, have been criticized for promoting global wealth inequalities and for negatively impacting the livelihoods of workers and citizens around the world (Stiglitz 2002).

Homogenous global economy? One starting point in an attempt to characterize the global economy is first to identify the world's major economies, their relationships to one another and to other countries and regions in the world, and how this has changed over time. This will help ground the various theoretical debates about globalization in reality. It might be surprising to note that up until the late nineteenth century, the world's biggest economies were China and India. Western Europe and North America only became the world's dominant economic blocs after that period, especially from 1900 when the USA became the world's largest economy (Dicken 2011: 15). The USA is still the largest economy in the world today, but China is re-emerging as the second largest economy after nearly a century – this will be discussed in more detail below. According to data from the World Bank and presented in Table 7.1, the largest economies in the world by **gross domestic product** (GDP) in 2013 are mostly from the Global North, but also include a number of rising

TABLE 7.1 Top ten countries by GDP in current prices (US$)

1961	1980	2000	2013
United States	United States	United States	United States
United Kingdom	Japan	Japan	China
France	Germany	Germany	Japan
Japan	France	United Kingdom	Germany
China	United Kingdom	France	France
Italy	Italy	China	United Kingdom
Canada	Canada	Italy	Brazil
India	Brazil	Canada	Russian Federation
Australia	Spain	Mexico	Italy
Sweden	Mexico	Brazil	India

Source: http://data.worldbank.org/indicator/NY.GDP.MKTP.CD (accessed June 2016)

powers like China, Brazil, Russia and India – the so-called BRICS – which we return to below. The list of largest economies has changed over time, being somewhat different in 2000 and especially since 1980 and 1960, although the USA remains on top throughout. What this data cannot show, however, is *how* globalized the world's economy is, or *how* globalization has happened; for that we have to turn to other indicators.

Key methodological issue: Gross domestic product

GDP refers to the total spending on goods and services in an economy plus any sales taxes and minus any subsidies. Using GDP is a very common way to calculate differences between economies, but it is important to note that it has been criticized and that it does not reflect a country's level of well-being or development. GDP is often calculated in different ways including: current prices to take account of inflation over time and make calculations comparable over time; nominal prices that do not take inflation into account; and purchasing power parities to take account of differences in spending power between countries since the cost of one thing in one country is not the same in another.

Source: World Bank

It is important to note that globalization is a contradictory process. On the one hand, production by businesses has become more fragmented across many countries as their supply chains have become more global; on the other hand, countries have become more integrated as trade and investment barriers have been removed through international treaties. These two trends are, obviously, related to one another, but in order to understand how integrated different countries are around the world it is useful to look at certain indicators like trade flows and **foreign investment**. A helpful resource in this regard is Peter Dicken's (2011) book *Global Shift*. In this book, Dicken (2011: Ch. 2) provides an enormous amount of information and detail on the transformation of the global economy over the late twentieth and early twenty-first centuries.

Definition: Foreign investment

Businesses in different countries do not simply trade with one another; they also make investments in other countries. These investments take two main forms: portfolio investment and foreign direct investment (FDI). Portfolio investment involves the purchasing of stocks and bonds in another country, while FDI involves the creation of subsidiaries or purchase of companies in a foreign country. The key difference between portfolio investment and FDI is the level of control that the investment provides, with the former representing an 'indirect' form of control while the latter is 'direct'.

According to Dicken (2011), the following major trends are important for understanding the global economy. First, the world's economy has become increasingly interconnected since the 1960s, creating a *global* economy as more and more countries trade with one another. For example, Dicken (2011: 18) argues that 'world merchandise trade increased almost twentyfold while world merchandise production increased just over sixfold'. Second, while trade has increased significantly, foreign direct investment (FDI) has increased even more (p.21), especially after 1985. Third, this increase in FDI is important because FDI represents direct means for controlling resources and assets by MNCs outside their home countries. Fourth, as a result of increasing FDI between one-third and a half of all trade is now intra-firm trade, involving businesses producing, assembling and retailing products in very different parts of the world (p.20). This necessitates an enormous amount of shipping and transportation between countries. Fifth, world trade and foreign investment flows predominantly happen between the global *triad* of world regions – Western Europe, North America and Asia – although this is gradually changing (p.19). It is important, therefore, to recognize that certain world regions are more *globalized* than others. Finally, although the global economy has become more interconnected since 1980, with rising levels of exports and FDI, it has also become increasingly volatile with significant rises and falls in levels of exports and FDI across years (pp.17, 21). Overall, when looking at these trends it is evident that only a few countries dominate the global economy. For example, just 15 countries represent 75 per cent of world manufacturing output, 80 per cent of world agricultural output and 80 per cent of outward FDI stock (p.25).

In light of the information presented by Dicken (2011), it is necessary to maintain a sceptical perspective about globalization as a real process *and* as a policy prescription for promoting economic development around the world (Stiglitz 2002; Chang 2008). However, what it also illustrates is that businesses now play a significant role in the organization, coordination and governance of the global economy.

Critical perspectives

Questioning globalization As can be seen from the preceding discussion in this chapter, globalization is a difficult concept both to define analytically and to identify empirically. Many critics of globalization take issue with at least three claims about globalization in these debates:

- *conceptual claims* that globalization is the best theory to explain the transformation of our economies over the last few decades;
- *empirical claims* that globalization has led to the end of geography through the erosion of the nation-state and national sovereignty; and

- *normative claims* that globalization is an inevitable and irreversible process we can do nothing about and which benefits everyone equally.

First, many critics of globalization point out that capitalism is a world-wide system (see Chapter 2) and that, therefore, globalization is not new – we have been here before. For example, a number of critics have suggested that there are at least two ages of globalization (McGrew 2011). These are outlined in Table 7.2.

TABLE 7.2 Two ages of globalization

Characteristics	First age of globalization	Second age of globalization
Time period	1820–1914	1950–present
Main countries	European colonial powers (e.g. UK, France etc.)	USA (plus Japan and China)
Dominant world power	British Empire	USA
Trade flows	Raw materials from colonial periphery to core imperial homeland; manufactured goods from core to periphery. British system of free trade	Raw materials and products from Global South to Global North; knowledge and services from Global North to Global South. Gradual international elimination of trade barriers
Investment flows	Portfolio investment in colonies by businesses. British system of free trade	Foreign direct investment by multinational corporations. Gradual elimination of capital controls
International governance	Gold standard enforced by British Empire	**Bretton Woods System** (until 1971) and then US$ dominance enforced by USA

Sources: Hirst and Thompson (1999); McGrew (2011)

Key global institutions: Bretton Woods System

The Bretton Woods System (BWS) was an international arrangement established after the Second World War by the Allied nations to organize the global economy and comprised a fixed currency exchange system pegged to the US dollar, the International Monetary Fund, the World Bank and the General Agreement on Tariffs and Trade. We discuss these in more detail in Chapter 8. When it came to trade, the BWS was based on the idea that all countries should trade with one another using a single currency – in this case the US dollar – so that no country could simply devalue their currency in order to gain a competitive advantage (i.e. their exports would be cheaper if they devalued their currency). It collapsed in 1971, however, when the USA withdrew its backing for the BWS.

Two of the most sceptical analysts of globalization are Paul Hirst and Grahame Thompson (1999) who's book *Globalization in Question* provided a detailed empirical critique of various globalization theories. They highlighted: similarity in trends in international trade and capital mobility between the nineteenth century and the last few decades; the dependence and embeddedness of MNCs in their home countries; and the lack of clear theoretical definition of a global economy. In particular, they showed that most international economic activity and integration was limited to the 'triad' of Western Europe, North America and Japan (also Hay 2011). While their empirical data is now out of date, Hirst and Thompson (1999) provided a much-needed test of hyper-globalist claims.

Second, critics have empirically questioned the idea that globalization has led to the erosion of **the nation-state** and national sovereignty as countries have converged on one economic system – namely, (neo-)liberal capitalism. There have been numerous claims that national governments, for example, have lost their capacity to create and enforce laws and regulations in their own territories as international organizations (e.g. IMF, World Bank, WTO etc.) have accumulated more power to govern the global economy (e.g. set rules on international trade). Moreover, there have been numerous claims that national governments are no longer as influential or important as global forces have led to the restructuring of national economies. These claims have been criticized for being wrong or too simplistic (Weiss 1998; Clark 1999; Brenner 2004; Hay 2011).

Definition: The nation-state

The state can be defined as an array of institutions, public and semi-public, that have sovereignty (i.e. legal authority) over a particular territory (i.e. geographical area). The state comprises institutions like the government, the civil service, the legal system, the police, the education system and so on.

The state has not withered away, nor has every country converged on one ideal model of the state. Colin Hay (2011: 325–326) argues, for example, that the state is still an important social actor and represents a significant proportion of national GDP in most developed countries; this ranges from 35 per cent in the USA to 54 per cent in Sweden in 2005. Since then, the role of the state became even more obvious as many countries bailed out their national banks during the global financial crisis – without this support, there was a chance that national economies would have totally collapsed (Varoufakis 2013). Hence, it is important to note that while there is no doubt the current era of globalization is shaped by the global activities of businesses, especially by MNCs and their strategic decisions in regard to production, trade and investment (Dicken 2011), this global dominance of business is supported *and* enforced by national governments, especially those in the Global North like the USA and UK (Helleiner 1994; Weiss 1998).

Third, critics have especially questioned the idea that globalization is either an unalloyed good – benefiting all and sundry around the world – or an inevitable and irreversible process we can do nothing about. A number of important thinkers like Anthony Giddens (1990) and Manuel Castells (1996) have argued for the need for a more nuanced analysis of global change; while they might agree that globalization is happening, they do not assume that it is wholly new or necessarily has positive impacts. Others, in a similar vein, argue that globalization is not some unstoppable behemoth that we cannot influence, but rather emphasize the continuing role of the nation-state in global policy-making through international institutions like the UN, EU, WTO and so on (Griffin 2003). What this implies is that globalization can benefit everyone if it is managed in the right way. One example is the international attempt to enrol MNCs in new forms of global governance through mechanisms like the **UN Global Compact**. The UN Secretary-General Ban Ki-moon describes the Global Compact thus:

> The Global Compact asks companies to embrace universal principles and to partner with the United Nations. It has grown to become a critical platform for the UN to engage effectively with enlightened global business.

Definition: UN Global Compact

Established in 2000, the UN Global Compact is an attempt to align the interests of business with internationally agreed upon principles of human, labour and environmental rights, as well as anti-corruption practices. It is an example of corporate citizenship and corporate social responsibility discussed in Chapter 5.

Not all critics agree with the idea that international organizations like the UN – or WTO, IMF and World Bank – are best placed to challenge the most egregious impacts of globalization since they are dominated by those governments which seek to spread the influence of markets and business most widely – see Richard Peet's (2007, 2009) criticisms of these institutions, for example. With all of these criticisms of globalization in mind, it is evident that the global economy is not homogenous or converging on one, best economic system; nor can it do so, conceptually, empirically or normatively. Rather, and as we illustrate next, the global economy and globalization are better understood as an interconnected and interdependent system of diverse, often national-centred, *capitalisms* – in the plural – which have their own distinct qualities and flaws.

Varieties of capitalism in a global economy The theory and reality of globalization are often very different from one another, as the above discussion should illustrate. This opens up two rather important questions: *how* has globalization impacted on different countries and *why* has it had different impacts? We think these two questions help us to understand the variety and diversity inherent in capitalism that often gets obscured in debates about globalization and the expected convergence of national economies to a free market ideal – often called '**neoliberalism**'. In answering these questions we can identify at least two different senses in which capitalism is varied and diverse: first, capitalism may go through different stages at different points in time (i.e. temporal diversity); and second, capitalism may be different in different places (i.e. geographical variety).

Key concept: Neoliberalism

Neoliberalism is a contested term used to refer to a range of things including: policy practices, economic system, political project and epistemic community. For ease, we use it here to refer to a political-economic system based on the idea that (free) market interactions – i.e. those with no or limited state or social intervention – are the most efficient way to organize the economy *and* to coordinate all social institutions. This does not mean, however, that the state plays no role in the economy; quite the opposite. The state's role is to create new markets, maintain the rule of law (especially when it comes to competition) and ensure social stability through penal policies. As such, neoliberalism does not simply imply 'de-regulation' of the economy, but rather its 're-regulation' as new rules are instituted.

Source: Birch (2015)

First, the idea that capitalism has changed over time is best exemplified in the notion that there was a shift from Keynesianism to neoliberalism in the early 1980s. While not everyone characterizes this shift as the emergence of neoliberalism, most scholars agree that there was a significant change following the 1970s. One important thinker in this regard is Bob Jessop (2002) who argues that the transformation of capitalism has been accompanied by the transformation of the state – in fact, the economy and state necessarily change together as the former is *regulated* – by which he means stabilized – by the latter. Jessop (2002) identifies several differences between what he calls the Keynesian National Welfare State (KNWS) and Schumpeterian Competition State (SCS). The former emerged after the Second World War and was centred on a national-centred form of capitalism supported by different social welfare systems. After the KNWS broke down during the 1970s, it was replaced by the SCS in which the state supported global capital mobility and global competition through policies like wage restraint, low taxation, employment flexibility and so on, all designed to attract international investment. While these are distinct forms of capitalism, it is notable that both stress the role of the state in buttressing the activities of business, rather than the erosion of the state altogether.

Second, there is a large body of literature discussing the 'varieties of capitalism' around the world, drawing on the work of Peter Hall and David Soskice (2001) and others like Bruno Amable (2003). In their work, Hall and Soskice (2001) argue that different countries sit on a spectrum from liberal market economies (LME) to coordinated market economies (CME). Anglo-Celtic economies, like the USA, UK, Canada and Ireland, are often contrasted with social democratic or coordinated economies in Scandinavia, Northern Europe and Japan (Amable 2003). Hall and Soskice (2001) examine the firm- or business-level characteristics of different countries in order to understand what differentiates the performance of different economies. For example, they look at industrial relations between management and workers, education and training systems, corporate governance – as discussed in Chapter 4 – and inter-business interaction (e.g. competitive or collaborative). What they argue is that LMEs are less regulated, less egalitarian, more competitive, more legalistic, lower taxed and more flexible than CMEs. In making these claims, academics like Hall and Soskice provide an important counter to the claims of hyper-globalists about the inevitable, irreversible and homogenizing forces of globalization. What is clear from the literature on the varieties of capitalism is quite the reverse in fact; many national economies have a strong, institutional heritage which is not simply wiped away by a global steamroller forcing every country to adopt one set of global market rules. Moreover, different countries, especially those in the Global North, have adopted very different policies in light of globalization, helping to alleviate the worst effects of global change.

Empirical example: the 'BRICS' countries

It is useful to look at a specific example in order to illustrate the notion that there are varieties of capitalism and not a homogenous global economy. While the global economy is still dominated by a small number of countries it is evident that things are changing. In particular, over the last few decades the Global South has become a more important site of economic development, trade and investment. According to data presented by Dicken (2011: 25; 2015: 25), for example, 'developing countries' grew from around 18 per cent of world GDP, 19 per cent of world exports and 21 per cent of world FDI in 1990 to around 35 per cent, 32 per cent and 35 per cent respectively by 2012. It is important, once again, to note that the growth in these three indicators reflects the emergence of a few countries, mainly in the Global South, as global players rather than all countries. In particular, Brazil, Russia, India, China and South Africa – the so-called BRICS – have witnessed significant growth in GDP, exports, FDI and production; they now represent around 15 per cent of world GDP, for example (Dicken 2011: 26). While the BRICS are increasingly important, they are not the same as each other. The economies of Brazil and Russia are based on commodity exports, especially agriculture (Brazil) and oil and gas (Russia), while China is a major product exporter and commodity importer, and India is a major services exporter.

Again, the BRICS can be distinguished from one another on the basis of differences in their economic system; they are also diverse forms of capitalism (Hall and Soskice 2001; Amable 2003). On the one hand, China is a totalitarian political system in which one party controls the state, while India is the largest democracy in the world. Although these political differences are important, it is also necessary to understand the political-economic characteristics of each country. What is interesting in light of (neoliberal) arguments about the need to adapt to globalization is that China and India, for example, did not adopt the policies promoted by the Washington Consensus, and yet they achieved significantly higher growth rates than those that did (Peet 2007). One example of the differences is the Chinese state's continuing control over its own currency – it is not free floating – and over new companies set up in China – they maintain a controlling share in them. Whether these growth rates are also a result of China and India's size is beside the point; they show that each and every country is different and should not be forced to adopt one set of (very prescriptive) policies. Development comes in many forms, it would seem.

Not only do the BRICS represent diverse forms of capitalism, their relationship to the rest of the world is not always as simplistic as sometimes presented in the globalization narrative. China is an interesting example in this regard. While we might think that China is now the workshop of the world, since most of the products we buy (e.g. apparel, electronics etc.) seem to have 'Made in China' stamped on them, this hides a complex set of international trade and investment relationships. China has positioned itself at a particular point in the **global value chain** as outlined by Dicken (2011) and Thun (2011).

Key methodological issue: Global value chains

There are various ways to study the global economy. One way is to conceptualize the process of production, distribution and retail as a 'value chain' in which different social actors capture value from the creation of a product or commodity as it moves between different locations around the world. For example, an iPhone may be sold in the USA or Canada, but its component parts were produced and assembled elsewhere (e.g. China, Taiwan, South Korea), while the raw materials used to make those parts come from somewhere else entirely (e.g. Democratic Republic of the Congo, Indonesia). Moreover, at each stage of the value chain workers and owners capture different levels of value depending on their relative power to one another. What this approach does is help researchers explore the social, political and economic dynamics behind the production, distribution and retail of goods and services, rather than assume that this is a neutral process from which everyone benefits.

Source: Thun (2011)

As an economy, China has grown at astonishing rates since the early 1990s and has become the second largest economy in the world. It is also the second largest manufacturer (after the USA), second largest merchandise exporter (after Germany) and third largest importer (Dicken 2011: 32). However, what these data obscure is that China is a major importer of raw materials *and* manufactured goods; it is not simply an exporter. We can explain this by noting that China is tied into a series of intra-Asian trade relationships through multinational business networks in which component or intermediate parts are produced in a variety of Asian countries (e.g. Thailand, Malaysia, Indonesia etc.) – and elsewhere – before being shipped to China for assembly and then final export to overseas markets like North America and Western Europe (Dicken 2011: 33). The Chinese economy, in this sense, is built on the back of foreign business investment in Chinese factories that seeks to exploit low Chinese labour (Thun 2011: 361).

Conclusion

In this chapter we sought to do a number of things. First, we have provided an outline of ongoing debates about the importance of globalization on our economies and societies, especially as this relates to how this era of globalization might be distinct and different from past eras. Second, we have discussed how globalization has been used to make particular claims about what is development, what is happening to the nation-state and what governments should do to restructure their societies. Third, we challenged these claims by outlining how globalization is a contested concept and process, and how we have to be careful when making normative claims about it. Fourth, we showed how it is more useful to represent the global economy as an interconnected and interdependent system of national *capitalisms* – a plural amalgam of diverse and varied economies, each with their own institutional heritage and state. What these insights should help us do is better understand the development of different economies and what kinds of development are actually beneficial and what kinds are not.

Suggested readings

- Ch. 1, Chang, H.-J. (2008) *Bad Samaritans*, London, Bloomsbury.
- Ch. 2, Dicken, P. (2015) *Global Shift* (7th Edition), New York, Guildford.
- Hay, C. (2011) 'Globalization's impact on states', in J. Ravenhill (ed.), *Global Political Economy* (3rd Edition), Oxford, Oxford University Press, pp.312–344.
- Ch. 2, Hirst, P. and Thompson, G. (1999) *Globalization in Question* (2nd Edition), Cambridge, Polity Press.
- Ch. 2, Peet, R. (2009) *Unholy Trinity* (2nd Edition), London, Zed Books.

Bibliography

Amable, B. (2003) *The Diversity of Modern Capitalism*, Oxford, Oxford University Press.

Birch, K. (2015) 'Neoliberalism: The whys and wherefores . . . and future directions', *Sociology Compass*, Vol.9, pp.571–584.

Brenner, N. (2004) *New State Spaces*, Oxford, Oxford University Press.

Castells, M. (1996) *The Rise of the Network Society*, Oxford, Blackwell.

Chang, H.-J. (2008) *Bad Samaritans*, London, Bloomsbury.

Clark, I. (1999) *Globalization and International Relations Theory*, Oxford, Oxford University Press.

Dicken, P. (2011) *Global Shift* (6th Edition), New York, Guildford.

Dicken, P. (2015) *Global Shift* (7th Edition), New York, Guildford.

Friedman, T. (1999) *The Lexus and the Olive Tree*, New York, Farrar, Straus & Giroux.

Friedman, T. (2005) *The World Is Flat*, New York, Farrar, Straus & Giroux.

Giddens, A. (1990) *The Consequences of Modernity*, Cambridge, Polity.

Griffin, K. (2003) 'Economic globalization and institutions of global governance', *Development and Change*, Vol.34, pp.789–807.

Hall, P. and Soskice, D. (eds) (2001) *Varieties of Capitalism: The Institutional Foundations of Comparative Advantage*, Oxford, Oxford University Press.

Harvey, D. (1989) *The Condition of Postmodernity*, Cambridge, Blackwell.

Hay, C. (2011) 'Globalization's impact on states', in J. Ravenhill (ed.), *Global Political Economy* (3rd Edition), Oxford, Oxford University Press, pp.312–344.

Held, D., Goldblatt, D. and Perratton, J. (1999) *Global Transformations*, Cambridge, Polity Press.

Helleiner, E. (1994) *States and the Reemergence of Global Finance*, Ithaca, Cornell University Press.

Hirst, P. and Thompson, G. (1999) *Globalization in Question* (2nd Edition), Cambridge, Polity Press.

Jessop, B. (2002) *The Future of the Capitalist State*, Cambridge, Polity Press.

McGrew, A. (2011) 'The logics of economic globalization', in J. Ravenhill (ed.), *Global Political Economy* (3rd Edition), Oxford, Oxford University Press, pp.275–311.

MacKinnon, D. and Cumbers, A. (2007) *An Introduction to Economic Geography*, Harlow, Pearson.

Ohmae, K. (1990) *The Borderless World*, London, Collins.

Peet, R. (2007) *Geography of Power*, London, Zed Books.

Peet, R. (2009) *Unholy Trinity* (2nd Edition), London, Zed Books.

Reich, R. (1992) *The Work of Nations*, New York, Vintage Books.

Stiglitz, J. (2002) *Globalization and Its Discontents*, London, W.W. Norton & Company.

Strange, S. (1998) *Mad Money*, Manchester, University of Manchester Press.

Thun, E. (2011) 'The globalization of production', in J. Ravenhill (ed.), *Global Political Economy* (3rd Edition), Oxford, Oxford University Press, pp.345–369.

Van Waeyenberge, E. (2010) 'Tightening the web: The World Bank and enforced policy reform', in K. Birch and V. Mykhnenko (eds), *The Rise and Fall of Neoliberalism*, London, Zed Books, pp.94–111.

Varoufakis, Y. (2013) *The Global Minotaur* (2nd Edition), London, Zed Books.

Weiss, L. (1998) *The Myth of the Powerless State*, Cambridge, Polity Press.

Williamson, J. (1993) 'Development and the "Washington Consensus"', *World Development*, Vol.21, pp.1329–1336.

8 | Global governance

Introduction

In early 2016 Greenpeace Netherlands released the negotiating text of the *Transatlantic Trade and Investment Partnership* (TTIP) between the EU and USA.[1] They released the draft document in order to highlight the deeply problematic effects it could have on governments and, by implication, on citizens in those jurisdictions. Negotiations on the TTIP began in 2013 between the EU and USA. The stated intention behind the TTIP, at least according to the European Commission (EC), is that it is expected to generate jobs and cut consumer prices.[2] Another rationale behind the pursuit of these sorts of *bilateral* or *multilateral* trade and investment agreements is that a truly *global* agreement cannot be reached on the form that global governance should take. That is, the national interests of many countries come into conflict with one another. For example, the World Trade Organization (WTO) has been mired in negotiations over agricultural subsidies since 2001, with little opportunity for a speedy resolution any time soon. That means that the TTIP and other agreements like the 13-country Trans-Pacific Partnership (TPP) and the Canada-European Comprehensive Economic and Trade Agreement (CETA) are likely to be the global shape of things to come.

Many politicians, policy-makers, media commentators and academics stress the benefits that these trade and investment agreements have for the countries involved; there is little reason for them otherwise. In May 2016, David Cameron, the British Conservative Prime Minister, called on all parties to the TTIP to find the 'political courage to get it over the line' (Mason 2016). While these comments refer to a specific agreement, they reflect a broader consensus around the idea that 'free' trade and investment benefit everyone involved, a view that stretches back to the heyday of British Empire in the nineteenth century (Polanyi 1944 [2001]). It is not uncommon to hear the same views parroted over a hundred years later in popular media like the TV show *The West Wing* (e.g. Season 2, Episode 16). Similarly, such topics are increasingly popular in universities, where there has been a proliferation of degrees and programmes on global studies, such as the University of Toronto's Munk School of Global Affairs.[3] No matter where it originates, this

---

1 Greenpeace TTIP Leaks: https://ttip-leaks.org/ (accessed May 2016).
2 European Commission: http://ec.europa.eu/trade/policy/in-focus/ttip/about-ttip/ (accessed May 2016).
3 Munk School of Global Affairs: http://munkschool.utoronto.ca/mga/ (accessed May 2016).

perspective reflects a particular view about the proper **governance** of the world's economy; that is, about how the global economy works and consequently how it *should* be coordinated.

Definition: Governance

Often compared with the concept of 'government' – which refers to the formal political system and formal authority – the term 'governance' is used to conceptualize the coordination of the political-economic system across an array of social actors and institutions (e.g. government, business, civil society etc.). Increasingly, governance is associated with the growing role and importance of private actors in political-economic decision-making, especially at the global scale.

Drawing on the work of Weiss (2013) and May (2015), we define this sort of *global governance* as the systematic and collective attempt to organize and coordinate global activities in the pursuit of common global goals, which would be beyond the capacity of any individual country to undertake. Furthermore, as Weiss (2013: 32) emphasizes, it involves 'the combination of informal and formal values, rules and norms, procedures, practices and policies, and organisations of various types'. In the previous chapter we stressed the need to adopt a nuanced perspective when trying to understand the global economy, taking into account the varied and uneven economic geography of globalization processes (Dicken 2015). The same could be said about global governance. Capitalism does not manifest the same way in every country around the world; in fact, so many countries, even neighbouring ones, are significantly different from one another that it has led academics to the idea that there are diverse or varied capitalisms (Whitley 1999; Hall and Soskice 2001). In our view, this is not despite the fact that there has been considerable effort to institute a specific form of global governance, especially when it comes to the economy and business; rather, it is because of the attempts to institute global governance that the world has such uneven economic geography. So, we want to highlight that the notion there are varieties of capitalism does not militate against the idea that there is a systematic and ongoing attempt to coordinate and govern the global economy and international economic exchange.

A key problem facing students grappling with the global political economy is that mainstream discourses around globalization and the relationship between business and society tend to ignore the economic geography of this relationship. In particular, popular and academic debates often forget about the positioning and configuration of business and business relations across different geographical scales (e.g. local, national and global). By this, we mean that these debates focus more on the global relationship between business and governments, rather than the role of business in making a global world.

In this chapter our aim is to discuss this perspective and then unpack it by looking at how global rules are made by business, and what implications this has for society.

Key discussion questions

- What is global governance?
- Why does global governance matter?
- What institutions are involved in global (economic) governance?
- How is the current system of global governance implicated in the development of problematic national policies?
- How does business help to make global governance rules?

Mainstream perspectives on global governance

It is somewhat surprising that there is so limited discussion of global governance in mainstream literature on business and society. For example, in an otherwise comprehensive introductory textbook, Carroll and Buchholtz (2015) do not have a chapter on global governance, nor do they reference topics like globalization and the WTO in the index. It might be the case that such textbooks do not address global governance because they assume that business is, by its very definition, already global – for example, these textbooks specifically discuss topics like global ethics, global competition etc. However, it is more useful, in our view at least, to consider multinational or transnational corporations as *global* social actors (see Ietto-Gillies 2014), distinct from *national* or *local* business more generally. In order to reflect on the mainstream treatment of global governance we start with a brief introduction to international relations (IR) before discussing the view of global governance as a result of inter-governmental arrangements and the examples of this view in contemporary global governance organizations.

Introduction to international relations and inter-governmental arrangements In order to understand global governance it is important to have a basic grasp of international relations between countries and their origins (Clark 2000). As a starting point, it is helpful to consider where national sovereignty comes from. By this we mean the power of a nation-state to pursue certain policies, enact specific laws, regulate particular activities, and so on. A quite simple question helps illustrate this point: why can one country not enact laws or regulations (e.g. labour or product standards) in another country? If asked this question, most political scientists would point to the emergence of national sovereignty from the seventeenth century onwards as the explanation. In particular, they would probably highlight the 1648 *Treaty of Westphalia* as the key historical event in the development of modern state sovereignty.

The Treaty was the culmination of the Thirty Years' War, which had ravaged Europe as the result of religious divisions and conflict between Catholic and Protestant Christianity.

One major treatise on the emergence and evolution of the (European) nation-state is the book *Shield of Achilles* by Philip Bobbitt (2002). In this book, Bobbitt outlines his view of the historical relationship between state sovereignty and national strategy; namely, he argues that sovereignty reflects strategic ambitions (e.g. war, conquest, colonialism etc.). As Bobbitt highlights with the emergence of the modern nation-state, geographically-specific territories (e.g. England, France, Spain etc.) became the focus of constitutional claims about nation-state sovereignty. This meant that only a state underpinned by a territorial designation could enact or introduce laws in that territory. As a result of this political development, nation-states increasingly had to find ways to coordinate their activities with one another in order to facilitate things like international trade. Today, this is especially the case as the result of the increasing technological, social, political and economic connectivity between countries around the world, and the increasing need to solve global problems like climate change (see Chapter 9).

In light of the common notion and definition of national state sovereignty we have just discussed, much of the mainstream discourse on global governance tends to treat the relationship between business and global governance in an unproblematic fashion. One example is the World Economic Forum (WEF), which is an organization that holds regular global policy-making meetings in Davos, Switzerland and elsewhere around the world. It describes its mission and activities as 'shaped by a unique institutional culture founded on the stakeholder theory [see Chapter 5], which asserts that an organization is accountable to all parts of society'. The WEF goes so far as to recognize that there is growing popular unease with economic globalization and corporate power, but at the same time stresses certain (business-friendly) solutions:

> Transformations are required in the fragmented governance of global value chains, competition policy and investment frameworks to slash investment uncertainty, the complexity of international commerce and the costs of business operation.[4]

In part the problem here is that organizations like the WEF assume that global governance is about inter-governmental arrangements, or the relations between nation-states. Such assumptions are reflected in academic debates as well. According to May (2015), for example, much of the academic literature on global governance – even the literature critical of the role of

---

4 World Economic Forum: www.weforum.org/global-challenges/international-trade-and-investment/projects/e15-initiative (accessed May 2016).

business in setting and influencing global rules (e.g. Hertz 2002) – tends to emphasize either (1) the impact of business – especially multinational corporations (MNCs) – on global institutions, or (2) the impact of those global institutions on business. As an example, May cites the work of Brühl and Hofferberth (2013) as representative of this tendency. In short, the mainstream discourse assumes that global governance is about the relationship between business and the state, where the latter is represented by intergovernmental arrangements or organizations at the global scale. It assumes, moreover, that global governance is about the impact of one on the other. We come back to May's criticism of these assumptions later in the chapter, but for now we want to outline the emergence of the current system of global governance.

Contemporary global governance The form that global governance takes today largely emerges from a meeting held by the Allied nations in 1944 at Bretton Woods, New Hampshire. This came to be known as the Bretton Woods Conference and set the stage for post-Second World War capitalism in countries like the USA, UK and Japan, as well in Western Europe and other parts of the world. It led directly to the establishment of three core global governance agreements or organizations: the World Bank, the International Monetary Fund (IMF) and the General Agreement on Tariffs and Trade (GATT), which turned into the WTO. These institutions as well as the fixed currency system underpinning them are called the Bretton Woods System (BWS), which lasted until 1971 in its original form. This BWS represents a cornerstone in what John Ruggie (1982) has called the 'embedded liberal' order that dominated the post-Second World War era, up until the 1970s at least.

The BWS was based on the growing dominance of the USA in the world capitalist economy at the end of the Second World War, reflected in its emergence as one of the post-Second World War superpowers alongside the USSR (see Chapter 10). At the time, the USA was the only major capitalist economy not severely damaged by the war, and it took on a major role in the global governance of the world's capitalist economies (Eichengreen 1996, 2006). The BWS was designed as a way to coordinate trade and investment activities between nation-states by controlling the flow of capital (i.e. money) between countries and promoting international trade by reducing tariffs. Capital controls were meant to reduce the economic volatility caused by the free movement of capital investment between countries; while tariff reductions were meant to increase trade between countries. The BWS incorporated a range of international organizations or agreements, which we discuss below, but was also based on a fixed exchange system dominated by the US dollar. In many ways, it was an attempt to return to the '**gold standard**', although it was largely controlled by the USA (Eichengreen 1996).

Key global institution: 'Gold standard'

The gold standard involves a government fixing the value of its currency in gold and redeeming its currency notes in gold on demand. This means that a person could exchange a certain number of dollar notes for their equivalent in gold at a bank. One advantage of such a system is that a country's money supply cannot outgrow its reserves of gold, something perceived to curtail inflation associated with excessive government spending.

A return to a form of gold standard underpinned the BWS established at the end of the Second World War. It worked through the fixing of the rate of exchange between a country's currency and the US dollar, while the dollar's value was fixed to a certain value of gold (US$35 per ounce). The system curtailed currency speculation because there were exchange controls which limited access to foreign currency.

The USA came off this modern 'gold standard' in 1971 when President Nixon sought to release government spending from the constraint of the need to retain significant gold reserves and because of the trade deficits – which, under the BWS, had to be backed by gold – that the US had accumulated with its trading partners. A system of fixed (but periodically adjustable) exchange rates gave way to a system, still in existence today, of floating exchange rates, whereby the value of a currency fluctuates in accordance with the demand for and supply of that currency. The system of floating rates also paved the way for financial globalization, whereby foreign currencies can be acquired without limit on currency markets.

Source: Eichengreen and Flandreau (1997)

There are a number of other international arrangements and organizations that constitute a part of global governance. Generally speaking, organizations like the United Nations (UN) represent one element in this global governance, but in this chapter we want to focus on the organizations charged with a primarily *economic* role; for example, organizations like the World Bank, IMF and WTO – more details of these organizations are contained in Table 8.1. It is important to acknowledge, though, that these supposedly *economic* organizations are as much political entities as they are economic; by this we mean that they influence the political process globally and in specific countries around the world. Moreover, this influence is highly uneven, a point we will return to below. However, in mainstream policy and academic discourses these organizations are often represented as mainly technical or politically neutral organizations, focused on establishing the global rules of the (capitalist) game and not interfering in sovereign political decisions (Friedman 1999; Acemoglu and Robinson 2013). Whether or not this is an accurate depiction of their activities is a key question we as individuals and societies need to ask, not only in this chapter but in our everyday lives.

TABLE 8.1 Global governance agreements and organizations

Name	Location	Founded	Role	Changes over time
Bank for International Settlements (BIS)	Basel, Switzerland	1930	Owned by central banks and set up to enable coordination of central banking around the world	Established Basel Accords (Nos. I, II and III) as regulatory frameworks for global banking (1988, 2004, 2019)
World Bank	Washington DC, USA	1944	Group of organizations set up to fund reconstruction of Europe after the Second World War	Mandate shifted to other countries after reconstruction of Europe
International Monetary Fund (IMF)	Washington DC, USA	1944	Organization set up to lend money to countries to cover short-term balance of payments problems	Shift in role from 'neutral' lender to active lender from 1970s; started requiring economic restructuring in exchange for loans (e.g. Structural Adjustment Programme)
General Agreement on Tariffs and Trade (GATT)	Geneva, Switzerland	1947	Agreement to reduce taxes on trade (i.e. tariffs) and other 'barriers to trade'	Converted into WTO in 1994
International Organization for Standardization (ISO)	Geneva, Switzerland	1947	Organization set up to promote spread of standards through coordination of national standards organizations	Not applicable
World Trade Organization (WTO)	Geneva, Switzerland	1995	Organization set up to regulate international trade	Stuck in 2001 'Doha Round' of negotiations over agricultural subsidies

Sources: Helleiner (1994); Peet (2007, 2009)

There is quite a range of international agreements and organizations tasked with a role in coordinating international economic activity, whether this is the promotion of international economic development or the stabilization of the global financial system. In Table 8.1 we highlight some of the most significant ones and of these the World Bank, IMF and WTO are probably the most well-known. Here we briefly outline their roles and activities:

- *World Bank*: the World Bank started as an organization to help reconstruct Western Europe after the Second World War, but its primary role nowadays is to provide development loans and guarantees for loans, as well as to support development through its advisory arm. Loans, guarantees and advice are designed to support countries in the restructuring of their economies in order to make them more pro-market and more internationally competitive. More recently, the World Bank has supported a range of poverty-focused policies, such as the Millennium Development Goals (Peet 2009; van Waeyenberge 2010).
- *IMF*: the IMF's mandate was to regulate currency exchange and enable members to resolve balance of payments problems (i.e. where imports exceed exports) through short-term loans. Over time, the IMF sought to add conditions to its loans as a way to push countries into adopting certain types of structural reforms to change their economies, with the aim that this would make them more internationally competitive and end any balance of payments problems (Peet 2009).
- *WTO*: a more recent organization, the WTO has its origins in the GATT. It is meant to operate as a way to reduce trade tariffs and thereby encourage international (free) trade. It also establishes a set of basic ground-rules for things like intellectual property rights (IPRs) and other forms of property protection – see Chapter 18 for more.

These organizations not only construct global governance, they also have their own internal governance structures which can work to the advantage of certain nations and interest groups. As an example of how important this internal governance structure is, it is helpful to compare the IMF and WTO:

- *IMF*: membership consists of 189 (of the nearly 200) nation-states of the world. Upon becoming a member, each nation pays a quota, and the number of votes a country has is proportionate to its quota. The main determinant of a country's quota is its GDP, while total population plays no part establishing a country's quota. Hence, between them, the US, UK, France, Germany, Italy, Japan and China hold over 45 per cent of the votes, with the US being the largest vote-holder (16.66 per cent of the total votes of the IMF). India, by comparison, holds only 2.66 per cent (see Barnett and Finnemore 2004).

- *WTO*: membership consists of 162 nation-states, each of which has one vote irrespective of its population, GDP, geographical location etc. Furthermore, most decisions are made on the basis of consensus, so each country has, in theory, veto power over each policy proposal (Eagleton-Pierce 2013; Footer 2006). Usually, however, representatives of richer countries and a few select developing countries set the WTO's agenda in so-called 'green room meetings' at which a 'take-it-or-leave-it' agenda is determined with developing countries' representatives being marginalized (Hoekman and Mavroidis 2016).

Global governance and global development Probably the main reason that these global organizations and agreements are so significant is because they directly impact on the economic development policies that countries do and can pursue around the world. Organizations like the World Bank, IMF and WTO support and promote a particular form of economic development, one which has been called the 'Washington Consensus' (Williamson 1990, 1993). The economist John Williamson (1993: 1334) came up with the term as a way to refer to 'the common core of wisdom' which was 'embraced by all serious economists' in the US administration (e.g. Treasury, Federal Reserve Board), international financial institutions (e.g. World Bank, IMF) and various US-based or international think tanks and policy groups.

The term Washington Consensus is used to define a range of commonly accepted economic policy reforms designed to support (free) trade and unrestricted capital mobility (i.e. foreign direct investment, FDI) from the 1980s onwards, especially in the Global South. Described as a 'golden straightjacket' by the likes of Thomas Friedman (1999), the Washington Consensus includes policy reforms like: tight fiscal discipline (i.e. public spending cuts); phase-out of subsidies; tax cuts; financial and trade liberalization; privatization; deregulation; strengthened property rights; and so on (Williamson 1993). Even though these sort of institutional reforms have been the subject of strong criticism (e.g. Chang 2008), they still represent a global policy *common sense* in many circles as evidenced by the popularity of books like *Why Nations Fail* by Daron Acemoglu and James Robinson (2013). In recent debates, the focus on institutions and institutional reform usually revolves around the strengthening of markets and market institutions (e.g. contract law, property rights), rather than around the problems engendered by capitalism or capitalist development – see Chapter 2 for more on these. Another example of this perspective is the work of the Peruvian economist Hernando de Soto (2000), whose book *The Mystery of Capital: Why Capitalism Triumphs in the West and Fails Everywhere Else* is premised on the idea that secure, formal property rights are the foundation of economic development.

As an example, Acemoglu and Robinson (2013) stress the importance of centralized government and liberal institutions to a country's economic success; conversely, they argue that 'extractive' governments and institutions are the reasons for economic failure. In this sense, then, their prescription for successful economic development is liberal, open and democratic institutions, especially ones that support and reinforce the (free) market. As a position it aligns well with the earlier Washington Consensus in which deregulation, privatization etc. are presented as purported solutions to ongoing problems with economic growth and development in the Global South. Through deregulation, which basically means cutting government rules, the argument is that the entrepreneurial spirit inherent in everyone will be released from the strictures of government red tape, thereby leading to economic growth, jobs and rising standards of living.

Critical perspectives on global governance

Critical perspectives on global governance tend to start from the position that existing and dominant global governance organizations and agreements are not open, not democratic and not even (economically) liberal (cf. Acemoglu and Robinson 2013). As Griffin (2003) notes, the world needs global governance in order to deal with global problems and in order to avoid forms of asymmetric globalization in which certain countries and people benefit from globalization while others do not. In order to deliver global governance, Griffin argues that global organizations and agreements need to become *more* democratic with representative democracy scaled up from the national to the global scale (e.g. individual people from all countries voting for representatives at global institutions like the UN, IMF, WTO etc.). In our current context, it is imperative to think about who gets to set global rules, how they get to set them and what this means for everyone else. Unlike the mainstream focus on the relationship between business and governments we outlined above (May 2015), this necessitates looking at the role of *both* government *and* business in the organization of global governance. In particular, it means examining how business activities come to configure global rules outside of government oversight. Before that, however, we want to outline the government-side of the equation.

Understanding global hegemony A particular problem with mainstream views of global governance is that they tend to ignore or downplay the role played by the USA as a global superpower, or *hegemonic* nation-state (Helleiner 1994). By dint of its economic, political and even cultural power, the USA is able to override or ignore global organizations and agreements (e.g. Kyoto Protocol), enforce its national interest more effectively than other countries (e.g. TTP) and generally dominate or drive global events (e.g. global financial crisis)

(Griffin 2003: 790–792). It is vital, then, to understand the place of the USA as a player in global governance, especially as this relates to the US state and government.

According to some thinkers, who we discussed in Chapter 2, capitalism is a 'world system' in which one country usually plays a hegemonic role, dominating the world's economy and, hence, dominating international decisions and activities. A good example of this perspective is Giovanni Arrighi (1994 [2010]) whose book *The Long Twentieth Century* provides an historical analysis of the evolution of capitalism from the thirteenth century onwards. Unlike the discussion in Chapter 1 of this book, however, Arrighi focused on the recurring cycles of capitalist expansion and development, and how these are manifested in the rise of one hegemonic power after another. For example, Arrighi outlined the hegemony of the Italian city-states of Genoa and Venice (c.1300–1600), then the Netherlands (c.1600–1750), then the UK (c.1750–1900), before the emergence of the USA as the global hegemon in the early-to-mid twentieth century. Each period of hegemony lasted for over a 100 years, during which time the dominant country was the centre of international production, trade and finance. This was in the European context initially, and then globally as these countries conquered and colonized other parts of the world (see Chapter 2). In the current period, Arrighi argued that the USA dominated the world economy through the expansion of American multinational corporations and the BWS of global governance after the Second World War.

As a result of its dominance of the world economy, the USA has been able to pursue certain policies and strategies that other countries could not do. Yanis Varoufakis (2011), Greece's ex-Minister of Finance, describes the US as a 'Global Minotaur' in his book of the same name. By this he means that the US remade the global order after the Second World War through the BWS and global governance organizations and agreements to ensure US military and economic hegemony. In particular, Varoufakis argues that the US sought to bind capitalist economies to US power through this global system. As it evolved, however, US dominance ensured that it could run a huge trade deficit *and* huge government budget deficit simultaneously; basically, it was 'based upon a constant flow of tribute from the periphery to the imperial centre' in Varoufakis' words (2011: 23). While this plan ensured US hegemony, it had implications for global stability in that many other countries and businesses became dependent on the US economy. For example, China and Germany depend on the US as an export market, and many businesses, especially oil companies, recycle their profits through investments in US stocks and bonds.

While the US state has had significant freedom in terms of the policies it can pursue, other countries are increasingly bound by the rules spread through the system of global governance introduced after the Second World War. Many of these rules originate in the work of the international financial institutions

(IFIs) like the World Bank, IMF and WTO, but they are equally supported and promoted by the US state (and other countries). As noted above, international development is dominated by this so-called Washington Consensus. Richard Peet (2007) argues that this consensus represents a powerful policy regime combining the political power of IFIs and US state agencies with the economic power of capitalist business (e.g. banks) and the ideological power of (neo-classical) economic ideas developed in elite universities and think tanks. As a policy regime, it promotes certain global rules and a specific form of global governance at the expense of alternative possibilities (see Chapter 16). Even when this consensus evolves to incorporate more progressive development goals (e.g. poverty reduction), Peet argues that these concerns simply hide more instrumental goals like national interests, or reflect simplistic notions of capitalist development (also see Chang 2008).

The Global South has been most impacted by the implementation of global rules and global governance based on the Washington Consensus. As the World Bank and IMF re-oriented their mandates during the 1970s and 1980s, they became more focused on lending to countries in the Global South – frequently defined as *developing* or *less-developed* economies. These IFIs have pursued an approach to development based on market principles in which conditions are attached to loans that are meant to alleviate economic crises or help countries integrate into the global economy. These conditions are commonly referred to as *structural adjustment programmes* (SAPs) and are meant to force countries to restructure their economy so it can better withstand global competition (Chang 2008). In his book *Unholy Trinity*, Peet (2009) describes the IFIs as global debt collectors who, through the introduction of SAPs in the Global South, ensure that capital investment is returned to businesses or governments in the Global North (also Harvey 2003). Citizens in the Global South end up paying for this debt through reductions in government spending (e.g. health care, education, social welfare etc.). As such, IFIs and the Washington Consensus cannot be thought of as simply neutral or technical rules of the (capitalist) game; rather, they are how the game is played and won by a limited number of countries, especially the USA, based in the Global North.

Private rules, private rule It might seem that governments, especially the US state, dominate global governance; however, that view is too limited and ignores the increasing importance of business and especially MNCs and MNEs in making and setting global rules. As May (2015) points out, the state-centric view (i.e. that government and business influence each other) misses the role played by business in actually creating international standards, rules, regulations and so on that configure the global economy. It is our intention in this section to raise a number of issues around the growing importance of private rules and the private governance of the global economy.

As we have already discussed in this book, the global economy has become more fragmented and more integrated at the same time (see Chapter 7). Supply chains are increasingly stretched across more and more national borders, fragmenting production in different geographical places; at the same time, though, MNCs and MNEs are increasingly integrating these fragmented supply chains in their operations (Dicken 2015). This has led to a complex array of business and corporate relationships between core companies (e.g. Apple) and their suppliers (e.g. FoxConn), across several national jurisdictions. It is important to understand that these supply chains are coordinated and governed by private social actors like MNCs and MNEs, rather than only or primarily through state regulations. As such, these relationships are governed by *private* global rules created and enforced by business through things like contract law, standard-setting, arbitration agreements etc. (May 2015). For example, corporate social responsibility (CSR), which we discussed in Chapter 5, represents a form of private regulation in that it is often created, regulated, monitored, enforced, audited etc. by private or quasi-private organizations (e.g. NGOs) in coordination with business, rather than by the state. This means that private organizations increasingly sit at the centre of global governance, which has implications for how international environmental, labour, social etc. regulations and standards are created and enforced.

Rather than (free) markets run amok, we want to stress that large, often monopolistic MNCs and MNEs have come to dominate how the global economy is organized and coordinated (Ietto-Gillies 2014). It is important to emphasize the role of business in creating new forms of private regulation and private rules because many critical commentators, journalists, politicians and academics claim that globalization, especially in the 'neoliberal' form promoted by the Washington Consensus, has led to a significant erosion of regulations (e.g. Bakan 2004; Klein 2007; Varoufakis 2011). This deregulation argument, however, on the one hand is too simplistic, and on the other hand ignores the role of business in creating new global rules and the implications of this for people, communities and countries (May 2015). A number of scholars have criticised the argument that globalization has gone hand-in-hand with deregulation (e.g. Vogel 1996). Here we want to highlight the work of John Braithewaite (2005), who argues that the growth of global business operations has necessarily been accompanied by a growth in global rules, although these are often *private* rules, as we noted above. This is important for a number of reasons: first, it means that citizens have less control over the regulation of business because these *private* rules no longer fall within the purview of the *public* state and democratic decision-making; and second, business and private interests increasingly determine the basis of *good* global governance, rather than the state.

All of this becomes obvious when we examine the internal politics of business or corporate entities. They are not, in themselves, open or democratic organizations. It is, in fact, the opposite. As David Ciepley (2004, 2013) points out in his work, most private business organizations have strict hierarchies in which employees are required to follow internal organizational rules and the orders of their superiors, wherever the employees are geographically in the organization – that is, organizational rules can be the same in different countries. At the core of these rules is managerial authority, which determines what managers and executives are able to do with the assets of the business and the authority they have over employees (Ciepley 2013). According to May (2015: 4), such private global governance often 'mimics legal structures', which means business ends up becoming a 'form of governing body'. As these arguments suggest, then, global governance ends up increasingly as a set of private rules to assert private control over resources, people and decisions. It is a form of corporate- or business-led governance, rather than government or democratic governance. We could argue, as both Barkan (2013) and Veldman (2013) do, that business, especially large corporations and businesses, should be understood in the same way as the state; they set rules, they govern lives, they negotiate international agreements and so on.

Conclusion

In this chapter we have sought to examine global governance and explore different ways to understand the coordination of the global economy. We outlined mainstream discourses around global governance, especially as these relate to global governance organizations and agreements like the World Bank, IMF and WTO. In so doing, we highlighted how this form of global governance, often characterized as the Washington Consensus, promotes a particular form of economic development. In turning to the critical perspectives of global governance, we wanted to highlight the need to understand global governance as both a state-led *and* business-led process. In particular, we highlighted the importance of understanding the increasing importance of private rules in global governance.

Suggested readings

- Brühl, T. and Hofferberth, M. (2013) 'Global companies as social actors: Constructing private business in global governance', in J. Mikler (ed.) *The Handbook of Global Companies*, Chichester, Wiley-Blackwell, pp.351–370.
- Ciepley, D. (2013) 'Beyond public and private: Toward a political theory of the corporation', *American Political Science Review*, Vol.107, pp.139–158.
- Griffin, K. (2003) 'Economic globalization and the institutions of global governance', *Development and Change*, Vol.34, pp.789–807.
- May, C. (2015) 'Who's in charge? Corporations as institutions of global governance', *Palgrave Communications*, Vol.1, pp.1–10.
- Ch. 4, Peet, R. (2007) *Geography of Power: The Making of Global Economic Policy*, London, Zed Books.

Bibliography

Acemoglu, D. and Robinson, J. (2013) *Why Nations Fail*, New York, Crown Business.

Arrighi, G. (1994 [2010]) *The Long Twentieth Century*, London, Verso.

Bakan, J. (2004) *The Corporation*, London, Random House.

Barkan, J. (2013) *Corporate Sovereignty*, Minneapolis, University of Minnesota Press.

Barnett, M. and Finnemore, M. (2004) *Rules for the World: International Organizations in Global Politics*, Ithaca, Cornell University Press.

Bobbitt, P. (2002) *The Shield of Achilles: War, Peace, and the Course of History*, New York, Alfred A. Knopf.

Braithwaite, J. (2005) 'Neoliberalism or regulatory capitalism', ANU: RegNet, Occasional Paper No. 5.

Brühl, T. and Hofferberth, M. (2013) 'Global companies as social actors: Constructing private business in global governance', in J. Mikler (ed.), *The Handbook of Global Companies*, Chichester, Wiley-Blackwell, pp.351–370.

Carroll, A. and Buchholtz, A. (2015) *Business and Society* (9th Edition), Stamford CT, CENGAGE Learning.

Chang, H.-J. (2008) *Bad Samaritans*, London, Bloomsbury.

Ciepley, D. (2004) 'Authority in the firm (and the attempts to theorize it away)', *Critical Review: A Journal of Politics and Society*, Vol.16, pp.81–115.

Ciepley, D. (2013) 'Beyond public and private: Toward a political theory of the corporation', *American Political Science Review*, Vol.107, pp.139–158.

Clark, I. (2000) *Globalization and International Relations Theory*, Oxford, Oxford University Press.

de Soto, H. (2000) *The Mystery of Capital: Why Capitalism Triumphs in the West and Fails Everywhere Else*, New York, Basic Books.

Dicken, P. (2015) *Global Shift*, New York, Guildford.

Eagleton-Pierce, M. (2013) *Symbolic Power in the World Trade Organization*, Oxford, Oxford University Press.

Eichengreen, B. (1996) *Globalizing Capital*, Princeton, Princeton University Press.

Eichengreen, B. (2006) *Global Imbalances and the Lessons of Bretton Woods*, Cambridge MA, The MIT Press.

Eichengreen, B. and Flandreau, M. (eds) (1997) *The Gold Standard in Theory and History* (2nd Edition), London, Routledge.

Footer, M. (2006) *An Institutional and Normative Analysis of the World Trade Organization*, Leiden, Martinus Nijhoff.

Friedman, T. (1999) *The Lexus and the Olive Tree*, New York, Farrar, Straus & Giroux.

Griffin, K. (2003) 'Economic globalization and the institutions of global governance', *Development and Change*, Vol.34, pp.789–807.

Hall, P. and Soskice, D. (eds) (2001) *Varieties of Capitalism: The Institutional Foundations of Comparative Advantage*, Oxford, Oxford University Press.

Harvey, D. (2003) *The New Imperialism*, Oxford, Oxford University Press.

Helleiner, E. (1994) *States and the Reemergence of Global Finance*, Ithaca, Cornell University Press.

Hertz, N. (2002) *The Silent Takeover: Global Capitalism and the Death of Democracy*, New York, The Free Press.

Hoekman, B. and Mavroidis, P. (2016) *World Trade Organization: Law, Economics, and Politics* (2nd Edition), London, Routledge.

Ietto-Gillies, G. (2014) 'The theory of the transnational corporation at 50+', *Economic Thought*, Vol.3, pp.38–57.

Klein, N. (2007) *The Shock Doctrine*, Toronto, Knopf Canada.

Mason, R. (2016) 'David Cameron calls for political courage to seal TTIP deal', *The Guardian*, 4 May: www.theguardian.com/business/2016/may/04/david-cameron-political-courage-ttip-trade-deal (accessed May 2016).

May, C. (2015) 'Who's in charge? Corporations as institutions of global governance', *Palgrave Communications*, Vol.1, pp.1–10.

Peet, R. (2007) *Geography of Power: The Making of Global Economic Policy*, London, Zed Books.

Peet, R. (2009) *Unholy Trinity: The IMF, World Bank and WTO*, London, Zed Books.

Polanyi, K. (1944 [2001]) *The Great Transformation*, Boston, Beacon Press.

Ruggie, J. (1982) 'International regimes, transactions, and change: Embedded liberalism in the postwar economic order', *International Organization*, Vol.36, pp.379–415.

Van Waeyenberge, E. (2010) 'Tightening the web: The World Bank and enforced policy reform', in K. Birch and V. Mykhnenko (eds), *The Rise and Fall of Neoliberalism*, London, Zed Books, pp.94–111.

Varoufakis, Y. (2011) *The Global Minotaur: America, the True Origins of the Financial Crisis and the Future of the World Economy*, London, Zed Books.

Veldman, J. (2013) 'Politics of the corporation', *British Journal of Management*, Vol.24, pp.S18–S30.

Vogel, S. (1996) *Freer Markets, More Rules*, Ithaca, Cornell University Press.

Weiss, T. (2013) *Global Governance: Why? What? Whither?*, Cambridge, Polity Press.

Whitley, R. (1999) *Divergent Capitalism*, Oxford, Oxford University Press.

Williamson, J. (1990) 'What Washington means by policy reform', in J. Williamson (ed.), *Latin American Adjustment*, Washington DC, Institute for International Economics.

Williamson, J. (1993) 'Democracy and the "Washington Consensus"', *Critical Perspectives on International Development*, Vol.5, pp.56–77.

9 | Global environmental change

Introduction

Nowadays we have a very romantic notion of nature, associating it with images of forests, mountains, streams and the wildlife that inhabit these places. Our understanding of nature is not only romantic, however; it also involves a series of assumptions about what it means to be 'natural' and – as importantly – what it means to be 'unnatural'. For example, forests are natural, but plastic is not; moose are natural, but cars are not; and humans are natural, but also not at the same time. The reason we have such a complex relationship with nature and the environment is because nature itself – and what it means to be natural – is constituted by a diverse set of human practices and knowledges ranging from the findings of scientific research through cultural representations of nature in film and other media to the organization of business within capitalism. This has led a number of human geographers to argue that, in a very real sense, our imaginations and our socio-economic practices actively shape nature and the natural world, not only in our minds but also in reality (e.g. Smith 1984 [2008]; Whatmore 2002). Thus, they argue, humans are both products of nature and the producers of nature.

This influence or impact of humans on the environment – which we define, for simplicity's sake, as the world's biosphere – has been well-documented over the last few decades, but awareness of our human imprint on the world and the implications this has for our livelihoods and survival has a much longer history. In fact it is possible to identify environmental movements as far back as the nineteenth century, when various peoples and groups sought to highlight the damaging impacts of industrialization on society. Examples include: the Romantic poets like William Wordsworth, Lord Byron and Percy Bysshe Shelley at the end of the eighteenth century and start of the nineteenth century; the Sierra Club established in 1892 in the USA; and the Garden City movement that sprang up at the start of the twentieth century. The modern environmental movement, however, emerged in the 1960s and 1970s as a response to a range of environmental issues and crises like chemical pollution, oil spills, anti-whaling campaigns, toxic waste, biodiversity loss, animal extinctions and so on (Millington and Pickerill 2005). One particular driving force was concerns about the 'limits to growth' – the title of an influential report in 1972 – of the world. Since the 1960s and 1970s there has been a growing interest in environmental change and human-environment interactions, leading many thinkers to start calling our current era the 'Anthropocene' – or, age of humans (Castree 2014).

The Anthropocene is especially dominated by the impacts of human activity on the world's climate. As a result of these impacts, one of the key global challenges facing us today is how to mitigate (i.e. stop) and adapt to (i.e. live with) **anthropogenic climate change**, especially the significant shifts in global and local temperatures (e.g. warmer winters, colder summers), increasingly violent weather events (e.g. hurricanes, floods, storms etc.), melting ice caps and permafrost, and so on. How we deal with climate change and its impacts is shaped by the assumptions we have about the environment; this is not only in terms of romanticized visions of a pristine, untouched nature, but also in terms of how nature is treated by the state and businesses as a private resource and a common dumping ground for pollution and waste. What we want to emphasize in this chapter is that capitalism has both created the environmental problems with us today and is also proposed as the solution to those problems by world leaders. It is important, in light of this contradiction, to consider what other perspectives we might bring to bear to resolve these issues.

Definition: Anthropogenic climate change

According to the UN Environmental Programme, anthropogenic climate change results from the release of greenhouse gas (GHG) emissions, especially carbon dioxide (CO_2), from human activity like the burning of fossil fuels (e.g. coal, oil, natural gas). Climate change is caused by the emission of GHGs *and* their concentration in the atmosphere. By 2016, the world passed 400 parts per million (ppm) of GHGs in the atmosphere. According to the Intergovernmental Panel on Climate Change (IPCC), global temperatures have already increased by 0.8 degrees Celsius since the late 1800s and will have risen by 2 degrees by 2100 if GHGs in the atmosphere reach 450ppm.

We cover several issues in this chapter relating to global environmental change. First, we look at mainstream perspectives on the environment, pollution, limits to economic growth and concepts of sustainable development. We also outline the main ways that capitalist businesses seek to resolve environmental problems. Second, we present a critical take on understanding the environment called *political ecology*. This approach incorporates notions of environmental justice and political-economic change that challenges prevailing and dominant business solutions. Third, we focus on climate change as an empirical example of a global environmental problem, one which has become a seemingly intractable problem.

133

Mainstream perspectives

What is the environment? What are its limits? The natural environment can be defined technically as the world's biosphere, its biomes and its diverse and varied ecosystems. The biosphere comprises three interconnected parts: the atmosphere, which is the air cover around the Earth; the hydrosphere, which is the surface-level (e.g. oceans) and below surface waters (e.g. aquifers); and the lithosphere, which is the upper levels of the Earth's crust and includes the soil, plants and animals. Within the lithosphere there are a number of different biomes; these are plants and animals that inhabit distinct areas of the Earth's surface (e.g. desert, grassland, rainforest etc.). Within the biomes there are smaller ecosystems of interacting, self-regulating animal and plant populations adapted to specific local climates, topographies etc. (Robbins et al. 2010). As we have mentioned already, this technical definition obscures the human shaping of the environment through economic actions and decisions like pollution, waste production, biodiversity loss, climate change etc. However, according to **Barry Commoner** (1971), there are four laws of ecology that humans cannot escape, no matter what they do to the environment.

Key thinker: Barry Commoner and the 'four laws of ecology'

Barry Commoner was an influential US biologist who came up with four laws of ecology that define the limits of human actions on the environment. First, the biosphere (i.e. world) is a system in which 'everything is connected to everything else'; second, if everything is linked then 'everything must go somewhere', which means waste does not simply disappear; third, 'nature knows best', so any attempts to change the environment simply leads to unforeseen problems; and finally, 'there is no such thing as a free lunch' since the use of natural resources will turn them into useless waste by-products.

Source: Commoner (1971)

Mainstream approaches to the environment are often dominated by the assumption that the natural world exists for humans to exploit and use as they see fit and with little regard for the consequences. John Bellamy Foster (2002) argues that this assumption is particularly strong in Western cultures (e.g. North America, Western Europe) and stretches back several centuries. The reason that global environmental change causes such concern nowadays is because the Earth is a finite space with finite resources – the environment and its resources are *scarce*, in this sense – while human population has expanded considerably in a very short period of time, in geological timescales at least. For example, a hundred years ago the world's population was below two billion people, and yet there now are over seven billion people on the planet, all of whom need resources to survive (e.g. food, housing, water, tools, energy etc.). It is important to note that these population concerns are not new. In the nineteenth century an Anglican priest from Britain called Thomas Malthus argued that the world simply could not sustain the massive rise in the British population following industrialization; in his view, the world was overpopulated and this would lead to famines, poverty, disease and wars as humans fought over the finite resources (Robbins et al. 2010). While Malthus' views have been disproved by subsequent events, such as the huge growth in the world's population, it still holds a strong popular and political appeal for its simplicity – that is, environmental problems result from too many people chasing too few resources and producing increasing levels of pollution and waste. This appeal is still evident in the revival of environmentalism since the 1960s and 1970s.

Recent environmental awareness and campaigns have led to growing international concern with global environmental change. The global environment has become a major focus of international policy debate and intervention over the last few decades (see Table 9.1), especially around the issue of climate change (see Example below). It is important to note, however, that these agreements and arrangements are not always successful. In part, these moves to resolve environmental problems stem from continuing fears about the limits of the natural world. For example, the Club of Rome, a global think tank, produced an influential report in 1972 called *Limits to Growth* in which they set out to examine the physical limits of continuing economic growth. The report's conclusions were that 'resource scarcities would push prices up and slow down the possibilities for future growth' and that 'the resource base itself would collapse' (Jackson 2009: 7). Similar concerns motivated the establishment of the World Commission on Environment and Development by the UN in 1983. This Commission produced a report called *Our Common Future* in 1987 – more commonly known as the *Brundtland Report* – in which they set out to define '**sustainable**

development' in an attempt to make capitalism and environmental sustainability compatible with one another.

TABLE 9.1 Timeline of major global environmental events and agreements

Date	Events and agreements
1968	UNESCO Biosphere Conference
1972	UN Conference on the Human Environment
	Limits to Growth report published by Club of Rome
1980	IUCN launches World Conservation Strategy
1987	*Our Common Future* report (aka *Brundtland Report*) published by World Commission on Environment and Development
1992	Rio Summit on Environment and Development
	UN Framework Convention for Climate Change (UNFCCC) created
1997	Kyoto Protocols established
2000	UN launches Millennium Development Goals
2002	World Summit on Sustainable Development
2009	Copenhagen UNFCCC Conference of the Parties (COP)
2011	Canada withdraws from the Kyoto Protocols
2015	UN Sustainable Development Goals established
	Paris UNFCCC COP

Source: adapted and updated from Millington and Pickerill (2005: 156)

Key methodological issue: Defining 'sustainable development'

Sustainable development is a contested term introduced by the *Brundtland Report* in 1987. It is a concept that seeks to combine the notion of (environmental) sustainability – that is, the idea that human actions should not negatively impact the environment – with economic growth under capitalist relations. It was defined as: 'development which meets the needs of the present without compromising the ability of future generations to meet their needs'. It has been criticized as too vague and compromised by its association with business and capitalism. It is, therefore, very difficult to identify and discuss sustainable development, especially from different conceptual perspectives.

Source: Millington and Pickerill (2005: 158)

Solving environmental problems with capitalism Now, it is important to note that the Anthropocene is not simply about the general impact of humans on nature (and vice versa), especially where this assumes these impacts result from overpopulation. It is about the specific impact of capitalism on nature and what this means for the environment (Smith 1984 [2008]). A good way to illustrate this impact is through the concept of 'the commons' (Ostrom 1990) – see Chapters 1, 16 and 18 for more discussion of the commons. We can define nature and the environment as part of the commons; this means it is something held in common by all peoples, since no-one created it, and it has certain characteristics that 'make it difficult to fully enclose and partition, making it possible for non-owners to enjoy resource benefits and owners to sustain costs from the actions of others' (Robbins et al. 2010: 52). Capitalism entails certain logics, processes and practices that erode the commons, meaning that our common environmental heritage faces particular pressures to adjust to capitalist imperatives. For example, since anyone can use the commons (e.g. graze common land) without cost, this means that some people can exploit the commons (e.g. over-graze common land) without anyone else being able to stop them. This leads to something Garrett Hardin (1968) called 'the tragedy of the commons'. Hardin argued that it is in the interest of each person to use as much of the common resource as they can for their own benefit, leading ultimately to the destruction of that common resource as everyone over-uses the resource.

These ideas, that there are limits to growth and numerous tragedies of the commons, have provided theoretical and normative support for the claim that capitalist markets and business are best able to provide solutions to various environmental problems (Bellamy Foster 2002). In particular, neoclassical economists argue that the market can *and* should be used to resolve environmental problems because it is the most efficient way to price and value the cost of environmental deterioration, degradation and destruction (Robbins et al. 2010). This has been described as 'market environmentalism' by a number of scholars (see Bailey 2007). The starting point for solving environmental problems with markets and business is understanding why there are environmental problems in the first place. For neoclassical economists and their ilk this requires an understanding of **externalities** as examples of **market failure**. Closely related to the tragedy of the commons, an externality is the effect of economic activity on everyone not directly involved in that activity – an example is the pollution or waste from factories. Neoclassical economists argue that environmental problems are simply externalities that can and should be incorporated into capitalist relations through a range of market and business solutions we outline below.

Definition: Externalities

An externality is the negative or positive impact of an economic activity that affects someone who is not directly involved in or benefiting from the economic activity. The classic example of an externality is pollution from a factory since everyone living near the factory suffers from the pollution, but may not benefit from the factory or its production of goods.

This form of environmentalism involves promoting three main market and business solutions to environmental problems, all of which are based on neo-classical economic assumptions (Coe et al. 2007; Leonard 2010; Robbins et al. 2010). These include privatization, commodification and marketization. We critique these three solutions in the next section, but for now we simply define them as the following:

- *Privatization*: this process involves turning the environment and natural resources into private property through changes to the law and regulations. The rationale behind this process is the assumption that only private owners (e.g. business) have an incentive to protect their property because it is valuable to them.
- *Commodification*: this process involves creating commodities out of the environment for sale or new technologies to improve resource efficiencies. The rationale here is the assumption that profit motivates everyone and that the market will efficiently determine how much everyone values the environment through their purchasing choices, and this will drive innovations to solve environmental problems.
- *Marketization*: this process involves the creation of new markets to achieve environmental goals (e.g. reducing greenhouse gas emissions). It is based on the assumption that markets are the most efficient mechanism to achieve these goals because markets promote new ideas and products through competitive pressures.

What these three processes illustrate is the emphasis on the market and business as the determinants of the value – or, more precisely, price – of natural resources and the environment, which ignores the environmental costs of many human activities – e.g. pollution, biodiversity loss, deforestation etc. (Coe et al. 2007). For example, while humans can extract oil from different places around the world, its extraction in some of those places, like Alberta, Canada (see Case Study), entails significant environmental consequences, now and in the future, that we cannot accurately calculate. This explains why its use, wherever it is extracted, has had and continues to have a significant impact on the world's atmosphere which we have not been able to resolve (see Example below).

138

> **Case study**
>
> Oil and the Athabasca tar sands, Canada
>
> *Biophysical characteristics*: oil is non-biological material extracted from specific locations in the world (e.g. Saudi Arabia, Canada). It is a finite resource, not being renewable in a human lifetime, and is consumed in use, producing greenhouse gas emissions (CO_2) when used.
>
> *Resource characteristics*: oil is an important natural resource since most economies are dependent on it for a range of things (e.g. transport fuels, chemicals, plastics, fertilizers). The amount of oil in the world includes proven reserves, which are economically accessible, and probable reserves, which cost too much, right now, to extract.
>
> *Unconventional oil*: as the world's economy has globalized over the last few decades, oil has become an increasingly important commodity because global trade and other global activities (e.g. travel) depend upon it. This has stimulated the exploration and extraction of new, unconventional sources of oil, including the tar sands in Alberta, Canada.
>
> *Tar sands*: oil is extracted from the Athabasca Basin in Alberta and Saskatchewan, Canada through a process of steam injection; it is then refined to separate the oil from the 'sand'. Both extraction and refining entail environmental problems (e.g. chemical run-offs in tailing ponds, GHG emissions), including a significant impact on the landscape.
>
> *Source*: Berners-Lee and Clark (2013)

Critical perspectives

Environmental justice and political ecology Like most scholarly debates, we can approach global environmental change from several different and distinct theoretical standpoints. For example, it is possible to conceptualize something like sustainable development on a continuum from *weak* sustainability to *strong* sustainability (Hopwood et al. 2005), where the former reflects a more business- and technology-centred view of the world and the latter a more egalitarian- and ecological-centred one. Where people sit on the continuum reflects not only their attitude to nature and the use of natural resources, it also reflects their attitude to issues of social justice, equality, redistribution and forms of social action (see Table 9.2). For example, who benefits from the extraction of natural resources and suffers from the resulting waste from production processes are ecological and socio-economic issues, not one or the other. They reflect an important distinction between environmental problems that involve the *over-use* of

TABLE 9.2 Two views of sustainability

Characteristics	Weak sustainability	Strong sustainability
Capitalism	Can solve environmental problems through markets	Causes environmental and socio-economic inequality and injustice
Technology	Provides solutions to problems	Cause of problems as much as solution
Nature	Nature as resources for human use (scarcity)	Inherent value in nature and ecological systems
Social justice	Largely irrelevant	Entwined with environmental problems
Social action	Market-based, individual consumer choice	Collective, democratic decision-making
Examples	Green capitalism (e.g. 'green' goods)	Deep ecology

Source: adapted from Hopwood et al. (2005)

natural resources and those that involve the over-burdening of ecological systems, or *sinks*, with waste outputs (Dicken 2011). Over-use by one group of people deprives others of access to that resource, while over-burdening the environment with pollution and waste always entails decisions about where those negative outputs go and which groups will be most impacted. Understanding these human-environment interactions is critical for understanding environmental justice and injustice.

Our aim here is to outline and illustrate one alternative approach that is critical of neoclassical economics and the solutions business and economists propose to solve environmental problems – as outlined in the above section. The approach we discuss is called *political ecology* and it seeks to combine insights from political economy – see the Introduction – with 'an understanding that nature and society are produced *together* in a political economy that includes humans and non-humans' (Robbins et al. 2010: 6). What this means is that to understand the environment involves understanding (1) human socio-economic relations, systems, processes, practices, knowledge claims and so forth – especially those related to business – *and* (2) ecological processes, systems, forces etc. The main strength of the political ecology approach is that it enables us to analyse the relationship between global environmental change and socio-economic change, especially where this raises normative questions about who *is* and who *should be* most affected by environmental problems and who is and who should contribute most to their resolution. Political ecology, therefore, provides a powerful tool to critique the claims of neoclassical economists when it comes to finding solutions to environmental problems, as we demonstrate below.

Rethinking environmental problems At the end of the previous section we identified three ways that the markets and business seek to resolve environmental problems. From a political ecology perspective, these solutions are deeply problematic for the following reasons:

- *Privatization*: this implies that there can and should be no commons, and that environmental protection depends upon turning *all* of nature into private property.
- *Commodification*: this depends on finding **techno-fixes** to turn nature into commodities (e.g. how do we commodify a beautiful landscape?) or to improve resource efficiencies. The latter is subject to something called **Jevons' Paradox**.
- *Marketization*: the creation of markets leads to the fragmentation of responses to environmental problems since it is left to individual businesses and consumers to drive change.

Definition: Techno-fix

This is another common assumption. Namely, that humans will solve all environmental problems through the development of new technologies. It is problematic because it promotes the idea that we do not have to change our behaviour or actions as there will always be a technological solution to any problems we create if we wait long enough. In that sense, it promotes the continued expansion of resource usage.

Definition: Jevon's Paradox

This describes the fact that increasing the relative efficient use of resources leads to an increase in the absolute use of that resource since it becomes cheaper to use the resource. For example, increasing the oil efficiency of cars means that more cars can be built because they use less petroleum, thereby leading to an overall increase in the consumption of oil.

First, transforming the environmental commons into private property involves changing laws and regulations in a country or globally; we want to emphasize that it is not an automatic or spontaneous process that magically happens when capitalist markets are unleashed. Since the environment is not created by humans it can be considered as another example of Karl Polanyi's *fictitious commodity* – see the Introduction. This is an important point because it means that any transfer of the environmental commons to a private individual or business is, effectively, a 'gift' of the state to that person or business

(Bellamy Foster 2002). Two things are important to note here. First, privatization is legitimated by a range of theories and claims, including Garrett Hardin's notion of the tragedy of the commons. Second, nature has to be *turned into* a resource since resources are social categories, not natural ones; as Bridge (2009) puts it, resources are 'a primary social category through which we organize our relationships with the non-human world'. From a political ecology perspective this means that we have to examine how the state turns nature into a resource and property, how it assigns or sells that resource, and how different resources entail different processes of privatization because of their different biophysical characteristics (see Table 9.3). Taken to the extreme, privatization implies the total conversion of nature into private property, which raises serious concerns about the potential for it to inflate conflicts over resource use between countries – e.g. Global North versus Global South – and between social actors – e.g. multinational corporations versus local social movements.

TABLE 9.3 Classifying resources

Non-renewable / stock			Renewable / flow	
Consumed in use	*Recoverable*	*Recyclable*	*Critical zone*	*Non-critical zone*
Oil	All minerals	Metallic	Fish	Solar energy
Natural gas		minerals	Forests	Tides, waves,
Coal			Soil	wind
			Water in	Water
			aquifers	Air

Source: adapted from Bradshaw (2008)

Second, mainstream approaches to environmental problems have gradually incorporated a wider range of factors in their models since the 1970s, moving away from a simple focus on population growth and resource use. For example, in the 1970s the ecologist Paul R. Ehrlich and others came up with something called the IPAT formula (Jackson 2009). This formula seeks to explain environmental problems as the outcome of three interacting elements:

I (environmental impacts) = P (population) × A (affluence, or consumption) × T (technology)

The IPAT formula avoids the assumption that population drives environmental problems, and highlights the role of consumption and technology – or what we define as the commodification of nature. It is important to incorporate these two factors because different countries consume different amounts of resources and create different types of new technology. However, from a political ecology perspective consumption and technology can simply reinforce environmental problems and environmental injustice. On the one hand, the commodification of nature produces new types of goods and services; for example, it might be possible to turn certain environmental elements (e.g. landscapes) into commodities for sale. However, this then limits access to the environment since consumption depends on a consumer's ability to pay. On the other hand, commodification might produce new technologies that improve resource efficiencies, a techno-fix; for example, new types of car that use less fuel. However, these efficiencies often entail Jevons' Paradox, which results from improvements in relative resource usage leading to increases in absolute resource usage so that more resources end up being used overall (Robbins et al. 2010). What these two issues illustrate is that commodification does not resolve environmental problems, it merely shifts them around or reinforces the original problem; for example, commodifying nature may mean certain groups end up losing their access to nature and natural resources (Castree 2003), while new technologies may end up increasing the overall use of natural resources (Leonard 2010).

Finally, the mainstream emphasis on market and business solutions to environmental problems – or 'market environmentalism' (Bailey 2007) – results in a number of problematic consequences. After the global financial crisis starting in 2007/08, policy-makers around the world proposed a Green New Deal to get us out of recession and address global environmental problems at the same time; an example of this policy proposal was the UNEP's Green New Deal (Jackson 2009). The underlying aim was to transition to a more sustainable version of capitalism, based on the assumption that replacing fossil fuels with renewable energy would solve environmental problems like climate change. While there is some potential in this proposal, it was never implemented. Why it was not pursued illustrates the problems with market environmentalism more generally. It is based on the assumption that the market will automatically and spontaneously promote new products and services *if* the cost of environmental problems is incorporated into existing prices of products and services. There are several criticisms we can make of this approach if we take a political ecology perspective (Bellamy Foster 2002). First, market environmentalism is based on a tension between individual, atomistic decision-making on the one hand (e.g. consumer choice), and collective, coordinated action on the other (e.g. enforcing environmental costs). Second, there is a lack of political agency as any collective action tends to be arrogated to international institutions (e.g. UN, WTO etc.) making 'technical' decisions about whether something meets certain criteria, rather than democratic deliberation amongst national electorates. Finally, the response to environmental problems is left in the hands of individual consumers and businesses as they make decisions about what to spend their money on. This reinforces existing inequalities in access to and use of resources and environmental benefits, since wealthier consumers can demand and receive better environmental conditions than poorer consumers. What these criticisms should show is that environmental problems are deeply bound up with human socio-economic institutions, practices and knowledge claims – we cannot separate one from another. Trying to reduce all actions to economic calculations misses the complexity of nature–society relationships.

Empirical example: climate change as an intractable global challenge?

We now turn to one example of a major environmental problem in order to illustrate the complexity in nature–society relations we stressed in the previous section. We focus on anthropogenic climate change because it is probably the biggest environmental problem facing the world today and will have significant implications for our futures. We can only provide a brief outline of climate change, and its causes and effects, here; we suggest reading Robbins et al. (2010: Ch. 9) for a more detailed discussion. Put simply, anthropogenic climate change is caused by the release of greenhouse gases (GHGs), especially carbon dioxide (CO_2), into the atmosphere as the result of burning fossil fuels (e.g. oil, natural gas, coal). The release of CO_2 into the atmosphere is not a problem *per se*, since this constitutes part of the carbon cycle; what is a problem is the rising CO_2 content of the atmosphere that has built up as humans have burned more and more carbon – it is now at over 400 parts per million (ppm). This means that it is important to understand both GHG emissions and the GHG content in the atmosphere when discussing climate change. This is because the GHG build-up in the atmosphere contributes to the greenhouse effect which regulates global temperatures.

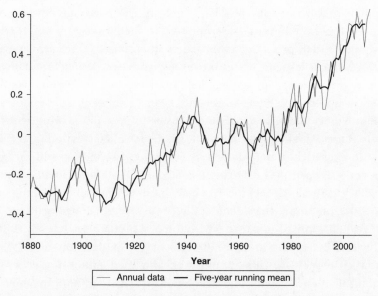

FIGURE 9.1 Rising global temperatures (°C) *Source*: www.giss.nasa.gov/research/news/20110113/ (accessed June 2016)

The build up of CO_2 and other GHGs from human activity has led to an increase in global temperatures of around 0.8 degrees Celsius since 1880 (see Figure 9.1), and will lead to global temperatures rising between one and four degrees by 2100 (Robbins et al. 2010). While this does not sound dramatic, the rise obscures the fact that some parts of the world will experience far more significant shifts in temperature than others, resulting in major changes in the environment. For example, predicted effects include drought, floods, declining sea ice and glaciers, sea level rises, amongst others. This is why at the 2015 Paris UN Climate Change Conference countries around the world agreed to limit global temperature rises to below 1.5 degrees Celsius. However, to limit temperature rises to below 1.5 degrees means that the world can only release a certain amount of CO_2 into the atmosphere before 2050, which we currently are not on target to meet. What is more, there are major economic constraints on achieving this goal because to limit our CO_2 emissions means 'burning less than half of the oil, coal and gas in currently commercial reserves' (Berners-Lee and Clark 2013). Contrary to what many fear about resource scarcities, especially when it comes to peak oil (Bridge 2013), our real problem is too many fossil fuel resources and too much economic and financial reliance on those resources. For example, if the world agrees to limit the burning of those fossil resources, then that would wipe out the wealth of fossil fuel businesses, governments reliant on fossil fuel incomes and individuals whose pensions and savings are invested in those fossil fuel companies. According to McKibben (2012) it would mean wiping out US$20 trillion of wealth, which 'makes the housing bubble look small by comparison'.

It might seem sensible, in light of the potential catastrophe looming large in our near future, that governments, businesses and people around the world agree on ways to mitigate (i.e. stop) and adapt to climate change. This has not happened, nor is it likely to happen in the near future. Why this has not happened is an interesting, if depressing, example of how partisan government, business and personal interests and ideologies can scupper collective attempts to find solutions for global problems. There is a growing literature on how conservative think tanks, politicians and business people, as well as certain businesses, have financed a campaign of **climate change denial** (e.g. McCright and Dunlap 2010; Oreskes and Conway 2010). This campaign against climate change has been very successful at convincing people that climate change is not happening, is not a big deal or is simply an environmentalist conspiracy to bring down capitalism (Klein 2014). It is, therefore, not surprising that governments around the world have found it difficult to agree on a plan of action, especially as the main polluter – the USA – is witness to the most vociferous climate denial. Instead, we are left with more versions of market environmentalism, such as carbon trading (Robbins et al. 2010). However, there are numerous problems with carbon trading which Lohmann (2010) outlines in his work. In particular,

Lohmann argues that it is, once again, another example of governments simply giving away resources to businesses, and then letting the market decide the value of carbon emissions – it does not, therefore, necessarily lead to a significant (if any) reduction in the emission of GHGs. Moreover, Lohmann highlights the global disparities and inequalities that result from carbon trading, especially in terms of the Global North simply buying more carbon credits, thereby stunting socio-economic development in the Global South.

Key methodological issue: Climate change denial – who to trust in climate debates?

There is a scientific consensus that climate change is happening and that it is caused by humans. This consensus is demonstrated by the work of the Intergovernmental Panel on Climate Change (IPCC), which is a global body set up by the UN and World Meteorological Organization in 1988. The IPCC collects and collates all the scientific research in the world and produces regular 'Assessment Reports' to help guide policy-making. Despite this global scientific consensus, however, many people, politicians, policy-makers etc. reject the idea that anthropogenic climate change is happening. Why they reject it is an important question. One answer is that there has been a concerted and coordinated effort to deny climate change pursued by right-wing and free market think tanks and funded by conservative business people and businesses. What this means is that when researching climate change it is important to examine who finances the literature you are reading, especially when it is not written by academics. There are several websites that help in this regard, including Exxon Secrets (www.exxonsecrets.org/maps.php).

Source: Oreskes and Conway (2010)

Conclusion

In this chapter we sought to raise several issues to do with global environmental change. First, we discussed the environment and how environmental problems are framed in neoclassical economics and then resolved in capitalism. We presented three key processes used to solve environmental problems: privatization, commodification and marketization. Second, we sought to question this mainstream perspective by introducing the concept of environmental justice and political ecology as an approach to understanding the interaction between humans and the environment. We then criticized the three mainstream solutions to environmental problems by highlighting several tensions, inconsistencies or problematic normative assumptions. Finally, we finished the chapter by examining climate change as a specific environmental problem which persists despite the need for an urgent response and despite several years of awareness of it as a problem and numerous global conferences, treaties and so on. We suggested that climate change is unlikely to be resolved precisely because it is being addressed through market-based measures like carbon trading.

Suggested readings

- Ch. 2, Bellamy Foster, J. (2002) *Ecology Against Capitalism*, New York, Monthly Review Press.
- Ch. 5, Jackson, T. (2009) *Prosperity without Growth*, London, Earthscan.
- McKibben, B. (2012) 'Global warming's terrifying new math', *Rolling Stone*, 19 July. www.rollingstone.com/politics/news/global-warmings-terrifying-new-math-20120719 (accessed September 2016).
- Millington, A. and Pickerell, J. (2005) 'Environment and environmentalism', in P. Daniels, M. Bradshaw, D. Shaw and J. Sidaway (eds), *An Introduction to Human Geography* (2nd Edition), Harlow, Pearson, pp.145–167.
- Ch. 4, Robbins, P., Hintz, J. and Moore, S. (2010) *Environment and Society*, Oxford, Wiley-Blackwell.

Bibliography

Bailey, I. (2007) 'Market environmentalism, new environmental policy instruments, and climate policy in the United Kingdom and Germany', *Annals of the Association of American Geographers*, Vol.97, pp.530–550.

Bellamy Foster, J. (2002) *Ecology against Capitalism*, New York, Monthly Review Press.

Berners-Lee, M. and Clark, D. (2013) *The Burning Question*, London, Profile Books.

Bradshaw, M. (2008) 'Resources and development', in P. Daniels, M. Bradshaw, D. Shaw and J. Sidaway (eds), *An Introduction to Human Geography*, Harlow, Pearson, pp.105–134.

Bridge, G. (2009) 'Material worlds: Nature resources, resource geography and the material economy', *Geography Compass*, Vol.3, pp.1217–1244.

Bridge, G. (2013) 'Geographies of peak oil: The other carbon problem', *Geoforum*, Vol.41, pp.523–530.

Castree, N. (2003) 'Commodifying what nature?', *Progress in Human Geography*, Vol.27, pp.273–297.

Castree, N. (2014) 'The Anthropocene and geography I: The back story', *Geography Compass*, Vol.8, pp.436–449.

Coe, N., Kelly, P. and Yeung, H. (2007) *Economic Geography*, Oxford, Blackwell.

Commoner, B. (1971) *The Closing Circle*, New York, Knopf.

Dicken, P. (2011) *Global Shift* (6th Edition), New York, Guildford.

Hardin, G. (1968) 'The tragedy of the commons', *Science*, Vol.162, pp.1243–1248.

Hopwood, B., Mellor, M. and O'Brien, G. (2005) 'Sustainable development: Managing different approaches', *Sustainable Development*, Vol.13, pp.38–52.

Jackson, T. (2009) *Prosperity without Growth*, London, Earthscan.

Klein, N. (2014) *This Changes Everything: Capitalism vs. the Climate*, Toronto, Simon & Schuster.

Leonard, A. (2010) *The Story of Stuff*, London, Constable.

Lohmann, L. (2010) 'Neoliberalism and the calculable world: The rise of carbon trading', in K. Birch and V. Mykhnenko (eds), *The Rise and Fall of Neoliberalism*, London, Zed Books, pp.77–93.

McCright, A. and Dunlap, R. (2010) 'Anti-reflexivity: The American Conservative Movement's success in undermining climate science and policy', *Theory, Culture, and Society*, Vol.27, pp.100–133.

McKibben, B. (2012) 'Global warming's terrifying new math', *Rolling Stone*, 19 July: www.rollingstone.com/politics/news/global-warmings-terrifying-new-math-20120719 (accessed September 2016).

Millington, A. and Pickerell, J. (2005) 'Environment and environmentalism', in P. Daniels, M. Bradshaw, D. Shaw and J. Sidaway (eds), *An Introduction to Human Geography* (2nd Edition), Harlow, Pearson, pp.145–167.

Oreskes, N. and Conway, E. (2010) *Merchants of Doubt*, New York, Bloomsbury Press.

Ostrom, E. (1990) *Governing the Commons*, Cambridge, Cambridge University Press.

Robbins, P., Hintz, J. and Moore, S. (2010) *Environment and Society*, Oxford, Wiley-Blackwell.

Smith, N. (1984 [2008]) *Uneven Development*, Athens GA, University of Georgia Press.

Whatmore, S. (2002) *Hybrid Geographies: Natures Cultures Spaces*, London, Sage.

10 | Markets and economic order

Mark Peacock

Introduction

All societies have some sort of economic mechanism through which people acquire their means to survive; the market is one such mechanism. All of us today rely on the market to acquire our means of survival. Few of the goods and services which a typical individual person consumes are made by that individual. Although market exchange has existed for much of human history, dependence on the market as we know it is a relatively new phenomenon. In Chapter 1, we saw how dependence on the market was brought about through the transition from feudalism to capitalism in England. But what sort of mechanism is the market? When does it work reasonably well and produce something we might call *economic order*, and when does it descend into something nearer to chaos?

Many theories of the market speak of the market producing *order* or *equilibrium*. Another way of putting this is that markets are *self-correcting* or *self-regulating*: if things start to go wrong or become disordered, the market will automatically or spontaneously correct such errors itself. This idea was discussed in Chapter 1 when we referred to Karl Polanyi (1944 [2001]). This self-corrective capacity of the market has an air of mystique about it and we investigate what is meant by it in this chapter. To understand the gist of the idea of self-correction, consider a ship at sea which has gone off course. The ship's course can be corrected, but the ship is not *self*-correcting; it is rather the captain who steers the ship back onto its true course. Those who believe the market to be self-correcting do not conceive the market as a ship, for the market has no captain who steers the market; the market somehow steers itself.

Whether and to which extent the market is self-correcting has policy implications. If markets generate order without external influence, this will have a bearing on our view about how much government intervention is required to correct for the market's failings. If the market generates order effectively and provides for people's needs quite well, the role of government in economic life might be minimal; if the market does not produce order, or does so imperfectly or slowly, the role of government might be considerable. Economic theories which one may call 'mainstream' and policy-makers who are influenced by orthodox economics hold that markets are efficient and produce order in ways which require little government intervention (see Chapter 11). This view is not shared by all economists as we discuss in Chapter 12 on 'heterodox economics'. However, before we look at the market economy, let us examine an economic system which might be deemed its opposite, one that is, like the ship depicted above, steered by a captain. This type of economy is called a **centrally planned economy**.

Key discussion questions

- Why are centrally planned economies sometimes called 'command economies'?
- What is the criterion of success in business and how might it guide people to make intelligent decisions about their avenue of work?
- What does it mean to say the markets produce order *ex post* or *a posteriori*?
- In which respects does market competition resemble the playing of a game?
- Outline Marx's distinction between the division of labour in society and the manufacturing division of labour (the latter is referred to as the 'internal division of labour' below).
- What do our views on the market's ability to bring about economic order imply for our views on government policy?

Different economic orders

Centrally planned economies With the following thought experiment we can ask how one would centrally plan an economy. Imagine that a team of politicians – the Politburo – was charged with the task of 'running' the economy, rather like a CEO runs a corporation. How would they go about this? Presumably by following something like these steps:

- First, the politicians would ascertain what sort of goods the people require and in which quantities.
- Second, they would set up factories to produce these goods, hopefully using inputs that are efficiently supplied (e.g. raw materials, machines, workers),

and they would instruct a certain number of workers to build cars, others to make clothes, grow food etc.

- Once the goods had been produced, they would distribute these goods to people. Perhaps, as was the case in actually existing 'socialist' countries, workers would be paid money wages and they would decide which goods to buy.
- At the end of the year, the politicians might discover that too many of some goods and not enough of others had been produced. This would lead them to adjust production targets in the following year.

Put like this, the task of central planning seems straightforward. Yet the history of planned economies tells a different story. Whilst everyone had a job in centrally planned economies, production was inefficient and incentives to be efficient were few (Dyker 1992). There was a chronic shortage of basic consumer goods, and centrally planned economies proved ineffective at meeting consumers' needs. Few people today support the type of planning which characterized countries like the USSR and today still characterizes aspects of China, Cuba and Vietnam.

One difference between a centrally planned economy and a market economy is that, in the former, the state usually owns the economic units of production – e.g. factories, machines, raw materials etc. There is no *private property* in the means of production in a centrally planned economy, something which reflects the socialist values of the countries which used central planning. A second difference between a market economy and a centrally planned one is that, in the latter, people are instructed what to do to a far greater degree. For this reason, centrally planned economies are sometimes called *command economies*: the government commands people to do certain things in accordance with its central plan (e.g. what to produce, how much, which production techniques to use, how much to pay the workers etc.).

In a market economy, by contrast, people are free to decide what to do. If a group of people decides to form a business which manufactures USB sticks, it is not because the government instructs them to do so. In a market economy, people are free to decide what to produce or which career to pursue. If some people decide to produce USB sticks, they themselves determine the number of USB sticks they produce per year, at what price they are to be sold, how much to pay the workforce, from where the materials for making USB sticks are sourced etc. But if people are free to decide what to do in a market economy, how can we be assured that the right number of USB sticks is produced and at what price? This brings us to the issue of the market's ability to 'self-correct'.

Markets, order and self-correction In what follows, we concentrate on one market, namely the labour market, and we ask how order is produced in this market and how the labour market might be said to correct disorder. We start with what Karl Marx calls the *social division of labour*. This term refers to the distribution of producers to different branches of production in society. Let us take a snapshot of the social division of labour in a country like Canada in the year 2014.

In 2014, about 18 million people had jobs in Canada. Of these, nearly 4 million worked in manufacturing, 370,000 in natural resources, 1.3 million in construction and 1.1 million in catering (Statistics Canada 2015a). This is not a full breakdown of the Canadian social division of labour as there are many other branches of production. Moreover, the branches of production just mentioned can be further subdivided; for instance, the natural resources sector is divided into forestry, mining, fishing, oil, quarrying and gas. Our question is: how does this social division of labour come about in a market society?

Let us first say how this social division of labour does *not* come about. The distribution of people to jobs is not centrally planned. That is, the government does not tell so many thousands of people to become miners, others to become arable farmers, others still to become computer programmers etc. Instead, individuals make up their own minds about which job they wish to pursue. Hence, the first step in the determination of the division of labour in a market society consists in the decisions of millions of people who use their freedom to decide which job to pursue. Marx (1867 [1976]: 476) wrote that this first step in the determination of the social division of labour follows 'the play of chance and caprice'. With this phrase, he tries to capture both the freedom people have to decide what to do and the uncoordinated or decentralized nature of the process of allocating people to jobs: people usually decide which job to look for independently of other people's decisions.

We all know, though, that getting a job as a carpenter or an architect is not simply about deciding to become a carpenter or an architect. Even people who are qualified to take on these jobs do not manage to find a job. Indeed, with an unemployment rate of about 7 per cent, over a million people in Canada were unable to find work in 2014. This might lead us to think that the market is not working very well – at least not for those people without work. Let us consider an example.

Assume a person, let us call her Béatrice, wishes to set up a business as a watchmaker. Her decision to manufacture watches is the way she tries to become part of the social division of labour. Before commencing business, Béatrice will probably make a business plan which will contain answers to the following questions:

- How many watches should I produce per year?
- Should I aim at a particular market segment – e.g. luxury, budget, women's watches etc.?

- How should I advertise my watches?
- From which suppliers should I acquire the component parts – e.g. batteries, leather for the straps, steel for the watch faces, etc.?
- At which price should I sell and how much profit do I aim to make?

There are many watchmakers in an economy, and, unlike in a centrally planned economy, the government in a market economy does not issue instructions which say: 'the country's watchmakers should produce 25,000 watches next year'. In a market economy, *nobody* plans or knows how many watches are to be produced in total; the number of watches produced results from the *decentralized* and uncoordinated decisions of many individuals who have decided to become watchmakers. But if every watchmaker decides how many watches to produce independently of other watchmakers, how can we be sure that the right quantity of watches is produced? How, in other words, from Marx's 'play of chance and caprice' can something like economic order emerge in the market?

Assume that Béatrice produces 1000 watches in year 1 of her business. Is this the right amount, too many or too few? At the beginning of year 1, Béatrice expects to sell 1000 watches to retailers, and this is the number she makes. At the end of the year, however, it transpires that she has only sold 200, and hence she has 800 unsold watches and a lot less profit than she had hoped. Something has obviously gone wrong, and Béatrice knows this because her expectations have been disappointed. Perhaps she underestimated how many people rely on their iPhone to tell the time and stopped buying wrist watches.

What should Béatrice do to ensure that year 2 might go better? There are many options:

- Béatrice might reduce the price of her watches so that more are bought; economists would say that, by reducing the price, more watches will be demanded, and so the supply of and demand for your watches will come into 'equilibrium' and, if Béatrice gets the price right, she will sell her entire stock. Lowering the price, however, will reduce her profit on each watch sold, and she might end up making a loss if she does not produce in a cost-efficient way.
- Alternatively, Béatrice could maintain the current price and embark on an advertising campaign, in the hope that more people will buy her watches.
- Instead, Béatrice might look at what her competitors are doing and copy their business strategy; have they found cheaper sources of components, for instance?

Béatrice could combine the above strategies or try out others, but whatever she does, it will be a matter of *trial and error*. Béatrice has no guarantee that her change of business plan will lead to success, and, if it does not, she will, eventually, confront the ultimate option of admitting failure and closing down her business.

Let us assume that other watchmakers are in a similar position to Béatrice at the end of year 1, and the unsuccessful businesses (including Béatrice's) all close down. Next year, in year 2, there will be fewer watches on sale; the market, one might say, has 'corrected' the oversupply of watches in year 1. This would be an example of 'self-correction'. What that means is that a number of suppliers have withdrawn from the market because of their unfavourable experience in year 1. The total number of watches produced in year 2 shrinks. Once again, this correction was not instructed by the government but is the result of the independent decisions of many separate watchmakers. The story does not end there. Imagine that market conditions in year 2 are different from those in year 1. During year 2, consumers buy more watches than they did in year 1, perhaps because wristwatches become more fashionable. In year 2, then, there will be greater demand for watches, and retailers will be looking for additional supplies of watches to sell to their customers. But the supply of watches has fallen in year 2 because Béatrice and other watchmakers shut down their businesses at the end of year 1. The increased demand for watches in year 2, together with the reduction in supply, means that watches have become scarcer, and this will increase their price. These higher prices in year 2 signal that watchmaking has become lucrative. Extant watchmakers will work overtime and produce more watches, and other producers will enter the market in the hope of making a profit.

Let us continue the story and assume that, following a period of unemployment after Béatrice closed her watchmaking business at the end of year 1, she re-enters the watchmaking business in year 3, having seen the watch business boom in year 2. In year 3 she gets lucky: she sells enough watches at high enough prices to make her desired level of profit. Something has gone right for Béatrice and she knows this because her expectation of sales, prices and profits have been met (possibly exceeded). The market, one might say, has corrected for the unexpected increase in demand in year 2 by indicating to producers, via price signals, that they should enter the watchmaking business. To Béatrice's disappointment, however, the spike in the demand for watches in year 3 is temporary; in year 4, people stop buying watches and watch manufacturers – including hers – cannot sell their stock at the profitable prices. Béatrice's business goes bankrupt again. This is another example of 'self-correction'; watches have become less scarce because there are too many watchmakers and not enough people to buy them in year 4. This leads some watchmakers to close their businesses. The story could go on and on, but we will take our leave of it here and pose and answer some questions about the scenario we have portrayed above.

Do markets create social order?

How does the social division of labour come about? We started with Marx's 'play of chance and caprice', that is, with the decentralized employment decisions of millions of people in an economy, including Béatrice's decision to become a watchmaker. Not all these decisions transpire to be practicable, and the social division of labour which results depends not only on Béatrice's decision to produce watches but on the decisions of other producers, who are in competition with Béatrice, and of consumers, who might but might not buy her watches. Once she has tried her hand at watchmaking, Béatrice will receive feedback from the market and this will guide her future decisions. If watchmakers' plans or expectations are not realized (e.g. if many do not make their desired level of profit), they will react by changing their business strategy. This might, but will not necessarily, move the market in a direction in which order is attained – fewer watchmakers making fewer watches. In our example, the exit of watch manufacturers from the market after their disappointment of year 1 is an instance of this. All this really means is that watchmakers react to the 'information' the market gives them, and if this information is not welcome (because their plans are disappointed), they will change their market behaviour. The social division of labour which exists at a given time is a product of the feedback which market competition provides to economic agents and their reactions to this feedback. What emerges is a pattern or order which reflects all these changes and movements in the market. The order which is thereby produced on the market is sometimes described as being created *ex post*; that is, *after* the process of competition has taken place.

How does anyone know whether becoming a watchmaker is a good idea, better than becoming a chef, a wine-taster or a manufacturer of USB sticks? A person like Béatrice might already possess watchmaking skills, and she might know things about the watch market that give her a certain competence in watchmaking. But despite all she knows about watchmaking, before she starts her business, she does not know whether it is a good decision to become a watchmaker. Even the most detailed and well-researched business plan will give you no guarantee that your business will succeed. The only way Béatrice can find out whether becoming a watchmaker is a good idea is to become one and to see if she is successful. Becoming a watchmaker and entering into market competition with other watchmakers is how she *discovers* whether becoming a watchmaker is a good idea. Some economists, like **Friedrich Hayek** (1976) talk of the market competition as a 'discovery procedure'; a person discovers whether it is a good idea to become a watchmaker by becoming one and seeing whether her expectations are fulfilled. Market competition is like a game which each player is trying to win. Before the game starts, nobody knows who will win, and only by playing the game does one find out who wins. And like a game, not only is the outcome of market competition unpredictable, but it is possible that someone with less skill, competence or knowledge than another player will win. The outcome of market competition, like the outcome of a game, is partly determined by luck.

Will there be enough watchmakers in your economy, too many or too few? Before people try their hand at watchmaking, nobody knows what the right number of watchmakers is. A sign that there are too many is that some of them will be unprofitable because they do not sell enough watches. One response to this market signal is that watchmakers will close down their businesses. But things are not quite so simple. If many watchmakers are unprofitable, it might not be because there are too many watchmakers in the market; rather it might be that they are making the wrong sort of watch. The best strategy for a watchmaker like Béatrice at the end of year 1 might not be to close down her business but to make a different type of watch, one which might be more attractive to consumers. What is the 'correct' strategy – close down, change the type of watch one produces or something else again? Nobody knows for sure, and the only way to find out whether a strategy is successful is to try it and see what happens. As we noted above, this is a process of trial and error.

What determines whether your watchmaking business is successful? Your business is successful if your hopes and expectations are realized (i.e. if you sell a certain number of watches and make the profits you hoped to make when you started your business). If these expectations are realized or surpassed, a watchmaker can, for the time being, say that it was a good idea to become a watchmaker. Before one starts one's business, though, there is no guarantee of success, as we noted when answering question two. Ultimately, whether a watchmaker's business is successful depends on whether the business is useful for other people. So the question each watchmaker must ask themselves is, 'will I produce something of use for other people at prices which those people find acceptable'? The people to whom one has to be useful are consumers. As we saw above, there are many other factors beyond a watchmaker's control which also determine whether a given watchmaking business is successful. Consequently, the success of a business is partly a matter of luck, just as success in playing a game is partly a matter of luck (e.g. against whom is one playing, which cards is one dealt, how the die falls when it is rolled?) (Hayek 1976). For instance, Béatrice's business might fail because she launched it in 2008, on the eve of a worldwide recession, a time when people are unlikely to buy new wristwatches. Or the launch of her business might coincide with the launch of a new line of well-marketed watches from a large international corporation, and Béatrice might be unable to compete against this corporation. Had she launched her business five years earlier, it might have succeeded, but market conditions have changed and Béatrice has the bad luck of starting her business at the wrong time. This is not her fault because she could not have predicted these market conditions, it was simply bad luck.

Does the market ever establish an order or reach an 'equilibrium' at which everything settles? Theoretically, it is imaginable that an equilibrium is reached at which every producer's and every consumer's expectations are realized such that nobody has an incentive to change her or his actions. In practice, though, market activity is too dynamic and subject to disturbances for this to happen. Entrepreneurs create new products, technicians and scientists invent new production techniques, consumers' tastes change, and shocks to the market, such as earthquakes, terrorist attacks, financial crises and wars, are forever upsetting the market system. Nevertheless, if individuals who operate in the market react to the market signals they receive, there will be movement toward the creation of order and there is some chance that people's plans and expectations will come into line with those of other people to a certain extent. But simply because people's plans and expectations are realized this year does not mean that the same will happen next year, and so economic agents must constantly react to feedback in the form of market signals and change their plans accordingly, in the hope that they can maintain whatever success they have had hitherto.

The internal division of labour

We have examined above two types of economic order – that which is centrally planned and is associated with command economies, and that which is decentralized and is associated with the free market. As we saw in the context of a market economy, a social division of labour arises as a result of the decisions of many independent producers like Béatrice. Not everyone, though, is an independent producer, that is, an entrepreneur who owns their own business. In fact most people are not self-employed. In 2014, there were 2.7 million self-employed people in Canada (nearly two-thirds of whom were men and one-third women) (Statistics Canada 2015b). So nearly 15 million of the remaining 18 million people employed in Canada in 2014 were employed in businesses not owned by themselves. These people are workers or employees. This gives rise to a second element to the division of labour, which Marx (1867 [1976]) calls the manufacturing division of labour. The manufacturing division of labour refers to the way labour is divided within a single workplace or business, not within society as a whole. I will refer to this as the *internal division of labour*, to make clear that this refers to the way in which labour is divided *within* a single business. For example, if a person, let us call him Egil, works for a car manufacturer, he will be responsible for perhaps one task only; for example, fitting doors onto the car's body or testing the car's safety features (e.g. brakes, seatbelts or airbags). Or if we consider a bank, the internal division of labour consists of all the positions the bank has; branch managers, tellers, personnel staff, customer advisors etc. The people who fill these positions all share a single employer, the bank. Once Egil is employed by a business, he and his fellow employees are what Marx calls 'part' or 'detail' workers (*Teilarbeiter*); each worker is responsible for perhaps a minute part of the corporation's activities, e.g. mounting doors onto the body of cars, or advising customers of a bank about their retirement savings plans. Normally the manager of the business assigns tasks to individual workers in the workplace. As a car worker, Egil is not free to choose what to do; he must obey the commands of his boss, and refusal to do so could result in him being fired.

There are some important differences between the social division of labour and the internal division of labour:

- As an independent producer, like the watchmaker Béatrice, one produces a commodity – watches – which, when she has made them, belong to her; they are Béatrice's property and hence they are hers to sell if she wishes. As a detail worker in a car factory, Egil does not make a commodity of which he is the owner; what he makes does not belong to him – it belongs to those who own the factory, the capitalists.
- The social division of labour is regulated through the market *ex post* or *a posteriori*. That is, *after* individuals have made their decisions about which job to pursue, market competition determines how many producers survive in each branch of business. Nobody plans or determines in advance of market competition how many taxi drivers, watchmakers or computer

programmers there should be in a society; it is only by observing the results of market competition that we know how many producers survive market competition in each branch of production. Within a business, by contrast, the division of labour is determined according to a plan. The business' owners (also called capitalists), or a representative of the owners in the person of a manager, formulate the plan. The plan stipulates who works at which task within the business, how many workers are required in each activity etc. The plan is conceived *ex ante* or *a priori*, that is, *in advance of production*. The manager's plan helps create the internal order of the business, for the manager not only creates the plan but has the authority to enforce it (recalling that refusal to obey the manager's commands can result in a worker being disciplined or fired). Adam Smith (1776: I.i.3) described the internal division of labour in pin manufacturing:

> One man draws out the wire, another straightens it, a third cuts it, a fourth points it, a fifth grinds it at the top for receiving the head; to make the head requires two or three distinct operations; to put it on, is a peculiar business, to whiten the pins is another; it is even a trade by itself to put them into the paper; and the important business of making a pin is, in this manner, divided into about eighteen distinct operations, which, in some manufactories, are all performed by distinct hands.

- The division of tasks within a factory is not chosen randomly and does not result from the 'play of chance and caprice'; rather it is worked out methodically and determined *a priori* by the manager whose will is backed up with the threat of discipline towards those workers who either disobey the manager or carry out their plan inadequately.
- Any worker who works for a business is therefore part of an internal division of labour, and is subject to the authority and commands of the owners of that business. Workers stand under the command of a boss and if they do not carry out their boss's instructions, they may lose their jobs. A business is a hierarchical order with sanctions for insubordination. Marx (1867 [1976]: 477) described the hierarchy of the business as a 'despotism', whereby the boss is the despot and the order within the business is imposed on workers. The economic order brought about in the social division of labour, by contrast, is characterized, Marx tells us, by 'anarchy', for, as we saw with Béatrice, our watchmaker, nobody dictates to people what jobs they are to pursue; watchmakers, like all other people in a market economy, are free to set up whatever business they like (within the bounds of the law). There are, of course, sanctions in the social division of labour, for market competition will tell a person whether their choice of occupation was good or bad. But these sanctions are not imposed by a boss, like they are within a business.

There are many debates about why the 'firm' is organized hierarchically according to a system of command and whether this is a fair form of organization (e.g. Ciepley 2013). Mainstream positions hold that hierarchically organized firms are efficient because they reduce the 'transactions costs' of production (see Chapters 3 and 4). Non-mainstream positions, by contrast, draw attention to the relations of authority within business entities and question whether it is legitimate that owners or managers have the power to command workers (Marglin 1974). These are not topics we pursue here, but ones which should be considered before one takes the relations of authority within a business as natural or given.

Types of economic order: from society to the business organization

We have considered the social division of labour and the internal division of labour. The latter, we observed above, is hierarchical; there is a chain of command from the business owners who, in many, particularly large, public corporations, employ managers. Managers are responsible for running the business or corporation for the purposes of furthering the interests of its owners, which usually means making as much profit for them as possible. To this end, managers issue commands to employees whose tasks are likewise organized with the aim of making profits for the owners.

One may ask whether the order created by the internal division of labour is fair. That is, what justifies the power of capitalists (or managers) to issue commands to workers? One answer might be that workers are never forced to work for a particular business; a worker, like everyone else in a market economy, is a free individual over whom a business has no authority unless the worker decides freely to work for it. Nobody can be compelled to work for Blackberry, Walmart or Microsoft against their will; workers who work for these or other businesses freely choose to do so. If people decide to work for Walmart, their work contract will place them under the command of a manager, but if the workers do not find the terms and conditions of the job acceptable, they can look for employment elsewhere. But recall what we said in Chapter 1 about workers and the freedom they enjoy. Workers are propertyless in that they do not own the means of production and, to become productive in any way, they rely on a capitalist to give them work. Without work, the worker has few options for survival, and so one might say that, despite their freedom to turn their backs on a given employer like Walmart, workers, in truth, are compelled to work and thus to submit to the dictates of some business or other. If they do not work for a business, workers might starve. Hence the circumstances in which workers find themselves do not give them effective freedom to avoid the hierarchy of command in a business, even if the worker finds the conditions of their workplace harmful, degrading or dangerous. All workers are free to set up their own businesses, as Béatrice did, but, as we saw when discussing the social division of labour, there is no guarantee of success, and, if one's business fails, one might have few or no options other than submitting oneself to the dictates of a business owner and thus becoming a worker.

Adam Smith was one of the keenest critics of the effects of the internal division of labour. He noted that, by being assigned 'to a few very simple operations' in the workplace, the worker 'becomes as stupid and ignorant as it is possible for a human creature to become' (Smith 1776: V.i.f.50). The division of labour, Smith argued, can lead to the moral and intellectual deformity of workers, and this could have grave consequences for the society in which we live. Today, still, people undertake jobs in which the tasks allow for little exercise of creativity and allow for no personal fulfilment. What effect does this have on such people and what is the role of people who consume the products they make and thus play an essential role in the perpetuation of harmful working conditions? There is good reason for consumers to be informed about more than the price and nature of the goods they buy; an essential part of what we buy includes the conditions under which goods are made. If we wish to be ethical consumers, we must pay attention to the conditions under which goods are produced and to the effects of consuming them (e.g. the effects on the environment and on the workers who produce the goods).

Conclusion

We have looked above at different types of economic order and how they are created. We have seen that the self-correcting features of markets really means little more than that individuals in the market react to the signals they receive and ask themselves: can I do anything to improve my economic situation such that the hopes I have of earning a living can be realized better than they are being realized at present? Only if what one does on the market proves to be useful to other people will one have any success either in getting a job or in running a business. We have also seen that order does not imply a movement to a stationary point from which nothing will change; rather, order is constantly in the making if individuals in the market react to market signals accordingly, but order is constantly disturbed and individuals in the market will constantly have to change their plans and seek new opportunities for making money.

There are many questions raised in discussions of economic order and these have implications for government policy and regulation. Consider again Béatrice, who at the end of the first year of business went bankrupt and became unemployed. Should the government support her financially whilst she is unemployed? Or is the best thing not to support her so that she sets about finding new employment as quickly as possible? Those who have faith in the market's ability to correct for disorder might say that unemployed people should adjust their expectations about which jobs they can get and at which rates of pay. Proponents of the market might say that if Béatrice finds herself without work, she is free to seek work in catering, cleaning, prostitution or another low-wage sector. If her watchmaking business closed, that might have been bad luck, but does she deserve state support whilst she is unemployed? Others would say that, precisely because Béatrice's lack of success as a watchmaker was bad luck, it would be harsh, perhaps inhumane, not to have a safety net which supports people like her whilst they are unemployed.

Suggested readings

- Ch. 10, Hayek, F.A. (1976) *Law, Legislation and Liberty*, volume 2, London, Routledge and Kegan Paul.
- Ch. 1, Heilbroner, R. and Milberg, W. (2002) *The Making of Economic Society* (11th Edition), New York, Prentice Hall.
- Ch. 4, Section 4, Marx, K. (1867 [1976]) *Capital: Volume 1*, London, Penguin.

Bibliography

Bleaney, M. (1988) *Do Socialist Economies Work?* Oxford, Blackwell.

Ciepley, D. (2013) 'Beyond public and private: Toward a political theory of the corporation', *American Political Science Review*, Vol.107, pp.139–158.

Dyker, D.A. (1992) *Restructuring the Soviet Economy*, London, Routledge.

Hayek, F.A. (1944) *The Road to Serfdom*, Chicago, Chicago University Press.

Hayek, F.A. (1976) *Law, Legislation and Liberty*, volume 2, London, Routledge and Kegan Paul.

Heilbroner, R. and Milberg, W. (2002) *The Making of Economic Society* (11th Edition), New York, Prentice Hall.

Marglin, S. (1974) 'What do bosses do? The origins and function of hierarchy in capitalist production', *Review of Radical Political Economics*, Vol.6, pp.60–112.

Marx, K. (1867 [1976]) *Capital: Volume 1*, London, Penguin.

Mirowski, P. and Plehwe, D. (eds) (2009) *The Road from Mont Pèlerin: The Making of the Neoliberal Thought Collective*, Cambridge MA, Harvard University Press.

Polanyi, K. (1944 [2001]) *The Great Transformation*, Boston, Beacon Press.

Smith, A. (1776 [1976]) *An Inquiry into the Nature and Causes of the Wealth of Nations*, Oxford, Oxford University Press.

Statistics Canada (2015a) 'Employment by industry': www.statcan.gc.ca/tables-tableaux/sum-som/l01/cst01/econ40-eng.htm (accessed 14 January 2015).

Statistics Canada (2015b) 'Self-employment, historical summary': www.statcan.gc.ca/tables-tableaux/sum-som/l01/cst01/labor64-eng.htm (accessed 21 January 2015).

11 | Economics, capitalism and business: the orthodoxy

Sonya Scott and Mark Peacock

Introduction

In the previous chapter, we looked at markets and economic order, but the 'theory' of market order was kept deliberately in the background. In this chapter, we examine an economic doctrine which dominates university curricula the world over and which was developed to understand markets. This mainstream doctrine goes under the name 'neoclassical' or 'orthodox' economics.

This doctrine is increasingly challenged by economists, as is evident in student-led movements such as Rethinking Economics and the International Initiative for Pluralism in Economics. It is nevertheless the dominant mode of thinking amongst economists and policy-makers around the world. What we consider below are only some aspects of this orthodoxy, most of which concern *microeconomics*. Microeconomics deals with individuals, their behaviour, decisions and motivation. It is based on a number of assumptions concerning human beings and deduces from these assumptions various theories about markets and the economy. We do not deal with *macroeconomics*, which concerns aggregate phenomena such as unemployment, economic growth and inflation.

In this chapter, we explore the origins of mainstream economics, and we consider whether it provides an accurate depiction of the way human beings act and make decisions. It is important to consider such matters because of the dominant position the orthodoxy holds in university curricula and in public policy. After examining mainstream economics in this chapter, the next chapter focuses on economists who dissent from the mainstream.

Key discussion questions

- What is mainstream economics?
- What are the differences between Smith's notion of self-love and Bentham's principle of utility?
- What are the characteristics of *homo economicus*?
- What does the term 'Pareto improvement' mean and how is it supposed to provide a normative foundation for market exchange?
- Why do economists use the term 'preference' to describe the underlying process of choice?
- What are interpersonal comparisons of utility and why might it be difficult to make them?

The mainstream perspective

When we talk about mainstream economics we are referring to the dominant form of economic reasoning today. It involves a set of ideas, methods and conceptions of human nature that guide economists. These ideas constitute an *orthodoxy*, or core set of principles, which form the basis of mainstream economics. If you were to take an *ECON 101* course at the vast majority of universities in the world, you would be taught mainstream economics and nothing else.

Most historians of economic thought trace one principle of mainstream economics to the work of Adam Smith (1723–1790) who was a major figure in the Scottish Enlightenment. Smith is an important political economist because he developed his ideas at the time when modern industrial capitalism was coming into existence in Britain. In 1776 he published *The Wealth of Nations*, which described the emerging capitalist economic order. Smith was concerned with understanding people's economic lives. Just as the structure of the economy was changing with the development of capitalism, so too was the way in which people lived and organized their lives. The shift from feudalism to capitalism – described in Chapter 1 – meant a whole new way of thinking. Instead of living rurally and engaging in agricultural labour, people moved in great number into towns and cities and organized their lives around jobs in factories. Within this emerging economic order, Smith grouped people into three classes – landlords, capitalists and workers. Each group, he explained, had a particular way of surviving: landlords lived by charging rent on land, capitalists by making profit and workers by earning wages from capitalists.

We might step back from history for a moment and ask how we would define ourselves as economic beings. Are you a scrupulous saver? A big spender? A workaholic? A philanthropist who donates to good causes? An investor with financial savvy and a keen sense of the market? For us the answers depend on our individual identity. For Smith, by contrast, the answers depend on the bigger question of 'human nature', itself a highly contentious notion.

Smith explained that capitalism depends upon a collection of people working in cooperation with one another, even if we are not aware of it, or not closely related with the majority of the people making the goods and services we buy. According to Smith, one distinguishing feature of contemporary civilization – and by this Smith meant Europe of the late eighteenth century – is the interdependence of human beings through the *division of labour*. More and more people in society come to rely on one another because no one person can produce all they need on their own. What had previously been a *subsistence* economy became an economy of mutual dependence. In this context, money became more and more necessary, so that individuals could buy those things they did not produce themselves.

We might think that this emerging society would be based upon a collective spirit of cooperation and goodwill because of this vast mutual dependence. Smith, by contrast, believed that capitalist society does not and does not need to depend upon goodwill. Rather it is our *self-interest*, or each person's desire to look after themselves first, that motivates us and is fundamental to our human nature. In a famous passage Smith wrote:

> It is not from the benevolence of the butcher, the brewer or the baker, that we expect our dinner, but from their regard to their own interest. We address ourselves, not to their humanity but to their self-love, and we never talk to them of our own necessities but of their advantages. (1776 [2000]: I.ii.2)

This statement seems to make a lot of sense. With it, Smith suggested that people respond to incentives; they are motivated by self-interest (or 'self-love' as Smith called it), rather than by selflessness; they are most likely to cooperate when it is to each person's advantage to do so.

At about the time that Smith was writing about the nature of capitalism, the British philosopher Jeremy Bentham (1748–1832) developed an ethical theory called *utilitarianism* based on the idea that human beings are driven by the pursuit of pleasure and the avoidance of pain (see Chapter 14). Bentham (1780 [2011]: 111–112) famously proclaimed:

> Nature has placed mankind under the governance of two sovereign masters, *pain* and *pleasure*. . . . They govern us in all we do, in all we say, in all we think: every effort we can make to throw off our subjection, will serve but to demonstrate and confirm it.

On the surface this looks like Smith's claim that human beings are motivated by self-interest. However, Bentham was making an entirely different point. He did not believe that we are selfish pleasure-seekers motivated by self-interest; instead he understood our motivations as a part of a broader social and moral theory. Indeed, as seekers of pleasure and avoiders of pain, each person should not act in his or her own interest alone; rather morality dictates that each of us act in the best interest of the *common good* – to seek the greatest good for the greatest number in society. This quest to seek the greatest good for the greatest number is called the *principle of utility* and it underpins utilitarianism (see Chapter 14). The principle of utility is not a description of self-interest but is rather a form of universal selflessness. For example, it may be important to sacrifice our immediate pleasure by giving up some of our income and paying taxes. As an individual we are contributing to the greatest good for the greatest number by allowing government to invest in public services like health care and education. If this sacrifice leads to an increase in happiness in society, Bentham would support it; that paying taxes is to an individual's personal disadvantage is not a good reason for tax evasion.

So while Smith believed that self-interested individualistic behaviour was part of human nature, and leads to social cooperation and interdependence, Bentham believed that conscious and calculated sacrifice of individual self-interest for the greater good was morally required. For example, Bentham argued that:

> an action may be said to be conformable to the principle of utility (meaning with respect to the community at large) when the tendency it has to augment the happiness of the community is greater than any it has to diminish it. (1780 [2011]: 113)

The same applies to the actions of government, and to the rule of law, which ought, as a matter of principle, to promote the greatest good for the greatest number. This idea is important in economic terms because it gives us a way to begin to measure the relationship between individual action and the welfare of the whole, as well as the role of the government in the economic affairs of the state.

Homo economicus Smith's idea of self-interest is a central principle of mainstream economics. It defines what economists call *homo economicus* or **'rational economic man'**. *Homo economicus* is the economist's characterization of a human being as:

- a free individual (assumed to be a man) who
- pursues 'his' own self-interest,
- knows what 'his' self-interest is, and
- can measure 'his' own self-interest in economic terms (e.g. in terms of price or cost) and act accordingly.

Whether we think these traits of *homo economicus* are plausible or not, even some mainstream economists believe that it is not always possible to behave like a *homo economicus*. For instance, we do not always have sufficient information to determine what is in our self-interest (Hill and Myatt 2010). When we make decisions about purchases it can be hard to know if a product is defective, if a house has hidden problems, or if the new model of a phone or laptop is actually worth the money. Another problem comes in the form of uncertainty about the future. Many people believe that it is in our self-interest to make financial investments, but knowing how to invest can be tricky given all the ups and downs of stock markets, house prices etc. An investment that might appear to be in your interest at the time you make it can actually result in a loss of savings, perhaps bankruptcy, as was the case for many in the financial crisis of 2008. Hence, real human beings are not always able to act like a *homo economicus*.

Key critique: Going beyond 'rational economic man'

Many feminist scholars hold that mainstream economics is biased towards men (see Chapter 12). They argue that the use of 'man' in the expression 'rational economic man' was intended specifically to refer to men, who were, at the time it was developed in Europe, considered to be the more rational, intelligent, and moral gender. While economics and philosophy have come a long way since the eighteenth and nineteenth centuries, and while women have gained many formal equalities in contemporary Western society, it is crucial to note the way in which this originally gendered conception continues to hold sway today. Attributes traditionally associated with men are still perceived to be the 'natural' and 'superior' characteristics of economic life – such as competitiveness, rationality and power. These assumptions play out both in economic writing and in the work world, where women face many systemic challenges including a systemic undervaluing of women's work (e.g. low pay for work associated with women, such as caring, nurturing and emotional support) and a relative absence from positions of power in the business world and in the economics profession.

Source: Ferber and Nelson (1993)

In order to understand mainstream economics better, we can ask questions like: how are we to understand this *homo economicus*? Does 'he' correspond to our true nature or is 'he' an absurd caricature of real human beings? Does 'he' represent the way we ought to behave as rational economic individuals, even if we fall short of 'his' standards in our less well thought through decisions? We suggest that *homo economicus* is not 'the truth' about what human nature really is, but is a device necessary for making economics into a 'science'. This assumption was popular in the late nineteenth century, when many thinkers began to render what was once called **political economy** into the modern 'science' of **economics**. This change was accomplished primarily through the use of mathematical models and reasoning. For example, assuming that most human beings are rational economic beings who possess the attributes of *homo economicus* makes it easier to fit them into mathematical models. This is why economics textbooks seem more like the study of mathematics than anything else; most mainstream economists assume that human beings think of their advantage and self-interest in terms of quantity and price, and since price can be measured, we can then start to think about economics in mathematical terms.

These mathematical models are based on *homo economicus* and the economic decisions 'he' makes about buying and selling. In other words, the 'people' who inhabit the mathematical models of economic economics are primarily consumers who wish to maximize their own utility. One of the most fundamental concepts of economics is *marginal utility*. This idea, developed in the 1870s and associated with the **Marginalist Revolution** in economics, helps to explain how individuals make decisions about what to buy or sell at different prices.

In order to illustrate what marginal utility means, it is helpful to consider an example. Imagine that a young athlete has injured her leg in training and cannot walk without a leg brace. A leg brace would be very valuable to her, and she might be willing to pay as much as $100 for it. But, if she were to be presented with a second leg brace, it would not be worth nearly as much, as a person can only use one brace at a time, and her problem would have already been solved. At $100 the athlete might not be willing to buy a second, but perhaps if there were a sale (buy one get the second 75 per cent off) she would consider buying the brace for $25 so that she had a back-up. Now consider the purchase of a third brace. What price would the athlete be willing to pay – $15? $10? Or perhaps she would be unwilling to buy a third brace at all. When we reason in this way we are reasoning at the margin, determining the subsequent value of each good as it satisfies our utility. This perspective can apply to any type of good or service. What is the next T-shirt worth? The next cup of coffee? The next loaf of bread? The next computer? This idea has become another key principle in mainstream economics as a way of assessing consumer demand and evaluating the appropriate level of prices.

We saw above that Bentham thought the principle of utility was a moral imperative which, through universal selflessness, aimed to achieve the greatest good or greatest *utility* for the greatest number. The assumptions which underpin mainstream economics, by contrast, are based on a different idea of utility; in mainstream economics, *utility* represents not the good of all people in society but the good of the individual whose decision is under examination. Hence, each economic agent or *homo economicus* asks not how 'he' should act to maximize utility in society at large but how 'he' should act so as to maximize

Key concept: The Marginalist Revolution

In the 1870s, three European economists independently developed the theory of marginal utility. William Stanley Jevons (Britain), Carl Menger (Austria) and Léon Walras (France) all endeavoured to link human desires to price through the theory of supply and demand. This theory, which is also termed *marginalism*, was appealing because it granted economics a new status as a science, much like astronomy or physics. The goal was to develop a system of thought that could explain the entire economic universe through a coherent set of laws. Today this development is called the 'Marginalist Revolution'. Léon Walras, who developed the most mathematical expression of this theory, famously proclaimed:

> The law of supply and demand regulates all these exchanges of commodities just as the law of universal gravitation regulates the movements of all celestial bodies. The system of the economic universe reveals itself, at last, in all its grandeur and complexity: a system at once vast and simple, which, for sheer beauty, resembles the astronomic universe.

Sources: Walras (1874 [1954]: 374); Scott (2013)

'his' own utility. Utility maximization, in mainstream economics, is a *behavioural postulate*. According to this postulate, people are self-interested and they pursue their self-interest in a calculating and rational way.

The normative foundation of market exchange In the previous chapter, we outlined how some thinkers believe that markets generate order. Here we pose a different question: what is so good about market exchange if we, for the sake of argument, take *homo economicus* as the starting point of our analysis? This is a *normative* question; that is, one which does not pertain to matters of fact but to what is good and what is bad (see Chapter 14). The answer to the question has far-reaching implications:

- Should we promote or restrict market exchange?
- If people are rational in the way described above, should we let them use their freedom unhindered to make whatever market transactions they wish?
- Should government ever intervene to restrict people from entering into certain market exchanges? If so, when?

First, though, let us analyse a simple market exchange. Consider two individuals, Ali, who wishes to sell his Chevrolet Sedan made in 1930, and Benedetta, who is a collector of classic cars. Ali and Benedetta will effect this transaction if they can agree on a mutually agreeable price. Let us say this price is US$15,000. Benedetta purchases the car in the belief that doing so will make her better off; she has a *preference* to have the car rather than keep the money. Similarly, Ali has a preference to relinquish the car and take the money because, by doing so, he expects to increase his utility. Ali and Benedetta *rationally* pursue their self-interest in this exchange; each, we may assume, wants to further their own self-interest, knows what is in their interest, and acts upon this knowledge through a calculation of the costs and benefits involved (each calculating what the value of possessing the car and what the value of having the money will be). As long as both parties are rational in this sense, we have good grounds for allowing them the freedom to decide for themselves what they wish to buy and sell in market exchange. There are, of course, exceptions to this such as when we believe that certain market transactions will harm the people making them. This is why the sale of narcotics is often illegal and also why we do not allow children to buy alcohol. But if it seems reasonable to assume that people know enough about themselves to buy and sell things such that their utility increases, we have little reason to intervene in their market affairs.

This illustrates a central normative principle of mainstream economics; what makes market exchange a good thing is precisely that neither Ali nor Benedetta is likely to be worse off as a result of Benedetta buying the Chevrolet from Ali for US$15,000. In fact, there is reason to believe that both are made better off; for example, if Benedetta thought the price were too high, she would have a preference for keeping the money and not buying the car. In the language of economic theory, the transaction leads to a *Pareto improvement*; that is, nobody is made worse off by the transaction and at least one person is made better off (Varian 2007). If we assume that this holds for each of the billions of market transactions made every day in the global economy, we can conclude that the billions of people who make these transactions are becoming better off every day through market exchange. And if every possible market transaction which led to a Pareto improvement were allowed to take place, we would reach a situation of *Pareto efficiency*, whereby there would be no way of increasing one person's utility through market exchange without reducing the utility of another person (Dixit 2014).

The market transactions which lead to a Pareto improvement include not only those we make as consumers (e.g. when we buy cars, electronic gadgets or cups of coffee); they include also the choices we make as producers, or as businesspeople and workers. Consider someone deciding to take a summer job at Walmart. If they are rational, they will calculate the advantages to themselves of earning the minimum wage for a certain number of hours a week; if they expect thereby to further their self-interest more than they would by, say, working on their BA Honours thesis, then they should take the job – it increases their utility. Similarly for their employer. If Walmart's managers believe that Walmart will be better off (i.e. more profitable) by employing the prospective employee, they will offer them a contract. Once again, if each party is able to choose freely to enter into this contractual relationship, both parties improve their situation and nobody becomes worse off as a result.

Economists use the Pareto principle not only to judge market exchanges, but also to judge public policy proposals. If a proposal is expected to make at least one person better off whilst making nobody worse off, it will be approved because it will bring about a Pareto improvement.

Key thinker: Vilfredo Pareto

Many university students have learned about Pareto efficiency and Pareto optimality, but less common is knowledge about Pareto himself. Pareto was an Italian civil engineer who worked in Tuscany with the railway and iron works for almost twenty years. In the late 1880s he took up economics and developed a purely mathematical theory thereof. He also defended the free market system. Later in his life, Pareto began to question his earlier theories. Notably, he doubted that rational self-interested behaviour was really as common as he and many other economists had assumed. His later sociological writings reflect this scepticism and focus on the irrationality and unpredictability of much social action.

Source: Amoroso (1938)

Individuals and preferences In the previous section, we used the term 'preference' when discussing how people make choices. Consider, once again, Ali, who has two mutually exclusive options: x (acquiring $15,000) and y (keeping his Chevrolet Sedan). If he thinks his utility will increase by acquiring the money, he *prefers* option (x) over option (y). One might think that saying 'Ali prefers option x to option y' is equivalent to saying 'Person A expects their utility will be higher if they choose x rather than y'. Even though the two formulations are similar, mainstream economists are more comfortable with the terminology of 'preference'. Here, it is necessary to discuss three characteristics of the notion of utility, as it is used by mainstream economists.

First, utility is subjective, a feeling of happiness which one derives from doing something pleasurable. This is not the sort of variable which can serve as a basis for a science of choice, as mainstream economists purport their discipline to be. We need something more objective, more easily observable for such a science. Preference, by contrast, is considered more objective because it is observable; we manifest our preferences in the observable choices we make, and this forms a better basis for what mainstream economists expect from their discipline, namely, that it be an empirical science. Second, talk of utility suggests that we derive an 'amount' of something which makes us happy when we pursue a pleasurable activity. Thinking of utility as a quantity of pleasure might lead to statements like: 'I get twice as much utility from x than I do from y'. Such judgements are of dubious exactitude (see Sandel 2009). It would be difficult, for example, to make utility comparisons between the following:

- a foot massage
- a morning cup of coffee
- watching a baseball game on TV
- watching a baseball game live
- reading a novel by Dostoevsky
- learning a foreign language.

Can we state that a morning cup of coffee gives a person twice as much utility as a foot massage? And is the foot massage 2.7 times more pleasurable than watching a live baseball game? Answering these questions might be difficult, if not impossible. Luckily, mainstream economics does not assume that people can answer them; it suffices that people are able to say that they prefer x to y, without any quantitative comparison beyond that.

Consider a trickier question which brings us to a third problem with the notion of 'utility'. Can a person ascertain whether the utility which Peter derives from drinking a glass of champagne is greater or less than the utility Petra derives from drinking it, or greater or less than the utility Joseph derives from going for an evening stroll? The difficulty involved here concerns making *interpersonal comparisons of utility*. Economists hold that such comparative judgements lack an objective basis, and some hold such judgements to be unscientific or even meaningless. How do we know how much utility Peter gets from the champagne and can we compare it to Petra's utility from drinking it? Mainstream economics does not actually rely on such comparisons, and economists have even declared that such comparisons are meaningless (Arrow 1963) or, as William Stanley Jevons, to whom we referred above, thought, impossible.

The terminology of preference allows us to move from some simple assumptions about human beings, to the analysis one finds in *ECON 101* courses (e.g. indifference curve analysis and demand curves). The two main assumptions made about people's preferences are:

- *Completeness*: for any two options, x and y, a given consumer can rank x and y such that either x is preferred to y, y is preferred to x, or the two are equally preferred.
- *Transitivity*: if, for a given consumer, option x is preferred to option y, and option y is preferred to option z, then (by transitivity) option x is preferred to option z.

From the assumptions of complete and transitive preferences, the world of microeconomic analysis opens itself and *homo economicus* unfolds in all its glory. That, though, is something to explore in the pages of elementary microeconomics textbooks.

Critical perspectives

We have stated already that mainstream economics, however dominant it might be as a doctrine, is not without rivals and detractors. We present some of these 'heterodox' approaches to economics in the following chapter. In the remainder of this chapter, however, we focus on some limitations of mainstream economics.

Selfishness 'Self-love', as Smith called it, has been a lasting legacy in economics, and although Smith's other great book, *The Theory of Moral Sentiments* (1759 [1976]), shows that he did not believe that individuals were motivated by self-interest alone, mainstream economists have been remarkably resistant to relinquish the assumption that people are, by nature, self-interested. But is everything we do motivated by self-interest? Many of our choices might be, but what about when one volunteers for a local community project or helps a friend move house? These do not seem to be self-interested acts. Helping others, however, does not contradict *homo economicus* as long as one's motive is to further one's own self-interest. Mainstream economists have become quite creative in explaining apparently 'selfless' acts in terms of *homo economicus* (see Becker 1974).

A particularly eloquent formulation of such explanations came long before mainstream economics came into existence. The English philosopher, Thomas Hobbes (1588–1679), was once asked why he gave money to a beggar in London. Hobbes replied: 'I was in pain to consider the miserable condition of the old man; and now my alms, giving him some relief, doth also ease me' (Aubrey 1975: 166). Hobbes explained his act of charity in self-interested terms. Although the money Hobbes donated improved the situation of the old man, this was not Hobbes' motive; Hobbes gave the money so that he himself would feel 'eased'. As such, it was for the sake of increasing his own utility that Hobbes gave the money. Mainstream economists sometimes speak of the 'warm glow' effect one receives from acting in a way which increases the utility of others. So, one answer to the question why we help our friends move house is that we derive a good feeling ('warm glow') from doing so; without this, the economist would have us believe, we would refuse to help.

The question is: does *homo economicus* provide a plausible account of our motivation? Many people, including many non-mainstream economists, think not. One alternative explanation focuses not on whether one derives a warm glow from helping one's friend but on one *reason* for acting. If we are asked why we helped a friend move house, a perfectly natural answer is: 'Because I wanted to help her – it was a nice thing to do'. It would be odd if you replied: 'Because I wanted to receive a warm glow which would increase my utility'. We might actually receive a warm glow as a by-product of helping a friend, but this need not be the *reason* for our action. Once we acknowledge that one can have reasons for acting which do not have to do with self-interest, we can account for actions which pretty obviously do not maximize one's utility. Here are some examples: fighting in a war of independence at risk to one's own life might not be what maximizes your utility, but perhaps one feels a duty to fight; likewise, accompanying an aged relative in the last stages of their life might be a very arduous and painful experience, but one might do it nevertheless because one thinks it is right (see Sen 1977). But 'right', here, does not mean that we act in our individual self-interest; it might go against our self-interest because it pains us and means that we have to sacrifice other pursuits, e.g. our social life or university studies.

Key concepts: Freedom and coercion

Many scholars have asked whether we are truly free in our economic decisions. For example, a poor person is only as free as their financial resources allow; their socio-economic status determines the degree to which they are free to be truly rational economic actors. It may make sense to buy in bulk, because you can save on each unit in the long run, but if you don't have the money to buy 24 cans of soup at once, for example, then you will have to buy one at a time, paying the higher (and less rational) price. Another challenge to our freedom is the coercion we encounter in everyday situations. Some coercion is easy to see and understand. When we are under threat we might act in a way that is not of our free choosing. If one attends an outdoor music festival and suffers serious dehydration, one will likely pay $8 for a bottle of water because there is no other option (see Chapter 18 on the notion of rent-seeking and *rentiership*). Some scholars have argued that even when we are not under direct threat, we behave in ways that are coercive because of social and cultural expectations. If we do not comply with these norms then we might be sanctioned – e.g. ridiculed, excluded or even held legally accountable. While we can easily see coercion in cases of emergency or threat, something like buying new clothing for one's wardrobe every season is rarely understood as part of a broader coercive circumstance dictated by the culture around us.

Source: Hanson and Yosifon (2003–2004)

Are we really free to choose?   The next question we address is whether maximizing your utility or choosing according to our preferences actually enhances our self-interest. Recall that *homo economicus* is conceived to be a *free* individual, free to make the choices 'he' thinks will further 'his' self-interest most. Is this always the case? As a thought experiment, imagine that, under hypnosis, a person is 'programmed' to believe that jumping up and down 100 times is in their best interest. The person remembers nothing about being hypnotized, but, sure enough, they find themselves jumping up and down several times a day for no apparent reason, other than that they think they are increasing their utility by doing so. We would probably say that the person has been manipulated, and that their interests are not really served by jumping up and down. Their preference for jumping, one might say, is not their own preference but has been imposed on them externally and against their will.

This example might seem far-fetched, but consider another, made by heterodox economist John Kenneth Galbraith (1908–2006). What if our preferences are somehow created or constructed by others? Galbraith (1958) thought that businesses and corporations do precisely this through advertising; they make you want to buy certain products. If this is true, businesses and corporations not only produce the goods we consume but also the preferences which make us want to buy those same goods.

These examples raise the question about where our preferences come from. Many mainstream economists do not feel competent to answer this question and they assume, for simplicity, that people's preferences are simply given. Once we have our preferences – wherever they come from – economists think it is a good thing if our preferences are satisfied, because satisfying our preferences increases our utility. But if our preferences are not chosen freely by us but are, instead, the product of some kind of manipulation or indoctrination, it is not clear that satisfying our preferences is such a good thing. The point applies not only to our preferences for consumer goods, but also for other aspirations and goals. Consider a female university graduate in the 1950s, the best student in her cohort. She has grown up with gender stereotypes imparted to her by family, school and media sources. The stereotype has drummed into her the view that pursuing a professional career is less important for a woman than for a man; if she wishes to pursue a career at all, an 'appropriate' career for a woman, she has been told, is elementary school teaching. She has been told that other careers, such as being a university professor, lawyer or politician, are not the sort of thing in which women should get involved. Our university graduate becomes a school teacher and she believes her choice was made freely, for nobody forces her to become a teacher. And she believes that she furthers her own interests best by becoming a teacher. The question is: does her preference to become a teacher really represent her true interests? If not, we have reason to doubt whether acting on one's preferences always furthers one's interests. This calls into question the trait of *homo economicus* which holds that people know their own interests and act upon that knowledge.

Normative economics and the Pareto principle We described above how mainstream economists adopt the principle of a Pareto improvement to justify market transactions. Whilst this principle arguably provides some normative grounding for market transactions, it is limited when applied to public policy. Consider, for example, a government which is proposing a new tax. The tax would introduce a new top-rate tax on the super-rich, those earning an annual income over $5 million. With the proceeds of the tax, the government proposes to build affordable social housing in deprived urban neighbourhoods. Many people support this sort of redistributive measure (e.g. taxing the very rich to benefit the poor). According to the principle of Pareto improvement, however, the tax is not justified because the tax will make the rich worse off. However much better off the tax would make the poorest people in society, it cannot be justified as a Pareto improvement if it makes the rich even a little worse off. Even transferring a mere $10 from a multibillionaire to a pauper is ruled out by the Pareto principle. The adoption of the Pareto principle poses a limit to the normative reach of mainstream economics, and some economists are eager to transcend this limit (e.g. Sen 1987).

Conclusion

From a self-interested *homo economicus* through the principle of Pareto optimality to the determination of our preferences, in this chapter we have looked at how mainstream economics has sought to explain markets and prices on the basis that human beings are ultimately utility maximizers. Taking a critical perspective, we have questioned some of these assumptions: are we always selfish in our motivations? Are we capable of knowing and acting upon our preferences? Does economic rationale like the Pareto improvement always lead to the greatest good for the greatest number?

Mainstream economic theory, which we have examined critically in this chapter, is highly influential. It is, as we have stated, taught in the vast majority of economics departments the world over, often to the exclusion of alternative economic theories (see the following chapter on such theories). Mainstream economics is also highly influential in policy circles, be it in shaping national governments' policies (e.g. 'austerity') or the policies of international organizations such as the IMF or the WTO.

Remarkably, though, mainstream economics does not dominate the study of business. Although mainstream economics boasts a 'theory of the firm', the syllabi of business schools are not dominated by the mainstream. For instance, theories of organizational behaviour draw on the work of Herbert Simon, himself an influential economist, though not one who falls into the mainstream. Simon's analysis of decision-making in administrative organizations, like firms, highlights limits to the rationality of decision makers, as we did when discussing *homo economicus* above. Simon developed a theory of 'bounded rationality' to capture the less-than-perfect rationality of real human beings (Simon 1957, 1961). Furthermore, empirical studies of the firm have often found that decisions made by managers do not conform to the principles of mainstream economics; even profit maximization is not as clear a goal as some would believe. Studies of corporate power and concentration and of structures of property and ownership play an important role in understanding business, and these are themes traditionally neglected by mainstream economics.

So while it can be said that mainstream economics is not predominant when it comes to the study of business, it nonetheless shapes the economic policies and institutional frameworks within which business is conducted. Thus, we have introduced some principles of mainstream economics in this chapter so that the reader can understand policy debates and the economic analysis of global economic activity.

Suggested readings

- Ch. 2, Chang, H.-J. (2014) *Economics: The User's Guide*, New York, Bloomsbury Press.
- Ch. 1, Hill, R. and Myatt, T. (2010) *The Economics Anti-Textbook: A Critical Thinker's Guide to Microeconomics*, London, Zed Books.
- Ch. 10, Hunt, E.K. (2002) *History of Economic Thought: A Critical Perspective* (2nd Edition), New York, M.E. Sharpe.

Bibliography

Amoroso, L. (1938) 'Vilfredo Pareto', *Econometrica*, Vol.6, pp.1–21.

Arrow, K.J. (1963) *Social Choice and Individual Values* (2nd Edition), New Haven, Yale University Press.

Aubrey, J. (1975) *Brief Lives*, London, Folio Society.

Becker, G.S. (1974) 'A theory of social interaction', *Journal of Political Economy*, Vol.82, pp.1063–1093.

Bentham, J. (1780 [2011]) 'Principles of Morals and Legislation', in *Selected Writings*, New Haven, Yale University Press, pp.102–151.

Dixit, A. (2014) *Microeconomics: A Very Short Introduction*, Oxford, Oxford University Press.

Ferber, M. and Nelson, J. (eds) (1993) *Beyond Economic Man: Feminist Theory and Economics*, Chicago, University of Chicago Press.

Galbraith, J.K. (1958) *The Affluent Society*, Boston, Riverside Press.

Hanson, J. and Yosifon, D. (2003–2004) 'The situation: An introduction to the situational character, critical realism, power economics and deep capture', *University of Pennsylvania Law Review*, Vol.152, pp.149–201.

Hill, R. and Myatt, T. (2010) *The Economics Anti-Textbook: A Critical Thinker's Guide to Microeconomics*, London, Zed Books.

Phillips, P. (2003) *Inside Capitalism: An Introduction to Political Economy*, Halifax NS, Fernwood.

Sandel, M.J. (2009) *Justice: What's the Right Thing To Do?*, New York, Farrar, Straus & Giroux.

Scott, S. (2013) *Architectures of Economic Subjectivity*, London, Routledge.

Sen, A.K. (1977) 'Rational fools: A critique of the behavioural foundations of economic theory', *Philosophy and Public Affairs*, Vol.6, pp.317–344.

Sen, A.K. (1987) *On Ethics and Economics*, Oxford, Blackwell.

Simon, H.A. (1957) *Models of Man: Social and Rational*, New York, Wiley.

Simon, H.A. (1961) *Administrative Behavior: A Study of Decision-Making Processes in Administrative Organizations*, New York, Macmillan.

Smith, A. (1759 [1976]) *The Theory of Moral Sentiments*, Oxford, Oxford University Press.

Smith, A. (1776 [2000]) *The Wealth of Nations*, Toronto, Random House.

Varian, H. (2007) *Intermediate Microeconomics: A Modern Approach* (7th Edition), New York, W.W. Norton.

Walras, L. (1874 [1954]) *Elements of Pure Economics or the Theory of Social Wealth*, Homewood IL, Richard D. Irwin.

12 | Political economy and critiques of capitalism: heterodox perspectives

Sonya Scott

Introduction

Now that we have discussed mainstream or 'orthodox' economics, we can turn to critical perspectives. While mainstream economics is widely accepted as the correct form of economic reasoning within universities today, there are other ways of doing economics and other valuable forms of economic knowledge. These different approaches can be grouped in the category of 'heterodox economics'.

Defining heterodox economics is not easy because so many different thinkers and schools of thought fall under its banner. Generally speaking, heterodox economics can be defined negatively; that is, in terms of what it is not. Some have even gone so far as to argue that 'the only widely recognized and accepted feature of all the heterodox tradition is a rejection of the modern mainstream project' (Lawson 2006: 485). It is safe to say that heterodox economics rejects some or even all aspects of mainstream economics. But why would anyone choose to reject the mainstream?

The reason people distinguish between mainstream and heterodox economics is both intellectual and political. In some cases it is a question of methodology – many heterodox economists disagree with the methods and models of mainstream economics because they believe that they are not useful in explaining or predicting economic reality. In other cases, the distinction is political – many heterodox economists believe that the mainstream economics entrenches existing power relations and gross injustices within capitalism. In this sense heterodox economics can serve as an alternative to the *status quo* (i.e. capitalism), and seeks actively to reshape our economy and society.

Now that we have seen some general indications of what heterodox economics is against, we want to note what it supports. Because of the great variety of heterodox thinkers this is not an easy issue to address. The goal of this chapter is to present the ideas of several key figures or theories in the heterodox tradition – both inside and outside of the classroom.

Dominant heterodox perspectives

The Marxian critique of capitalism   The first and most historically significant heterodox theorist is Karl Marx (1818–1883). Chapter 1 dealt with some of Marx's ideas in detail, exploring his theory of the emergence of capitalism. In Chapter 10, we discussed the Marxian understanding of the social division of labour. Here we look at Marx from two perspectives. First, we explore his criticism of the mainstream rational economic man (*homo economicus*) and, second, we explore how this criticism develops into an indictment of an economic system based on exploitation and alienation.

Many people associate Marx with socialism and communism, and some even read him only in light of the many socialist regimes which have sprung up in the twentieth century such as the USSR, Cuba and China. But Marx's work focused primarily on the capitalist system that was transforming the world and the lives of all those who came into contact with it in his time. In fact, Marx was mainly concerned with relationships that people experience in capitalism; he argued that despite the fact that 'economic' relationships look like rational and free-willed interactions between individuals as described by mainstream economists (see Chapter 11), they are actually class relations, because each individual is part of a larger group called a *social class*.

Class, for Marx, was defined by the way in which we relate to *capital*. Capital can be thought of, roughly speaking, as the money and resources needed to conduct and finance business (e.g. property, factories, equipment and money). But none of these things represent capital if they are not also part of a social relationship, or part of a structure of ownership and power. Those who own and control capital are members of the capitalist class, or capitalists; Marx also referred to this class as the *bourgeoisie*. In nineteenth-century Europe they would have been the owners of factories and industry. Those who do not own and control capital, having only control over their own person and capacity to work, are the working class, or the *proletariat*. The bourgeoisie requires the proletariat to work in their factories and for their businesses in order to produce and return a profit. The proletariat requires work in the factories in order to receive a wage.

Marx criticized what he termed 'bourgeois economics' – or, the mainstream economics of his day – for basing its system of thought on the false claim that the individual is free. Instead, he argued that our position in the class structure of society – that is, as either worker or capitalist – is not the result of the superiority of one person's skill or work effort over that of another. This is due not only to the fact that the worker is bound by their class to agree to work for the capitalist, but also to the fact that paid work (or wage labour) is a special kind of relationship. An employee does not simply make an agreement of employment; instead they sell their own labour power, time and vital energies, as a commodity for the capitalist to use in the production process. This labour, when put into action in the production process, will produce surplus – goods worth more than the component parts that went into them in the first place. This idea is called the *labour theory of value* – and it is the foundation of Marx's economics. It is not simple exchange – buying cheap and selling dear – that produces profit in a capitalist system, but rather the labour of workers that does so, but they do not get to keep this surplus. At its heart, the fundamental relationship of capitalism is *exploitation* – the use of the worker's labour to make profit for the capitalist (Marx 1867 [1976]).

Within capitalism, competition is held to be of paramount importance. Many have argued that competition in perfectly free markets will promote creativity, innovation and efficiency (e.g. Smith 1776 [2000]; Hayek 1948 [1992]; Freidman 1962). Marx, however, attacked this belief, arguing instead that 'competition isolates individuals, not only the bourgeois but even more the proletarians, despite the fact that it brings them together' (Marx and Engels 1845–1846 [1947]: 142). Even though people both live and work in close proximity, the relationship between people becomes more functional, instrumental and isolating. The feeling of isolation and anonymity that one can feel in a big city is a perfect example of this. Thinkers like Marx call this isolation *alienation*. According to Marx, there are four fundamental forms of alienation in a capitalist economy:

- *Alienation from the product of one's labour*: once workers exchange their labour for a wage, they *alienate* (or give up) their right to control the things they produce.
- *Alienation from the labour process*: the very process of working is controlled by employers (or capitalists). As a result Marx commented that workers often become an 'appendage of the machine', like tools to be used in the production process.

- *Alienation from oneself*: Marx believed that labour is the very essence of human nature. Thus, when we sell our labour to another we sell the most vital aspect of our selves.
- *Alienation from others*: in a society divided by class, workers are rarely able to connect with one another in a meaningful way due to alienating working conditions, long hours and the isolation of modern life.

Given Marx's belief that *homo economicus* was a fiction which conveniently served the interests of the capitalist class as it justified an exploitative relationship by calling it 'free' or designating it merely a question of contract, and given that he believed that the fundamental structure of capitalism was based on exploitation and alienation, many have read Marx's work as a call to change an unjust system. In fact, few political or economic thinkers have had as much influence on the world, inspiring resistance and revolution against the capitalist system.

An American critique: institutional economics In the late 1800s the USA underwent significant social and economic change. As we discussed in Chapter 3, the US experienced the rise of a new business model – that of the modern corporation. In the midst of these changes, some historians, legal scholars and economists started to insist upon the need to understand the economy historically, as part of a broader evolution. The development of neoclassical economics at the same time (see Chapter 11) took the individual as its starting point and did not consider historical context, instead trying to establish universal and objective economic laws. A number of *institutional economists* challenged this idea, focusing specifically on the role of institutions in the economy, hence the name 'institutional economists'. The institutional economist John R. Commons (1931: 649) defined institutions as follows:

> Collective action ranges all the way from unorganized custom to the many organized going concerns, such as the family, the corporation, the trade association, the trade union, the reserve system, the state. The principle common to all of them is greater or less control, liberation and expansion of individual action by collective action.

There are several important thinkers who are part of this tradition, most notably Thorstein Veblen (1857–1929) and John R. Commons (1862–1945). Veblen was famous for his critique of what he termed 'the leisure class' – those who lived by the labour of others and actively flaunted their wealth in order to maintain their status and power through leisure activities and lavish patterns of '**conspicuous consumption**' (Veblen 1899). Commons was a labour economist concerned with the legal system and the way that law could influence the development of the economy and vice versa (Commons 1931). Both thinkers challenged the idea that the individual acts in such a way as suggested by mainstream economics. As humans, they claimed, we are embedded in social, historical and legal institutional contexts.

> **Key concept: 'Conspicuous consumption'**
>
> Veblen developed a theory of the leisure class at the end of the nineteenth century. This theory gives us insight as to how and why some of the most wealthy and powerful players in the US economy would behave in a way that appeared to be irrational and 'wasteful' of both time and resources. He argued that engaging in leisure activities, refraining from work and consuming luxury goods was not an activity of simple preference or personal indulgence. Instead consumption was a notably 'conspicuous', or publicly obvious, performance in order to establish social status and power:
>
> > Since the consumption of these more excellent goods is an evidence of wealth, it becomes honorific; and conversely, the failure to consume in due quantity becomes a mark of inferiority and demerit. (Veblen 1899 [1994]: 74)
>
> Lavish parties and galas, the finest furnishings and fashions, all were part of a social and political practice to demonstrate superiority over those who had to labour or merely had enough to survive. Given the importance of conspicuous consumption in the formative stages of US industrialism we might question what traces of these practices have affected mainstream consumer society today.
>
> *Source*: Veblen (1899 [1994])

Common to these 'old' institutional economists (not to be confused with *new institutional economics*, which developed in the 1980s and has very different objectives) are six fundamental beliefs about how we should understand capitalism. These are listed in Table 12.1.

TABLE 12.1 Principles of 'old' institutional economics

The individual	Economic behaviour is not independently self-motivated; it is shaped by the institutional environment of the individual.
History	History is evolutionary, economics is evolutionary as well. Change is what defines our society and economy.
Technology	Technological development is a crucial consideration when analysing the nature of the economy. Our technologies shape our history and are shaped by our history.
The market	The market is characterized by competition and conflict. It is not harmonious or self-regulating as the mainstream approach might suggest.
Institutions	Institutions can be shaped and altered to better serve the needs of people in society.
Economics	Economic analysis depends upon more than mathematical models alone. Instead, disciplines such as psychology, anthropology and law can be used to more fully understand human economic behaviour.

Source: Mercuro and Medema (2006)

Institutional economics has had a lasting influence on legal activism, the labour movement and on proponents of the welfare state. Perhaps the most important idea of its legacy is that economics is not an arena of human activity to be understood separately from other aspects of society, but rather that it is actively shaped, defended or changed through institutions, such as law and government regulation (see Chapter 13). Instead of self-regulating markets which will inherently take care of themselves and all of those who live in any particular economy, we have human institutions that can define and defend structures that respond to human needs.

A mainstream alternative: Keynesian macroeconomics John Maynard Keynes (1883–1946) was a British economist who had a tremendous influence on the discipline of economics and on economic policy from the 1930s until the 1970s. In this section we focus on the way Keynes challenged many assumptions regarding our economic natures and the nature of the economy. He is notorious for challenging the mainstream belief that humans are fundamentally rational, and even more so for questioning many of the core principles of *laissez-faire* economics by promoting government investment in the economy during times of recession (Keynes 1936).

Unlike mainstream economists who tend to argue that we know and act upon our preferences when making economic decisions (see Chapter 11), Keynes claimed that our economic reality is marked by uncertainty (Scott 2013). Two undeniable aspects of the human condition are *time* and *ignorance*. Time, because decisions made today are usually made with certain expectations of the future, and ignorance, because we cannot be certain of what the future might hold. For example, a government may choose to dedicate its resources to investing in and promoting an industry like oil with the expectation that oil prices will remain high, but then face plummeting oil prices and its consequences (e.g. unemployment).

We are not simply the victims of the future, however, because we are constantly revising our expectations based on new inputs. As a whole, this makes for a rather complex system:

> the state of expectation is liable to constant change, a new expectation being superimposed long before the previous change has fully worked itself out; so that the economic machine is occupied at any given time with a number of overlapping activities, the existence of which is due to various past states of expectation. (Keynes 1936: 50)

With so much uncertainty and constantly changing expectations, what might prompt people to make economic decisions at all? The decision to buy this or that good might seem relatively harmless, but what about the decision to start a business, to invest, to take a risk? While Keynes did believe that individuals were free to make their own choices, he did not think that rationality was the sole driving factor behind our free economic choices. Instead an internal 'spontaneous optimism', what Keynes called our *animal spirits*, prompts individuals to take risks and make risky economic choices. This inherent characteristic of our economic nature is so important, he argued, that it is essential for the very operation of a capitalist economy (Scott 2013).

On a structural level, Keynesian economics differs from the mainstream, resting upon the fundamental belief that private decisions alone will not necessarily lead to the most successful or stable economy. Sometimes government decisions are required in order to temper market forces. As a result, the idea that government must borrow in tough times in order to increase productivity and maintain employment in the economy became standard across Western economies between 1945 and the late 1970s. The shift to neoliberal economic principles since the 1980s and 1990s unseated Keynes as the dominant macroeconomic theorist, though the great financial crisis of 2008 has reinvigorated support for Keynesian economic policy in some quarters (Krugman 2011).

Alternative heterodox perspectives

The above-mentioned approaches are all critical of capitalism and the mainstream economics that supports and promotes it. Some are anti-capitalist, such as Marx, while institutionalists and Keynes were working to make capitalism more equitable yet leaving its basic structure intact. The same range of positions can be found in more recent heterodox perspectives, which we turn to next.

Feminist political economy Feminism is popularly associated within the Western liberal tradition with equal gender rights – that is, the right to vote, to hold office, to own property, to make decisions regarding reproductive health and so on. Yet many civil liberties struggles have extended well beyond the scope of political rights into the realm of economics. Feminist scholars and activists like Barker and Kuiper (2003), Ferber and Nelson (2009) and Fraser (2013) argue that despite women acquiring many political and social rights, economics remains a site of deep inequality within contemporary gender relations. This is primarily because formal rights – rights that see women and men as equal under the law – are of little importance if the economic situation of women does not practically allow for equal opportunity, education, freedom from domestic violence and financial security to raise children with dignity.

We should be careful here when we talk about 'women'. The situation of women within the Global North, for example, varies with that of women in the Global South (Walby 2009), as does the experience of women within their societies (see Chapter 15). In other words, the experience of women varies across countries, across classes, across ethnicity, race and sexuality. Even in societies where women enjoy a high degree of formal freedom, women's experience may be highly dependent upon their socio-economic status. Women who are privileged are more likely to be educated, to have professional careers and to hire help to offset traditional women's labour such as housekeeping, cooking and child-rearing. Women who are marginalized are more prone to bear the uneven brunt of poverty, often obliged to work several jobs and take care of domestic labour. Of course this disparity is further exacerbated when we consider the many social barriers posed by racism (Bullock 2013). Consider that within the Global North women of colour make up a disproportionate percentage of the most poorly paid and most precarious workforce (Fuller and Vosko 2008). Women in the Global South are responsible for more labour than their male counterparts but are rarely rewarded with wages, social prestige or political rights. In fact, the great majority of the one billion poorest inhabitants of the world today are women (United Nations Womenwatch 2015).

Part of the reason for the state of affairs is the structural history of *patriarchy* – which sees wealth and family lineage pass along the male line, and divides labour and worth accordingly. Not all societies have been patriarchal throughout human history, as there are instances of matrilineal and shared political regimes. Prior to European colonization, for example, the Iroquois/Haudenosaunee of North America had a matrilineal social structure, which saw kinship determined along the mother's line, and had shared responsibility for political power (Baskin 1982). Patriarchy, however, is the dominant form in most contemporary capitalist societies, and was instrumental in shaping the labour relations between men and women as the Industrial Revolution unfolded.

Another reason for the persistence of gendered inequality has to do with the way that mainstream economics measures value. Marilyn Waring (1999) has brought the issue to public attention through her studies of national accounting practices. She argues that only certain types of activities and resources are given economic value; for example, when calculating the sum total of economic activity of a nation (i.e. GDP), only certain types of activity get counted. We can count goods bought and sold, along with wages paid, but the activities such as bearing and raising children, teaching them social skills and values, doing housework and caring for family members – what is called **social reproduction** – often remains invisible. In mainstream economic terms, these activities have 'no value' because they are not measured and accounted for.

The invisibility of domestic labour is important for several reasons. First, it lies at the very heart of the mainstream economic method. As we saw in the previous chapter, mainstream economics became a mathematical 'science' by rendering economic phenomena quantifiable through price. Unpaid labour, since it has no price, is not considered part of the general economic activity of a nation. This may seem natural, as we have internalized the idea that things

Key concept: Social reproduction

Social reproduction refers to the labour required to maintain people in our society. The term was specifically developed by Marx in order to identify the task of *reproducing* the working class so that they could *produce* for society. In feminist terms the concept of social reproduction then refers to the specific labour of raising and caring for people – raising and educating children, imparting social values and knowledge, providing a clean environment, food, shelter, clothing and care, and the emotional support needed to cope with daily life. This labour has traditionally been gendered labour – that is, labour carried out by women. It has also been (and continues to be) typically unpaid labour, carried out in the private sphere of the home instead of the public realm of the formal labour market.

Source: Bezason and Luxton (2006)

like cooking, cleaning, raising children and taking care of the elderly should bear no discernible cost. But this is a socially constructed and historically situated belief. Many feminists have argued that there is no scientific basis upon which one can assert that women are better at caring for and cleaning up after their families than men (Davis 1983; Guillaumin 1988). The notion that work involving 'caring' and other domestic tasks is 'unskilled' has led to the consistent undervaluation of work in traditionally female professions such as nursing, early childhood education and many jobs within the service industry (Fudge and Vosko 2001).

The second reason this is so important is because the national accounting system helps to determine government objectives and national budgets. Because childcare is invisible, national governments often do not invest in affordable public daycare, meaning that women, especially those with low to middle incomes, cannot afford to go out and work in order to gain financial and personal independence. If the labour of women in the Global South is almost completely invisible, while war is extremely profitable, then why would wealthy nations focus on aid, fair trade and debt relief instead of war and military initiatives? Feminist political economists argue that we must redefine value and begin to make the invisible visible in order to change society (e.g. bell hooks 2000).

Anarchist economics Anarchism is commonly associated with political movements instead of economics (see Chapter 16). But, as with all heterodox economic traditions, anarchist thought involves a consideration of the state, the market and the nature of economic relationships. Emma Goldman (1869–1940) was an influential anarchist activist and thinker in the US and Canada in the early twentieth century. She defined anarchism as the fundamental liberation from many of the constraints imposed by the capitalist system and the state:

> Anarchism, then, really stands for the liberation of the human from the dominion of religion; the liberation of the human body from the dominion of property; liberation from the shackles and restraint of government. Anarchism stands for a social order based on the free grouping of individuals for the purpose of producing real social wealth, an order that will guarantee to every human being free access to the earth and full enjoyment of the necessities of life, according to individual desires, tastes, and inclinations. (Goldman 1910: 68)

A common feature of anarchism, therefore, is the shared goal of freeing human society from the institutions which govern by hierarchy and power, such as the government, the system of unequally distributed wealth and the Church. Goldman was not the first to express such ideas. She was influenced by several important classical European anarchist thinkers such as Pierre-Joseph Proudhon (1809–1865), Mikhail Bakunin (1814–1876) and Peter Kropotkin (1842–1921).

All three of these thinkers critiqued both capitalism *and* state power, at the same time that they were imagining new and more equitable forms of socio-economic organization. For example, Proudhon is famous for his denunciation of private property (see Introduction) and his advocacy of *mutualism*, a system of economic cooperation where workers control the means of production and exchange with one another on the basis of what each has produced. His system promoted worker associations as a way to ensure cooperation, credit and exchange (Marshall 1993). Bakunin also developed a form of anarchism that was fundamentally social. He ardently opposed the hierarchical power exercised by the state and by capitalist business; he nonetheless proposed to organize economic activity with cooperative principles (see Chapters 16 and 17). Finally, Kropotkin developed a theory of evolutionary anarchism that built upon scientific theories of the nineteenth century. Unlike Social Darwinists, however, who use evolutionary theory to argue that humans are inherently competitive, Kropotkin argued that *mutual aid* and *cooperation* are the most important features of our evolutionary past:

> we maintain that under *any* circumstances sociability is the greatest advantage in the struggle for life. Those species which willingly or unwillingly abandon it are doomed to decay; while those animals which know how best to combine have the greatest chances of survival for further evolution. (1902 [1939]: 60–61)

Contemporary anarchist thought is quite diverse and overlaps with many other schools of thought. In the popular imagination it is most often associated with the 'alter-globalization' movement that began to gain considerable momentum in the late 1990s and early 2000s (see Chapter 16), and with other protest movements today, like Occupy Wall Street (el-Ojeili 2014). But anarchist economics are not fundamentally about protest movements. Instead, anarchist economics focuses on developing alternative models of social organization, production and distribution (Parker et al. 2007). While there are a great number of contemporary anarchist movements, including those that focus on questions of ecology and the environment (Bookchin 1986), and those that focus on freedom for traditionally marginalized groups such as women and people of colour (Dark Star Collective 2012), the most developed school of anarchist economic thought focuses on *participatory economics*, also known as *parecon*. People like Michael Albert (1997) emphasize the importance of 'economic vision', which involves actively conceptualizing goals and values rather than simply conforming to current models or the *status quo*. Participatory economics relies on five basic principles in its plan to *transform* the economy into an economy that relies upon active participation of its members:

> 1) social rather than private ownership; 2) worker and consumer . . . councils
> rather than corporate workplace organizations; 3) remuneration for effort and
> sacrifice rather than for property, power or output; 4) participatory planning
> rather than markets or central planning; 5) participatory self-management
> rather than class rule. (Albert 2003: 84)

While no society runs upon these principles yet, some of these guiding ideals can be seen at work in cooperative organizations and worker-managed industries (see Chapter 16).

Common property resource economics As we discuss in Chapter 9, environmental issues and sustainability are undoubtedly a part of our public consciousness today (Klein 2014). Here we take up the question of how ecological concerns interact with mainstream economic ideas, specifically by looking at the question of 'the commons' (also see Chapters 16 and 18), or common property resource economics.

Elinor Ostrom (2009), a Nobel Prize-winning economist and advocate of the institutional management of natural resources, famously wrote about ways in which to manage 'common pool resources' (such as forests, fisheries, water sources, oil reserves etc.) without relying strictly on the market or on government agencies. In other words, she sought to resolve what Garrett Hardin (1968) described as the 'tragedy of the commons'. Hardin used the example of a pasture that was open to all, where each individual would increase their own use to the detriment of others. The logic of individual benefit, unlike the theory presented by Adam Smith, is in fact what results in a detrimental impact on society:

Therein is the tragedy. Each man is locked into a system that compels him to increase his herd without limit – in a world that is limited. Ruin is the destination toward which all men rush, each pursuing his own best interest in a society that believes in the freedom of the commons. (Hardin 1968: 1244)

In contrast, Ostrom's studies, based on a new institutional approach, focused on the ways in which institutions can mitigate the logic of individual appropriation while not resorting to whole-scale state control. Much like the definition of institutions that we saw with the old institutional economists such as Veblen and Commons, this notion of institution is inherently evolutionary and does not provide a blueprint for the management of common public resources. The mixture of public and private solutions to the management of collective resources forces us to go beyond the belief that privatization can solve all problems, or that government is the only reliable manager of common goods. Institutions can thus be a source of economic order that escape the traditional market–state dualism discussed in Chapter 10. For example,

---

Case study

'Idle No More' campaign, Canada

In 2012, after the tar sands of Northern Alberta and Saskatchewan (see Chapter 9) became a hot-button issue in Canada and the USA, a popular indigenous movement arose to confront the logic of the private appropriation of land and natural resources in Canada. Named 'Idle No More' by its founders, and using traditional (pre-colonial) knowledge of land use and strategies of political participation, the movement challenges the profit-oriented logic of the mainstream. Tens of thousands have participated in sit-ins, marches and rallies across Canada and the United States, and millions have now visited their website. In their manifesto they write:

> The state of Canada has become one of the wealthiest countries in the world by using the land and resources. Canadian mining, logging, oil and fishing companies are the most powerful in the world due to land and resources. Some of the poorest First Nations communities (such as Attawapiskat) have mines or other developments on their land but do not get a share of the profit. The taking of resources has left many lands and waters poisoned – the animals and plants are dying in many areas in Canada. We cannot live without the land and water. We have laws older than this colonial government about how to live with the land.

The historical context of Idle No More's critique is very important, as the movement works to undo many of the assumptions of mainstream economics insofar as these assumptions drove the economic strategies of European settler-colonialism in the Americas. As Coulthard (2014: 152) has pointed out in his recent work on colonial relations in Canada, 'settler-colonialism is territorially acquisitive in perpetuity'. What this means is that the colonial relationship which began when European colonial forces

Ostrom (1990: 185) argued that in many cases small communities can 'supply themselves with new rules, gain quasi-voluntary compliance with those rules, and monitor each other's conformance to the rules' in order to use and share natural resources in a sustainable and collectively beneficial manner. This can often influence larger-scale institutional change at the regional or national levels, but is fundamentally based upon the principle of actively making rules and living with the consequences of these rules (i.e. creating dynamic institutions) in an immediate and locally managed setting, with sustainability and renewability as goals instead of profit alone (see Case Study on the 'Idle No More' campaign in Canada).

Taking the debate out of the classroom There has been a growing popular and academic movement against mainstream economics since 2000. In 2000–2001 French professors of economics and their students started a public campaign against university curricula requiring students to learn mainstream

---

settled North America in the seventeenth century was based on the acquisition of land and resources at the expense of the indigenous populations and their ways of life. The appropriation continues today and often manifests itself concretely through the erosion of treaty rights that were historically established to secure certain pieces of territory and resources for indigenous peoples, and through changes in environmental legislation regarding the use of natural resources.

Idle No More was founded as a direct response to Canadian legislation passed in December 2012 called *Bill C-45*. This Bill included revisions to environmental legislation and the *Indian Act*, redefining the way in which business is conducted, and making the use and acquisition of indigenous territory and resources easier for big business. Coulthard (2014: 160) explains:

> from the perspective of many Indigenous people and communities, the changes contained in Bill C-45 threaten to erode Aboriginal land and treaty rights insofar as they reduce the amount of resource development projects that require environmental assessment; they change the regulations that govern on-reserve leasing in a way that will make it easier for special interests to access First Nation reserve lands for the purposes of economic development and settlement; and they radically curtail environmental protections for lakes and rivers.

While this legislation enables the mainstream logic of growth and private resource appropriation to gain greater ground in the Canadian economy, Idle No More has brought many of these issues into public consciousness, and many hope that some of the incursions into indigenous land and rights will be resisted and that alternative forms of economic development will be sought.

Sources: www.idlenomore.ca; Coulthard (2014)

economics without allowing for alternative viewpoints or methods. This movement was called the 'post-autistic economics' movement and it critiques the inward-looking and dogmatic nature of the economics discipline. In one of their petitions, the French students explain the problem with the way mainstream economics is taught in universities:

> This approach is supposed to explain everything by means of a purely
> axiomatic process, as if this were THE economic truth. We do not accept this
> dogmatism. We want a pluralism of approaches, adapted to the complexity
> of the objects and to the uncertainty surrounding most of the big questions
> in economics (unemployment, inequalities, the place of financial markets,
> the advantages and disadvantages of free-trade, globalization, economic
> development, etc.).[1]

This movement gained popularity throughout many parts of Europe and North America, and the inclusion of heterodox economics is starting to take place especially in interdisciplinary departments and programmes. But this movement is only one side of a contemporary tendency to challenge the mainstream, one that has started in the place where the mainstream is most powerful, the university. Others have taken the case against mainstream assumptions out of the classroom and into the realm of public protest (Newman 2014).

Economic crises, such as the 2007–2008 global financial crisis (GFC), often draw attention to the state of economic thought. After all, when things go very wrong, we often question whether our beliefs and assumptions are accurate. In the case of the GFC, much attention was focused on the nature of the distribution of wealth in society. After a long process of financial deregulation, where entire industries and forms of investment were left to a free and self-making marketplace, many started to question the role of the neoclassical economists who promoted deregulation, low corporate taxation, tax shelters for the ultra-rich and governments who bailed out risky and reckless industries with public monies. Many also started to see the correlation between these practices and the growing gap in the distribution of wealth worldwide (Piketty 2014).

As a result, several popular movements against inequality have arisen. This includes the Occupy Wall Street movement, which started in New York in 2011 following the financial meltdown and the resulting increase in rates of unemployment, loss of middle-class savings and cuts to government spending on social services (van Gelder 2011). It also involves the anti-austerity movements in Europe, especially prominent in Spain and Greece. Both of these countries suffered massive economic turmoil and the imposition of harsh cutbacks in government spending and social welfare (termed 'austerity measures'). These movements have raised a public voice against many of the practical results of

1 Real World Economics: www.paecon.net (accessed June 2016).

mainstream economics. They point to the irony of intensifying the practices of neoliberalism, which uses mainstream principles as its justification, to alleviate the very problems caused by neoliberal policies (Flassbeck and Lapavitsas 2015).

Conclusion

This chapter has explored some of the most historically influential proponents of heterodox economics. While we have shown that heterodox economics encapsulates a great variety of ideas and approaches, we also want to emphasize that it is united in its critique of mainstream economics. Contemporary movements are putting many heterodox ideas into practice, calling for other values, such as environmental sustainability, gender and racial equality, democratic accountability and the reduction of global inequality, to enter into public consciousness and policy debate. How these voices will impact future economic policy and our democratic landscape remains to be seen.

Suggested readings

- Ch. 10, Marx, K. (1859 [1990]) *Capital: A Critique of Political Economy, Volume One*, trans. Ben Fowkes, New York, Penguin.
- Ch. 4, Veblen, T. (1899 [1994]) *Theory of the Leisure Class*, New York, Penguin.
- Chs. 12 and 15, Keynes, J.M. (1936) *The General Theory of Employment, Interest and Money*, London, Macmillan.
- Ch. 9, Fraser, N. (2013) *Fortunes of Feminism: From State-managed Capitalism to Neoliberal Crisis*, New York, Verso.

Bibliography

Albert, M. (1997) *Thinking Forward: Learning to Conceptualize Economic Vision*, Winnipeg, Arbeiter Ring.

Albert, M. (2003) *Parecon: Life after Capitalism*, New York, Verso.

Barker, D. and Kuiper, E. (eds) (2003) *Towards a Feminist Theory of Economics*, New York, Routledge.

Baskin, C. (1982) 'Women in Iroquois society', *Canadian Women Studies*, Vol.4, pp.42–46.

Bezanson, K. and Luxton, M. (2006) *Social Reproduction*, Montreal, McGill-Queen's University Press.

Bookchin, M. (1986) *Post-Scarcity Anarchism*, Montreal, Black Rose Press.

Bullock, H. (2013) *Women and Poverty: Psychology, Public Policy and Social Justice*, Chichester, Wiley Blackwell.

Commons, J.R. (1931) 'Institutional economics', *The American Economic Review*, Vol.21, pp.648–657.

Coulthard, G.S. (2014) *Red Skin, White Masks: Rejecting the Colonial Politics of Recognition*, Minneapolis, University of Minnesota Press.

Dark Star Collective (2012) *Quiet Rumors: An Anarcha-Feminist Reader*, San Francisco, AK Press.

Davis, A. (1983) *Women, Race and Class*, New York, Vintage Books.

el-Ojeili, C. (2014) 'Anarchism as the spirit of contemporary anti-capitalism? A critical survey of recent debates', *Critical Sociology*, Vol.40, pp.451–468.

Ferber, M. and Nelson, J. (eds) (2009) *Beyond Economic Man: Feminist Theory and Economics*, Chicago, University of Chicago Press.

Flassbeck, H. and Lapavitsas, C. (2015) *Against the Troika: Crisis and Austerity in the Eurozone*, New York, Verso.

Fraser, N. (2013) *Fortunes of Feminism*, New York, Verso.

Friedman, M. (1962) *Capitalism and Freedom*, Chicago, University of Chicago Press.

Fudge, J. and Vosko, L. (2001) 'Gender, segmentation, and the standard employment relationship in Canadian labour law, legislation and policy', *Economic and Industrial Democracy*, Vol.22, pp.271–310.

Fuller, S. and Vosko, L. (2008) 'Temporary employment and social inequality in Canada: Exploring intersections of gender, race and immigration status', *Social Indicators Research*, Vol.88, pp.31–50.

Goldman, E. (1910) 'Anarchism: What it really stands for', in *Anarchism and Other Essays*, New York, Mother Earth Publishing.

Guillaumin, C. (1988) 'Race and nature: The system of marks: The idea of a natural group and social relationships', *Feminist Issues*, Vol.8, pp.25–43.

Hardin, G. (1968) 'The tragedy of the commons', *Science*, Vol.162, pp.1243–1248.

Hayek, Friedrich (1948 [1992]) *Individualism and Economic Order*, Chicago, University of Chicago Press.

hooks, bell (2000) *Where We Stand: Class Matters*, New York, Routledge.

Keynes, J.M. (1936) *The General Theory of Employment, Interest and Money*, London, Macmillan.

Klein, N. (2014) *This Changes Everything: Capitalism vs. the Climate*, New York, Simon and Schuster.

Kropotkin, P. (1902 [1939]) *Mutual Aid: A Factor in Revolution*, Harmondsworth, Penguin.

Krugman, P. (2011) 'Keynes was right', *The New York Times*, 29 December.

Lawson, T. (2006) 'The nature of heterodox economics', *Cambridge Journal of Economics*, Vol.30, pp.483–505.

Marshall, P. (1993) *A History of Anarchism*, London, Harper Perennial.

Marx, K. (1867 [1976]) *Capital: Volume 1*, London, Penguin.

Marx, K. and Engels, F. (1845–1846 [1947]) *The German Ideology*, ed. R. Pascal, New York, International Publishers.

Mercuro, N. and Medema, S. (2006) *Economics and the Law: From Posner to Post-Modernism and Beyond* (2nd Edition), Princeton, Princeton University Press.

Newman, J. (2014) 'Governing the present: Activism, neoliberalism and the problem of power and consent', *Critical Policy Studies*, Vol.8, pp.133–147.

Ostrom, E. (1990) *Governing the Commons: The Evolution of Institutions for Collective Action*, New York, Cambridge University Press.

Parker, M., Fournier, V. and Reedy, P. (2007) *The Dictionary of Alternatives: Utopianism and Organization*, London, Zed Books.

Piketty, T. (2014) *Capital in the Twenty First Century*, Cambridge MA, Harvard University Press.

Scott, S. (2013) *Architectures of Economic Subjectivity*, London, Routledge.

Smith, A. ([1776] 2000) *The Wealth of Nations*, New York, The Modern Library.

United Nations Womenwatch (2015), www.un.org/womenwatch (accessed September 2016).

van Gelder, S. (ed.) (2011) *This Changes Everything: Occupy Wall Street and the 99% Movement*, San Francisco, Barrett-Koehler.

Veblen, T. (1899 [1994]) *Theory of the Leisure Class*, New York, Penguin.

Walby, S. (2009) *Globalization and Inequalities: Complexity and Contested Modernities*, London, Sage.

Waring, M. (1999) *Counting for Nothing: What Men Value and What Women Are Worth* (2nd Edition), Toronto, University of Toronto Press.

13 | Business, regulation and policy

Richard Wellen

Introduction

There are few more important and controversial topics for public policy than the regulation of business. At a general level, we can say that regulation is the set of rules, norms and enforcement (or sanctioning) mechanisms that are used by the state – or other authorities – to control and steer socially important activities such as business. Regulation itself is not always performed by the state, but the most common use of the term tends to refer to state regulation of the activities of business and, of course, other institutions such as schools, professional associations, prisons etc. Politicians and policy-makers are responsible for creating business regulatory systems and establishing the agencies that supervise, monitor and sanction businesses. Nevertheless, regulators themselves are typically quasi-independent, non-elected administrators who work in specialized public agencies delegated to perform regulation.

In the broadest sense business regulation is part of a complex set of political, legal and organizational norms and sanctions that are designed to pursue the public interest, or, in other words, align business practices with social priorities. As we shall see below, business regulation that is seen through a 'public interest' lens is meant to correct 'market failures' or social harm not sufficiently contained by the forces of the market.

In Chapter 6 we saw how corporate power can impact social institutions and the economy in problematic ways, not just by undermining efficiency but also by concentrating power and creating relationships of inequality among social groups. In this chapter we will see how regulation has emerged as a means for societies to address many of these problems. The success of regulation has been questioned by many, and since the late 1970s there has been a deregulatory backlash against the perceived excesses of 'big government'. Part of this is due to the observed capture of regulators and the supposed tendency of government to stifle innovation and business competitiveness (Ogus 2004). This has led to the dismantling of many forms of industry protection and the deregulation of telecommunications and other industries. More recently, rising inequality, corporate scandals and financial crises have led to a revival of policy interest in regulation, both within states and at the international level.

After discussing the contending theories of regulation, we turn to surveying the various forms of regulation such as mandates, restrictions, standard setting and information requirements. Finally, we address important cases of business regulation and policy-making including new approaches like 'nudging' and pressures on regulations and policy resulting from processes like innovation and globalization.

Key discussion questions

- What is regulation?
- Is regulation best understood in terms of its public interest? Or is it better to understand regulation in terms of government failure?
- What are market failure and government failure?
- What types of regulation exist?
- How have recent social, technical and economic changes impacted on regulation?

Mainstream theories of regulation

It has been commonplace to see regulation as synonymous with government intervention in the market. Of course, regulation is not the only policy instrument that governments use to control and influence economic and business activities and institutions. Government can also enact the policies in conjunction with – or as alternatives to – regulation, or as indirect forms of regulation (Stiglitz and Sappington 1987). These include:

- *Inducements*: imposing taxes or levies on businesses and individuals to discourage certain activities, or the subsidizing of selected activities (such as clean technologies) to encourage them.
- *Compensation*: redistributing wealth and income through government assistance or insurance (like employment insurance).
- *Direct service provision*: government often provides services and products which would otherwise not be provided by private business or in a socially desirable way by private sector business firms.

While we cannot ignore these other forms of government intervention, since they are close cousins to regulation or function as indirect regulations, in this chapter, however, we focus on theories of government regulation. In particular, we examine two key mainstream theories that emphasize the 'public interest' and 'government failure' aspects of regulation.

Public interest theory The classic economic argument in favour of government regulation of the economy is based on the idea of market failure. According to the standard economic model, the market is the most efficient and welfare promoting way of coordinating our economic activity (Smith 1977). Yet this model is an idealization. It assumes that the costs and benefits of anything we produce or consume ultimately get reflected in its price in a competitive market. Broadly speaking, Stiglitz (2010a) argues that the market's efficiency – and its ability to serve the public interest – is premised on three assumptions that are often not met:

- that there will be a competitive market;
- that people will have adequate information about what they are buying in that market; and
- that the costs are all absorbed (and benefits enjoyed) by the people participating in the market exchange.

When these conditions are not met then it is said that markets 'fail' and government regulation or intervention may be needed to correct those market failures. In other words, the *invisible hand* of the market does not always lead to the best result for society and government regulation may be necessary to ensure that the public interest can be served (Leight 2010; Stiglitz 2010a).

To see the role of regulation according to the 'public interest' theory, we need to look more closely at the causes of market failure that this theory tries to address. These include negative externalities (unaccounted for costs), imperfect information and limits to competition. We spell out each of these in turn.

First, negative externalities are costs associated with economic transactions which one of the parties can shift on to another person or group without paying for them. Negative externalities are literally the 'unpriced costs' of a market activity or transaction. Most economists agree that negative externalities undermine the efficiency of markets that neoclassical economic theory prizes so highly (Bakan 2004). When there are negative externalities at least some of the costs of producing or consuming a product are not reflected in the price. Water pollution is a good example of a negative externality because making a product that pollutes the water supply imposes an unpriced cost on those who like or depend upon clean water. Business firms that pollute or exhaust the clean water of streams, lakes and rivers are getting these resources for free, as are those who dump waste without paying to clean it up (see Chapter 9 for more on this). In fact, they are really receiving a subsidy from society because in the end society is bearing the cost of making the product (Stiglitz 2010a).

There are many ways governments have addressed externalities. One way is to tax the industry that is causing the social harm so that the producers – and consumers – internalize the cost of the externality. This forces both consumers and producers to pay a price that is closer to the true cost of the harm-causing behaviour, which is often called the 'polluter pays' principle; cigarette or gasoline taxes are good examples of this as they give people an incentive to make other decisions. Or government can simply prohibit or limit the harm-causing behaviour by setting safety or pollution standards for an industry, as we see in the case of many product categories such as children's toys or electrical products. In either case, public interest theorists say these government interventions are more welfare-promoting than if we were to rely on the invisible hand of the market alone to direct our economic activities (Pigou 1938).

Second, mainstream economic models assume markets will be efficient because people will have all the information needed to know the value of what they are buying (see Chapters 10 and 11). The problem is the market is not a good mechanism to ensure that people are informed or have the 'right' information to make good choices – that is, people may have 'imperfect information'. Many products are technically complex and so it is hard for consumers to acquire information; and even if the information is available at an affordable price, it is costly in terms of time and effort to acquire. Perhaps more importantly, information about products in the market is a public good, which means if one person produces it, many other people can acquire it as well without paying for it (Stiglitz and Sappington 1987). Because information is subject to this 'free-riding' behaviour, people who might otherwise produce it lack an incentive to do so. Instead, producers will primarily provide information that is designed to convince consumers to buy products (e.g. advertising) rather than inform them of the full range of costs, benefits and alternatives. This is another market failure and many government regulations try to address it by prohibiting false advertising or requiring certain kinds of information be provided to consumers which would not be voluntarily provided by businesses. For example, most countries will only allow the sale of pharmaceutical drugs upon submission of a prescription notice from a physician, and a number of countries restrict advertising of prescription drugs, cigarettes and so on. Major government agencies such as the USA Food and Drug Administration (FDA) supervise these kinds of regulations. Imperfect information is also addressed by many other forms of reporting requirements as well as ongoing government inspection or certification activities (Baldwin et al. 2012).

Third, another type of market failure involves 'limits to competition' (Stiglitz 2010a). Many of today's wealthy countries such as the UK, USA and Canada attribute their economic development to the invisible hand of the free market (see Chapter 3). This means that the power of firms would always be limited by the possibility that other firms could provide a better or cheaper product or service. By the end of the nineteenth century, however, large businesses – often public corporations – came to dominate many markets, sometimes due to economies of scale and the efficiencies caused by mass production and vertical integration. For example, at the end of the nineteenth century US Steel, Standard Oil and other corporations in transportation and communication industries had become large enough to control their markets and create limits to competition (Furner 2010). In many cases the business elites who owned or managed these firms were seen as having undue influence over politicians, and in some cases were able to use their non-market power to influence government to undermine labour actions and strikes. Many of these firms grew so large that they could decide what price could be charged for their products, thereby removing what many economists see as the necessary market incentives to make the product cheaper or better.

One response to this was the set of policies that grew out of the so-called *Progressive Movement* in US politics which began in the 1890s and lasted more than two decades (Nace 2003). Some governments began to listen to social reformers who observed that many business firms had become monopolies or groups of firms formed cartels and trusts which allowed several firms to collude and fix prices. These were all instances of market failure which called forth legislation such as the US *Sherman Act* of 1890 which provided tools for government to restore competition by forcing the breakup of monopolistic companies or to tightly control or regulate industries where there was a concentration of power in a few firms (Ogus 2004). In many cases economic reformers and progressives acknowledged that some business enterprises were large because it was more efficient for them to be so. Progressives argued that such 'natural monopolies' that emerged in some industries such as radio broadcast should be closely regulated (Baumol 1977; Furner 2010).

Theory of government failure Public interest theory tends to focus on the benefits of controlling or reducing the social costs of business through government regulation. Yet the rise of the interventionist state during the twentieth century has always been controversial, especially among conservative supporters of business. By the 1970s many policy-makers and academics in countries like the US and UK were looking for explanations for the economic turbulence caused by rising energy prices, competition from low wage countries and so on (Furner 2010). This emboldened many supporters of the free market who opposed extensive regulation to criticize the interventionist regulatory state. For example, George Stigler (1971), a professor at the University of Chicago and a well-known *public choice theorist*, helped to solidify these ideas by developing a model of 'government failure' in opposition to concerns about market failure expressed by public interest theorists.

Following other public choice theorists like Mancur Olson (1965), Stigler posited a built-in tendency of democratic systems in capitalist societies to promote the interests of organized groups over less organized groups. These theorists observed that regulatory systems are steered by politicians who are motivated by the desire to be elected and re-elected to office. These politicians have a great incentive to favour the interests of established businesses which provide jobs in their communities, donate money to their campaigns and compete against rival firms from other communities or countries. Realizing that every regulatory system creates winners and losers, politicians are likely to be as opportunistic as anyone else in such a situation. From this perspective, if aligning themselves with influential corporations will help them, politicians will choose the regulations that help those corporations even if it comes at the expense of the public interest in the long run or the emergence of new firms using new technologies.

This also creates a phenomenon Ogus (2004) and others call 'regulatory capture' in which regulators fall under the influence of the industry they are supposed to control, inspect and monitor. Indeed, some studies during this period showed that there was a 'revolving door' between industry and government where many regulators in government agencies actually ended up taking jobs in the industry they regulated (Mitnick 1980).

The general point is that phenomena like regulatory capture may mean that the 'political market' is even less efficient than the economic market. Democratic politics is structured to favour those economic actors who have the loudest voices rather than those who might make the economy work better. The political market is also dysfunctional because members of the general public are not good at organizing to pursue policies that will really achieve the public interest. Public choice theorists say this is because anyone who wants to be engaged or become very informed about a specific public issue must make a very large investment with a small expected payoff. As a result, citizens tend to become 'rationally ignorant' (Downs 1957); that is, ordinary citizens do not have a big enough stake in any one issue related to business regulation to justify the enormous effort required to seriously rival professional lobbyists hired by business. Conversely, businesses which can gain by concentrating their government lobbying efforts on one or two problems that matter a great deal to them have a great advantage. Ordinary citizens stand to gain more from general policies which bring better jobs, or have more say in the workplace, yet governments tend to focus on areas where there is opportunity for capture by special interests, which typically reinforces the business bias of government. This is why some leading critics of capitalism often oppose the regulatory state as much as those trying to free business from the intervention of government (Novak 2014).

Widespread cynicism towards the public interest mandate of government reached its heyday with the rise of the governments of Margaret Thatcher (UK) and Ronald Reagan (USA) during the 1980s. These political leaders promoted the ideas of individual responsibility and the economic superiority of the market. The deregulation movement of the 1970s owed much to the influential analysis of the causes of government failure and its argument that government interference typically has a worse outcome than letting the market operate freely. Academics like Ronald Coase (1960) influenced the deregulatory movement by arguing that disputes about the impact of economic activities are not about the public interest, or about bad businesses harming innocent bystanders, but rather ultimately about disputes among private parties who want different goals. After all, a price can be put on any behaviour, so we could (and should) set up a kind of market that would let people decide how much they want to pay to pollute or let people who might be affected by the pollution negotiate a price that could be paid by those who have an interest in making a mess. Coase assumed that such a market-oriented approach would often allow people to find a way of resolving problems better than government. In particular, it would avoid having government engage in paternalistic, top-down regulation of economic activity and instead encourage bargaining between the private parties that are potentially affected by each other's behaviour.

Assessing the two leading theories On the one hand, public interest theory does need to be tempered by realism. Bruce Yandle (2011) argues that the most convincing theory of regulation is one that includes elements of both the public interest and private interest theories. He points out that regulation is often the product of interest alignment between promoters of public interest regulations and the businesses that are regulated. The process of regulation may start with pressure groups trying to influence government about addressing some negative externality. The government will then actively consider regulations in response to these demands. While some businesses may oppose the prospect of any regulatory initiative, other firms may see some kinds of new regulations as a market opportunity. This is especially true if those businesses have some kind of technological head start or other advantage that puts them in the best position to compete in the market once a specific set of regulations are in place. For this reason, not all businesses want to suppress regulation, and they may in fact be allies with the pressure groups that want to bring changes to the industry. For example, Yandle says this might explain why General Motors lobbied government to bring in stricter fuel standards at a time when it was further along than other American car manufacturers in shifting production to smaller, more fuel-efficient cars.

On the other hand, the problem with the public choice theory of government failure is its categorical distrust of both government and constructive approaches to public issues. It starts from the fictional assumption that all participants in the political process inherently prioritize their economic self-interest above all else and that citizens are inherently under-informed or easily manipulated 'consumers' in the political 'marketplace'. This is clearly problematic as we see today the number of civic groups and other participants who involve themselves in public interest campaigns and are motivated by the power of ideas and even social justice. One would have to adopt a very narrow model of human action and rationality to say that people – including politicians – are incapable of coming together to deliberate effectively about what policies would best contribute to the public good (Furner 2010).

Forms of regulation and their challenges

Having surveyed mainstream debates around regulation, we want to review different forms of regulation as they relate to specific areas of economic life and industries where state regulation typically applies. In this chapter we cover: (1) restrictions on business, (2) mandates, licensing and standard-setting and (3) disclosure rules.

Restrictions Restrictions on businesses stipulate what kinds of activities that business firms and their agents cannot perform or limits they cannot exceed. This is perhaps the most well-known and controversial form of government regulation. Anti-trust laws, for example, prohibit certain activities on the part of business that might limit competition in the market. A recent well-known case brought by the US Department of Justice and global regulators led to a 2015 guilty plea by some of the world's largest banks (e.g. JP Morgan Chase, Royal Bank of Scotland, Citigroup) for the serious offence of fixing foreign exchange prices. The case resulted in fines of over \$5.7 billion (Henning 2015). Earlier accounting scandals in 2001 involving Enron and WorldCom corporations – discussed in Chapter 6 – prompted the US government to pass a package of regulatory laws known as the 2002 *Sarbanes-Oxley Act* (Soederberg 2008). The Act criminalized the perpetration of certain types of financial irregularities, and also set up new conflict of interest guidelines applying to financial auditing firms with the hope of reducing incentives to exaggerate corporate earnings – or conceal corporate losses – from outsiders.

Some people see restrictive regulations and bans as unwarranted interference with private business decision-making. Business leaders often warn that regulations could create 'red tape' and expensive compliance procedures that would create inefficiencies and stifle innovation and thus offset their intended benefits. Economists who dislike restrictive regulations often cite their 'paternalistic' character, which means that they rely on using government as a 'nanny state' (Le Grand and New 2015) and treating workers or consumers as children unable to learn how to look after their own safety or become informed about risks (Joskow 2011). Even critics of business are sometimes sceptical of regulations, saying they are often selectively enforced or too lax for fear of harming industry. These critics also say that regulations tend to scratch the surface of corporate behaviour without having any real impact on the structural factors such as power relations that cause concentrations of wealth and various forms of harm and risk for consumers, workers and communities (Glasbeek 2002). Indeed, businesses are often characterized as 'one step ahead' of regulators since politics and technical complexity make it hard for regulations to be fully comprehensive or systematic and to account for all possible externalities.

Mandates, licensing and standard setting In many cases, governments may want to ensure that a specific – and presumably desirable – public goal is achieved by businesses operating in a particular industry by positively mandating actions or requiring a certain level and type of service provision or safety feature. For example, in some countries banks must provide certain services that are deemed to be important to the public, such as access to loans for poorer communities or, as in the case of Ireland and the UK, free access to all ATMs. Telecommunications companies may be required to provide certain services as well. In many countries phone companies must provide universal landline telephone services to all communities at a standard rate even though in remote or sparsely populated regions many such services are so expensive that they would never be provided if end users had to pay the full cost.

In many industrial sectors, businesses not only are overseen by specialized agencies but also must be licensed by those agencies. This is the case in areas like media broadcasting, taxi services and legalized cannabis production. In Canada, for example, the Canadian Radio and Television Corporation (CRTC) requires cable TV providers as well as TV networks to provide a certain minimum amount of Canadian content in order to 'level the playing field' against the flood of US content that has the advantage of being imported from one of the world's largest markets (Edwardson 2008).

Critics of these kinds of policies often point to the fact that government cannot legislate for good or safe or beneficial behaviour. Others say that by licensing an industry or mandating certain standards of provision the government is stifling competition and innovation in ways that are actually harmful to the public interest. For example, the CRTC in Canada has long been criticized for assuming its Canadian content rules can actually encourage viewers or listeners to watch Canadian content (Hunter et al. 2010).

Disclosure On the surface, one of the best ways of regulating is to require businesses to provide information and transparency of the potentially harmful business activity or product. A good example is food labelling (Howells 2005). If consumers are made aware of the excessive sugar content of a breakfast cereal, then the consumer of the product has the power to avoid the potentially harmful consequences. This solution avoids paternalism and leaves it in the hands of each individual to determine which consequences they want to avoid. No product is perfectly safe, and each person assigns a different weight to different values such as safety, enjoyment and so on. Hence, rather than restricting or banning products, perhaps it is more efficient for government to simply require producers to provide full information for consumers.

Mainstream economists tend to prefer disclosure over other forms of regulation because it simply builds upon and restores the power of choice at the foundation of the competitive market. Nevertheless, we know that information by itself is not the same as providing for social needs and providing alternatives for people who lack resources to attain them (Howells 2005). Governments around the world require cigarette marketers to inform people they might suffer illnesses from smoking. Yet there is strong evidence that even when warnings exist, certain groups of people maintain a high rate of smoking. In fact, there is a higher prevalence of smoking among people from lower socio-economic groups, which suggests that the problem is not one of good information but rather deeper structural issues such as lack of access to the social supports conducive to healthy behaviour (Hiscock et al. 2012).

Different approaches to regulation and policy-making

Theories of regulation, of whatever type, influence politicians and policy-makers by providing legitimation and justification for new policies or approaches to new societal issues (see Case Study on banking regulation). In this section we want to address an example of each of these things. First, we examine the emerging policy approach based on theories of 'nudging' people's behaviour; and second, we examine the policy approaches to innovation and globalization (see Chapter 7).

Libertarian paternalism and nudging policy There is an emerging and popular policy approach called 'libertarian paternalism', which seeks to influence and regulate people's behaviour by drawing on insights from behavioural economics. It has proved particularly popular in the UK and US (Salazar 2012). The basis of this approach is that individuals have cognitive biases which lead them to act in irrational ways, defined as against their own self-interest (see Chapter 11). It departs from other rational choice theories since it does not assume that consumers and other market participants act rationally to maximize their self-interest. Rather, it is based on the theory that we need policy interventions – what Thaler and Sunstein (2008) call 'choice architecture' – to enable people to overcome their cognitive biases and enhance their self-interest. According to Thaler and Sunstein (2008: 6), a 'nudge' includes:

> any aspect of the choice architecture that alters people's behaviour in a predictable way without forbidding any options or significantly changing their economic incentives. To count as a mere nudge, the intervention must be easy and cheap to avoid. Nudges are not mandates. Putting the fruit at eye level counts as a nudge. Banning junk food does not.

Nudging is a policy approach that aims to change 'self-destructive' behaviour into 'self-interested' behaviour without restricting individual freedom

Case study

The 2007–2008 global financial crisis and banking regulation

The issue of regulating the banking sector re-emerged in the wake of the 2007–2008 global financial crisis. Of course, regulation of banking and finance has always been an important matter because the stability of the financial system is extremely important to society as a whole. For example, banks perform the function of creating money through lending to consumers, lending capital to businesses and linking lenders and borrowers, all of which are crucial to the market economy. At the same time, the financial intermediaries who perform these functions are in a position to make large gains by taking risky bets with other people's money. As a result the economy as a whole – and the larger public interest – can come under threat without a strong financial regulatory system (Stiglitz 2010b).

Government therefore is called upon to manage risks that the market itself cannot. For example, financial regulators in most countries with developed stock markets have the power to investigate and limit the practice of 'insider trading' so that people with privileged information cannot engage in unfair manipulation of markets. Assurance against such manipulation is necessary to ensure that there is sufficient trust in the financial system, which in turn can create a more efficient flow of investment and cheaper access to capital. Other regulations are meant to discourage excessive risk-taking.

One of the major causes of the 2008 financial crisis was weakened US banking regulations which allowed almost anyone to take out a sub-prime mortgage (Stiglitz 2010b). When the house price bubble burst, unsuspecting investors around the world were left holding worthless financial assets that most financial rating agencies had classified as highly rated investments. The way the complex financing schemes were structured ensured that large profits could be made upfront by the sellers of these financial assets, and when the market collapsed (due to loan defaults) the pain would be spread among many types of investors around the world (Morgenson and Rosner 2011).

Many of the world's largest investment banks like Goldman Sachs, JP Morgan and CitiBank were themselves exposed to these so-called 'toxic' investments, but those institutions were not ordinary victims. Rather, they were bailed out by governments after they were deemed 'too big to fail'. In fact, the extreme risk-taking behaviour that caused the crisis was almost certainly made possible in the first place by the fact that these banks knew that government knew they could not afford to let them fail. To this day it is not clear that regulators have been able to curb the incentives for socially dangerous private risk-taking on the part of the financial industry (Stiglitz 2010b).

and without altering the behaviour of individuals who already act in a self-interested manner (Salazar 2012). Consequently, it is meant to preserve freedom of choice and legitimate policy-makers and others in their promotion of particular policies (based on notions of self-interested, rational action) (Thaler and Sunstein 2012). An example might be changing where 'healthy' foods (e.g.

fruit) appear in a cafeteria or shop, so that they appear before 'unhealthy' foods (e.g. cake). Placing fruits before desserts steers consumers towards healthy food without removing choice.

In policy terms, nudging is appealing over other policy options (e.g. institutional change) because it offers a seemingly simple and low-cost solution that does not require primary legislation. As such, nudging can replace formal regulations, mandates or bans, while imposing no extra cost on citizens (i.e. no extra taxation is needed). Policy-makers and politicians might find this attractive because it implies that public health, for example, can be improved without extra spending in terms of both regulatory cost and taxation while avoiding the typical failures of a 'nanny state'.

While it might appear benign, nudging can be highly problematic as a policy solution. Nudging can simply induce short-term cosmetic behavioural changes, predominantly amongst more savvy and informed – that is, affluent – consumers. It does not address important problems like consumers misperceptions; income inequality; resource access; structural lifestyle decisions; existing knowledge, attitudes and values that hinder long-term behavioural change; the influence of business marketing; and so on. Ignoring these sorts of problem means that nudging policy intervention can raise unrealistic expectations of societal change and welfare, which downplays other important regulatory interventions (e.g. bans) (Salazar 2012).

Policy-making and regulation in a technological, global world It is important to note that policy-making and regulations are not static; they are, necessarily, dynamic and evolving rules for at least three reasons. First, new innovations and technologies call into question the applicability of old regulations. For example, the internet and World Wide Web have had significant implications for the viability and legitimacy of many television regulations and licensing requirements. Television regulations controlling content seem increasingly out of place in an age of internet streaming (Mansell 2014). Other examples might include new services like UberX that allow car owners to become freelance taxi drivers in the so-called 'sharing economy' (see Chapter 18). A question arising with UberX is whether it should be regulated like traditional taxi services on the basis of licensed and insured drivers. For example, with UberX, who is responsible when safety standards go wrong – the company or the driver? In California a court has ruled that UberX should actually be seen as an employer, not simply a service linking self-employed drivers to passengers (Alba 2015).

Second, new technologies can give businesses new powers to write the rules about how much privacy should be given up in order to provide increased convenience. For example, the 'Internet of Things' (the world of interconnected and networked devices) has made it possible to share and generate enormous amounts of data, thereby creating 'smart' systems and highly customized services with a speed and efficiency never before imagined and in a way that some observers say will radically transform business systems and models (Rifkin 2014). Yet the only way this can occur is by handing over vast swathes of information about our behaviours and preferences to businesses. The regulatory challenges around privacy, security, information access and corporate power and responsibility are difficult to manage (Brynjolfsson and McAfee 2014).

Third, state-based regulation has been strongly challenged by the globalization of business whereby firms increasingly subcontract production and services across borders (see Chapters 7 and 8). Major multinational corporations (MNCs) like Nike, The Gap and Apple have been accused of 'regulatory arbitrage' because they allegedly globalize their operations to take advantage of relaxed labour, safety and environmental standards in less regulated economies (Vogel 2010). Regulations are meant to make business more accountable to societal needs, and globalization is seen as a process that has meant government regulation is becoming less effective. Conversely, MNCs have also pushed for transnational business laws that are stronger than national regulations and protect their investments around the world. International investment agreements proliferated throughout the 1990s and 2000s and often limit governments' abilities to introduce policies that respond to the needs and demands of their citizens (e.g. the Trans-Pacific Partnership mentioned in the Introduction). Pursuant to such agreements, MNCs have sued host governments for perceived interferences with their investments, and these hearings are held before non-state arbitral tribunals that are often criticized for being ideological, biased, costly and uncertain as they lack an appeal process (Grant 2015). These lawsuits against regulating governments have resulted in the state having to pay extremely expensive compensations to foreign investors and to restrain itself from further regulating the economy.

In response, many theorists of business and society have heralded the prospects of non-state or civic regulation (Bakan 2004), whereby NGOs, students, labour activists and others hold corporations accountable through non-state actions, organizations and campaigns. Such initiatives involve persuading business to adopt voluntary codes and standards, or promoting consumer markets for products with eco-labels and fair trade certification (see Chapter 16). Clearly civic regulation may be effective in establishing market and reputational rewards for socially beneficial business practices and also helps to legitimize and professionalize business practices that are more socially aware. Yet civic regulation has also been criticized as opening opportunities for insincere 'greenwashing', allowing corporations to selectively adopt a few new policies or practices to brand themselves as socially responsible without embracing more meaningful changes (Cherry and Sneirson 2010). It is probably safe to conclude that civic regulation is an important complement to government regulation, filling in some of the gaps and shortcomings of the latter, especially in a more complex world of globalized production and networked activists and socially aware consumers in the public sphere.

Comparing regulatory approaches among countries Although we have made a number of generalizations about major regulatory trends it is important to recognize that different countries often take different approaches to regulation. David Vogel (2012) has pointed out that before 1990 the USA imposed much stricter regulations than European countries did in addressing product safety and environmental risk. After 1990 that pattern reversed itself as European countries are now more assertive than the USA in monitoring safety, restricting food ingredients and proactively addressing climate change. A major reason for this change has been the pressure from those countries with stronger regulations to harmonize regulations with other member states within the European Union (EU). Vogel (2012), for example, points to the fact that EU regulators have restricted genetically modified organisms (GMO) in the food industry, while very few restrictions exist in the USA. He explains this by showing that US policy-makers over the years have become more insulated from 'public pressures' and have instead followed strict cost-benefit analysis and risk assessment procedures where the burden of proof falls on those proposing restrictions and regulations. By contrast, in the last three decades in the EU there has been a strong interest in legitimizing European integration, and this has led to a demand for EU institutions and regulators to become more precautionary as they need to demonstrate responsiveness to strongly voiced public pressures (Vogel 2012: 278). This shows that different systems of economic governance can lead to very different regulatory approaches, even in societies facing otherwise similar types of risks and business practices.

Conclusion

Business regulation is often intended as a way of protecting the interests of society from potentially harmful business activity or overly powerful corporations. Yet as we have seen, it is perhaps too simplistic to see regulation as simply a limitation imposed on business activity. Rather, regulations are political-legal instruments that fundamentally shape business opportunities and activities, and even help explain how business structures and practices have evolved and adapted to political-legal instruments. Our discussion of the forms of business regulation and the debates and controversies about them drives home one of the key points of this book, namely that business must be understood as an institution that involves a dynamic interplay of economic, social and political factors (see Introduction).

Suggested readings

- Lecture 16, Atkinson, R.H. and Stiglitz, J. (1980) *Lectures on Public Economics*, New York, McGraw Hill.
- Part I, Baldwin, R., Cave, M. and Lodge, M. (2012) *Understanding Regulation: Theory, Strategies and Practice*, Oxford, Oxford University Press.
- Chs. 6 and 7, Le Grand, J. and New, B. (2015) *Government Regulation: Nanny State or Helpful Friend?*, Princeton, NJ, Princeton University Press.

Bibliography

Alba, D. (2015) 'In California, Uber loses another round in driver debate', *Wired*, 10 September: www.wired.com/2015/09/california-uber-loses-another-round-driver-debate/ (accessed 26 October 2015).

Bakan, J. (2004) *The Corporation*, London, Random House.

Baldwin, R., Cave, M. and Lodge, M. (2012) *Understanding Regulation: Theory, Strategies and Practice*, Oxford, Oxford University Press.

Baumol, W. (1977) 'On the proper cost tests for natural monopoly in a multi-product industry', *American Economic Review*, Vol.67, pp.809–822.

Brynjolfsson, E. and McAfee, A. (2014) *The Second Machine Age*, New York, W.W. Norton.

Cherry, M. and Sneirson, J. (2010) 'Beyond profit: Rethinking corporate social responsibility and greenwashing after BP oil disaster', *Tulane Law Review*, Vol.85, pp.983–1038.

Coase, R.H. (1960) 'The problem of social cost', *The Journal of Law and Economics*, Vol.3, pp.1–44.

Downs, A. (1957) *An Economic Theory of Democracy*, New York, Harper.

Edwardson, R. (2008) *Canadian Content: Culture and the Quest for Nationhood*, Toronto, University of Toronto Press.

Furner, M.O. (2010) 'From "state interference" to the "return of the market": The rhetoric of economic regulation from the old gilded age to the new', in E. Balleisen and D. Moss (eds), *Government and Markets: Toward a New Theory of Regulation*, New York, Cambridge University Press, pp.92–142.

Glasbeek, H. (2002) *Wealth by Stealth*, Toronto, Between the Lines.

Grant, K. (2015) 'The ICSID under siege: UNASUR and the rise of a hybrid regime for international investment arbitration', Osgoode Legal Studies Research Paper Series, Paper 108.

Henning, P. (2015) 'Guilty pleas and heavy fines seem to be cost of business for Wall St.', *The New York Times*, 10 March: www.nytimes.com/2015/05/21/business/dealbook/guilty-pleas-and-heavy-fines-seem-to-be-cost-of-business-for-wall-st.html?_r=0 (accessed September 2016).

Hiscock, R., Bauld, L., Amos, A. and Platt, S. (2012) 'Smoking and socio-economic status in England: The rise of the never smoker and the disadvantaged smoker', *Journal of Public Health*, Vol.34, pp.390–396.

Howells, G. (2005) 'The potential and limits of consumer empowerment by information', *Journal of Law and Society*, Vol.32, pp.349–370.

Hunter, L., Iacobucci, E. and Trebilcock, M. (2010) *Scrambled Signals: Canadian Content Policies in a World of Technological Abundance*, Toronto, C.D. Howe Institute: www.cdhowe.org/sites/default/files/attachments/research_papers/mixed/commentary_301.pdf (accessed September 2016).

Joskow, P. (2011) 'Market imperfections versus regulatory imperfections', *CESifo DICE Report*, pp.3–7.

Leight, J. (2010) 'Public choice: A critical reassessment', in E. Balleisen and D. Moss (eds), *Government and Markets: Toward a New Theory of Regulation*, New York, Cambridge University Press, pp.213–255.

Mansell, R. (2014) 'Global media and communication policy: Turbulence and reform', in *Global Community: Yearbook of International Law and Jurisprudence*, Oxford, Oxford University Press, pp.3–26.

Mitnick, B. (1980) *The Political Economy of Regulation: Creating, Designing and Removing Regulatory Forms*, New York, Columbia University Press.

Morgenson, G. and Rosner, J. (2011) *Reckless Endangerment*, New York, Henry Holt and Co.

Nace, T. (2003) *Gangs of America*, San Francisco, Berrett-Koehler.

Novak, W. (2014) 'A revisionist history of regulatory capture theory', in D. Carpenter and D. Moss (eds), *Preventing Regulatory Capture: Special Interest Influence and How to Limit it*, New York, Cambridge University Press, pp.25–48.

Ogus, A. (2004) 'Whither the economic theory of regulation? What economic theory of regulation?', in J. Jordana and D. Levi-Faur (eds), *The Politics of Regulation: Institutions and Regulatory Reforms for the Age of Governance*, Cheltenham, Edward Elgar, pp.31–44.

Olson, M. (1965) *The Logic of Collective Action: Public Goods and the Theory of Groups*, Cambridge MA, Harvard University Press.

Pigou, A. (1938) *The Economics of Welfare* (4th Edition), London, Macmillan.

Rifkin, J. (2014) *The Zero Marginal Cost Society: The Internet of Things, the Collaborative Commons and the Eclipse of Capitalism*, New York, Palgrave Macmillan.

Salazar, A. (2012) 'Libertarian paternalism and the dangers of nudging consumers', *King's Law Journal*, Vol.23, pp.51–67.

Smith, A. (1977) *An Inquiry into the Nature and Causes of the Wealth of Nations*, Chicago, University of Chicago Press.

Soederberg, S. (2008) 'Deconstructing the official treatment for "Enronitis": The Sarbanes-Oxley Act and the neoliberal governance of corporate America', *Critical Sociology*, Vol.34, pp.657–680.

Stigler, G. (1971) 'The theory of economic regulation', *Bell Journal of Economics and Management Science*, Vol.3, pp.3–18.

Stiglitz, J. (2010a) 'Government failure vs. market failure: Principles of regulation', in E. Balleisen and D. Moss (eds), *Government and Markets: Toward a New Theory of Regulation*, New York, Cambridge University Press, pp.13–51.

Stiglitz, J. (2010b) *Free Fall: America, Free Markets and the Sinking of the World Economy*, New York, W.W. Norton.

Stiglitz, J. and Sappington, D. (1987) 'Information and regulation', in E. Bailey (ed.), *Public Regulation*, London, MIT Press, pp.3–43.

Thaler, R.H. and Sunstein, C. (2008) *Nudge: Improving Decisions about Health, Wealth and Happiness*, New Haven, Yale University Press.

Thaler, R.H. and Sunstein, C. (2012) 'Behavioral economics, public policy, and paternalism: Libertarian paternalism', in S. Holland (ed.), *Arguing about Bioethics*, London, Routledge, pp.386–91.

Vogel, D. (2010) 'Private regulation of global corporate conduct', *Business and Society*, Vol.49, pp.68–87.

Vogel, D. (2012) *The Politics of Precaution: Regulating Health, Safety and Environmental Risks in Europe and the United States*, Princeton, Princeton University Press.

Yandle, B. (2011) 'Bootlegers and Baptists in the theory of regulation', in D. Levi-Faur (ed.), *Handbook on the Politics of Regulation*, Cheltenham, Edward Elgar, pp.25–33.

14 | Ethics and business

Co-authored with Richard Wellen

Introduction

To a large extent, this book has been concerned with *positive* issues – by which we mean descriptive statements about what 'reality' *is*. While we might argue about whether one theoretical perspective or another (e.g. neoclassical economics, institutionalist, feminist etc.) describes reality better or not, we can assess all of them on the basis of whether they create a coherent and consistent relationship between theory and description. For example, if neoclassical economists argue that everyone is self-interested, we can unpack that theoretical claim *and* test it in the 'real world' (e.g. are people actually self-interested?). However, and alongside descriptive claims, people also make *normative* claims about a range of issues – by which we mean statements about how we think society (or something else) *should* be organized or managed or run or what-have-you. In contrast to positive claims, though, normative arguments entail understanding the social values and norms that underpin social and legal rules. It is here that we need to think about the **ethics and morality** of business, markets and capitalism.

> **Definition: Ethics and morality**
>
> Although often considered interchangeable, ethics and morality are distinct things. Ethics represent the principles and rules people use to determine (and govern) how people should act in society, while morality represents the social norms or values of society that underpin ethics. For example, killing someone is generally considered to be immoral in most societies, yet different societies have different rules and principles about when it is ethical to kill or not kill someone (e.g. warfare, euthanasia, capital punishment, self-defence etc.). It is important to remember that ethics and morality are not the same as the law, which may differ from both.

Positive and normative statements are frequently confused and conflated, leading to what David Hume – a Scottish philosopher from the eighteenth century – called the 'is-ought problem' (Herman 2003); that is, we often think that our positive descriptions of the world (e.g. 'people *are* self-interested') also reflect normative principles (e.g. 'people *should* be self-interested'). We have already come across one example of this is-ought problem in Chapter 5 with the discussion of Milton Friedman's (1970) perspective on the responsibility of business. He claimed that business people only have one responsibility – which is to make profit – because that is what is implied by the theory that says the business manager is the agent of shareholders not society (who are the principals). From this 'positive' observation, according to Friedman at least, we can derive the 'normative' claim that business *should* only pursue profit. There are problems with Friedman's framing of business ethics, which we discuss in this chapter and elsewhere (e.g. Chapter 5), and the other principles that underpin the ethics of doing business.

Of course, there are many cases where positive observations (i.e. explanations and descriptions) do not tell us what normative claims or prescriptions can be justified. For example if we know why income inequality is increasing in our society, we have a basis for designing policies to address that inequality, but such knowledge cannot tell us how important it is to fight inequality or what priority those policies should be given in comparison to other policies. From this perspective, normative inquiry is really an attempt to fill the gap between our forms of knowledge that help us explain the world and the moral controversies and 'value choices' we may face once we have that knowledge. This gap has even led moral relativists to say that ethical claims cannot be rationally grounded since they are based on subjective and arbitrary choices among competing values. Whether or not one agrees with moral relativism, this problem of the variety and pluralism of ethical perspectives will be important in our discussion.

In this chapter, we consider the specific issues that relate to the field of applied ethics called *business ethics*, which is the dominant perspective taught in business schools around the world. Our aim in this chapter is to provide a brief introduction to business ethics and then to criticize how it is applied to business practices. We then discuss three key ethical perspectives – utilitarianism, rights theory and social justice – in order to offer a range of normative viewpoints that can be used to analyse business practices, business ethics and the social values that underpin societal attitudes to business, more broadly.

Key discussion questions

- What is the difference between 'positive' and 'normative' issues?
- What is business ethics?
- What are the problems with business ethics?
- What influences the principles underpinning business ethics?
- What do different ethical perspectives say about business practices?
- Can business be ethical?

What is business ethics?

Business ethics In order to understand business ethics, we need to consider ethical theory in general and applied ethics in particular. Ethical theory itself is the enterprise of engaging in moral reasoning and discourse aimed at justifying or legitimizing certain practices, policies or actions. Ethical issues emerge wherever a possible action or choice we face might lead to a violation of moral standards or harm people in a way that could be avoided (Velasquez 2012: 11–12). Sometimes our actions and choices appear not to have moral implications because we do not have information about what those choices entail or we simply do not have the power to influence other people's lives in a given way. For example, if we lack information about the implications of using fossil fuels to generate energy then a decision between using solar power or coal-fired electricity may lack a moral dimension. We may agree that we have a responsibility to future generations, but we do not know how our energy use relates to such a responsibility. In this way scientific inquiry and technological progress have opened up many new types of moral problems because they have extended human capabilities and made us aware of areas of responsibility that did not exist before. See Chapter 9 on environmental issues and Chapter 18 on technological ones.

Business ethics follows the familiar ethical principle of 'ought implies can', which means that an agent's moral responsibility is relative to – or conditional upon – their capacity and power to act. This of course applies to the activities of businesses which control a great deal of resources and exhibit a strong degree of power to affect the lives of workers, communities and consumers. For example, it is noteworthy that reports about the widespread use of child labour in hazardous underwater gold mining in the Philippines do not blame the parents who send their children to these mines, but rather the people who exploit those children and families (Human Rights Watch 2015). Ethical inquiry often starts from abstract principles about our duties and obligations to others, but it also requires concrete and even critical knowledge of a given social context, such as an understanding of which groups have power over whom.

As highlighted in Chapters 5 and 13, public attitudes to business have changed numerous times throughout the last century and a half, almost certainly due to the growth of corporate power and the understanding of the importance of business decision-making over so many aspects of our lives. This is why so many ethical controversies have developed over time with respect to business practices that are quite long-standing such as child labour, discrimination against particular social groups such as women, ethnic minorities, sexual minorities (see Chapter 15), or environmental pollution (see Chapter 9). Consequently, it is evident that morality and ethics are centrally implicated in the activities of business and decisions of business people, since they relate to the so-called 'social licence to operate' (Gunningham et al. 2004). Without this social licence, businesses would find it difficult to sell their products and services (because they might face boycotts), recruit employees (because people might not want to work for them) and avoid stringent restrictions on their activities (because politicians might find it wins votes to create new regulations).

The risks to business of losing their social licence mean that business has to be concerned with ethics and morality. As a result, business ethics has emerged as an important area over the last hundred years or so (De George 1987; Parker 2002). Its origins can be traced back to the corporate revolution – discussed in Chapter 3 – and the attempt to bind public corporations to the social good, especially in countries like the USA. For example, Rakesh Khurana (2007), a professor at Harvard Business School, argues that public fears about big business at the end of the nineteenth century led business leaders to encourage the alignment of business with broader social goals like employment, economic growth and so on. This was achieved through newly emerging business schools and management programmes that emphasized the importance of the social role of business, especially public corporations, as social and public institutions in American society.

However, as the twentieth century progressed, especially during the 1970s and 1980s, business leaders asserted another view, that business should only be concerned with profit – business school programmes soon followed suit. The idea and form of **business changed**, in this sense. From this later perspective, the science of management should focus on the firm's bottom

---

Key methodological issue: Changing forms of business

An important 'positive' and 'normative' issue in business ethics is what do we mean by concepts like 'business' and 'corporation' – and here we leave aside all the other variety of social economy organizations in operation (see Chapter 17). While we defined these organizational forms in the Introduction of this book, it is vital to highlight that the form that (for-profit) businesses and corporations take has changed over time. The corporation, for example, started out as a public institution designed to undertake specific tasks that could not be done by the state or privately-owned businesses (e.g. building a canal). During the nineteenth century, business and the corporation were transformed by new laws and regulations (e.g. general incorporation, limited liability), which we discussed in Chapter 3. Since the 1970s the corporate form has been transformed again by new demands based on the idea of shareholder primacy (see Chapter 4). What this means is that when we discuss business ethic, we have to be careful to distinguish what we mean by 'business'.

Source: Avi-Yonah (2005)

line, including how to improve the firm's market fortunes measured by its financial results or returns to investors. Yet as Bowie (1986) and De George (1987) explain, it is also in the 1970s and 1980s that business ethics itself began to emerge as an academic subfield of management studies, as the field's first scholarly journals were published, textbooks written and specialized academic programmes set up. These business ethics scholars showed how business decision-making has a large impact on society and 'stakeholders' (workers, consumers, community members), and therefore raises significant moral implications that cannot be avoided in the study and practice of business management.

Understanding business ethics Today, we can, generally speaking, unpack business ethics in at least two ways. First, in terms of the scale at which we might want to understand the ethics of business; and second, in terms of how ethics is shaped by economic theories of the market. We will deal with each in turn.

On the one hand, we can think of business ethics as operating on different levels or scales. According to Velasquez (2012: 15), for example, business ethics can be used to examine (1) *systemic*, (2) *corporate* and (3) *individual* issues. First, business ethics can be used to produce normative analyses of social institutions and of capitalism in general; we might want to ask whether capitalism is moral or not, for example. Second, it can also be used to focus on a particular organization, like a specific business or corporation (e.g. Walmart, Nike, Apple). At this level, ethics relates to the activities of the organization in question; we might want to look at whether a particular decision adhered to certain principles or not. Finally, we can look at the ethics of individuals in business; for example, we could analyse the decisions and choices of managers and executives. We might want to ask how and why they made certain decisions – that is, what is the motivation behind individual ethical choices.

While a range of issues might be open to discussion in business ethics in this line of thinking, some academics like Martin Parker (2002: 97) have criticized business ethics for adopting an individualistic and economistic approach to ethics – that is, focusing on single issues (e.g. should a business sell certain products) and ignoring collective or political considerations (e.g. should we simply ban certain products). Consequently, no matter what level or scale is analysed, according to Parker, business ethics does not lead to significant changes. Part of the reason for this is that business ethics has emerged from and continues to form an important part of business education, especially in business schools; it is important, in this context, to understand how **people learn ethics** and not just what ethical principles might be best suited to particular business activities.

Key ethical issue: How do we learn ethics? The role of the business school

One question that needs to be considered when it comes to the relationship between ethics and business is how people, especially managers and executives, learn business ethics. As we have mentioned already, business schools have played an important role in training managers and executives and, consequently, they have played a key role in shaping the field of business ethics. In this sense, we can examine business schools and the principles they teach as a way to understand how and why business people enact specific ethical practices in their workplaces. Notably, examining this relationship reveals something rather worrying. As the work of Ferraro et al. (2005) and others illustrate, people who receive their education at business schools – and in (neoclassical) economics programmes more generally – tend to end up believing that everyone is self-interested and acting upon that belief by acting more selfishly themselves. There are even studies that show that managers and executives who have received MBAs from business schools are more likely to commit unethical acts than those who have not. Consequently, it is important to think about how ethics is taught as much as the content of it.

Sources: Ferraro et al. (2005); Khurana (2007)

When it comes to the influence of economic theories on ethics, we want to highlight two positions: (1) the 'strong' position and (2) the 'pragmatic' position.

First, the strong position reflects the perspective that markets are the optimal allocators and distributors of societal resources – we discuss this in Chapters 10 and 11. In particular, this position is associated with market fundamentalists – often called 'neoliberals' – who contend that the market is the best and most moral way to organize society – see Hayek (1944 [1994]) and Friedman (1962) for example. This view is often traced back to Adam Smith and his contention that individual self-interest – or selfishness, generally considered to be immoral – can lead to a greater, public good – in this case, economic growth (see Foley 2006). While the causative relationship between individual actions and societal outcomes is contested, this perspective forms the basis of a market-centred approach to business ethics.

In 1970, Friedman wrote a famous essay entitled 'The Social Responsibility of Business Is to Increase Its Profits', which was published in the *New York Times Magazine*, a publication with wide readership in the general public. In it he pleaded against the growing chorus of claims that managers and executives should consider their social responsibility when making business decisions (see Chapter 5). He insisted that such an approach would not only ignore the responsibility of managers and executives to act as 'agents' of shareholders, but it would also weaken the contribution of business to society. According to Friedman, asking managers and executives to be socially responsible is akin to asking them to do a job they are neither authorized to perform nor qualified to do. People elect politicians to look after the public interest and make laws accordingly. With those laws in place, and market forces pressuring managers and executives to look after the interests of both consumers and investors, there is no need to assign a special social or moral 'responsibility' to business other than to try to make a profit (within the limits set by laws enacted by governments). A manager or executive who tries to promote social values – like a clean environment – is really acting like a politician, who is supposed to do those things, rather than looking after the money of investors, which managers are supposed to do according to Friedman (1970: 122). Friedman even said that managers and executives who pursue social interests with investors' money are actually doing harm to society by usurping the role of politicians who are elected and accountable to the people in a democracy. As a market fundamentalist, Friedman insisted that when businesses try to make as much profit as possible, and keep their noses out of the democratic political process where social policy and priorities should be determined, they will make the greatest contribution to the well-being of society.

There are others who take a more 'pragmatic' stance on business ethics, such as Manuel G. Velasquez (2012), who has written a major textbook on the subject called *Business Ethics: Concepts and Cases*. By pragmatic we mean that his position is not driven by a set of first principles (e.g. people are self-interested, markets are optimal allocators of resources etc.), but rather by what specific decisions will solve what particular problems. In his book, for example, Velasquez argues that:

> ethical behavior is the best long-term business strategy for a company – a view that has become increasingly accepted during the last few years. This does not mean that occasions never arise when doing what is ethical will prove costly to a company . . . Nor does it mean that ethical behavior is always rewarded or that unethical behavior is always punished . . . To say that ethical behavior is the best long-range business strategy just means that, over the long run and for the most part, ethical behavior can give a company significant competitive advantages over companies that are not ethical. (2012: 7)

Velasquez's position is very different from the likes of Friedman or other market fundamentalists. For Velasquez, ethical decisions are advantageous for a business, but ethical decisions are not always obvious; consequently, managers and executives need help making those decisions, which is where business ethics plays an important role. In a sense, business ethics helps managers and executives make decisions on a case-by-case basis, ensuring that their decisions are principled and not simply self-interested. Indeed, as Velasquez reminds us, ethics has an important function of building trust, which in turn is an important ingredient in making organizations effective.

Critique of business ethics As should be obvious from this brief summary, designing a special type of applied ethics for business is particularly challenging due to the fact that many actions that are praiseworthy in business can be seen as ethically problematic in other contexts. For example, competition and competitiveness are seen as a plus in the business world, but not necessarily in other parts of our lives (e.g. personal relationships). Even within the same business organization there may be competition for advancement and other rewards that give people an incentive to be aggressive and ruthless (Boatright 2003). This might explain why business is an arena for a specialized version of ethics. On the one hand there are good 'business' reasons for businesses to be ethical, if for no other reasons than that this will help them gain the trust of consumers. On the other hand, managers and executives may expect their employees to be aggressive in maximizing sales opportunities and to be ethical mainly insofar as doing so reinforces those opportunities.

Alongside these issues, it is possible to make a number of critical comments about business ethics as a specific form of applied ethics. Here we draw on Martin Parker's (2002) book, *Against Management*, to highlight a few of these criticisms. First, Parker argues that business ethics is really a way to legitimate business, rather than a way to encourage business to be ethical. Basically, he argues that business ethics is a way to side-step serious scandals by offering to make business more effective by dealing with the problems identified in each corporate scandal. Second and as already mentioned, Parker argues that business ethics is dominated by individualistic rather than collective conceptions of ethical behaviour; as a result, it does nothing to challenge dominant economic ideas in business, like self-interest, which might be ethically problematic. As a result, it reinforces the notion that morality is a private decision rather than a political issue. This also entails something called the 'loyal agent' argument which stresses that it is implausible to make employees accountable for the socially beneficial and ethical outcomes of business within a hierarchy of command. Indeed, there is controversy around whether we can make clear assignments of responsibility within large and formal impersonal organizations like corporate bureaucracies (Michalos 1995). Third, Parker (2002) argues that business ethics helps to establish the limits within which business and business people are meant to operate (e.g. profit motive), it does not challenge those limits. For example, when it comes to employment relations, we might see drug tests as violations of privacy in non-business contexts, but in business a mandatory drug test might be seen as a legitimate way to increase the performance of employees. Here, business performance can legitimate certain actions that would not be acceptable otherwise.

Understanding ethical theory outside business ethics

If business is a special kind of 'ethics of economic relations', as Boatright (2003) claims, it is nevertheless strongly influenced by the general principles of ethics that have been developed over many centuries by leading moral philosophers and thinkers. Consequently, it is helpful, we would argue, to consider the leading moral frameworks and theories that can be used to justify and guide ethical decision-making. We discuss three of these next – utilitarianism, rights theory and social justice – before considering how to apply these ethical theories to the problems and dilemmas which business ethics tries to address.

Utilitarianism Utilitarianism is based on the idea that the actions and choices that are most ethical are those which contribute most to the overall good of society (Velasquez 2012). The eighteenth-century philosopher Jeremy Bentham is the original exponent of utilitarianism (Snoeyenbos and Humber 2002). Bentham proposed that the best decision from a moral point of view is the one that produces the 'greatest good for the greatest number'. In other words, the goal of those designing policies and making decisions is to bring about the greatest 'net' happiness. Utilitarianism starts from the assumption that it is not the job of moral theory to tell people what kind of goals or preferences they should have or what kinds of values are most important. Instead moral theory only needs to take people's goals and preferences as a given – much like economists typically do, as we discussed in Chapter 11 – and try to satisfy the greatest number, with the knowledge that not all can be satisfied. In this sense, utilitarianism is a 'consequentialist' ethical approach because it does not rank actions and policies as morally good or bad based on the quality of the actions themselves or what values those actions might promote, but rather on whether they lead to the best results or consequences for individuals and society. Utility is an impartial standard since the best result is not what satisfies my goals or yours, but the most goals overall, no matter what those goals are (Velasquez 2012). In light of these qualities, utilitarianism is closely associated with liberal pluralist ideas and society, where many of our moral challenges involve finding effective approaches to social cooperation among people with different values.

Many of the attempts to defend the capitalist market that we have reviewed in this book such as Adam Smith's 'invisible hand' – discussed in Chapter 3 – rely on utilitarian reasoning, but utilitarianism does not necessarily support the market fundamentalist view (Boatright 2003; Velasquez 2012). It is important to note that the normative claims of Smith's theory rest on a contestable descriptive claim, namely, the assumption that the price mechanism of the market is the best way of ensuring that society's resources are put to their most valuable use. Alternative theories of economic relations, however, might show that cooperative economic relationships may produce more socially desirable results than market competition – see discussion of anarchist economics in Chapter 12. In this case, then, utilitarian reasoning might support policies that favour making available economic resources as public goods or organizing economic relations using cooperative principles.

Rights theory The concept of a 'right' is another important basis for ethical theory. One of the key proponents of the theory is Ronald Dworkin (1984) who argued that rights represent 'trumps' over other ethical claims. We can say that rights are entitlements for individuals and groups to be treated with respect in regard to their interests, freedoms, capacities or choices. There are many types of rights: human rights, natural rights, legal rights, rights created by contracts and so on. We do not have the space to review all of these, but it is important to see that if someone has a right to something it means that other people have a duty to treat that person in a certain way. For example, if a customer has a right to privacy then that means a business has a duty not to collect and share their information with others without consent. Indeed, privacy rights have been used as a justification for policies that limit the surveillance powers of large organizations such as businesses and governments. As with other ethical principles outlined in this chapter, rights can be enforced through regulations and laws (see Chapter 13), or they can be recognized and affirmed through voluntary actions and decisions.

There are many types of rights as well. The seventeenth-century English philosopher John Locke claimed that humans have a 'natural right' to property based on what we create through our labour as individuals (see Chapter 18 for more discussion of this). Locke's approach has been used as a moral argument against government interference with the economic choices and behaviour of individuals and businesses, and even as an argument against the legitimacy of taxation. From the *libertarian* end of the political spectrum, for example, property rights legitimate 'negative' rights of non-interference with each person's freedom (Nozick 1974). Other types of rights in liberal-democratic societies are characterized differently; for example, as 'positive' rights to enable individual freedom. This includes the right to be treated equally under the law, as provided by the Fourteenth Amendment of the US Constitution and many other similar provisions in other societies, for example. This right has been used to justify policies of non-discrimination or affirmative action in hiring and recruitment. Equality under the law has also been cited as a reason to roll back progressive income taxes on the grounds that high income earners should not be taxed at a rate higher than low income earners.

Rights-based ethics is not consequentialist, but rather 'deontological', which means that the moral justification for an action has to do with whether it adheres to a rule or obligation, and not whether its consequences are good or bad. Another important feature of rights is that they often conflict with other rights. A good example of this relates to employment rights. The political scientist David Ciepley (2004, 2013) points out that workers, in the US context at least, give up their rights (e.g. free speech, free association etc.) when they enter the workplace. A business can enforce workplace rules that conflict with basic human rights. According to Ciepley (2013) this is not an anomalous arrangement, rather businesses are legally given the authority to enforce these rules, almost like government has delegated its power to them.

Justice A third major area of ethics involves theories of justice. At a general level, justice means giving people what they deserve based on their status, situation or circumstances. We often say that an ethical problem involves a question of justice or fairness when there is moral pressure to address the inequalities and disadvantages that certain groups and types of people have. Distributive justice deals with how – and according to what principle – good or valuable things should be allocated among people (Velasquez 2012). An early formulation of justice comes from the writings of the ancient Greek philosopher Aristotle, who gave the most general formulation of distributive justice by describing it as 'treating equals equally and unequals unequally' (Aristotle 2014). In the nineteenth century, Karl Marx articulated a radically egalitarian theory of economic justice expressed in the principle: 'from each according to his abilities, to each according to his needs'.

Many challenges arise, however, once we try to give concrete content to this abstract principle. For example, should 'unequal need' be a basis for distribution? In many cases we would say yes, but certainly not all. For example, most people would say that a student who asks a professor for a higher mark on a test because they 'need' a good grade average to get into law school does not deserve a positive response. On the other hand, justice based on need may be warranted in contexts such as reversing important types of social disadvantage or workplace policies that accommodate people with illness or disability. Liberal justice, by contrast, is based on rewarding people for their contributions or investments, which can lead to great inequality. Affirmative action in hiring is one attempt to reverse historical disadvantage and inequality. Based on these and other examples we can see that claims based on theories of justice are powerful and compelling. At the same time they can be controversial as they often challenge established economic patterns and institutions and may require significant change to the priorities within organizations and society more generally.

Applying ethical theories to business

Equity–efficiency tradeoff? As we noted, Adam Smith's concept of the invisible hand is an attempt to justify the market on utilitarian grounds (Foley

2006). Many proponents of the invisible hand argue that inequality is morally acceptable on the grounds that a successful and growing economy needs to reward the most talented and productive people by allowing them to earn high incomes (Sayer 2015). This creates a potential conflict with egalitarian justice: if society taxes the wealthy to pay for redistributive policies then there might be fewer incentives for the most productive people to contribute, undermining the economic growth from which even the poor may benefit. Others have argued that this market incentives approach ignores the fact that money has 'declining marginal utility' for individuals. In other words, once people have a lot of income or wealth, further amounts of income become less valuable to them. If the 'declining marginal utility of money' view is true, then egalitarian justice would not be incompatible with a growing economy (Le Grand 2002). Whether inequality and efficiency are convergent or divergent values can partially be answered empirically. In fact, some recent studies give support to the idea that societies which pursue egalitarian redistributive social policies can also be more economically efficient and productive (Ostry et al. 2014).

Utility–rights tradeoff Many business ethics scholars have raised privacy issues associated with online businesses like Google and Facebook and their social networking and search engine technologies. The very qualities that give a Google search its power depends upon the ability of those companies to share, link and sell information about the users of their services. According to Rifkin (2014), the next stage in this process is the so-called 'Internet of Things' (IoT) which will create another level of connectivity and data sharing through embedded sensors and usage tracking devices that are already pervading more of our everyday activities and interaction with objects and technologies. The capacity of the IoT to profile and rate users and their behaviours provides a basis for creating more efficient ways of delivering services and allowing 'on demand' customization of those services to our needs.

One concern has been that people will lose control over their personal information, making it hard to know how to balance the loss of privacy against the convenience or utility of customized services and richer connections that these technologies provide. Clearly those concerned with rights have pointed to the privacy concerns mentioned above while a utilitarian could make the argument that the value created by improved services and products and new opportunities for collaboration and sharing outweighs the privacy concerns. In practice utilitarianism recommends that we search for optimal trade-offs between different goals, and this concern about how to balance these ethical considerations has been the subject of much regulation and court challenges.

Justice–rights tradeoff The emergence of capitalism is associated with the breaking down of status-based societies (e.g. feudalism) and the promotion of merit-based ones (Herman 2003). Consequently, business is often assumed to be based on the level of effort people put into it and rewards commensurate with that effort – this assumption is used to justify, for example, inequality (di Muzio 2015). On the one hand, and taking the Lockean view, this makes sense because people are rewarded for their work and talents; that is, they can claim property rights to the results of their labour and work. On the other hand, however, this claim ignores the social basis of work in that all forms of human activity are the result of social inheritance and context. As we noted in the Introduction and Chapter 12, anarchist thinkers have argued that all human activity builds on the work of previous generations, which means that we all benefit from this inter-generational investment in our social systems, laws, norms, values, technologies and so forth that enables us, in the here and now, to create something. Language represents a useful example. Without language – which has developed over many generations – the content of books, articles, magazines, blogs etc. would have no value, because we would not have a common language to share our ideas. Consequently, any written work we create owes a debt to previous generations of people who have helped to create and sustain the language we use.

Conclusion

In this chapter we have covered mainstream versions of business ethics, provided some critical commentary on its underlying assumptions, and then introduced a number of ethical theories in order to illustrate a range of normative issues in business. We want to finish by emphasizing that normative analyses, like those we discuss here, are an important part of any consideration of the relationship between business and society. Moreover, normative assumptions can underpin a range of supposedly positive claims, which means that it is important to consider what might be a normative claim and what might not.

Suggested readings

- De George, R. (1987) 'The status of business ethics: Past and future', *Journal of Business Ethics*, Vol.6, pp.201–211.
- Ferraro, F., Pfeffer, J. and Sutton, R. (2005) 'Economics language and assumptions: How theories can become self-fulfilling', *Academy of Management Review*, Vol.30, pp.8–24.
- Ch. 5, Parker, M. (2002) *Against Management*, Cambridge, Polity Press.
- Ch. 1, Velasquez, M.G. (2012) *Business Ethics: Concepts and Cases* (7th Edition), New York, Pearson.

Bibliography

Aristotle (2014) *Nichomachean Ethics*, trans. C.D.C. Reeve, Indianapolis, Hackett.

Avi-Yonah, R. (2005) 'The cyclical transformations of the corporate form: A historical perspective on corporate social responsibility', *Delaware Journal of Corporate Law*, Vol.30, pp.767–818.

Boatright, J. (2003) *Ethics and the Conduct of Business*, Upper Saddle River NJ, Prentice Hall.

Bowie, N. (1986) 'Business ethics', in J. DeMarco and R. Fox (eds), *New Directions in Ethics*, New York, Routledge, pp.158–172.

Ciepley, D. (2004) 'Authority in the firm (and the attempt to theorize it away)', *Critical Review: A Journal of Politics and Society*, Vol.16, pp.81–115.

Ciepley, D. (2013) 'Beyond public and private: Toward a political theory of the corporation', *American Political Science Review*, Vol.107, pp.139–158.

De George, R. (1987) 'The status of business ethics: Past and future', *Journal of Business Ethics*, Vol.6, pp.201–211.

Di Muzio, T. (2015) *The 1% and the Rest of Us*, London, Zed Books.

Dworkin, R. (1984) 'Rights as trumps', in J. Waldron (ed.), *Theories of Rights*, Oxford, Oxford University Press, pp.153–167.

Ferraro, F., Pfeffer, J. and Sutton, R. (2005) 'Economics language and assumptions: How theories can become self-fulfilling', *Academy of Management Review*, Vol.30, pp.8–24.

Foley, D. (2006) *Adam's Fallacy*, Cambridge MA, Belknap Press.

Friedman, M. (1962) *Capitalism and Freedom*, Chicago, University of Chicago Press.

Friedman, M. (1970) 'The social responsibility of business is to increase its profits', *The New York Times Magazine*, 13 September, pp.122–125.

Gunningham, N., Kagan, R. and Thornton, D. (2004) 'Social license and environmental protection: Why businesses go beyond compliance', *Law & Social Inquiry*, Vol.29, pp.307–341.

Hayek, F. (1944 [1994]) *The Road to Serfdom*, Chicago, Chicago University Press.

Herman, A. (2003) *The Scottish Enlightenment*, London, Fourth Estate.

Human Rights Watch (2015) *What if Something Went Wrong?: Hazardous Child Labour in Small-Scale Gold Mining in the Philippines*: www.hrw.org/sites/default/files/report_pdf/philippines0915_brochure_web.pdf (accessed September 2016).

Khurana, R. (2007) *From Higher Aims to Hired Hands*, Princeton, Princeton University Press.

LeGrand, J. (2002) *Equity and Choice: An Essay in Economics and Applied Philosophy*, London, Routledge.

Michalos, A. (1995) *A Pragmatic Approach to Business Ethics*, Thousand Oaks CA, Sage.

Nozick, R. (1974) *Anarchy, State and Utopia*, New York, Basic Books.

Ostry, J., Berg, A. and Tsangarides, C. (2014) 'Redistribution, Inequality and Growth', IMF: www.imf.org/external/pubs/ft/sdn/2014/sdn1402.pdf (accessed September 2016).

Parker, M. (2002) *Against Management*, Cambridge, Polity Press.

Rifkin, J. (2014) *The Zero Marginal Cost Society: The Internet of Things, the Collaborative Commons and the Eclipse of Capitalism*, New York, Palgrave Macmillan.

Sayer, A. (2015) *Why We Can't Afford the Rich*, Bristol, Policy Press.

Snoeyenbos, M. and Humber, J. (2002) 'Utilitarianism and business ethics', in R. Frederick (ed.), *A Companion to Business Ethics*, Oxford, Blackwell, pp.17–29.

Velasquez, M. (2012) *Business Ethics: Concepts and Cases* (7th Edition), New York, Pearson.

15 | Business and social exclusion

Caroline Shenaz Hossein

Introduction

Understanding how people participate in the business world is important. In Chapter 2, we explored how European countries extracted resources from the Global South as part of their own wealth accumulation. Walter Rodney (1982) illustrates the role of corporate capitalism in the under-development of the Global South and the implications of this for racialized people in other parts of the world. But there are other ways of understanding business and its impact on the world, and one of these is through the complex ways that people participate in the 'economy' (see Gibson-Graham 1996, 2006; Hossein 2013; Roelvink et al. 2015). Van Staveren (2015) argues that since the 2007–2008 global financial crisis, many people have been exploring new ways to think about the economy to ensure that business is more embedded in social relations. The 2015 Greek financial crisis also alerted citizens around the globe to the attitudes of business and government elites, and triggered action to reclaim the kind of markets people want to see in their societies.

In this chapter we want to examine some of the ways that people engage with business, both as workers and entrepreneurs in the Global South and as racially marginalized groups in the Global North. While people commonly participate in capitalist markets as wage earners, they can also be producers or entrepreneurs. In the Global South, businesses often take the form of owner-operated legitimate but unregistered businesses, often very small in scale, that are part of the **informal economy** (see Chapter 17). At times these businesses can provide the means for people to manage their exclusion from mainstream capitalist markets and create economic opportunities. In this chapter, we examine two ways of doing business: one that exploits and excludes the poor as workers; and another that can liberate them through some forms of self-employment. The question driving this chapter is: how can some forms of business be oppressive and other forms liberating? We want to stress that it is important to focus on how marginalized groups create alternative business opportunities, rather than simply see them as victims of capitalism.

As we have noted already (see Chapter 7), people's experience of business is different in different countries. Some countries have laws and regulation in place to manage diversity, equity and equality issues in the workplace, and others do not. It is important to note that discrimination in business affects people in all countries, although in different ways. For example, a person's

Definition: Informal economy

The informal economy is defined as a diversified set of economic activities, enterprises, jobs and workers that are not regulated or protected by the state. The concept originally applied to self-employment in small unregistered enterprises. According to Hart et al. (2014), the discourse on the informal economy can also include people in unprotected low-wage employment.

Source: Hart et al. (2014)

identity (e.g. their social class, gender or race) can limit access to business resources, leading to the marginalization of certain groups in the economy and in the wider society (Hossein 2014b, 2015). This raises the issue of **social exclusion**. Yet, business can be liberating as well if it is people-focused (Gordon-Nembhard 2011; Hossein 2016). At the global level, capitalist firms engage in exploitative employment practices, but at the small- and micro-business level, people can be viewed as creating and managing their own livelihoods.

Key concept: Social exclusion

Social exclusion is defined as both the structure and processes of inequality among groups in society, and particularly inequality in the structural access to resources of those disadvantaged groups. In the book *Canada's Economic Apartheid*, Galabuzi (2006) argues that social exclusion refers to the inability of racialized Canadians to participate fully in society and the economy due to structural inequalities in access to social, economic, political and cultural resources.

Source: Galabuzi (2006)

In this chapter, as noted above, we examine two ways of doing business: as employees or as entrepreneurs. The examples consider the role of identities in business and how people react to social exclusion. For instance, it is important to look at diverse experiences, such as the cooperative enterprises of Canada's Aboriginal people in the hinterlands or racialized women working as employees in an MNC in the Global South. In analysing business and social exclusion, we have to recognize that while mainstream business can be used as a tool to subjugate and control different social groups (e.g. racialized people, women), economically and politically, it can also be co-opted by marginalized people as a way to resist capitalism (see also Chapter 16). Our objective in this chapter, then, is to consider how business can be simultaneously oppressive and freeing.

Identities are seldom analysed in mainstream business because markets are believed to be immune from racial, class and gender bias. By contrast, we locate the contextual environment and examine the identities of marginalized people, arguing that these do matter in market environments. Considering identities in business enables us to move away from a one-dimensional view of marginalized people as victims of an unsustainable economic system to seeing them as a group of people who resist oppressive economic models. It is important to look at the innovative ways marginalized people engage in commerce to meet their livelihood needs. This is a more realistic way of understanding the varied activities within the economy.

Key discussion questions

- What is social exclusion in the marketplace?
- How are people exploited as workers?
- What are some gender-specific risks in MNCs?
- How can the MDM theory explain social exclusion in Global South countries?
- Can business be viewed as a form of resistance for marginalized groups?

Untangling mainstream and critical perspectives

Modernization theory is a clear set of prescriptions that emanated from North American and Western European countries, forcing a programme of 'free' trade and 'free' markets on the Global South (see Chapter 2). This enforced spread of capitalism by the Global North is associated with the 'Washington Consensus' (Williamson 1993), which we discuss in Chapters 7 and 8. Often associated with neoliberalism, the Washington Consensus shaped how the Global South was supposed to develop (Harvey 2007), as outlined in the Case Study of Indonesia and Chile. The Washington Consensus was based on the enactment of a series of fiscal reforms and structural adjustment programmes (SAPs) that were meant to set 'underdeveloped' countries on the right track to economic growth and prosperity. These reforms and SAPs were underpinned by an assumption that for the countries of the South to develop economically, they had to shift from being traditional and communal societies to more scientific, rational, secular and individualized societies.

The market fundamentalism promoted by the Washington Consensus has been disastrous for many countries around the world; the push for economic growth has come at a great cost. The negative effects have been particularly glaring in Southern countries in the aftermath of SAPs. Countries have adopted a pro-business system of low taxation, reduced welfare spending, privatization, trade liberalization and so on, which has had an adverse effect

227

Case study

Modernizing experiments: Indonesia Inc. and the Chicago Boys in Chile

The Global North's political and business elites 'tested' their economic reforms in countries like Indonesia and Chile.

The first major meeting to divide up the domestic economies of the Global South was in 1967 at a meeting in Switzerland. There, global capitalist elites decided how to parcel out key sub-sectors, such as banking, forestry, minerals and manufacturing in Indonesia. This meeting is commonly known as 'Indonesia Inc.', as political leaders as well as the Rockefeller Foundation, Lehman Brothers, Chase Manhattan Bank and international financial institutions (IFIs) met to determine the legal infrastructure for foreign investment in the country. This expansion of multi-national corporations (MNCs) into the country was supported by Indonesia's president, General Suharto (1967–1998). As a result of these investments, the Suharto family became one of the richest in Indonesia.

A few years later, another 'development' experiment was carried out in Chile after the 1973 overthrow of socialist president Salvador Allende by General Augusto Pinochet – supported by the US government. This is perhaps the most famous experiment of neoliberal 'reform', seen as a success story by many neoliberal thinkers. The experiment was led by Chilean alumni of the University of Chicago's Department of Economics who had returned home to try to implement neoliberal economic reforms. These men, who became known as the 'Chicago Boys', adopted the theories of Milton Friedman and other Chicago economists, and were able to implement these theories during Pinochet's authoritarian dictatorship (1973–1990).

Both countries implemented a 'development' agenda that embraced an anti-state position favouring capitalist business models, which gave business owners the right to use labour and capital as they pleased with few impediments. The result of these 'modernizing' experiments has contributed to the exclusionary nature of business in these societies and elsewhere.

Source: *New Rulers of the World* (2001), 53 minutes, directed by Alan Lowery

on vulnerable groups, especially women, elderly and children. SAPs totally ignore the complex social and historical terrain of the Global South, especially the experiences of enslavement and colonization that has instituted a colour-coded economic pyramid in which local elites (e.g. whitened elites through miscegenation [racial intermingling] or tribes favoured by colonizers) inherited land, money and power at the expense of others. SAPs miss this historical component that explains persistent social and economic exclusion.

As a result, business in many parts of the Global South has ended up controlled by local elites who exclude others from engaging in business. In her book *World on Fire: How Exporting Free Market Democracy Breeds Ethnic Hatred and Global Instability*, Amy Chua (2004) argues that the free market mantra promoted by the Global North is dangerous because it does not consider this historical bias embedded in former colonized countries. Unrestrained capitalism manifests itself in a way that enables local elites in both business and politics to collude and manage investments to the exclusion of the indigenous masses. Chua (2004), a Filipina-American of Chinese ancestry, recounts a personal story in the book in which servants in the Philippines slit her aunt's throat in an expression of ethnic hatred. Chua developed the concept of market-dominant minorities (MDMs) to understand these colonial histories, basing it on the observation that the elite business class is usually composed of a distinct racial or ethnic group. These political and economic elites collude with the IFIs and MNCs to reinforce existing inequalities in society. An example of MDM is the 250,0000 Lebanese that live in West Africa (The Economist 2011); rich Lebanese businesspeople have made payments to politicians like Sierra Leone's Siaka P. Stevens (1967–1985) and Liberia's Charles Taylor (1997–2003) in exchange for exclusive rights to the diamond mines. The MDMs concept is useful because it helps explain how history has created a highly classed and racialized private sector in many countries around the world, where economic elites who are a distinct racial or ethnic group exploit the labour of the other racial or ethnic groups.

In contrast to critics like Chua, business professor C.K. Prahalad (1941–2010) argued, in his 2006 book *Fortune at the Bottom of the Pyramid: Eradicating Poverty through Profits*, that the private business sector can create economic opportunities for people in the Global South. According to Prahalad's 'bottom of the pyramid' (BOP) theory, engaging with the world's four billion poorest people as consumers could shift the poor upwards from the BOP, creating a range of business opportunities for the majority of people. The BOP theory is controversial as it illustrates how business can be used to promote the fortunes of the majority, but ignores the structural inequalities embedded in a system. Prahalad (2006) claimed that multi-national businesses miss an opportunity when they discount the BOP and that the dominant logic of business has to change to work with businesses in the Global South. Many CEOs of MNCs do not see the poor as participating in the economy other than as beneficiaries of charity. Supporters of the BOP theory argue that it helps business to change their perceptions of the poor, highlighting how they are not only consumers but also producers and entrepreneurs.

Are global firms exclusionary or an opportunity?

Early development experiments in Indonesia (1967) and Chile (1973) – see Case Study – set in motion market fundamentalism for the Global South. Since then, MNCs have been on the move in search of cheap labour and inputs (see also Chapter 7). The Washington Consensus is firmly embedded in the South and in the IFIs, such as the World Bank, that promote market reforms. As a result, Southern countries compete amongst themselves and local elites strive to make their countries more appealing to foreign investors by lowering labour and environmental regulations (see Chapter 13), reducing tax levels and supplying cheap unskilled labour.

These development polices have embraced an anti-state argument and pushed capitalist business models that reinforce social divisions among people. This is particularly glaring in the Global South in the aftermath of SAPs imposed by IFIs. The negative effects of SAPs are not felt equally. For example, the market reforms of the 1980s required countries to adhere to a pro-business regime of low taxation, reduced welfare spending and the elimination of subsidies for things like fuel and food, which adversely affected the most vulnerable people, especially women and children. Market fundamentalism has ended up exacerbating historically rooted social conflicts. Issues of social exclusion are particularly well documented in the aftermath of SAPs. In her work, Oxford professor Francis Stewart (1991) has argued that women are the ones most affected by fiscal restructuring. Because of cutbacks to social services, women put extreme pressure on localized forms of **social capital**. In the aftermath of market reforms, women have the triple burden of work, family and community responsibility in order to fill in the gaps left by the withdrawal of government support (Stewart 1991). In her case study of Latin America, Molyneux (2002) also shows that responsibility for adjusting to restructuring falls most heavily on poor women, who have to figure out how to feed communities without their labour being compensated by the state or NGOs. For example, the poorest women are the ones who organize collectively on top of their paid workload to create soup kitchens or kitchen gardens in order to feed each other.

Key concept: Social capital as a contested concept

Social capital is a contested concept. It has been embraced by both the left and the right. Social capital represents human relationships either as personal 'assets' held by individuals or as social 'assets' held by social groups. It has been used to represent a variety of social phenomena, including social norms (e.g. the bonds that bind communities together), social networks (e.g. the linkages that bring diverse communities together) and social diversity (e.g. the differences between communities). Harriss (2002) in *Depoliticizing Development* points to the concept as an important tool of the World Bank in carrying out infrastructure and development projects in the Global South. While the concept has been criticized, it has also proved to be an influential idea that has been mainstreamed into government policies, business practices and the social economy (see Chapter 17).

Sources: Woolcock (1998); Harriss (2002)

Former Filipino President Ferdinand Marcos pushed women into precarious and dangerous work with the ultimate goal of increasing state revenues and his personal income (Pyle 2001). Women were forced into the informal economy as sex trade workers, domestics (e.g. nannies and maids) and factory workers. In the case of factory work, several studies have found that MNCs prefer young female workers in their twenties because they are viewed as compliant, docile, fearful of male authority and less likely to complain about wages, working conditions and long work hours (Stewart 1991; Pyle 2001). The mistreatment of the poor in MNCs value chains is well documented, and there is much debate about the benefits of MNCs to poor countries.

There is a counter perspective of MNCs, however, and it does not come from modernizers alone: critical feminists, particularly from the South, have also promoted the idea that MNCs can be beneficial to the people who secure employment through these firms. For the pro-market modernizers, MNCs are viewed as important investors in the poorest countries in the world. The argument is that MNCs not only create jobs, but their presence also creates a demand for local value chains, thereby leading to the growth of locally owned subcontracting firms and scores of independent home-based businesses. Naila Kabeer (2004) questions liberal (Western) feminists who support the boycott of MNCs, maintaining that they can provide income and social benefits to working women in poor countries. A rush to regulate and boycott MNCs can have dire consequences for local economies, with damaging impact for the very people that liberal feminists intend to help. In countries where women have few opportunities due to tradition and customs that inhibit them from pursuing a career, these low-paying jobs provide them with a new form of confidence, status and leadership. The thinking here is that regulations to improve working conditions have to come from within a country in order to be effective. In a *New York Times* video, for example, Kalpona Akter, executive director of the Bangladesh Center for Worker Solidarity, argues that policy-making designed to improve the working conditions of people must come from inside the country, as the act of shaming international firms might deter them from investing in the country.

Short video: Local women speak out! – *Made in Bangladesh*

Some Bangladeshi women are not convinced that firms hiring four million people should be expelled from the country. This video clip (3.12 minutes) suggests that although women value the work they are doing, some of them agree there has to be legislation that also protects their rights as workers. In this short video, the journalists look at the conditions of female workers in garment factories in the wake of the 2011 fire at Rana Plaza, which claimed 1100 lives. The debate remains over how to best regulate MNCs and local sub-contractors to ensure people do not lose their jobs.

Source: *New York Times* (2013). *Made in Bangladesh*: www.nytimes.com/video/world/asia/100000002231544/made-in-bangladesh.html?ref=asia (accessed September 2016)

Can business be a form of resistance? A critical perspective

In *The Great Transformation*, Karl Polanyi (1944 [2001]) argued that capitalist markets are not free or self-regulating (see Introduction). In fact, he argued that markets are socially constructed, especially by the state, to serve elite interests. Polanyi warned that privileging economic life over social life would be disastrous. He argued that it would lead to a social backlash, or 'double movement', as people would protest the social disruption caused by disembedding markets from society (see Chapters 16 and 17). This Polanyian perspective, based on the notion that markets are embedded in society, helps us to put the welfare of people before profit. The idea of 'putting people first' and markets second challenges the mainstream perspective that profit should override other considerations in business – see the discussion of shareholder primacy in Chapter 4, for example. A contemporary example of this is Muhammed Yunus (2010), the 2006 Nobel Peace Prize winner, who questioned the role of banks in modern capitalism and set up the Grameen Bank three decades ago. 'Grameen' is a Bengali term for village. The aim of the bank was to put people first and to reorganize financial services in the form of group 'micro-banking'.

In the 1970s, Yunus, like many other Southern activists, was intent on changing elitism in commercial banks, a goal that he pursued through the Grameen Bank. In his efforts to make micro-banking socially inclusive, Yunus (2010) calls into question the kind of markets that exclude ordinary people from access to finance. Providing loans to very poor, pre-literate, rural women in the Global South in the 1970s would have seemed quite extraordinary at a time when an educated Western woman had difficulty getting a bank loan without her husband's approval. Three decades after its inception, Yunus' microfinance movement, first energized in the South, proved that people-focused institutions can do banking differently, that is, through solidarity economics.

Despite positive experiences, however, commercialized microfinance has faced significant criticism for failing to offer actual alternatives to capitalism (see Roy 2010; Hossein 2014b, 2015). Feminist Rankin (2001) was one of the first critics of microfinance, arguing that it is simply a strategy to make Nepali women 'rational economic actors' who fit into neoliberal economics. In her view, it did not change the systemic bias against poor women in the society at all. While the 'Bangladesh Consensus', which was the South's response to the Washington Consensus (Roy 2010), failed to turn the tide of neoliberal politics, it offers an alternative vision of business that can be socially inclusive through a group model. As we detail in Chapter 17, the significance of the social economy (including non-profits, cooperatives, self-help groups, associations, foundations etc.) demonstrates that business can be undertaken in ways to work for people.

In the South and in racially marginalized communities in the North, people have innovated within exclusionary business environments to make business

232

inclusive. Hossein's (2016) work shows how black 'Banker Ladies' in the Caribbean engage in a financial system that is collective and community-focused. These forms of alternative and cooperative economics were central concerns in the work of liberation scholars like Booker T. Washington, W.E.B. Du Bois and Marcus Mosiah Garvey, all three of whom are important but neglected theorists in the social economics of excluded people. Booker T. Washington (1856–1915) was born into slavery and rose to prominence as an African-American leader, founding Tuskegee University. He strongly promoted the movement of black people into trades and business. W.E.B. Du Bois (1868–1963) was the first African-American to receive a PhD from Harvard University and co-founded the National Association for the Advancement of Colored People (NAACP). In *Souls of Black Folk*, Du Bois (1903 [2007]) showcased the business acumen of Africans and their concern for community. He also outlined the dislocation caused by African-American's experience of enslavement, as well as the persistent and cruel forms of discrimination, exclusion and alienation in US society. In *Economic Co-operation among Negro Americans*, Du Bois (1907), through his concept of group economics, urged African-Americans to draw on African traditions to create solidarity businesses. Finally, **Marcus Mosiah Garvey** (1887–1940) was a Jamaican-born moral philosopher and entrepreneur who put forward ideas of self-reliance in business for the African diaspora (Martin 1983). His theory of Pan-African economic cooperation is followed by black communities such as the Nation of Islam and Rastafarians.

Key thinker: Marcus Mosiah Garvey (1887–1940)

Marcus Garvey is an early example of a 'social entrepreneur' – someone who uses business in the pursuit of social goals. His press, Negro World, published articles that mattered to the disenfranchised African-American community in the USA. He founded the Universal Negro Improvement Association (UNIA) and the African Communities League (ACL) to create one of the largest member-owned institutions for the African diaspora in the world. Garvey also founded a shipping firm, Black Star Line, through which he focused on maritime trade with Africa as well as cooperative-run laundries, restaurants and doll-making factories. The UNIA and ACL were created to uplift the lives of oppressed people through collective businesses. However, this idea of pursuing black self-reliance and independence through business threatened white America, and Garvey was subject to economic sabotage and accused of mail-fraud by the US government.

Source: Martin (1983)

The goal of liberation theorists who advocate for inclusive markets is to co-opt business so that it creates opportunities for excluded and marginalized groups and allows these groups to seek freedom through economic independence in their own collective enterprises – enterprises that prioritize the needs of community – rather than simply working in white-owned businesses. It should be noted that Garvey, Du Bois and Washington were influenced by their own life experiences; and while they quarrelled with one another in terms of how to uplift an impoverished group, they all believed in diverse, alternative and cooperative economics.

Doing business in and for marginalized groups can be seen as a form of resistance to the negative impacts of capitalism, and it requires significant courage (also see Chapter 16). African-American feminist economist Jessica Gordon Nembhard (2014) argued, in *Collective Courage: A History of African American Cooperative Economic Thought and Practice*, that economic sabotage, lynching and murder were very real threats that African-Americans faced as they tried to create cooperative economies for themselves. One of the most dangerous of these was the Underground Railroad, which 'smuggled' hundreds of people out of slavery through informal collectives (Du Bois 1907). The Underground Railroad between America and Canada was a collective effort and a sharing of resources. Human rights activist and former slave Harriet Tubman was a remarkable heroine in this movement, assisting hundreds of slaves to freedom in Canada. African-Americans and racialized people have been threatened since slavery, throughout the Jim Crow era, and into modern times, and the way people resisted oppressive system was through self-managed cooperatives, but these institutions were (and still are) viewed as subversive.

Short video: Organizing business by racially marginalized groups in the United States

America's black citizens have endured violent attacks since slavery right up to the modern day. These racially marginalized people have been pioneers in the cooperative movement in the US. In this interview from *The Laura Flanders Show*, City University of New York's (CUNY) Jessica Gordon-Nembhard discusses the ways African-Americans have engaged in both informal and formal collectives throughout history and into modern times, shaking up the idea that cooperatives originated in Europe.

Source: www.youtube.com/watch?v=_TVIghQMkBg#t=11 (accessed 23 October 2015)

Being an entrepreneur is not easy. Excluded groups in the Global South and North will turn to self-employment not only as a way to cope, but also as a way to contribute to the business sector on their own terms (Knight 2004; Mirchandani 2002). Immigrant and diaspora groups also turn to entrepreneurship in order to improve their independence and economic well-being. Feminists have argued that social exclusion in business has prompted excluded people to create community economies, one such example being women workers in MNCs. Self-employment can also open up the economic possibility of determining one's own future. Here, we present three examples that illustrate the business exclusion of Haitians, Aboriginal Canadians and people in the Global South, and how people react to such business exclusion.

First, the film *Poto Mitan: Haiti Women, the Pillars of the Global Economy* (2009) documents the lives of several Haitian women living in Cité Soleil (one of the largest slums in the Caribbean) and working in American sweat-shops for local sub-contracting firms. These women rejected these low-wage jobs because they were precarious, unsafe, demeaning and lacked benefits, and turned to self-employment. As outlined in Hossein's (2014a) work, Haitian women engage in collective commerce through the *caisses populaires* (credit unions) in order to support each other in business. They run their businesses out of their homes and in this way are able to take care of their children. While their incomes remain low, the women are no longer subject to harassment or maltreatment in the workplace. Moreover they have the flexibility to engage in socially conscious-raising events that address the poverty and gender-based violence in the community.

Second, in *Living Rhythms: Lessons in Aboriginal Economic Resilience and Vision*, Wanda Wuntunee (2010) describes the various ways Aboriginal peoples in Canada pursue their economic livelihoods. Aboriginal peoples, while one of the fastest growing racial groups in Canada, are plagued by poverty and social exclusion in the hinterlands and cities. In turning to business, some Aboriginal peoples pursue profit, while others are more concerned with community well-being. The multifaceted ways people choose to do business illustrate how business can be liberating for some people – even if not for others, as we outline elsewhere in this book. In the empirical example below, we use Arctic Co-operatives Limited to show how group economics can help communities. For Aboriginal Canadians, turning to business does not mean undermining social life, but finding a balance between respecting the social world and doing business (Wuntunee 2010; Southcott 2015).

Finally, in *Portfolios of the Poor: How the World's Poor Live on $2 a Day*, Collins et al. (2009) show that low-income people in Bangladesh, India and South Africa have complex financial lives with an array of devices to meet their economic needs, despite their financial exclusion. One of the most important financial supports for people who are excluded from mainstream business services is rotating savings and credit associations (ROSCAs) (Geertz 1962; Van Staveren 2015). ROSCAs or self-help banking groups rely on mutual aid to allocate financial resources to members. Hossein (2013, 2016) argues that people of the African diaspora, deeply affected by the legacy of slavery, have made conscious decisions to engage in money pools for centuries. Community economies have always been a part of our world, and socially excluded people form businesses that work for them in spite of market fundamentalism

(Gibson-Graham 1996, 2006; Roelvink et al. 2015). The most marginalized people rely on the support of friends and family to help them engage in entrepreneurial or personal projects. In this way, people are able to translate social capital – that is, their personal relationships, networks and contacts – into businesses aimed at caring for the well-being of people rather than profit alone.

Empirical example: The Arctic Co-operatives Limited, Canada

We draw on a specific example from Canada in order to illustrate this chapter's arguments that racially marginalized people can co-opt business to support their own lives and communities. The Arctic Co-Operatives Limited (ACL), based in Manitoba, Canada, is an economic organization set up over 55 years ago to support the Inuit Dene and Métis peoples. The discussion below is drawn from the Canadian Community Economic Development Network, an association of community groups and individuals.[1]

ACL is a service federation, owned and controlled by 31 Inuit and Dene community-based co-operative business enterprises located in Nunavut and the Northwest Territories. These co-operatives include retail stores, hotels, cable television operations, construction, outfitting, arts and crafts production and property rentals. The role of ACL is to coordinate resources, consolidate purchasing power and provide operational and technical support to the co-operatives. ACL enables local co-operatives to provide a wide range of services to their over 18,000 local member-owners in an economical way. ACL's democratic governance structure is designed to support the local ownership and control of each co-operative. Co-operative members take ownership in their local community business and have an equal share in the business affairs of the co-operative, as they adopt a 'one member, one vote' policy. Members are encouraged to participate in the operation of their co-operative by contributing ideas and making decisions on the policies and future direction of the co-operative.

For the Inuit Dene peoples in Canada's Arctic, cooperation and collaboration are incorporated into the traditions and cultural contexts that frame everyday life. Survival in this harsh climate has always been a struggle, requiring informal family and group cooperation. As contact increased with Europeans, the former became aware of the co-operative business model and saw the fit with their own values and cultures. These early co-operatives were based on arts and craft production, fur harvesting and commercial fisheries, aspects of life important to Aboriginal peoples.

In 1965, 14 local co-operatives joined together with the Government of Canada to form an Inuit art marketing organization – Canadian Arctic

1 Canadian Community Economic Development Network: www.ccednet-rcdec.ca/ CEDprofiles and www.arcticco-op.com/ (accessed June 2016).

Producers. In 1981, two existing co-operative federations, the Canadian Arctic Producers Co-operative Limited and The Canadian Arctic Co-operative Federation Limited, joined together to form Arctic Co-operatives Limited (ACL). Founders had certain goals that they felt were best met by using the co-operative business model. For example, members did not want people from outside their communities coming in and establishing businesses to sell products and provide services, which would drain local income from the community and would not keep money circulating locally. It made sense to develop the services themselves co-operatively, and retain the profits from any businesses for their own opportunities and priorities. In this way, the profits could be used to develop new and better services and enterprises, which would create additional employment opportunities for both co-op and Aboriginal members of the society.

The ACL symbolizes the importance of cultural preservation and the tra-ditional values of cooperation and collaboration through business within northern communities. This cooperative business model has proven extremely successful. The ACL is an example of a cooperative business that hires 800 people and has revenues of all member businesses of nearly $179 million (as of 2009). It is an important story of Aboriginal Canadians co-opting business to preserve culture and respect their social lives.

Conclusion

Business and social exclusion need not only concern the various ways in which market fundamentalism alienates people from their labour and lives. It is also important to understand that commerce, markets and business differ around the world (see Chapter 7). The Polanyi Institute at Concordia University in Montreal, Canada, is home to a group of community economy scholars who are interested in tackling cultural influences on markets and looking for business alternatives that are more amenable to human life. Community Economies Research Network (CERN) is a global network of activists and researchers committed to publishing on diverse economies and to unravelling the idea that there is only one way to do business. People participate in markets in a variety of ways, as employees as well as entrepre-neurs (Gordon-Nembhard 2011). In the globalization of extreme versions of free market capitalism, it is also important to note that many business people are co-opting business concepts and models to resist corporate capitalism.

In discussing business and social exclusion, this chapter introduced less well-known critical thinkers who argue for economic alternatives to business exclusion. These thinkers shed light on the Polanyian double-movements occurring in today's world, where people collectively organize counter-movements to show that business can be carried out in ways that are respectful of people. The ACL, an Aboriginal cooperative, is an important example of a racially marginalized group creating a social-purpose business to share indigenous culture as well as to provide jobs for its people. Another positive contribution in business is made by the self-managed banking groups called ROSCAs, which people turn to and use alongside mainstream business services (Hossein 2013, 2016). People will opt out of commercial banking systems and participate in community-driven banking systems they know and trust.

By taking stock of the small things people do to resist mainstream business practices, we give power back to people, and by recognizing the diverse economies people come up with, we can correct the assumption that most people are simply passive victims of business and markets. The everyday counter-movements ordinary people are taking to protest mainstream capitalism are happening in different ways around the globe. The Poto Mitans in Haiti are a striking example of people's resilience in finding market alternatives. Collective economics speak to the many and diverse ways people will mobilize local resources to create people-oriented economic opportunities considerate of the community.

Suggested readings

- Introduction, Chua, A. (2004) *World on Fire: How Exporting Free Market Democracy Breeds Economic Hatred and Global Instability*, New York, Anchor Books.
- Chs. 3 and 4, Galabuzi, G. (2006) *Canada's Economic Apartheid: The Social Exclusion of Racialized Groups in the New Century*, Toronto, Canadian Scholars Press.
- Ch. 2, Gibson-Graham, J.K. (1996) *The End of Capitalism (As We Knew It): A Feminist Critique of Political Economy*, Oxford, Blackwell Publishers.
- Introduction, Gordon-Nembhard, J. (2014) *Collective Courage: A History of African American Cooperative Economic Thought and Practice*, Pennsylvania, Penn State University Press.
- Ch. 1, Prahalad, C.K. (2006) *The Fortune at the Bottom of the Pyramid: Eradicating Poverty through Profits*, Upper Saddle River NJ, Wharton School Pub.
- Introduction, Wuntunee, W. (2010) *Living Rhythms: Lessons in Aboriginal Economic Resilience and Vision*, Kingston ON, McGill Queens University Press.

Bibliography

Chua, A. (2004) *World on Fire: How Exporting Free Market Democracy Breeds Economic Hatred and Global Instability*, New York, Anchor Books.

Collins, D., Morduch, J., Rutherford, S. and Ruthven, O. (2009) *Portfolios of the Poor: How the World's Poor Live on $2 a Day*, Princeton, Princeton University Press.

Du Bois W.E.B. (1903 [2007]) *The Souls of Black Folk*, Minneapolis, Filiquarian Publishing.

Du Bois W.E.B. (1907) *Economic Co-operation among Negro Americans*, Atlanta GA, Atlanta University Press.

The Economist (2011) 'Lebanese in West Africa: Far from home', 20 May: www.economist.com/blogs/baobab/2011/05/lebanese_west_africa (accessed 21 October 2014).

Galabuzi, G. (2006) *Canada's Economic Apartheid: The Social Exclusion of Racialized Groups in the New Century*, Toronto, Canadian Scholars Press.

Geertz, C. (1962) 'The rotating credit association: A middle rung in development', *Economic Development and Cultural Change*, Vol.10, pp.241–263.

Gibson-Graham, J.K. (1996) *The End of Capitalism (As We Knew It): A Feminist Critique of Political Economy*, Oxford, Blackwell Publishers.

Gibson-Graham, J.K. (2006) *A Postcapitalist Politics*, Minneapolis, University of Minnesota Press.

Gordon Nembhard, J. (2011) 'Microenterprise and cooperative development in economically marginalized communities in the USA', in A. Southern (ed.), *Enterprise, Deprivation and Social Exclusion*, New York, Routledge, pp.254–276.

Gordon-Nembhard, J. (2014) *Collective Courage: A History of African American Cooperative Economic Thought and Practice*, Pennsylvania, Penn State University Press.

Harriss, J. (2002) *Depoliticizing Development: The World Bank and Social Capital*, London, Anthem.

Hart, K., Laville, J.-L. and Cattani, A.D. (2014) *The Human Economy*, Cambridge, Policy Press.

Harvey, D. (2007) 'Neoliberalism as creative destruction', *The Annals of the American Academy of Political and Social Sciences*, Vol.61, pp.21–44.

Hossein, C.S. (2013) 'The black social economy: Perseverance of banker ladies in the slums', *Annals of Public and Cooperative Economics*, Vol.84, pp.423–442.

Hossein, C.S. (2014a) 'Haiti's *Caisses Populaires*: Home-grown solutions to bring economic democracy', *International Journal of Social Economics*, Vol.41, pp.42–59.

Hossein, C.S. (2014b) 'The exclusion of Afro-Guyanese in micro-banking', *The European Review of Latin America and Caribbean Studies*, Vol.96, pp.75–98.

Hossein, C.S. (2015) 'Government-owned micro-banking and financial exclusion: A case study of small business people in east Port of Spain, Trinidad and Tobago', *Canadian Journal for Latin American and Caribbean Studies*, Vol.40, pp.393–409.

Hossein, C.S. (2016) 'Money pools in the Americas: The African diaspora's legacy in the social economy', *Forum for Social Economics* (forthcoming).

Kabeer, N. (2004) 'Globalisation, labor standards, and women's rights: Dilemmas of collective (in)action in an interdependent world', *Feminist Economics*, Vol.10, pp.3–35.

Knight, M. (2004) 'Black Canadian self-employed women in the twenty-first century: A critical approach', *Journal of Canadian Woman Studies*, Vol. 23, pp.104–110.

The Laura Flanders Show. Interview with Jessica Gordon-Nembhard: www.youtube.com/watch?v=_TVIghQMkBg#t=11 (accessed 23 October 2015).

Martin, T. (1983) *Marcus Garvey, Hero: A First Biography*, Dover MA, The Majority.

Mirchandani, K. (2002) 'A special kind of exclusion: Race, gender and self-employment', *Atlantis*, Vol.27, pp.25–38.

Molyneux, M. (2002) 'Gender and the silences of social capital: Lessons from Latin America', *Development and Change*, Vol.33, pp.167–188.

New Rulers of the World. 2001. Film: 53 minutes. Prod. Alan Lowery.

New York Times (2013). *Made in Bangladesh*: www.nytimes.com/video/world/asia/100000002231544/made-in-bangladesh.html?ref=asia (accessed September 2016)

Polanyi, K. (1944 [2001]) *The Great Transformation*, Boston, Beacon Press.

Poto Mitan: Haitian Women, Pillars of the Global Economy. 2009. Film: 60 minutes. Prod. Tet Ansanm.

Prahalad, C.K. (2006) *The Fortune at the Bottom of the Pyramid: Eradicating Poverty through Profits*, Upper Saddle River NJ, Wharton School Pub.

Pyle, J. (2001) 'Sex, maids and export processing zones: Rules and reasons for gendered global production networks', *International Journal of Politics, Culture, and Society*, Vol.15, pp.55–76.

Rankin, K. (2001) 'Governing development: Neoliberalism, microcredit and rational economic women', *Economy and Society*, Vol.30, pp.18–37.

Rodney, W. (1982) *How Europe Underdeveloped Africa*, Washington DC, Howard University Press.

Roelvink, G., St. Martin, K. and Gibson-Graham, J.K. (2015) *Making Other Worlds Possible: Performing Diverse Economies*, Minneapolis, University of Minnesota Press.

Roy, A. (2010) *Poverty Capital: Microfinance and the Making of Development*, New York, Routledge.

Southcott, C. (2015) *Northern Communities Working Together: The Social Economy of Canada's North*, Toronto, University of Toronto Press.

Stewart, F. (1991) 'The many faces of adjustment', *World Development*, Vol.19, pp.1847–1864.

Van Staveren, I. (2015) *Economics after the Crisis: An Introduction to Economics from a Pluralist and Global Perspective*, New York, Routledge.

Williamson, J. (1993) 'Development and the "Washington Consensus"', *World Development*, Vol.21, pp.1329–1336.

Woolcock, M. (1998) 'Social capital and economic development: Towards a theoretical synthesis and policy framework', *Theory and Society*, Vol.27, pp.151–208.

Wuntunee, W. (2010) *Living Rhythms: Lessons in Aboriginal Economic Resilience and Vision*, Kingston ON, McGill-Queens University Press.

Yunus, M. (2010) *Building Social Businesses: The New Kind of Capitalism That Serves Humanity's Most Pressing Needs*, New York, Perseus Book Group.

16 | Resistance and alternatives to corporate capitalism

Introduction

The *autonomist* Marxist professor John Holloway (2005: 1) starts his book *Change the World without Taking Power* with the phrase: 'In the beginning is the scream. We scream'. He goes on: 'Faced with the mutilation of human lives by capitalism a scream of sadness, a scream of horror, a scream of anger, a scream of refusal: NO'. As a critic of capitalism, Holloway is concerned not only with dissecting capitalism and corporate power, he also wants to think about resistance and revolution as ways to find alternatives that do not fall into the same trap as previous generations – a point to which we will return below. In particular, the emphasis he places in the title of his book on *not* 'taking power' reflects his concern that alternatives to capitalism simply replace one form of authoritarian or totalitarian political-economic regime with another one, as happened with the major socialist revolutions of the twentieth century. As Holloway (2005: 12) argues, the socialist countries that emerged in the twentieth century – like the Union of Soviet Socialist Republics (USSR) discussed in Chapter 10 and the People's Republic of China – have done 'little to create a self-determining society or to promote the reign of freedom'. Consequently, it is necessary to look beyond these examples in order to think about resistance and alternatives to capitalism and corporate power.

It is perhaps pertinent to start this chapter with the criticisms laid at the door of capitalism. While there are many well-known critics of capitalism, like Karl Marx from the nineteenth century and Karl Polanyi from the twentieth century, who we have already discussed in this book, there are many, many more we cannot cover in the space available. In light of this fact, we refer to a few recent examples here, especially people critical of the corporate form of power (or *corporate capitalism*). For example, the legal scholar Joel Bakan (2004) wrote a well-known book called *The Corporation* in the early 2000s, which was subsequently turned into a film of the same name. In this book, Bakan argues that the corporation is a 'pathological institution' because its organizational structure and governance compels people to act in ways similar to a psychopath. Others like Birch (2007) argue that the corporation is a 'totalizing institution' that colonizes other social institutions (e.g. family, school, community etc.). As a result, corporate capitalism comes to infiltrate our lives in often insidious ways. Finally, the anthropologist David Graeber (2011) argues in his book *Debt: The First 5000 Years* that informal, reciprocal and everyday economies are only transformed into formal markets, including capitalist ones, through state-led violence.

As these ideas demonstrate, there are many ways to criticize corporate capitalism; equally, there are a many alternative visions, alternatives practices, and alternative organizational structures to corporate capitalism (see Gibson-Graham 1996). In a recent article, the sociologist Erik Olin Wright (2016) divides the 'logics of resistance' into alternatives that involve '*taming*', '*smashing*', '*escaping*' or '*eroding*' capitalism. First, 'taming' involves working within capitalism through the development of political and policy strategies to ameliorate the worst impacts of capitalism (e.g. Keynesianism, social democracy). Second, 'smashing' relates to the revolutionary resistance engendered by capitalism (e.g. the Bolshevik revolution in Russia). Third, 'escaping' is closest to forms of economic democracy (e.g. co-operatives) we discuss in the next chapter. And finally, 'eroding' involves finding new ways of organizing the economy that gradually promote and support the emergence of a whole new economic system. As these four logics suggest, alternatives to capitalism and corporate power come in many shapes and sizes.

In this chapter, our aim is to consider both resistance *and* alternatives to corporate capitalism. We start with a history of resistance, stretching back in history to a range of examples like the seventeenth-century Diggers movement and the nineteenth-century labour movement. We then turn to contemporary forms of resistance, especially evident in the rise of the so-called anti-globalization movement, which is better thought of as the *global justice movement*. We then finish with a discussion of a range of alternatives to corporate capitalism, such as fair trade, local exchange trading systems and social economy – the last of these we discuss in more detail in the next chapter.

Key discussion questions

- Does capitalism automatically generate resistance?
- Are there key moments in the history of resistance to capitalism?
- What are the alternatives to corporate capitalism?
- What is the Global Justice Movement?
- Is fair trade an alternative to corporate capitalism?
- Can you conceive of a world without capitalism? What would it be like?

Resistance and revolution

History of resistance to capitalism Ever since capitalism first started to emerge at the end of the medieval period, it has engendered criticism and resistance. As Karl Polanyi (1944 [2001]) noted, capitalism and capitalist markets are *instituted* rather than natural; that is, they are created through the transformation of existing social relations to force people to act in certain ways. For example, in the early days of capitalism people had to be forced to seek a wage for their labour by throwing them off the land which provided them with subsistence. This required the institution of private property (see Chapter 18). As a result, capitalism always involved a 'double movement' according to Polanyi. The transformation of society that resulted from capitalism, especially the dis-embedding of the economy from society, led to a counter-movement as people sought to re-embed the economy in social relations.

An early example of this double movement is the resistance and response to the English enclosures movement that started in the fifteenth and sixteenth centuries. We have already discussed the enclosures in Chapter 1, but it is important to emphasize how significant it was in terms of the social dislocation it caused to peasants who were thrown off land they had used for centuries with no alternative means of subsistence. Resistance to enclosures was commonplace, with frequent riots during this period. However, more concerted and organized resistance arose during the English Civil War (1642–1651) with social movements like the Levellers and, especially, the Diggers (Kennedy 2008). The Diggers were established in 1649 by Gerrard Winstanley as a religious political group that directly challenged the creation of private property through the enclosure of land. The Diggers, in particular, highlighted the exploitation of unlanded workers by land owners, arguing for a return to common ownership and working of land (Kennedy 2008). As such, they reflected the logics of 'escaping' and 'eroding' capitalism outlined by Wright (2016), which we discuss above.

Other historical examples of resistance to capitalism include the emergence of the labour movement in the nineteenth century, particularly across the European capitalist heartland. The labour movement involved the collective and voluntary forms of social organizing to create organizations – especially **trade unions** – that were controlled by neither the government nor capitalist business. As such, they represent an example of the social economy, which we come back to in the next chapter. Such collective organizing and bargaining was often made illegal and harshly punished in countries like the UK, where the 1799 *Combination Act* banned trade unions; although these Combination laws were repealed in 1825, it was not until 1872 that trade unions were then legalized in the UK (Marx 1867 [1976]). Although associated with key revolutionary figures, who we discuss next, the labour movement would fall into the 'taming' capitalism logic of resistance (Wright 2016), since it has often focused on the need to improve working conditions and wages. That is not always the case, however, as we discuss next.

Definition: Trade union

A trade union is a collective and voluntary organization which represents the interests of workers in bargaining with employers and protecting workers' rights (e.g. health and safety, working conditions, labour organizing etc.). Originally banned and repressed by capitalist countries when they first emerged in the eighteenth and nineteenth centuries, they were eventually legalized after years of struggle. In some countries (e.g. Germany, Japan), they were integrated in the management of the economy through particular forms of corporate governance or representation – see Chapter 4.

A number of political parties emerged directly out of this labour movement, including parties following socialist, communist, and anarchist ideologies. Despite their differences, these groups generally had a common goal in the elimination of private property and, consequently, of capitalist social relations. As such, they represent an example of the 'smashing' logic outlined by Wright (2016). The political parties that emerged from the labour movement were often at the forefront of resistance and revolution in Europe, including the 1848 Revolution in France that inspired Karl Marx and Friedrich Engels to write the *Communist Manifesto* (Marx and Engels 1848 [1985]). Subsequently, people like Marx, Engels and the anarchist **Mikhail Bakunin** helped to establish the International Workingmen's Association in 1864, bringing together socialists and anarchists from a number of European countries. Although the International eventually split as a result of disagreements between socialists and anarchists, it had an enormous influence on the world. A number of revolutions or political changes in the early twentieth century have their roots in these political movements. For example, socialist and communist parties came to power in a number of countries, including: Russia (1917), North Korea

Key thinker: Mikhail Bakunin

Mikhail Bakunin (1814–1876) was a major anarchist thinker who lived at the same time as Karl Marx. Born in Russia, Bakunin spent much of his life traveling around Europe supporting a range of revolutions or movements against capitalism. Arrested in 1849, Bakunin spent eight years in prison and was exiled to Siberia, from where he escaped in 1861. As an anarchist, Bakunin was committed to the idea that individual people are responsible for their own destinies, meaning that he rejected the ideas of Marx and others that history has an inevitability to it which leads to social change. One of his most well-known written works is the book *God and the State*, which was not published until 1882, six years after his death. In it, Bakunin rejects authority and hierarchy in all its forms, from the religious to the political.

Source: introduction, by Paul Avrich, to *God and the State* by Bakunin (1970)

(1948), China (1949), Vietnam (1954) and Cuba (1959) (Hobsbawm 1995). Despite achieving significant industrial and technological progress, however, these socialist regimes descended into totalitarianism, eradicating freedom and oppressing their people (Holloway 2005; Wright 2016).

From social democracy to post-capitalism? While these totalitarian regimes are not suitable visions for our futures, they represented enough of a threat to capitalist governments in the early- to mid-twentieth century to ensure that these governments sought to establish social safety nets for their citizens/ subjects – another form of 'taming' capitalism in Wright's (2016) terms. The creation of welfare states followed on from attempts to create forms of social democracy in which capitalism was aligned with broader social goals like eradicating poverty, uncertainty and insecurity (Malleson 2014). As the dominant capitalist regime from the end of the Second World War until the 1970s, social democracy was underpinned by the economic ideas of John Maynard Keynes and the social and political philosophies of politicians like William Beveridge and philosophers like John Rawls. It is often associated with a so-called 'golden age of capitalism' lasting from the end of the Second World War until the early 1970s (see Varoufakis 2011).

Since then, and as we have mentioned a number of times in this book, critical scholars have generally argued that we have entered a 'neoliberal era' (e.g. Harvey 2005). Neoliberalism is often seen as a return to nineteenth-century *laissez faire* thinking, but it is better thought of as a combining of the state *and* market instead. Since the 1970s, for example, the state has not got significantly smaller in many countries in the Global North (Birch 2015: 158); in many cases, in fact, it has got considerably bigger. Neoliberalism has generated all sorts of resistance and is often blamed for the mess left by the 2007–2008 global financial crisis. Our interest in this chapter, however, is not with neoliberalism *per se*. As we outline in the Introduction to this book, we think that the critique of and focus on free markets that underlies critical perspectives of neoliberalism often means that people miss or ignore how important business – which is, by definition, not a market – continues to be to any understanding of capitalism. Hence why we focus on corporate capitalism in this chapter.

More recently, and with corporate capitalism creating all sorts of social, political, economic and ecological problems, several thinkers have begun to posit the idea that we are fast approaching the emergence of a 'post-capitalist' era – that is, the erosion of capitalism altogether posited by Wright (2016). Largely inspired by technological developments and their implications for the organization of the economy, people like Peter Drucker (1993), Jeremy Rifkin (2014), and Paul Mason (2015) have all argued that capitalism is facing a major challenge as the result of capitalism's internal contradictions in light of things like: the declining cost of production, the increasing consumption of information rather than material products, the rise of network technologies (e.g. Facebook, Twitter etc.) and the profound changes these are having on work and workers. While the hyperbole around post-capitalism might be a bit rich in some cases, it is still worth considering these ideas and their implications to the future of capitalism as we will experience it in the twenty-first century. According to Mason (2015), for example, the oppression of workers that characterizes neoliberalism has stalled capitalism's dynamism, while production and consumption have become blurred with new information technologies (e.g. Facebook users create the content that makes it valuable to advertisers). We come back to some of these issues in Chapter 18, but wanted to raise them here as a potential trajectory for capitalism in the future.

Everyday alternatives to corporate capitalism

Tinkering around the edges or finding alternatives to corporate capitalism? While it is important to think big when it comes to imagining how the world could be otherwise, it is also important to bring ourselves back to the day-to-day world in which we live if we want to pursue those alternatives. As this book should have demonstrated already, many people have tried to find ways to tame the worst excesses of capitalism and corporate power. Many others have simply sought to sell it to us as the only political-economic system that works. This defence of capitalism is now a veritable industry; around the world there are thousands of think tanks (e.g. Fraser Institute, Canada), foundations (e.g. Coors Foundation, USA), policy networks (e.g. Atlas Research Network, USA), international fora (e.g. World Economic Forum, Switzerland), journals and magazines (e.g. *The Economist*), newspapers (e.g. *The Financial Times*) and much more besides, all directed at buttressing the supposedly unassailable logic and legitimacy of corporate capitalism. This defence goes back decades to books like Neil Jacoby's 1973 *Corporate Power and Social Responsibility*, which sought to counter a radical critique of capitalism in US public discourse (cited in Parker 2002: 177). Moreover, this defence of capitalism is well-funded and institutionalized in university business schools, economics departments and other academic units. All of it, from business ethics and CSR through the WEF to *The Economist*, represents the problems of corporate capitalism as requiring only a little tinkering at the edges; they claim that nothing at the core of capitalism or corporate power is inherently problematic, only the most egregious actions of the worst outliers (e.g. Enron, Lehman Brothers etc.).

The problem is that tinkering with corporate capitalism can only extend so far; taming capitalism only does so much, as Wright (2016) argues. In particular, when focusing on business, tinkering does not extend into changing or challenging the inner workings or regulations of corporations and businesses. Here, as David Ciepley (2013) highlights, the private rules and laws of business still hold sway; for example, a business employer can determine what an employee has to wear (e.g. uniform), how they have to work (e.g. labour process) and what they can say (e.g. discipline), no matter what the rules and laws are in wider society more generally. As such, things like freedom of speech do not apply inside the walls of capitalist business. Should we desire economic democracy or diverse economies, as promoted by the likes of Gibson-Graham (1996), then we have to find ways to go beyond this political-economic confinement. Despite what many people tell us, the brazen trumpeting of capitalism does not mean there are not many other ways to organize our economies and many alternatives to corporate capitalism we could pursue. For example, Parker (2002) provides a typology of protest, resistance and alternatives with many examples of each that we have adapted and updated here in Table 16.1. Parker's typology covers a range of activities, groups and structures, and we discuss several of them in more depth in the rest of this chapter.

Alternatives to corporate capitalism In this section we are going to outline five alternatives to capitalism: (1) the alter-globalization or global justice movement, (2) alternative production and trade, (3) alternative currencies, like local exchange trading systems (LETS), (4) alternative property systems, like open source and (5) alternative organizational structures, like economic democracy. Because we look at the last two in more detail in the next two chapters, we only provide a limited discussion of them here. We focus, therefore, more on the first three. It is important to stress that these five alternatives are not, by any means, the only or main alternatives to corporate capitalism in

TABLE 16.1 Resistance to corporate capitalism

Contestation and reform	Globalization from below	Delinking / relocalization
Fighting structural adjustment	Environmental	Anarchy
	Labour	Sustainable development
Peace and human rights	Socialism	Small business
Land reform	Anarchism	Sovereignty
Anti-corporate	Anti-free trade protests	Religious nationalism
Cyber-libertarian	Zapatista	Local alternative organization
Jubilee 2000	Greenpeace	
Amnesty International	Trade unions	Slow food
Peasants, squatters, indigenous	Political parties	Alternative food network
	Co-operatives	Local trading, community credit
Boycotts (e.g. Nike, Monsanto)	Occupy movement	Anti-colonial, independence movement
Hackers, open-source		Religious fundamentalism

Source: adapted and updated from Parker (2002)

the world. There are many other alternatives, as people like Gibson-Graham (1996), Parker et al. (2007) and Parker et al. (2013) illustrate in their work. However, since we have limited space in a book like this, we choose to focus on a few examples.

ALTER-GLOBALIZATION: THE GLOBAL JUSTICE MOVEMENT As anyone who has read a newspaper in the last few years should realize, there is considerable resistance to particular forms of global governance defined and conceptualized as the Washington Consensus, or 'neoliberal' globalization – see Chapter 8. Since we have already outlined the characteristics of the Washington Consensus in this book, we are not going to go over it again here. It is important to remember, however, that it involves the imposition of things like structural adjustment policies on countries in the Global South, and hence it has stimulated significant resistance in the Southern hemisphere. Consequently, we want to outline examples of resistance to the Washington Consensus and the alternatives that this resistance has generated. Although often described as an 'anti-globalization' movement, it is better to think of this movement as an 'alter-globalization' or 'global justice' movement (Routledge and Cumbers 2009; Chatterton 2010) because the people in the movement are not against globalization *per se*, but rather against a particular form that supports corporate capitalism.

While the global justice movement (GJM) burst into mainstream consciousness with the Seattle protests against the WTO in November 1999, it emerged earlier in the mid-1990s. According to Seoane and Taddei (2002), the GJM began to coalesce after the 1994 uprising in Chiapas, Mexico by the Zapatista Army of National Liberation against the signing of the NAFTA agreement. The Zapatistas established an autonomous zone in Chiapas and during 1996 and 1997 invited activists from around the world to come to Chiapas and share their experiences (Holloway 2005; Routledge and Cumbers 2009). The Zapatistas still occupy Chiapas to this day. Following the Zapatista uprising, several other events helped consolidate the growth of the GJM including the founding, both in 1998, of ATTAC (Association for the Taxation of financial Transactions and Aid to Citizens) in France and the creation of an NGO-led coalition against the Multilateral Agreement on Investment (MAI).[1] Both, in their way, were attempts to reduce the influence of multinational corporations (MNCs) on national governments. First, the goal of ATTAC was to campaign for taxes on international financial transactions in order to reduce currency speculation, which has a huge impact on the ability of countries to determine their own policies; and second, the campaign against the MAI was driven by the fear that it would enable corporations to hold national governments to ransom when it came to policy-making, because MAI gave corporations the

1 ATTAC: www.attac.org/ (accessed June 2016).

right to sue governments that interfered with the profitability of their investments (Seoane and Taddei 2002). All of this discontent came to a head in November 1999 at the WTO meeting in Seattle where activists, trade unionists and others blockaded and derailed the WTO negotiations.

After Seattle there was a sense of optimism within the GJM. Subsequent meetings of 'neoliberal' global governance institutions were targeted by activists and others, leading to a series of major demonstrations and protests (see Routledge and Cumbers 2009: 108). These included, but were not limited to:

- January 2000: Davos, Switzerland against the World Economic Forum
- September 2000: Prague, Czech Republic against the World Bank and IMF
- June 2001: Gothenburg, Sweden against the European Council
- July 2001: Genoa, Italy against the G8
- September 2003: Cancun, Mexico against the WTO
- July 2005: Scotland, UK against the G8.[2]

More recent examples, although taking a different approach, include the Occupy Wall Street (OWS) protests that began in a number of cities around the world in 2011 (Worth 2013). Well before OWS, the GJM had been criticized for lacking a clearly definable and achievable political goal. Partially in response to this, there have been attempts to create more formal spaces and structures for promoting alternative forms of globalization. The main one is the World Social Forum (WSF) set up in 2001 in Porto Alegre, Brazil as a direct response to the World Economic Forum (WEF) we discussed in Chapter 8 (see Seoane and Taddei 2002). Since 2001, the WSF has been held in a different country each year, with the latest event happening in Montreal, Canada in 2016.[3] The WSF brings together activists, campaigners, NGOs and others in a range of activities designed to support and promote global civil society, while adhering to a political position that no-one can speak for the whole (Worth 2013). Whether or not the WSF or wider GJM has achieved its goals, it has definitely raised awareness about the impacts of neoliberal globalization to the extent that the IMF has now even repudiated that form of globalization (Ostry et al. 2016).

ALTERNATIVE PRODUCTION AND TRADE Dominant forms of business-led globalization, which the global justice movement seeks to challenge, are based on the idea of breaking down trade and investment barriers in order to encourage

2 See Wikipedia for list of protests: https://en.wikipedia.org/wiki/List_of_demonstrations_against_corporate_globalization (accessed June 2016).
3 World Social Forum: https://fsm2016.org/en/ (accessed June 2016).

the supposed win-win benefits of international production and trade. However, these stated goals have rarely matched reality (Stiglitz 2002). Instead, multinational corporations (MNCs) have benefited from easier access to cheap labour and cheap resources in the Global South, as well as easy access to consumers in the Global North. It is, therefore, pertinent to consider whether there are any viable alternative forms of production and trade, since our daily purchases represent one area where we could make a difference on a daily basis. One alternative is fair trade, which the World Fair Trade Organization (WFTO) – originally established in 1989 as the International Federation of Alternative Trade (IFAT) – defines as:

> Fair Trade is a trading partnership, based on dialogue, transparency and respect, that seeks greater equity in international trade. It contributes to sustainable development by offering better trading conditions to, and securing the rights of, marginalized producers and workers – especially in the South. Fair Trade organisations have a clear commitment to Fair Trade as the principal core of their mission. They, backed by consumers, are engaged actively in supporting producers, awareness raising and in campaigning for changes in the rules and practice of conventional international trade.[4]

As this definition illustrates, fair trade is underpinned by a series of non-profit principles. According to Nicholls and Opal (2005), these include: minimum pricing, even above 'normal' market rates; development and social focus, so that a certain proportion of trade earnings are directed to development projects; direct, transparent and long-term supply chains in order to reduce volatility and the exploitation of suppliers; co-operative rather than competitive relations amongst producers; democratic organization through joint efforts at certification, labelling and such like; and sustainability to support the environment. Some academics like Laura Raynolds (2000: abstract) have even argued that fair trade represents an example of Polanyi-like 're-embedding of international commodity production and distribution in equitable social relations'.

The 'fair trade' movement – in opposition to notions of 'free trade' promoted by global financial institutions like the World Bank, IMF and GATT/WTO – has its origins in the mid-twentieth century and has a rather complicated history which we can only briefly sketch out here (Fridell 2007). According to Nicholls and Opal (2005), fair trade as we know it today evolved through a series of key historical moments. First, fair trade began in the aftermath of the Second World War with charities like Oxfam (UK) and Mennonite Central Committee (USA) importing craftwork from the Global South. Then it involved the establishment of alternative trading organizations like IFAT to

4 WFTO: http://wfto.com/fair-trade/definition-fair-trade (accessed June 2016).

enable producers from the Global South direct access to markets in the Global North without having to go through intermediaries like charities. Finally it was driven by certain businesses (e.g. Co-operative Group, UK) in the Global North buying and selling fair trade branded products in their stores, as well as certification schemes like the International FAIRTRADE Certification Mark. Fair trade is now a major global phenomenon involving worldwide sales of £4.4 billion (US$6.3 billion) in 2014, which was an increase of 13 percent above 2013 (Smithers 2014), and there are numerous fair trade products in the market including food (e.g. bananas), beverages (e.g. coffee) and apparel (e.g. university-branded clothing).

Although it is possible to think of fair trade as an alternative to corporate capitalism, it has also been criticized on a number of counts for failing to really challenge corporate power (e.g. Fridell 2006). It is helpful to look at a specific example in order to unpack these criticisms. For example, Carroll and Buchholtz (2015: 317) discuss the international coffee MNC Starbucks as a business that has integrated 'ethical concerns into its corporate strategies', specifically through 'ethical' sourcing of their coffee and the purchasing of fair trade coffee since 2000. While Starbucks claimed that 95 per cent of its coffee was 'ethically sourced' in 2013, the proportion of fair trade coffee was only 8.4 percent.[5] Their corporate strategy involves defining 'ethical sourcing' themselves, rather than purchasing coffee through fair trade channels. There are several important issues that this example, and others like it, raise for fair trade. First, it is often difficult to differentiate the varied fair trade value chains, meaning that fair trade can be easily diluted and co-opted as a brand through corporate dominated licensing and retailing arrangements (Doherty et al. 2015). Second, it is evident that fair trade principles often come into conflict with pricing decisions, with the former usually losing out to the latter (Fridell 2007). Finally, the participants in fair trade supply chains often have very different motivations, from creating new markets to transforming markets altogether (Jaffee 2014). How these divergent interests are managed is critical for ensuring that there is no compromise between ethics and market expansion (Renard 2005).

ALTERNATIVE CURRENCIES: LOCAL EXCHANGE TRADING SYSTEMS The third alternative is Local Exchange Trading Systems or LETS. These are networks based on a local, often virtual, currency. LETS are typically small, with a membership in double figures, at most, a few hundred. Members buy and sell goods and services to and from one another. Often the items for sale are of a craft or hobby nature, though some members offer services which they also sell

5 Starbucks: http://globalassets.starbucks.com/assets/98e5a8e6c7b1435ab67f2368b 1c7447a.pdf (accessed June 2016).

professionally on the formal market. LETS may be described as 'moneyless' to the extent that formal currency (e.g. dollar notes and coins) do not physically change hands; instead, a member's LETS account is credited (if they are a seller) or debited (in the case of the buyer) for the cost of the good or service exchanged; the transaction is recorded virtually by the system's administrator.

LETS often attract people from the alternative anti-capitalist and 'green' scene who wish to foster a local form of economy over which they have control. Members value the greater intimacy of exchanging with those in a community or neighbourhood, and they seek to reduce their reliance on corporations whose products are manufactured along supply chains which stretch across the world. Such local currencies have a long history (Peacock 2014), and many protagonists of LETS take inspiration from the impressive experiments with local money in the municipalities of Schwanenkirchen (Germany) and Wörgl (Austria) in the inter-war period. These experiments proved successful in getting unemployed people back to work, and involved not only private consumers and business, but also local government. However, the Austrian Constitutional Court saw the issuing of an alternative currency as a threat to the central bank's monopoly on currency issue and hence the Wörgl experiment was declared unconstitutional in 1933; the experiment in Schwanenkirchen had already been outlawed in 1931.

Both the Schwanenkirchen and Wörgl experiments were influenced by the work of Silvio Gesell (1862–1930), an anarchist of German origin whose name is often cited by supporters of LETS. Gesell's magnum opus, *The Natural Economic Order* (1934), propounds the idea that money should 'rust'; that is, money should be subject to periodic (monthly) devaluation so that people do not have the incentive to hoard money. Instead, people would spend it quickly (before it becomes devalued) and, by doing so, promote employment. Although something of a maverick monetary theorist, Gesell's work has not been without influence. He was cited with approval by John Maynard Keynes (1936) and remains a notable figure amongst heterodox economists.

The modern LETS movement was born in British Columbia in 1983. Few LETS today are borne of the economic hardship which gave rise to Schawankirchen and Wörgl, as many members of LETS, who are often well-educated, affluent and gainfully employed in the formal economy, seek an alternative economic lifestyle in LETS, rather than a way of earning a living. As a result, LETS rarely offer the poor and unemployed new avenues to make up for lost income from the formal economy (Peacock 2000). An exception is the Argentine barter network, Red de Trueque, the largest in the world, with hundreds of branches across the country. It was initiated in the 1990s in light of economic recession and involved between two and three million members.

ALTERNATIVE BUSINESS ORGANIZATION: ECONOMIC DEMOCRACY There is a growing interest in alternative forms of economic organization, which is often associated with the idea of the 'social economy' discussed in the next chapter. As an alternative to corporate capitalism, alternative business organizations are premised on a very different set of principles and structures. They are founded on the idea that the economy is always, and necessarily, embedded in social relations (Gibson-Graham 1996; Amin et al. 2002). It might have made more sense to have called this book *Business in Society* to reflect this perspective. It is problematic to conceptualize the economy as distinct and separate from society because that would ignore the fact that our economic lives, livelihoods, choices, preferences and so on are profoundly shaped by our social, political and material circumstances; that is, our lives are patterned by centuries of inherited beliefs, habits and values. It is the reason that so many people spend so much money at certain events or times of the year, like birthdays, Christmas and other cultural moments. Thomas Malleson (2014) argues that taking on board these sorts of ideas means we can rethink our economies to promote *economic democracy* so that we can attain more control over the direction and shape of our working (and personal) lives. It is possible, from this viewpoint, to organize work differently so that we do not give up our rights as we currently do when we enter a capitalist corporation or business (see Ciepley 2013). There are many organizational examples representing this vision of economic democracy, which we discuss in more detail in Chapter 17. An example we include here is a Case Study of 'worker recovered enterprises' in Argentina.

ALTERNATIVE PROPERTY RIGHTS: OPEN SOURCE Capitalist property regimes have gone through a major shake out over the last few years as a consequence of social and technological changes, especially the rise of the internet, file-sharing, Web 2.0 and so on. As businesses, corporations and governments have grappled with the implications of these changes, they have promoted and supported increasingly stringent property rights, especially around intangible things like information and knowledge (Drahos and Braithewaite 2002). So-called intellectual property rights (IPRs) have been extended internationally by global governance institutions like the WTO. In response to the increasing privatization and commodification of knowledge, especially software, the open source and open access movements have sought to support free access to and exchange of knowledge and information (Wellen 2013). For example, the open source movement started in 1985 as a response to early attempts to make software code proprietary so that consumers could not alter it. Over time, the open source movement has expanded to include new forms of open property rights (e.g. Copyleft), the support for open access to research (e.g. Science Commons) and challenges to corporate-dominated IP laws (e.g. Pirate Party, Sweden). For more on these issues turn to Chapter 18.

Case study

'Worker recovered enterprises' (or ERTs), Argentina

'Worker recovered enterprises' – or ERTs, derived from the Spanish *empresas recuperada por sus trabajadores* – represent an example of an alternative business organization. These ERTs emerged as a response to the 'neoliberal' policies of the 1990s that saw much of the country's national industry sold off and the economy opened up to foreign direct investment. This led to a high unemployment rate, increasing poverty and economic instability, which culminated in a full-scale economic crisis in 2001 marked by the largest sovereign-debt default in history.

ERTs are a strategy pursued by workers, primarily as a way to retain employment in factories and businesses that had gone bankrupt or been closed by their owners due to the 2001 crisis. While each factory or business has its own story, in general workers used the only resource left to them – their labour power – to restart the factories and businesses previously managed by private owners. According to Ruggieri and Vieta (2014: 78) 'the main distinguishing feature of ERTs is the recuperation of practices of self-management by workers themselves'.

Instead of a hierarchical, internal structure with a boss telling workers what to do, ERTs are organized and managed by the workers themselves. This sort of internal structure is often described as a 'horizontal' organizational structure since workers make decisions about production and management through general assemblies and democratic decision-making processes, rather than having instructions passed down through a chain of managerial command.

Argentina boasts the greatest number of ERTs today with over 312 that employ nearly 14,000 workers. Some particularly successful examples of ERTs include: FaSinPat – a name which is short for *Fábrica sin Patrones*, or a factory without bosses – which is a ceramics factory in western Argentina; IMPA, which is an aluminium products factory in Buenos Aires famous for its pioneering work in the movement and for its cultural centre and community-based high school courses, held symbolically in the old boss's office space; and Hotel Bauen, which is a four-star hotel in downtown Buenos Aires boasting excellent occupancy rates and frequent academic and cultural events. These types of ERT tend to be deeply embedded in the communities from which they emerged with 68 per cent of ERTs engaging in community-based activities according to Kasparian (2013). For more on these worker recovered factories and businesses, it is worth watching the 2004 film *The Take* – written by Naomi Klein and directed by Avi Lewis.

Since 2001, ERTs have spread to other countries in Latin America including Uruguay, Brazil and Venezuela, and have even inspired some factory occupations in countries of the global North such as the US, Turkey, Greece, Spain, Italy and France (Ruggieri and Vieta 2014). However, ERTs still face many challenges given that they must work within the law and compete within capitalist markets. As such, ERTs still operate within a legal system which privileges private ownership and property rights.

Conclusion

In this chapter we have outlined the diversity and variety of resistance and alternatives to corporate capitalism. As we noted, resistance to capitalism has a long history, stretching back to its origins in the enclosure of land (see Chapter 1). It has emerged again and again over the years, and is perhaps most obvious today in the various alter-globalization or Occupy protests that entered public consciousness with the Seattle protests in 1999. Resistance has also entailed the development of everyday alternatives to corporate capitalism. In this chapter we outlined a few examples, including: the global justice movement, fair trade, local exchange trading systems, economic democracy and the open source movement. In the next two chapters we cover two key alternatives in more depth, the social economy and rethinking ownership.

Suggested readings

- Ch. 1, Malleson, T. (2014) *After Occupy: Economic Democracy for the 21st Century*, Oxford, Oxford University Press.
- Peacock, M. (2014) 'Complementary currencies: History, theory, prospects', *Local Economy*, Vol.29, pp.708–722.
- Raynolds, L. (2000) 'Re-embedding global agriculture: The international organic and fair trade movements', *Agriculture and Human Values*, Vol.17, pp.297–309.
- Seoane, J. and Taddei, E. (2002) 'From Seattle to Porto Alegre: The anti-neoliberal globalization movement', *Current Sociology*, Vol.50, pp.99–122.
- Wright, E.O. (2016) 'How to be an anti-capitalist for the 21st century', *Journal of Australian Political Economy*, Vol.77, pp.5–22.

Bibliography

Amin, A., Cameron, A. and Hudson, R. (2002) *Placing the Social Economy*, London, Routledge.

Bakan, J. (2004) *The Corporation*, London, Random House.

Bakunin, M. (1970) *God and the State*, New York, Dover Publications.

Birch, K. (2007) 'The totalitarian corporation?', *Totalitarian Movements and Political Religions*, Vol.8, pp.153–161.

Birch, K. (2015) *We Have Never Been Neoliberal*, Winchester, Zero Books.

Carroll, A. and Buchholtz, A. (2015) *Business and Society* (9th Edition), Stamford CT, CENGAGE Learning.

Chatterton, P. (2010) 'Do it yourself: A politics for changing our world', in K.

Birch and V. Mykhnenko (eds), *The Rise and Fall of Neoliberalism*, London, Zed Books, pp.188–205.

Ciepley, D. (2013) 'Beyond public and private: Toward a political theory of the corporation', *American Political Science Review*, Vol.107, pp.139–158.

Doherty, B., Bezencon, V. and Balineau, G. (2015) 'Fairtrade International and the European market', in L. Raynolds and E. Bennett (eds), *Handbook of Research on Fair Trade*, Cheltenham, Edward Elgar, pp.316–332.

Drahos, P. with Braithewaite, J. (2002) *Information Feudalism*, London, Earthscan.

Drucker, P. (1993) *Post-Capitalist Society*, New York, HarperCollins.

Fridell, G. (2006) 'Fair trade and neoliberalism: Assessing emerging perspectives', *Latin American Perspectives*, Vol.33, pp.8–28.

Fridell, G. (2007) *Fair Trade Coffee: The Prospects and Pitfalls of Market Driven Social Justice*, Toronto, University of Toronto Press.

Gesell, S. (1934) *The Natural Economic Order*, San Antonio TX, Free-Economy Pub.

Gibson-Graham, J.K. (1996) *The End of Capitalism (As We Knew It): A Feminist Critique of Political Economy*, Oxford, Blackwell Publishers.

Graeber, D. (2011) *Debt: The First 5000 Years*, Brooklyn NY, Melville House.

Harvey, D. (2005) *A Brief History of Neoliberalism*, Oxford, Oxford University Press.

Hobsbawm, E. (1995) *Age of Extremes*, London, Abacus.

Holloway, J. (2005) *Change the World without Taking Power*, London, Pluto Press.

Jaffee, D. (2014) *Brewing Justice: Fair Trade Coffee, Sustainability, and Survival*, Oakland CA, University of California Press.

Kasparian, D. (2013) 'De alianzas y solidaridades. Las articulaciones no mercantiles en las empresas recuperadas de la Ciudad de Buenos Aires', *Observatorio Social sobre Empresas Recuperadas y Autogestionadas*, Vol.8, pp.1–16.

Kennedy, G. (2008) *Diggers, Levellers, and Agrarian Capitalism*, Lanham, Lexington Books.

Keynes, J.M. (1936 [1973]) *The General Theory of Employment, Interest and Money*, London, Macmillan.

Malleson, T. (2014) *After Occupy: Economic Democracy for the 21st Century*, Oxford, Oxford University Press.

Marx, K. (1867 [1976]) *Capital: Volume 1*, London, Penguin.

Marx, K. and Engels, F. (1848 [1985]) *The Communist Manifesto*, London, Penguin Books.

Mason, P. (2015) *Postcapitalism*, London, Allen Lane.

Nicholls, A. and Opal, C. (2005) *Fair Trade: Market-Driven Ethical Consumption*, London, Sage.

Ostry, J., Loungani, P. and Furceri, D. (2106) 'Neoliberalism: Oversold?', *Finance and Development*, Vol.53, pp.38–41.

Parker, M. (2002) *Against Management*, Cambridge, Polity Press.

Parker, M., Fournier, V. and Reedy, P. (2007) *The Dictionary of Alternatives: Utopianism and Organization*, London, Zed Books.

Parker, M., Cheney, G., Fournier, V. and Land, C. (eds) (2013) *The Companion to Alternative Organization*, London, Routledge.

Peacock, M. (2000) 'Local exchange trading systems: A solution to the employment dilemma?' *Annals of Public and Cooperative Economics*, Vol.71, pp.55–78.

Peacock, M. (2014) 'Complementary currencies: History, theory, prospects', *Local Economy*, Vol.29, pp.708–722.

Polanyi, K. (1944 [2001]) *The Great Transformation*, Boston, Beacon Press.

Raynolds, L. (2000) 'Re-embedding global agriculture: The international organic and fair trade movements', *Agriculture and Human Values*, Vol.17, pp.297–309.

Renard, M.-C. (2005) 'Quality certification, regulation and power in fair trade', *Journal of Rural Studies*, Vol.21, pp.419–431.

Rifkin, J. (2014) *The Zero Marginal Cost Society*, Basingstoke, Palgrave Macmillan.

Routledge, P. and Cumbers, A. (2009) *Global Justice Networks*, Manchester, Manchester University Press.

Ruggieri, A. and Vieta, M. (2014) 'Argentina's worker-recuperated enterprises,

2010–2013: A synthesis of recent empirical findings', *Journal of Entrepreneurial and Organizational Diversity*, Vol.4, pp.75–103.

Seoane, J. and Taddei, E. (2002) 'From Seattle to Porto Alegre: The anti-neoliberal globalization movement', *Current Sociology*, Vol.50, pp.99–122.

Smithers, R. (2014) 'Global Fairtrade sales reach 4.4bn following 15% growth during 2013', *The Guardian Online*, 3 September: www.theguardian.com/global-development/2014/sep/03/global-fair-trade-sales-reach-4-billion-following-15-per-cent-growth-2013 (accessed September 2016).

Stiglitz, J. (2002) *Globalization and Its Discontents*, New York, W.W. Norton.

Varoufakis, Y. (2011) *The Global Minotaur: America, the True Origins of the Financial Crisis and the Future of the World Economy*, London, Zed Books.

Wellen, R. (2013) 'Open access, megajournals and MOOCs: On the political economy of academic unbundling', *SAGE Open*, Vol.3, pp.1–16.

Worth, O. (2013) *Resistance in the Age of Austerity*, London, Zed Books.

Wright, E.O. (2016) 'How to be an anticapitalist for the 21st century', *Journal of Australian Political Economy*, Vol.77, pp.5–22.

17 | Social economy

Co-authored with J.J. McMurtry

Introduction

Over the last decade or so, there has been an increasing emphasis on the potential that business has for solving our social problems; that is, things like unemployment, poverty, poor health, inequality, environmental degradation etc. As we highlighted in Chapter 5, it has become commonplace for business and corporate organizations to pursue a range of corporate social responsibility (CSR) activities as part of this agenda – although it is important to note that there have been significant criticisms of these sorts of CSR activities (Shamir 2004). This chapter is not about CSR though; it is about how business organizations (e.g. the firm), business practices (e.g. entrepreneurship) and business logics (e.g. profit) have colonized (civil) society and government. However, we also want to stress that there is another vision of the economy as *always* embedded in society (see Polanyi 1944 [2001]), never distinct from social or cultural relations, logics and practices, which has important implications for how we understand the economy as always and necessarily *social*.

Popular terms like *social entrepreneurship* and *social innovation* are used to refer to the extension of business into society and government (e.g. Dees 2001). They reflect both conceptual arguments about the benefits of using business methods to solve social and environmental problems, and actually existing attempts to implement those abstract ideas. Examples include *philanthro-capitalism*, which we already mentioned in Chapter 5 (McGoey 2015); micro-finance as a solution to poverty and unemployment, especially in the Global South (Hossein 2016); and social enterprise policies as a way to regenerate deprived communities, especially in the Global North (Whittam and Birch 2011). In all these cases, and more besides, there is an assumption that business is inherently more efficient and more effective than either government or society at resolving a range of issues. It is also underpinned by an assumption that business and markets are more ethical because they are more responsive to individual preferences.

In contrast to this perspective, we want to emphasize that the economy, markets and business are embedded in their societies and cultures. Business does not, in this sense, represent a distinct or *asocial* set of organizations, practices and logics; rather, business is necessarily social. Thinkers like Karl Polanyi (1944 [2001]) stressed that attempts to dis-embed the economy from society – which he argued was attempted in the nineteenth century – always entail a 'double movement' in which society seeks to re-embed the economy in social relations. Consequently, it is not surprising that many thinkers and activists have argued that we need to think of the economy in terms of it being a **social economy** – always embedded in society – rather than in neoclassical economic terms like *homo economicus* (see Chapter 11). As such, the social economy problematizes the very idea that anyone can, or should, be a rational, self-interested individual, rather than a member of and participant in a broader social group of some sort (e.g. family, community, class, nation, religion etc.). As importantly, the concept of the social economy provides a political rallying point for people to question the hegemony of (corporate) capitalism in our lives by highlighting how social, cultural, political and spiritual values still play a central role in shaping our actions and choices. As such, it is important to remember two things here. First, there are alternatives to business and capitalism, as we discussed in the last chapter (see also Parker et al. 2007). Second, alternatives like the social economy have been marginalized in government policy and academic discourse, despite their popularity in practice. For example, the popularity of the social economy is evident in the size of the global co-operative movement, which today employs an estimated 250 million people and has over US$2 trillion of economic activity; yet this economic activity is largely invisible to government, the public at large and the academy.[1]

Key concept: Social economy

The social economy is generally defined in certain ways, focusing most frequently on the pursuit of certain types of economic activity. For some it represents a range of 'economic activities carried out by co-operatives and related enterprises, mutual societies and associations' who have a particular set of principles (e.g. member driven, independent, democratic etc.) (quoted in Defourney 2001: 6); for others, the social economy is best 'understood as commercial and non-commercial activity largely in the hands of third-sector or community organizations that gives priority to meeting social (and environmental) needs before profit maximization' (Amin 2009: 4); and others again argue that it is 'Economic activity neither controlled directly by the state nor by the profit logic of the market; activity which prioritizes the social well-being of communities and marginalized individuals over partisan political directives or individual gain' (McMurtry 2010: 4).

In this chapter we unpack these issues by exploring the popularity of social entrepreneurship as a concept and the importance of the social economy in understanding our place in the 'economy' and the world. In particular, we

1 International Co-operative Alliance: http://ica.coop/en/facts-and-figures (accessed May 2016).

want to stress that the interest in business as a solution to social problems belies the broader and long-standing entanglement of social and political goals that underpin a range of alternative social-economic organizations like co-operatives, not-for-profits, voluntary organizations etc. (Parker et al. 2007). To do this we outline the conceptual and historical development of the social economy, and consider its implications for the future.

Key discussion questions

- What is social entrepreneurship?
- Are there any problems with the ideas and examples of social entrepreneurship?
- What is the third sector? What is the social economy?
- What kinds of social economy organizations are there?
- What characteristics define the social economy?
- In what ways is the economy embedded in society?

Mainstream perspectives

In this section we want to introduce you to a number of mainstream ideas about the contribution of capitalism and business to solving social and other problems. While many people might argue that capitalism generally leads to social benefits like rising standards of living, rising life expectancy and so on, others have outlined more specific benefits of business methods in resolving societal issues.

From philanthropy to social entrepreneurship and social innovation As discussed in Chapter 5, businesses and business people have been involved in different forms of philanthropy throughout the history of capitalism. By philanthropy we mean the voluntary gifting of money and other resources to support the pursuit of particular *non-economic* (e.g. social, political, religious etc.) causes or goals. Now generally associated with charity and charitable giving, the motivation behind philanthropy has changed significantly over the centuries. In nineteenth-century Britain, for example, charitable giving was often associated with particular moralistic views on poverty, notably the idea that it was a moral failing of the people affected rather than any sort of systemic consequence of capitalism (see Amin et al. 2002). In contrast, in nineteenth-century America philanthropy was often driven by wealthy businessmen – and they were almost all men – seeking to cement their legacies through their gift-giving (Trachtenberg 2007). This is the reason that there are so many universities named after businessmen, including Vanderbilt, Carnegie Mellon, Rockefeller and Stanford amongst others.

More recently, *philanthropy* has been recast as one pillar of CSR according to people like Carroll and Buchholtz (2015). As such, it is not uncommon to see businesses donate money or other resources to a range of causes. Examples of this sort of activity abound. It is also increasingly associated with the notion that philanthropy involves a form of 'social investment' in which gift-giving is *and* should be considered as more like a business practice (*The Economist* 2006). In part, this reflects a critique of charitable organizations and foundations as inefficient in their activities and unresponsive to their donors. It does, however, also reflect the fact that the extent and depth of charitable giving has grown significantly over the last few years (Bishop and Green 2008), meaning that business and business people have had an increasing influence over the direction of societal solutions to major, seemingly intractably global problems (e.g. climate change, poverty, hunger, disease etc.). Importantly, this influence has been without any democratic oversight of their decision-making.

Although philanthropy has an important place in business history, a more recent trend has been the focus on *social entrepreneurship* as a way to solve social problems. As a term, social entrepreneurship was not frequently used until the 1970s, but since then it has become an increasingly popular term. The concept and practices of social entrepreneurship have been promoted by people like: Bill Drayton, founder of the Ashoka Foundation which finances social entrepreneurs; Jeff Skoll, former president of eBay and founder of the Skoll Foundation (est. 1999), which supports social entrepreneurs; and Charles Leadbeater, author, social commentator and political advisor to the British prime minister Tony Blair. Social entrepreneurship has also found an institutional home in university business schools with the founding of several university centres: for example, Skoll Centre for Social Entrepreneurship (est. 2003), University of Oxford; Canadian Centre for Social Entrepreneurship, University of Alberta; and Center for Advancement of Social Entrepreneurship, Duke University. All in all, social entrepreneurship has become a major field of university study as well as significant area of government and business interest (Nicholls 2006).

It is important to get a good sense of what social entrepreneurship actually means in order to think about it critically. There is a vast array of literature out there, so it is impossible to provide more than a brief introduction to the concept here. One of the most well-known definitions comes from J. Gregory Dees (2001), a professor at Stanford University. He argues that any definition of social entrepreneurship 'should reflect the need for a substitute for the market discipline' and that social entrepreneurs '*play the role of change agents in the social sector*' (2001: 3, 4: emphasis in original). As such, social entrepreneurship is often aligned with a particular set of behavioural characteristics. For example, Thompson et al. (2000) emphasize the importance of vision, leadership and capacity; Mair and Marti (2006) note that social entrepreneurship is often associated with notions of ethical motivation, personal fulfilment and social relationships; and Peredo and McLean (2006) argue that social entrepreneurs involve risk-taking, normative motivation and the resourcefulness to take advantage of opportunities. Across all these definitions, the key issue seems to be the idea that social entrepreneurship involves forms of innovation in the transformation of society.

Following from social entrepreneurship, there is an increasing interest in the idea of *social innovation*. Although an overlapping concept, social innovation does not necessarily entail the same sort of social or ethical motivation that supposedly underpins social entrepreneurship. According to Phills et al. (2008), social innovation is defined as 'the process of inventing, securing support for, and implementing novel solutions to social needs and problems'. As such, it does not entail a particular vision of social transformation, and can fit wholly within wider capitalist imperatives (e.g. profit-making) or government policy (e.g. reducing public spending). Moreover, its proponents argue that it can emerge from anywhere, since social innovation is defined by the creation of social value and not by any particular social or political-economic perspective. The exemplar of social innovation, according to Phills et al. (2008), is microfinance since it is meant to solve the problem of poverty by providing access to financial resources to marginalized groups (see Chapter 15).

Alternative perspectives: the social economy

Is capitalism all around us? As we have noted elsewhere in this book (e.g. Chapter 15), we often forget that capitalism is not necessarily *the* dominant socio-economic force in our lives – consequently, capitalist business practices and methods are not, then, necessarily the only ways to resolve societal problems or meet societal needs, or even live our daily lives. Consequently, when things like social entrepreneurship and social innovation come into vogue in mainstream debates, it is worth asking why. Our view is that they do not threaten existing structures and discourses of social power; in fact, the very emphasis on business-like terminology (i.e. entrepreneurship and innovation) might be said to reinforce it. As such, these concepts do not challenge the assumption that capitalism surrounds us and dominates our lives, nor do they challenge the capacity of wealthy individuals and businesses to influence the visions of social worth or social good. It is important, in our view, to explore other perspectives in order to step outside these everyday assumptions.

Feminist scholars like J.K. Gibson-Graham (1996) argue, for example, that capitalism only represents the tip of the iceberg of *economic* activity in which we engage. When they talk about 'economic' activity what they mean is the provisioning of goods and services in order to live our lives. In fact, Gibson-Graham argue that the economy has to be thought of as encompassing far more than wage labour, which they see as the defining characteristic of capitalism. For example, the economy also includes unpaid work, self-employment, gift-giving, volunteering, friendship, lending, illegal work, co-operatives, non-profit activities, and so on. A significant proportion of the economy, from this perspective, is actually about sharing, co-operation and solidarity – or what has been called *mutual aid* (Kropotkin 1902 [2012]). In this section we explore these issues by outlining the concept of the social economy, as well as the practices and politics of the social economy.

Between market and state? Conceptualizing the social economy As a starting point to the discussion of the concept of the social economy, we agree with Bouchard and Roussilière (2015: 15) that it 'is sufficiently distinct to constitute a "sector" or domain of the economy' because of its particular 'organizational characteristics, institutional rules and particular relationships with the state and the market'. Although the concept itself has a long history, that does not mean that it is an uncontested term. The idea of a social economy first began to emerge at the end of the eighteenth and beginning of the nineteenth century as European societies experienced profound social, political and economic changes (Moulaert and Aelinei 2005). Early advocates of the social economy included socialists and anarchists such as Joseph Fourier, Robert Owen, Pierre-Joseph Proudhon and Henri de Saint-Simon; they were all critical of the negative social impacts arising as a result of capitalism at that time (e.g. poverty, inequality etc.). Subsequently, the social economy became an important part of the social fabric of civil society in several countries by the early twentieth century, especially in countries like France (Lindsay and Hems 2004).

While the social economy has a long intellectual pedigree, stretching back to the nineteenth century at least, it re-emerged in the 1970s, according to Amin et al. (2002: 3–4), as a response to the 'cracks' that eventually shattered the consensus of post-Second World War Fordism. More recently, a number of scholars argue that the social economy has been mainstreamed into government policy as a way to address the problems engendered by 'neoliberalism' (e.g. Graefe 2007; Haugh and Kitson 2007; Birch and Whittam 2012). In what follows, we outline two ways to think about the social economy: first, one based on the idea of it representing a 'third' sector between the public and private sectors; and second, one based on the idea that it represents a particular form of socio-economic practice and politics.

First, the social economy can be thought of as a component in the wider socio-economic system – see Table 17.1 for an outline. From this perspective, discussed in Birch and Whittam (2008), the social economy represents a part of the broader third sector, so-called because it is distinct from the public and private sectors. The third sector also includes the *informal economy* and *household economy*. The informal economy includes economic exchange that is not regulated or overseen by the state, such as illegal markets (e.g. narcotics), cash-only employment etc. Quite a few countries have larger informal economies than formal ones. The household economy includes unpaid household and care work that is so important to the operation and reproduction of capitalism (see Chapter 12). In this framework, the social economy represents a more formal range of organizations that have certain structures and principles distinguishing them from the public sector and private sector, as outlined in Table 17.1. On the one hand, social economy organizations are characterized by organizational structures that are independent from the state, non-profit or not-for-profit, democratic and with mixed sources of income (e.g. sales, donations, in-kind, grants etc.); on the other hand, they are characterized by organizational principles that include social objective (e.g. social need), voluntary involvement, sustainability and mutual aid. However, from this perspective the social economy ends up as only representing another component in capitalism, focused more on social issues rather than profit. This has led people like Peter Graefe (2007) to criticize the social economy as a way to 'shore up' capitalism rather than challenge it.

TABLE 17.1 Organizational form and principles in the social economy

Organizational form	Organizational principles
Not-for-profit / non-profit	Social objective (e.g. unmet need)
Democratic	Voluntary
Mixed financing	Sustainable
Independent (i.e. non-state)	Mutual aid

Source: Birch and Whittam (2012)

Second, the above outline of the social economy only goes so far, in that it provides a descriptive or definitional conception of the social economy. We want to stress that it is important to think of the social economy in broader terms as a set of visions, practices, and politics for social transformation (McMurtry 2004, 2010). In this sense, the social economy is not simply another way to resolve social problems; rather, the social economy is a way to change society. This perspective is underpinned by the analytical position that social problems (e.g. unemployment, poverty, social exclusion etc.) are caused by capitalism and capitalist organization (i.e. private, for-profit business). Consequently, the only way to resolve these things is to undertake and support forms of political and normative practice that will lead to the transformation of society. In Moulaert and Nussbaumer's (2005: 2079) terms, then:

> . . . the social economy is that part of the economy . . . that
>
> • organises economic functions primarily according to principles of democratic co-operation and reciprocity . . .

- guaranteeing a high level of equality and distribution, and organising redistribution when needed . . .
- in order to satisfy human basic needs, in a sustainable way.

Such a conception of the social economy would obviously come into conflict with the intellectual, political and normative assumptions of capitalism and capitalist business. As a force for social transformation, the social economy is really about supporting forms of non-market and non-state activity, thereby strengthening civil society and the autonomy of individuals from both the state and capitalist business (Amin et al. 2002). As such, the social economy is not a substitute for when the 'normal' capitalist economy fails, it is a distinct 'economic circuit in its own right' and not an attempt at the reform of capitalism (Amin et al. 2003).

In any discussion of the social economy, then, it is important to remember that there is no single or agreed upon conceptual definition of the term. This can have both positive and negative impacts for our understanding of the social economy and for its practice:

- *Pros*: it creates space in and for communities, regions and countries to develop a wide range of practices, initiated by the people of those regions without any pressure to conform to a single idea of the social economy. This has led to widespread innovation and entrepreneurial creativity in addressing the needs of a wide variety of communities.
- *Cons*: it means that social economy practices and solutions have not always been resourced appropriately in the achievement of their ends. Further, as the idea of the social economy has gained public attention in recent years, governments and social actors looking for guidance and clarity on the practices and theories of the social economy find few simple answers, which can be alienating.

Social economy in practice Many academics, officials and activists see debates about the definition of the social economy as a significant distraction to 'getting things done'. While the reasons for these debates remain important, as they are reflections of the practice of the social economy as it has developed historically, they are not the end point for thinking about the social economy. In this section we discuss the various practices that form the framework of debates about the social economy. There is a need, therefore, to discuss the different conceptions of the social economy, as we have done above, but we also need to think about how the social economy is manifested in particular practices and organizations as well.

Whichever perspective you take for understanding the social economy, it is important to remember that it represents an incredibly diverse set of practices and organizations, ranging from religious institutions (e.g. churches) through community and charitable groups to different types of co-operatives. We have outlined some of these different organizations in Table 17.2. In their work, Moulaert and Ailenei (2005), Parker et al. (2007), Birch and Whittam (2008, 2012), Bouchard (2010) and Bouchard and Rousselière (2015) all highlight this incredible diversity. Some organizations are ancient, like religious orders and institutions; others were set up in response to the depredations of eighteenth- and nineteenth-century capitalism, like consumer co-operatives set up to provide workers with reasonably priced goods (e.g. The Rochdale Society of Equitable Pioneers, est. 1844) (Monaghan and Ebrey 2012); and more recent examples include attempts to counter corporate power, like the Benefit Corporation in the USA (Derber 2000). The literature cited above and the details in Table 17.2 provide a brief introduction to the variety and diversity in the social economy, and below we go into more depth with regards to some of these organizations.

Since there is such a dizzying array of practices and organizations within the social economy (e.g. Parker et al. 2007), it would be impossible for us to examine them in exhaustive detail. Moreover, ideas, practices and organizations are constantly emerging and the differences within them can be almost as diverse as those between them. That said, we think there are some historically significant and important social economy practices and organizations that provide scaffolding upon which to develop a deeper understanding of

TABLE 17.2 Social economy organizations

Organization	Objectives	Structure
Christian sects	Religious	Organized around utopian beliefs about bringing the 'kingdom of heaven' to earth
Charities	Assistance	Organized around the provision of assistance supported by donations; originally associated with moral judgements about those in need of assistance
Voluntary organizations	Mutual	Organized around the common interests of the members (e.g. trade union, trade association etc.)
Co-operatives	Solidarity	Organized around the idea of democratic decision-making, self-help amongst members, voluntary membership and equality amongst members
Social enterprises	Social	Organized around specific social objective and meeting social need through business activities (e.g. sales)

Sources: Parker et al. (2007); Bouchard and Roussiliere (2015)

the social economy. We discuss five of these here: (1) co-operatives, (2) micro-credit, (3) non-profits, (4) charities and (5) social enterprise.

First, co-operatives are one of the oldest and most developed of all the formalized practices and organizations within the social economy. Not only are they an organizational form which has been adopted in almost every country around the world, with hundreds of millions of members around worldwide, they have an international sectoral organization – called the International Co-operative Association (ICA) – and have developed an internationally recognized set of principles of co-operation (Birchall 1997). Co-operatives focus on economic democracy, community and member development as opposed to shareholder profit and privatized ownership (Malleson 2014). Co-operatives operate in almost every sector of the economy from agriculture to high-tech, services to self-help, but are defined normally by their membership. In this sense, we can identify four basic types of co-operative:

- *Worker co-operatives*: the workers own and govern the co-operative, with the most famous example being the Mondragon Worker Co-operative in Spain.
- *Producer co-operatives*: the producers of the goods own and govern the co-operative and the most common examples of this type of co-operative can be found in the agricultural sector such as the Oromia Coffee Co-operative in Ethiopia.
- *Consumer co-operatives*: these are owned and governed by the consumers of the products, with the Han group of co-operatives in Japan being an emblematic example.
- *Multi-stakeholder co-operatives*: these are owned and operated by more than one of the groups mentioned above and often have a community membership as well. The social co-operatives of Italy are perhaps the most notable of these types of co-operative.

Second, micro-credit organizations have a long history within the social economy as a means for marginalized groups to access capital or credit, which we cover in more detail in Chapter 15. Beginning with credit unions in the nineteenth century, the micro-credit movement has expanded rapidly over the course of the twentieth century (MacPherson 2010). Perhaps the most important and popular example in recent years is the Grameen Bank in Bangladesh founded by the 2006 Nobel Prize winner Muhammad Yunus. The principle innovation of the Grameen Bank was the idea of 'lending circles' where loans are made to low-income women – in order to finance entrepreneurial activities or home improvements – not as individuals but as part of a group who are all responsible for the loan. While there have been many critiques of the micro-credit form (e.g. Bateman and Chang 2012), it is undeniable that the model of self-finance, especially in its co-operative credit union form, has had a significant impact on community economic development. There have also been innovations amongst marginalized communities themselves to address their exclusion from formal circuits of microfinance (Hossein 2016; and Chapter 15). If there is sufficient community control (as Grameen has recently tried to institute) and a focus on community benefit rather than profit, the practice of micro-credit has a significant role to play in the social economy.

Third, non-profit businesses are another popular form of social economy organization, more prevalent in the Anglo-American world than in other places. Essentially the non-profit or not-for-profit business is an organization that incorporates as a business in order to achieve a social goal. When these organizations participate in economic activity, they can be considered a significant component of the social economy. In the North American and UK contexts it is increasingly popular for non-profit organizations to develop business activities in order to finance their social goals (McMurtry and Brouard 2015). While there are concerns that adoption of market-based methods by non-profits reflects a creeping capitalist logic in the social economy, there can be little doubt that the intention of the organizations themselves to serve a social good drives their activities (McMurtry and Brouard 2015). By focusing on social goals and dealing with marginalized populations through not-for-profit principles, these organizations form another important part of the social economy.

Fourth, charities are likewise an important component of the social economy, especially when they are active in funding or providing capacity to communities to address the inequality and poverty created by capitalism. Many of these charities, including religiously motivated organizations, participate in the social economy as a result their normative beliefs and principles. An illustrative example of this kind of organization can be found in the charity Oxfam, founded in 1942 in Oxford, UK.[2] Focused on poverty alleviation, this charity participates in community economic development around the globe and has been a major force in developing alternative business such as the Fair Trade Label. Again, and like non-profits, charities play an often under-appreciated role in socio-economic life, since they are focused on community well-being and participation, key features of the social economy, rather than profit.

Finally, and an area of the social economy that is receiving the most recent attention from academics and policy-makers, both negative and positive, is social enterprise (Birch and Whittam 2008). While it should be no surprise to readers of this chapter that there is no single accepted definition of social enterprise, social enterprises can be generally defined as business organizations with a social purpose, although there is disagreement about how to balance the social and business sides of social enterprise. It is not always clear whether the pursuit of a social goal, such as reducing greenhouse

2 Oxfam: www.oxfam.org/en (accessed May 2016).

emissions, through profit-oriented methods actually represents the principles that underlie the social economy (e.g. mutual aid, democratic control, autonomy etc.). We deal with similar issues in previous chapters (e.g. Chapters 5 and 14). Most relevant to social economy advocates, however, is the sudden interest of governments and capitalist businesses in this form of social economy and how it might fit into a larger neo-liberal paradigm of the retreat of the welfare state (Graefe 2007; McMurtry and Brouard 2015). However, despite this interest, it is not always clear whether government policy and legislation actually supports the social economy. That being said, we need to be mindful of the fact that social enterprise is still an emergent organizational form and activity, and the future is unclear as to how these debates will play out in practice.

Politics of the social economy: the solidarity economy Having outlined the concept and practice of the social economy, we now consider the politics underpinning it. Before we do so, however, we want to stress that the concept, practice and politics of the social economy cannot be treated in isolation from one another; all three aspects of the social economy help to define what the social economy is – even if this is contested. Here though, we want to return to the concept of mutual aid mentioned earlier in the chapter. It is an idea that can be traced back to the Russian anarchist thinker Peter Kropotkin who lived in the late nineteenth and early twentieth centuries. In his work, like the book *Mutual Aid*, Kropotkin (1902 [2012]) argued that humans are inherently or naturally co-operative, in stark contrast to the neoclassical economics view that humans are selfish and self-interested (see Chapter 11). If humans are co-operative, as Kropotkin and other anarchists contend, then we need to think carefully about the social, political and economic implications of this view.

One way to think about the implications of this view is to position concepts like mutual aid in a broader political context. As a concept, it helps frame the notion of a 'solidarity economy' (see Moulaert and Ailenei 2005). This concept emerged in a Latin American context as an attempt to politicize the concept and practices of the social economy. It gained popularity with the growth and spread of the World Social Forum (see Chapter 16), and represents an attempt to improve living standards through the social economy rather than capitalist development (Gibson-Graham 1996). For advocates of the solidarity economy, the social economy has too often been co-opted by policy-makers and businesses to strengthen rather than disrupt the advancement of capitalism and its endemic inequality (Graefe 2007). As with the social economy, the solidarity economy is a contested concept; however, despite this, many of its advocates see it as a political process, rather than a specific set of policies or practices. The key is that the solidarity is focused on societal transformations, rather than on simply changing specific forms of economic activity or organization. For example, Miller (2010: 3) defines it thus:

alternatives are everywhere and our task is to identify them and connect them in ways that build a coherent and powerful social movement for another economy. In this way, solidarity economy is not so much a model of economic organization as it is a process of economic organizing; it is not a vision, but an active process of collective visioning.

Central to this conceptualization is the specific attempt to envision the social economy as a political process; that is, as a way to transform society rather than a set of practices to ameliorate the worst impacts of capitalism. Other authors have argued for a similar politicization of the social economy; for example, Fontan and Shragge (2000: 27) argue that the social economy can be understood in political terms as operating along a continuum from the 'pragmatic/reformist' tradition on the political right to the 'utopian/social change' tradition on the political left. This political continuum is important for understanding the contested nature of the social economy, as pre-existing political beliefs often underlie the debates about what defines the social economy, what objectives it can achieve and how it should try to achieve those objectives.

The solidarity economy is important in debates about the social economy because of the increasing importance of the social economy in Latin America and other parts of the world over the last few decades. As mentioned above, while the social economy has existed in various forms for nearly two centuries, it has never been the dominant or even ascendant form of political-economic system. This has changed over the past few decades in Latin America, in particular, where countries with diverse governments, histories and social movements, such as Brazil, Venezuela, Cuba, Bolivia, Argentina, Peru and Ecuador, have incorporated the ideas of the solidarity economy, to differing degrees, into their political-economic planning (Laville 2010). The variety of ways in which these ideas have been taken up is broad, but ideas such as participatory budgeting, usufruct (i.e. the right to use land) and economics in the service of the *'buen vivir'* – or good life – have taken hold and are being put into policy. This can be seen, alongside the expansion of social economy policies in the Global North, as some of the first attempts to actualize the social economy in government policy and as an alternative to capitalism.

Conclusion

In this chapter we have discussed the concept, practices and politics of the social economy. In many ways, the social economy represents *the* key alternative to capitalism and capitalist business practices and organization. The social economy helps us to rethink the way that the economy is and can be organized, such that it provides individuals and communities with the resources, products and services they need to pursue a life they have decided to pursue. It is founded on principles of democratic control, mutualism, reciprocity, equality and autonomy; it is a set of organizations, practices and politics in which individual people take collective responsibility for their lives and livelihoods. Consequently, it represents a significant challenge to capitalist logics and assumptions.

Suggested readings

- Birch, K. and Whittam, G. (2012) 'Social entrepreneurship', in D. Deakins and M. Freel, *Entrepreneurship and Small Firms* (6th Edition), Maidenhead, McGraw-Hill, pp.105–123.
- Ch. 1, Bouchard, M. and Rousselière, D. (eds) (2015) *The Weight of the Social Economy: An International Perspective*, Brussels, Peter Lang.
- Dees, G. (2001) 'The Meaning of "Social Entrepreneurship"': https://entrepreneurship.duke.edu/news-item/the-meaning-of-social-entrepreneurship/ (accessed May 2016).
- Graefe, P. (2007) 'Social economy policies as flanking for neoliberalism: Transnational policy solutions, emergent contradictions, local alternatives', in S. Lee and S. McBride (eds), *Neo-liberalism, State Power and Global Governance*, Netherlands, Springer, pp.95–110.
- Ch. 1, McMurtry, J.J. (eds) (2010) *Living Economics*, Toronto, Emond Montgomery Publications.

Bibliography

Amin, A. (2009) 'Locating the social economy', in A. Amin (ed.), *The Social Economy: International Perspectives on Economic Solidarity*, London, Zed Books, pp.3–21.

Amin, A., Cameron, A. and Hudson, R. (2002) *Placing the Social Economy*, London, Routledge.

Amin, A., Cameron, A. and Hudson, R. (2003) 'The alterity of the social economy', in A. Leyshon, R. Lee and C. Williams (eds), *Alternative Economic Spaces*, London, Sage, pp.27–54.

Bateman, M. and Chang, H.J. (2012) 'Microfinance and the illusion of development: From hubris to nemesis in thirty years', *World Economic Review*, Vol.1, pp.13–36.

Birch, K. and Whittam, G. (2008) 'Critical survey: The third sector and the regional development of social capital', *Regional Studies*, Vol.42, pp.437–450.

Birch, K. and Whittam, G. (2012) 'Social entrepreneurship', in D. Deakins and M. Freel, *Entrepreneurship and Small Firms* (6th Edition), Maidenhead, McGraw-Hill, pp.105–123.

Birchall, J. (1997) *The International Co-operative Movement*, Manchester, Manchester University Press.

Bishop, M. and Green, M. (2008) *Philanthrocapitalism: How the Rich Can Save the World*, London, Bloomsbury Press.

Bouchard, M. (ed.) (2010) *The Worth of the Social Economy*, Brussels, Peter Lang.

Bouchard, M. and Rousselière, D. (eds) (2015) *The Weight of the Social Economy: An International Perspective*, Brussels, Peter Lang.

Carroll, A. and Buchholtz, A. (2015) *Business and Society* (9th Edition), Stamford CT, CENGAGE Learning.

Dees, G. (2001) 'The Meaning of "Social Entrepreneurship"': https://entrepreneurship.duke.edu/news-item/the-meaning-of-social-entrepreneurship/ (accessed May 2016).

Defourney, J. (2001) 'Introduction: From third sector to social enterprise', in C. Borzaga and J. Defourney (eds), *The Emergence of Social Enterprise*, London, Routledge, pp.1–28.

Derber, C. (2000) *Corporation Nation*, New York, St. Martin's Press.

The Economist (2006) 'The birth of philanthrocapitalism', *The Economist*, 23 February: www.economist.com/node/5517656 (accessed May 2016).

Fontan, J.-M. and Shragge, E. (2000) 'Tendencies, tensions and visions in the social economy', in E. Shragge and J. Fontan (eds), *Social Economy: International Debates and Perspectives*, Montreal, Black Rose, pp.1–15.

Gibson-Graham, J.K. (1996) *The End of Capitalism (As We Knew It): A Feminist Critique of Political Economy*, Oxford, Blackwell Publishers.

Graefe, P. (2007) 'Social economy policies as flanking for neoliberalism: Transnational policy solutions, emergent contradictions, local alternatives', in S. Lee and S. McBride (eds), *Neoliberalism, State Power and Global Governance*, Netherlands, Springer, pp.95–110.

Haugh, H. and Kitson, M. (2007) 'The Third Way and the third sector: New Labour's economy policy and the social economy', *Cambridge Journal of Economics*, Vol.31, pp.973–994.

Hossein, C. (2016) *Politicized Microfinance*, Toronto, University of Toronto Press.

Kropotkin, P. (1902 [2012]) *Mutual Aid*, New York, Dover Publications.

Laville, J.-L. (2010) 'The solidarity economy: An international movement', *RCCS Annual Review*, Vol.2: Online since 1 October 2010, http://rccsar.revues.org/202 (accessed 13 June 2016).

Lindsay, G. and Hems, L. (2004) 'Sociétés coopératives d'intérêt collectif: The arrival of social enterprise within the French social economy', *Voluntas*, Vol.15, pp.265–286.

McGoey, L. (2015) *No Such Thing as a Free Gift: The Gates Foundation and the Price of Philanthropy*, London, Verso.

McMurtry, J.J. (2004) 'Social economy as political practice', *International Journal of Social Economics*, Vol.31, pp.868–878.

McMurtry, J.J. (ed.) (2010) *Living Economics: Canadian Perspectives on the Social Economy, Co-operative, and Community Economic Development*, Toronto, Emond Montgomery Publications.

McMurtry, J.J. and Brouard, F. (2015) 'Social enterprises in Canada: An introduction', *ANSERJ: Canadian Journal of Nonprofit and Social Economy Research*, Vol.6, pp.6–17.

MacPherson, I. (2010) *Hands across the Globe: A History of the International Credit Union Movement*, Victoria BC, TouchWood Editions.

Mair, J. and Marti, I. (2006) 'Social entrepreneurship research: A source of explanation, prediction, and delight', *Journal of World Business*, Vol.41, pp.36–44.

Malleson, T. (2014) *After Occupy*, Oxford, Oxford University Press.

Miller, E. (2010) 'Solidarity economy: Key concepts and issues', in E. Kawano, T. Masterson and J. Teller-Ellsberg (eds), *Solidarity Economy I: Building Alternatives for People and Planet*, Amherst MA, Center for Popular Economics, pp.25–42.

Monaghan, P. and Ebrey, C. (eds) (2012) *The Co-operative Revolution: A Graphic Novel*, Oxford, New Internationalist Publications.

Moulaert, F. and Ailenei, O. (2005) 'Social economy, third sector and solidarity relations: A conceptual synthesis from history to present', *Urban Studies*, Vol.42, pp.2037–2053.

Moulaert, F. and Nussbaumer, J. (2005) 'Defining the social economy and its governance at the neighbourhood level: A methodological reflection', *Urban Studies*, Vol.42, pp.2071–2088.

Nicholls, A. (ed.) (2006) *Social Entrepreneurship*, Oxford, Oxford University Press.

Parker, M., Fournier, V. and Reedy, P. (2007) *The Dictionary of Alternatives: Utopianism and Organization*, London, Zed Books.

Peredo, A. and McLean, M. (2006) 'Social entrepreneurship: A critical review of the concept', *Journal of World Business*, Vol.41, pp.56–65.

Phills, J., Deiglmeier, K. and Miller, D. (2008) 'Rediscovering social innovation', *Stanford Social Innovation Review*, Fall: http://ssir.org/articles/entry/rediscovering_social_innovation (accessed May 2016).

Polanyi, K. (1944 [2001]) *The Great Transformation*, Boston, Beacon Press.

Shamir, R. (2004) 'The de-radicalization of corporate social responsibility', *Critical Sociology*, Vol.30, pp.669–689.

Thompson, J., Alvy, G. and Lees, A. (2000) 'Social entrepreneurship: A new look at the people and the potential', *Management Decision*, Vol.38, pp.328–338.

Trachtenberg, A. (2007) *The Incorporation of America: Culture and Society in the Gilded Age*, New York, Farrar, Straus and Giroux.

Whittam, G. and Birch, K. (2011) 'Market madness or the road to salvation? A critical review of the social enterprise agenda', in A. Southern (ed.), *Enterprise, Deprivation and Social Exclusion*, London, Routledge, pp.239–253.

18 | Rethinking ownership: the market vs. the commons

Introduction

What we own (property) and how we own it (property rights) are central concerns for anyone interested in capitalism and its alternatives (Mann 2013; Malleson 2014; Sayer 2015). While it may seem natural to think that the things we possess – our clothes, our shoes, our electronics etc. – are inherently ours to do with as we please, it is not actually as simple as this, as we will show in this chapter. History, for example, illustrates that there are a diverse range of property systems including communal or group ownership (e.g. Anglo-Saxon England), hierarchical and inherited ownership (e.g. feudal primogeniture), common ownership (e.g. common land), private ownership (e.g. capitalist labour market) and open ownership (e.g. open source software). Moreover, there are varied social, political and economic aspects to these property systems, including: limits on female ownership (e.g. feudal primogeniture), limits on male ownership (e.g. Iroquois/Haudensaunee), racialized slavery (e.g. pre-Civil War USA), non-racialized slavery (e.g. Rome) and so on. While we do not directly address these latter issues, we do want to highlight them here as integral to systems of ownership and property.

Our focus, in this chapter, is on capitalist forms of ownership. A number of scholars, political thinkers and philosophers have argued that capitalism only emerged as the result of the institution of private property, especially in European societies, through the dispossession of peasants from land they had held in common or as a customary right. We have already discussed some of these thinkers in previous chapters (e.g. Chapter 1), as well as this process of land enclosure (e.g. Marx 1867 [1976]; Polanyi 1944 [2001]; Wood 1998; Harvey 2003). What these thinkers emphasize is that private property and ownership as we understand them today have their origins in the violent instituting of new property laws that enabled certain people (i.e. the most powerful members of society) to take, own and sell land as they saw fit. For one, Marx (1867 [1976]) provides a graphic history of these enclosures, defining it as a form of 'primitive accumulation'. Building on Marx, the geographer David Harvey (2003) calls this process 'accumulation by dispossession' because the accumulation of capital, which is the very basis of capitalism, happens as the result of dispossessing people of the land, natural resources, knowledge etc. that they rely on for their lives and livelihoods, and turning it into private property to be traded and sold. Dispossession, in this sense, does not involve the usual risks associated with capitalist production; for example, uncertain or rising production costs, uncertain or declining demand and such like.

In this chapter then, we focus on a number of issues to do with property, property rights and ownership. First, we discuss mainstream perspectives of property, including those in law, political economy and neoclassical economics. In doing so, we highlight how private property, which is specific to capitalism, has been extended to more and more parts of the economy through privatization, new property rights etc. Second, we consider several critiques of private property and several examples of alternatives to it, including the commons, open access movement and the sharing economy. Finally, we consider the specific example of private property relating to intellectual activity, what are called intellectual property rights (IPRs), in order to show how notions of private property are contested and contestable.

Key discussion questions

- What is private property?
- What are property rights? Do they make sense?
- What things can we own? What things can we not own?
- How might you create property rights for something currently held in common?
- What are the critiques of private property?
- What are other forms of ownership?

Mainstream perspectives

What is property? What is ownership? Like most things, there are a number of ways to define property and ownership. When doing so, references to property rights can refer to *real property* – or things that are immovable like land – and to *personal property* – or things that are movable like commodities, money etc. Increasingly, we also make reference to *intellectual property* – for things that are intangible (e.g. copyright). Capitalist property rights – which we define here as *private property* – involve a bundle of rights, including: (1) the *use* of something, within certain legal limits; (2) a claim to the *returns* on the use of something, including sale, rent and interest; and (3) the right to *alienate* (i.e. to separate legally from other people) something through its use (e.g. consume) or through its transfer (e.g. sale) to other people (Boutang 2011). In order to understand property and ownership, we are going to explain how property in general is defined (1) in legal terms, (2) as political-economic phenomena and (3) in neoclassical economics.

Starting with the legal definitions, it is notable that property is an important legal right – sometimes defined as a human right – in many national constitutions, including those of the USA, UK and Canada. In the USA, the right to property was built into the Declaration of Independence, although it was euphemistically called 'the pursuit of happiness', and incorporated into the Constitution, especially in the Fourth and Fifth Amendments (1791), and then Fourteenth Amendment (1868). The last of these played a significant role in the *corporate revolution* discussed in Chapter 3 (Nace 2003). In the UK, property rights have a long history and evolution from group ownership (*allodial*) common in Anglo-Saxon England through Norman laws of primogeniture inheritance to the mass enclosure of land from the sixteenth century that Marx (1867 [1976]) linked to the emergence of capitalism – see Chapter 2. Finally, in Canada property rights are bound up with the historical agreements between the Crown and the First Nations. As a result, nearly all land is officially Crown Land, although individuals can still own it, while there are a range of legal claims to the rest by various First Nations. Worldwide, property rights are included in international doctrines like the 1948 United Nations *Universal Declaration of Human Rights*. According to Article 17, for example, 'Everyone has the right to own property alone as well as in association with others' and 'No one shall be arbitrarily deprived of his [sic] property'.[1] This highlights that the right to own property refers to both individuals and businesses or other organizations (i.e. association). While these legal rights to property may seem natural today, they have emerged over a long period of time and as the result of significant debates and struggles about who has certain rights and who does not.

Obviously, property rights do not simply arise from legal doctrines, and this is where political-economic understandings and definitions of property come in. A number of philosophers and political thinkers over the last few centuries, as capitalism emerged and consolidated (see Chapter 1 and 2), have helped to define and legitimate, through their definitions, the *private* property rights that underpin capitalism. Of particular importance in this regard is the English philosopher **John Locke** (1632–1704), especially his 1689 *Two Treatises on Government*. In this work, for example, Locke provided a justification for private property rights and ownership – and critique of feudal property rights (e.g. primogeniture inheritance) – by arguing that private property rights are derived from 'mixing one's labour' with nature (quoted in McMurtry 2002: 67). Private property, in this Lockean sense, can be considered as the right to whatever we produce through our own labour or work. As such, this conception contrasted sharply with existing theories of feudal property based on rights of inheritance. While this Lockean perspective of private property may seem, intuitively at least, reasonable – i.e. we merit rewards for our effort

1 United Nations *Universal Declaration of Human Rights*: www.un.org/en/universal-declaration-human-rights/index.html (accessed June 2016).

– it has been naturalized in a particular form under capitalism. According to Marx (1867 [1976]: 1084), private property in capitalism legitimates the appropriation of work through the centralization of production: '*Ideologically* and *juridically* the ideology of private property founded on labour is transferred without much ado to property founded on the *expropriation of the immediate producers*'. What this denotes is the legal, social and political capacity of capitalists, as producers who centralize work in business enterprises, to expropriate the work of individuals and then claim it as rightfully their own. The take away message is that we should not think of property rights as natural in any way; they are the constructs of human choices.

Key thinker: John Locke

John Locke (1632–1704) was an English philosopher whose political philosophy stands in the 'social contract' tradition which, amongst other things, attempts to justify the legitimate sphere of government. In his *Two Treatises on Government* (1689), Locke tried to justify private ownership of property. Locke's political philosophy has exercised an important influence on contemporary Libertarian philosophy. His work is held, by some, to aim to justify the European settlement of the 'New World' and the securing of property rights over land claimed by First Nations peoples.

Sources: Tully (1994); Bishop (1997)

This brings us to the final definition, that in neoclassical economics. In order to illustrate this we draw on the work of Ronald Coase (1937, 1960) – who we mention in Chapter 3. There are two sides to Coase's work relevant to this discussion of property; the first relates to his 'theory of the firm' and the second to his so-called 'problem of social cost'. First, Coase's theory of the firm provides the foundation for neoclassical conceptions of business organization, especially as it relates to notions of corporate governance (see Chapter 4). Later economists, especially key figures like Alchian and Demsetz (1972) and Jensen and Meckling (1976) stress that the firm is best characterized as a bundle of property rights, nothing else. A business, from this perspective, is nothing more than a 'nexus of contracts' between a number of property owners, especially workers as owners of their own labour and investors as owners of money. Second, Coase's discussion of the problem of social cost reflected the broader implications of these ideas. From this perspective, economic decisions are most efficient when private property owners are free to negotiate the value of their property *rights* with one another, without the intervention of the state or government. Basically, Coase suggested that property rights provide their individual holders (i.e. owners) with the proper incentives that ensure the efficient use of aggregate resources, because individual owners are able to make the best judgements about what has most value when it comes to conflicts over the use of property. In contrast, Coase argued, governments cannot make these decisions efficiently.

Property, property everywhere: private property as efficiency In this section we outline how private property can seem to resolve all sorts of problems in our societies. To do this, we have to start with a discussion of 'the commons' (Ostrom 1990; Robbins et al. 2010). We have already come across this concept in Chapters 1 and 9, but it is important to provide a brief recap here in order to ground the rest of the discussion in this section. As we stated before, the commons refers to anything held in common – collectively – by a group of people; it is usually held in common for the following reasons: (1) no-one created it themselves, and therefore cannot claim to have 'mixed their labour' with nature (*à la* Lockean property rights); (2) it is difficult, if not impossible, to enclose or partition through property rights (e.g. the oceans, the air, humour, love etc.); (3) there are overlapping social, ethical and legal claims to it from different people; and (4) it provides benefits to non-owners that cannot be restricted by (current) property rights (e.g. street lighting).

Despite what we have noted above, the commons is a contested notion, which explains why, over the years, different people have sought either to transfer things into common or public ownership, or into private hands – this is especially the case when it came to debates between left-wing and right-wing political parties after the Second World War (Cumbers 2012). As we have already mentioned, one argument against common ownership is that it leads to a 'tragedy of the commons' because it is in the economic interest of everyone who can use a commonly-held thing to use it as much as they can (Hardin 1968). Thus common property ends up over-used and eventually destroyed. According to the likes of Hardin (1968) and others, private property rights provide the correct incentives to owners because they force owners to take care of their property to ensure that it does not deteriorate or end up getting overused. More broadly, economists tend to argue that private property is essential for the proper functioning of market because it enables people to price their decisions accurately, and thereby make rational – and thereby efficient – choices (see Crouch 2011: Ch. 2). These perspectives of private property have had significant societal impacts in at least two main areas.

One trend has been the increasing privatization of once commonly-held things over the last few decades, primarily evidenced in the sale or transfer of public assets (e.g. railways, utilities etc.) to private businesses or other non-government organizations. For example, Clifton et al. (2006) detail the waves of privatization that happened across the European Union; Cumbers (2012) and Birch (2015) provide accounts of privatization in the UK; McBride and Whiteside (2011) focus on Canada; and Birch and Siemiatycki (2016) discuss diverse forms of privatization and pseudo-privatization (or 'marketization') around the world. While there are certainly ideological reasons behind privatization, often associated with neoliberalism, it is more generally justified in relation to higher efficiencies inherent in private business operations – especially competitive pressures – in contrast to public or government management (Vickers and Yarrow 1991). Whether or not privatization has led to efficiencies is debatable; what it has done definitively is transfer an increasing proportion of production, distribution and service delivery to the private sector.

A second major trend has been the extension and strengthening of private property rights over intellectual or intangible activities – e.g. science, innovation, culture, art, music etc. (Drahos and Braithewaite 2002; May 2010). So-called **intellectual property rights** (IPRs) are important because societies in the Global North have become, or are becoming, *knowledge-based economies* in which consumers are increasingly consuming 'content' rather than products (e.g. television shows and not televisions). For example, Jeremy Rifkin (2014) argues that value is no longer derived from the production of goods and services; rather, it is derived from access to knowledge, culture, relationships etc. (i.e. content). As a result, there has been a significant political and economic drive to extend and strengthen IPRs in order to provide the means to capture this value and stimulate further content development. This has been reinforced at the international level through agreements like the Trade-Related Aspects of Intellectual Property Rights (TRIPS) of the World Trade Organization (WTO) (Drahos and Braithewaite 2002), which we discuss in more detail below.

Key concept: Intellectual property rights (IPRs)

IPRs cover a range of legal property rights to knowledge, artistic creations, cultural products and so on. According to the WTO, they include the following: *copyright* for written, creative or performance works (e.g. books, films, music, software etc.), which lasts for the lifetime of the author and then 50 years after their death; *trademarks* and *geographical indications* for products, which last indefinitely as long as protected; *patents* for new inventions and designs, which last for a minimum of 20 years and are meant to stimulate innovation; and *trade secrets* which last as long they can be kept.

Source: www.wto.org/english/tratop_e/trips_e/intel1_e.htm (accessed June 2016)

It is important to note several things about property rights, private or otherwise. First, property is often characterized as a bundle of rights (e.g. Coase 1960); in that sense, we hold rights and *not* absolute physical control over things. Most property rights, for example, are really rights of exclusion which allow property owners to exclude others from using their property.

Second, then, property rights, in and of themselves, do not give the right to property owners to use their property in any way they see fit; for example, as Tom Malleson (2014: 146) points out, owning a car does not give someone the right to drive at any speed they choose. Governments can place certain limits on the use of property; increasingly, businesses can also place limits on the use of the products they sell us as well, an issue we will come back to in the chapter's example below. Third, ownership and property rights differ between jurisdictions (i.e. countries) and between different historical periods; we emphasize this again to reinforce the point that ownership and property rights are constructs of human decisions, they are not natural or the result of natural rights (cf. Locke). Finally, our societies have a range of different property rights, even though it may seem like private property is the dominant form; other examples include, common ownership, group ownership and open ownership.

In summary, we have sought to outline several conceptions of property and ownership, and then discuss why private property in particular is presented as the best way to organize society. In the next section we criticize these arguments and present alternative forms of ownership that enable different forms of economic organization (e.g. cooperatives, open systems, sharing etc.).

Critical perspectives

The discussion in the last section leaves a number of key issues unresolved and, in fact, unresolvable. It should be obvious that we find the characterization of private property as inherently beneficial to be problematic. Part of the problem with mainstream perspectives is that they do not define property rights as a social relation. Rather, they tend towards juridical, naturalistic or economistic assumptions; for example, property rights are an inherent human or natural right, or form the basis of the socially efficient allocation and distribution of resources. In this section we take a critical look at property and ownership.

Critique of private property We want to start this section by returning to the notion of the tragedy of the commons and the idea that private property resolves problems with the use and distribution of societal resources. We start by highlighting three key issues, and then discuss a number of issues in more depth. As a starting point, then, there are three issues with mainstream perspectives:

- *Privatize everything*: according to some economists, it makes sense to privatize everything since the capitalist market is the most efficient allocator and distributor of societal resources, but only if everything can be priced (Crouch 2011). And to price everything necessitates everything being owned, with clear private property rights (e.g. Coase 1960). However, this raises a question . . .

- *The commons*: . . . can all of the commons be privatized? Not simply in economics terms, but as a political institution and social relation. For example, national or regional art and culture, social values and norms, taste and fashion, knowledge and science etc. are all part of the commons, yet privatizing them would entail significant – and regressive – limits on people's lives, behaviour, decisions etc. (e.g. banning people from appreciating beauty, stopping people from choosing how they wear clothing etc.) See the Case Study. An important example of this specific issue concerns IPRs, which we will return to below.

- *Collective property*: many things are held as collective property, legally or ethically, because ownership rights have long-lasting effects and implications in their use, disposition and deterioration. For example, the world's biosphere will be essential for anyone who is born after us, which problematizes the idea that anyone can own it *now* and do as they see fit (e.g. destroy it, use it up etc.) without considering future generations (see Chapter 9 on the environmental consequences of this perspective).

Case study

Selling a beautiful landscape

Some economists have speculated that we could turn everything into private property, and that this would solve all societal problems. If we try hard enough, we could turn anything into a commodity, i.e. something for sale. We have to think about what it is we are trying to monetize – or sell – and what socio-technical arrangements we then need to turn it into private property. An extreme example might be something like the *view* of a beautiful landscape – it is important to note that this does not mean *owning* the landscape itself, just the view of it. While we can all enjoy this view at present if we simply look, it could also be turned into private property with the right kind of socio-technical arrangements. For example, all windows in all the buildings overlooking the landscape could be replaced with new glass that is opaque until you pay for it to turn transparent. The price you pay would reflect the cost of upkeep of the view of the landscape.

Next, we want to outline, briefly, some of the main criticisms of private property. Due to space constraints, we are going to focus on four main criticisms: (1) the notion that ownership is derived from work, (2) the problem of the divorce between ownership and control, especially as this relates to businesses and corporations, (3) the idea that common ownership implicitly entails a tragedy of the commons and (4) the problem with economic rents derived from ownership rights, especially of assets.

The first two issues relate to the idea that private property is justified by the work entailed in ownership (i.e. the Lockean notion). First, as several scholars have pointed out, much of ownership, and hence private property, does not derive from an individual's work, but from the instituting of new laws to dispossess people of resources they need to live. As we outlined in Chapter 2, capitalism emerged as a result of this sort of dispossession. People like Marx (1867 [1976]) and Polanyi (1944 [2001]) outlined the history of land enclosures in England, and then Britain, which threw thousands of peasants off the land they had previously farmed. More recently, Sayer (2015) argues that dispossession includes the privatization of utilities companies (e.g. water, electricity etc.), which transferred once publicly-owned services into private monopolies. As such, privatization dispossessed citizens of their ownership and control over very basic services and infrastructure (e.g. water, power, roads, railways etc.). Dispossession has nothing to do with labour or effort, it is merely power. Second, as a result of the evolution of business forms, especially corporate organization and governance (see Chapter 3 and 4), there has been a separation of ownership from control. Sayer (2015) also argues that this separation illustrates the growing importance of unearned income, by which he means income not earned as the result of individual labour or effort. The corporate form has been a key institution in this process.

The last two issues relate more to the tragedy of the commons argument. First, there are legal scholars like Heller (1998, 2008) who argue that there is actually a 'tragedy of the anti-commons'. This concept relates to the extension of private property rights, especially IPRs, to more and more areas of our lives. As a result, it becomes more difficult to actually undertake creative production because to do so requires coordinating the property rights of so many individuals and businesses. In his book, *Gridlock Economy*, Heller (2008) argues that the anti-commons (i.e. private property rights) means that it is no longer affordable to develop new drugs, new music and so on. Second, it is increasingly evident that ownership and property rights, especially IPRs, are constructing new, private monopolies – that is, private property rights over important assets (e.g. infrastructure, public services, knowledge etc.). This entails **economic rent-seeking**, or **rentiership**, rather than entrepreneurial activities. As Frase (2013) highlights, IPRs, for example, extend ownership rights from a particular object to all versions of that object – limiting the ability of competitors even to compete and turning that competition into a winner-takes-all process (Keen 2015). There is a deep contradiction here between notions of 'free' markets, underpinned by the free circulation of goods, people and money, and monopoly protections (Deibel 2014).

Key concepts: *Rentiership* and economic rent-seeking

An economic rent can be defined as the cost incurred by a producer, and hence a consumer, that is not part of the cost of production of a product or service (i.e. the money or labour needed). Originally defined by David Ricardo in the nineteenth century to refer to the economic rents extracted by landowners through their ownership of land, which was not seen as productive or capitalist, it can now be linked to various forms of private or public ownership that enables the extraction of money (i.e. economic rent) without an investment in production. Examples range from land, as in Ricardo's day, through bank fees and charges, to product brands. As a result, it is possible to argue that modern capitalism is underpinned by rentiership as opposed to entrepreneurship; that is, from the identification of rent extraction as opposed to capitalist production.

Commons-based production and ownership The extension of private property rights to new areas of human activity, like IPRs in information and communication technologies, has not gone uncontested; there is always conflict between different interests, social relations and groups. New forms of production and ownership are emerging around the world, and old forms are being dusted down once again. Here we will discuss commons-based production and commons-based property rights, while in the next section we discuss the specific notion of the sharing economy which has become popular in the last few years. We can split up non-proprietary production and ownership into forms of commons-based access, ownership and production as outlined in Table 18.1; we will go through each in turn.

TABLE 18.1 Commons-based access, ownership and production

Access	Ownership	Production
Open access (journals) Massive Open Online Courses (MOOCs)	GNU Public License (software) Copyleft (general)	Distributed computing Wiki-platforms (e.g. Wikipedia)
Pre-competitive research (e.g. Innovative Medicines Initiative, EU)	Creative Commons (general) – CC BY – CC BY-SA – CC BY-NC-SA – CC BY-NC-ND	Crowdsourcing 'Sharing economy' (e.g. Airbnb)

Sources: Wellen (2013); Deibel (2014); Keen (2015); Skågeby (2015)

283

As our economies have become more knowledge-based, the issue of access to knowledge – as opposed to physical things – has become an important political, social and economic issue. On the one hand, governments and businesses, especially in the Global North, have sought to extend private property over knowledge and other intangibles, as we highlight in this chapter. But, on the other hand, there is a movement to provide open access to knowledge (May 2010; Wellen 2013). The rationale behind open access is that knowledge is and should be a common good, especially when it relates to knowledge that might help countries and people resolve significant problems (e.g. agriculture, disease, health etc.). A few examples of open access include: open access journal publishing to make knowledge freely available (with internet access), which has been growing over the last few years (Wellen 2013); massive open online courses (MOOCs) run as partnerships by universities and businesses, although these MOOCs do entail payment for credit in taking the course (Wellen 2013); and 'pre-competitive research' initiatives designed to support research that businesses will not fund because it is not profitable (Birch et al. 2014). These three examples illustrate a few attempts to widen access to resources (e.g. knowledge, education, research) that are blocked by private property rights (e.g. journal paywalls).

The key recent example of commons-based ownership is the open source software movement which first emerged in the 1980s (Hope 2008; Boutang 2011; Wellen 2013; Deibel 2014). Since then there have been several attempts to use existing property laws to create free or open ownership licences. An early example was the GNU Public License, which was meant to support and extend the development of free software (Hope 2008). Other forms of non-proprietary rights have been created, the most important of which include Copyleft and Creative Commons licences (Deibel 2014). Creative Commons licences, for example, cover more than software and include a range of different licence options: for example, *attribution* (BY) requiring acknowledgement of the original producer; *share-alike* (SA) requiring that any adaptation of the original creation has to be distributed using the same licence; *non-commercial* (NC) requiring that use, distribution etc. are all for non-commercial purposes; and *non-derivative* (ND) requiring no adaptation of the original creation. While these non-proprietary ownership rights can be criticized, the fact that they are deemed necessary contradicts the simplistic, naturalistic and economistic assumptions that private property is the most efficient way to organize capitalism, let alone any other economic system. As Boutang (2011: 87) points out, the existence of these non-proprietary forms of ownership, 'raises a serious paradox: market exchange turns out to be less efficient and more expensive than cooperation outside the market'.

A final set of issues involves production itself. There are a growing number of examples of commons-based production, ranging from distributed computing – where individual's computers are linked together to undertake large projects – through various Wiki-platforms – of which Wikipedia is the most well-known – to things like crowdsourcing and the sharing economy. We come back to the last of these below, so focus on the others here. These different forms of production are based on the non-proprietary ownership rights we discussed in the last paragraph. What they entail are forms of collective, communal production that sit outside, or on the edge of, formal market exchange; some, like crowdsourcing, are more embedded in capitalist social relations than others, but they still involve direct relations between producers and users that bypass large businesses or corporations (Haiven 2014). A number of autonomist Marxists have argued that these forms of production help to radically alter production and property relations, thereby challenging the standard conception of the private firm as the key organizational form in capitalism (e.g. Boutang 2011). Other forms are more than just possible, they may actually be more efficient – or effective – because they enable the release of each individual's creativity rather than the subsumption of that creative potential to bureaucratic, corporate culture (see Malleson 2014).

The sharing economy Next, we want to discuss the so-called 'sharing economy' because it is held up as a significant alternative to modern capitalism. The sharing economy reflects the expansion of the internet as a site of human activity, socializing and interaction – basically as a 'place' where we now share our lives, our emotions, our desires and fears, our ideas and thoughts and so on (Skågeby 2015). With the advent of Web 2.0, as it is called, the internet has been transformed into a more interactive media; that is, the production of content on the internet is increasingly dominated by consumers themselves, rather than content providers (e.g. media companies, internet companies etc.). We can see this most obviously in social media websites and businesses like Facebook – which, as of mid-2015, has nearly 1.5 billion users worldwide – and YouTube (owned by Google) – which has over 1 billion users worldwide. These two websites, as with many others (e.g. Google, Amazon, Twitter, LinkedIn, Instagram etc.), only generate value because of the activities of their users and not because the businesses themselves necessarily sell us any products or services. In fact, the business model for these companies is often based on giving away their product or service (e.g. software) for free and then capturing value from the information provided by users (e.g. preferences, likes and dislikes etc.); or what is becoming known as Big Data (Keen 2015).

According to Skågeby (2015), the sharing economy, as distinct from Web 2.0, has its origins in earlier versions of file-sharing over the internet (e.g. Napster). While people sharing music, films etc. was gradually criminalized, framed as an act of 'piracy', the more recent description of the sharing economy involves a reframing of sharing as renting out our resources – or, more specifically, assets – to one another. Hence, we can use Airbnb to rent a room from someone, or Uber to hire them as a taxi. The trick, as it were, with this business model is the framing of monetary transactions (e.g. renting a room) as sharing between individuals, rather than buying a service from a business; this hides the fact that the sharing economy is tied to forms of economic rent-seeking – that is, *rentiership* – by intermediary businesses which run the networks through which people rent or hire resources from each other. Each time people transact with one another, the business takes a cut as owner of the network that brought the people together.

The sharing economy is based on this rentiership business model; according to Keen (2015: 37–39), for example, it is about identifying something to monetize and then creating the socio-technical means to capture value from that monetization. Key examples include new businesses like Airbnb and Uber, but we could also include Google, Facebook, Twitter etc., since they are essentially extracting value from our habits, desires, preferences, relationships, thoughts etc. A number of thinkers, called autonomist Marxists, actually argue that we should really think of ourselves as 'prosumers' since so much of our consumption generates value for internet businesses (Boutang 2011; Marazzi 2011). While this might all sound slightly harmless, it is important to remember that the internet, the Web and its underlying software and physical infrastructure were all financed by public investment from governments, especially the US government (Mazzucato 2013); that means that the internet was established as a commons, a collectively-owned thing, and not as the result of private investors taking a risk with their investment (Keen 2015).

Empirical example: intellectual property rights

The main, and in some ways iconic, example of the ongoing conflict over private property and ownership in contemporary, global society is the critique of intellectual property rights (IPRs). While IPRs have existed for centuries – e.g. patents and copyright to at least the seventeenth century in the UK – their current ubiquity, implementation and manifestation is different in kind as much as degree. For example, they now cover things like animals (e.g. Harvard's OncoMouse), plants, software, management practices, amongst other things. A number of scholars have discussed the changing political economy of IPRs in the last few decades, including Drahos and Braithewaite (2002, 2004), Hope (2008), Tyfield (2008), May (2010), Mirowski (2011) and others.

Of particular importance to this changing political economy of research and innovation is the globalization of IPRs through the Trade-Related Aspects of Intellectual Property Rights (TRIPS) agreement incorporated into the World Trade Organization. This agreement seeks to harmonize IPRs around the world, not only in terms of length of the property rights, but also necessary enforcement measures countries need to follow. As such, Drahos and

Braithewaite (2002) argue, it institutes measures that are beneficial to certain countries, like the USA, since only certain countries have significant intellectual property to protect. This has meant that these global rules have led to a huge increase in licensing profit for the Global North at the expense of the Global South, since the former owns more IP than the latter.

While there are global equity issues involved with IPRs, there are also a number of more general criticisms of this extension of private property to intellectual activities. First, IPRs entail a form of dispossession in which publicly-generated and supported knowledge (e.g. internet) is gradually enclosed behind private ownership (Mazzucato 2013). Second, IPRs are essentially monopoly rights, given to certain people such that they can acquire economic rents from their ownership (Boutang 2011). Finally, as mentioned already, IPRs extend private property from a particular thing (e.g. chair) to how that thing is used (e.g. copyrighted music that cannot be copied) (Frase 2013).

While our points may seem esoteric, IPRs have everyday consequences for you and everyone else. An example might help to illustrate this. Recently, several businesses, including John Deere and General Motors, have sought to limit the rights of people to change the software and other electronic elements in the tractors and cars they sell. According to these businesses, the IPRs behind the software and electronics gives them the right to stop how buyers use or adapt the tractors and cars. In fact, the businesses claim that any attempt to interfere with the machine would be an infringement of IPRs. As Wiens (2015) writes, 'John Deere and General Motors want to eviscerate the notion of ownership. Sure, we pay for their vehicles. But we don't own them. Not according to their corporate lawyers, anyway'.

Conclusion

In this chapter we have tried to illustrate some of the issues that arise with the extension and strengthening of private property, especially as this relates to the intangible, intellectual, relational and emotional aspects of our lives. First, we outlined how property and ownership are understood in a number of orthodox perspectives, including law and neoclassical economics. Second, we provided a critique of these perspectives and discussed some alternatives to capitalist property rights; these included commons-based production and the sharing economy. While neither is perfect, it is clear that commons-based production and ownership represents a clearer alternative than the sharing economy; the latter largely reflects existing assumptions about private property and new forms of rent-seeking, or rentiership. Finally, we discussed the growth of IPRs and the implications they have for our lives. We suggested that IPRs are unlikely to encourage the outcomes desired of them – e.g. greater innovation and creativity – and might even lead to the opposite – e.g. stagnation.

Suggested readings

- Drahos, P. and Braithewaite, J. (2004) *Who Owns the Knowledge Economy?*, The Corner House Briefing Paper 32: www.thecornerhouse.org.uk/resource/ who-owns-knowledge-economy (accessed May 2015).
- Frase, P. (2013) 'Property and theft', *Jacobin* (September): www.jacobinmag. com/2013/09/property-and-theft/ (accessed May 2015).
- Hardin, G. (1968) 'The tragedy of the commons', *Science*, Vol.162, pp.1243–1248.
- Heller, M. (1998) 'The tragedy of the anticommons: Property in the transition from Marx to markets', *Harvard Law Review*, Vol.111, pp.621–688.
- Introduction, May, C. (2010) *The Political Economy of Intellectual Property Rights*, London, Routledge.

Bibliography

Alchian, A. and Demsetz, H. (1972) 'Production, information costs and economic organization', *American Economic Review*, Vol.62, pp.777–795.

Birch, K. (2015) *We Have Never Been Neoliberal: A Manifesto for a Doomed Youth*, Winchester, Zero Books.

Birch, K. and Siemiatycki, M. (2016) 'Neoliberalism and the geographies of marketization: The entangling of state and markets', *Progress in Human Geography*, Vol.40, pp.177–198.

Birch, K., Levidow, L. and Papaioannou, T. (2014) 'Self-fulfilling prophecies of the European knowledge-based bio-economy: The discursive shaping of institutional and policy frameworks in the bio-pharmaceuticals sector', *Journal of the Knowledge Economy*, Vol.5, pp.1–18.

Bishop, J. (1997) 'Locke's theory of original appropriation and the right of settlement in Iroquois territory', *Canadian Journal of Philosophy*, Vol.27, pp.311–337.

Boutang, Y.M. (2011) *Cognitive Capitalism*, Cambridge, Polity.

Clifton, J., Comín, F. and Díaz-Fuentes, D. (2006) 'Privatization in the European Union: Pragmatic, ideological,

inevitable?', *Journal of European Public Policy*, Vol.13, pp.736–756.

Coase, R. (1937) 'The nature of the firm', *Economica*, Vol.4, pp.386–405.

Coase, R. (1960) 'The problem of social cost', *Journal of Law and Economics*, Vol.3, pp.1–44.

Crouch, C. (2011) *The Strange Non-death of Neoliberalism*, Cambridge, Polity.

Cumbers, A. (2012) *Rethinking Public Ownership*, London, Zed Books.

Deibel, E. (2014) 'Open generic code: On open source in the life sciences', *Life Sciences, Policy and Society*, Vol.10, pp.1–23.

Drahos, P. with Braithewaite, J. (2002) *Information Feudalism*, London, Earthscan.

Drahos, P. and Braithewaite, J. (2004) 'Who Owns the Knowledge Economy?', The Corner House Briefing Paper 32: www.thecornerhouse.org. uk/resource/who-owns-knowledge-economy (accessed May 2015).

Frase, P. (2013) 'Property and theft', *Jacobin*, September: www.jacobinmag. com/2013/09/property-and-theft/ (accessed May 2015).

Haiven, M. (2014) *Crises of Imagination, Crises of Power: Capitalism, Creativity and the Commons*, London, Zed Books.

Hardin, G. (1968) 'The tragedy of

the commons', *Science*, Vol.162, pp.1243–1248.

Harvey, D. (2003) *The New Imperialism*, Oxford, Oxford University Press.

Heller, M. (1998) 'The tragedy of the anti-commons: Property in the transition from Marx to markets', *Harvard Law Review*, Vol.111, pp.621–688.

Heller, M. (2008) *Gridlock Economy*, New York, Basic Books.

Hope, J. (2008) *Biobazaar*, Cambridge MA, Harvard University Press.

Jensen, M. and Meckling, W. (1976) 'Theory of the firm: Managerial behavior, agency costs and ownership structure', *Journal of Financial Economics*, Vol.3, pp.305–360.

Keen, A. (2015) *The Internet Is Not the Answer*, New York, Atlantic Monthly Press.

McBride, S. and Whiteside, H. (2011) *Private Affluence, Public Austerity*, Halifax NS, Fernwood.

McMurtry, J. (2002) *Value Wars*, London, Pluto Press.

Malleson, T. (2014) *After Occupy: Economic Democracy for the 21st Century*, Oxford, Oxford University Press.

Mann, G. (2013) *Disassembly Required: A Field Guide to Actually Existing Capitalism*, Oakland and Baltimore, AK Press.

Marazzi, C. (2011) *The Violence of Financial Capitalism*, Los Angeles, semiotext(e).

Marx, K. (1867 [1976]) *Capital: Volume 1*, London, Penguin.

May, C. (2010) *The Political Economy of Intellectual Property Rights*, London, Routledge.

Mazzucato, M. (2013) *The Entrepreneurial State*, London, Anthem Press.

Mirowski, P. (2011) *ScienceMart*, Cambridge MA, Harvard University Press.

Nace, T. (2003) *Gangs of America*, San Francisco, Berrett-Koehler.

Ostrom, E. (1990) *Governing the Commons*, Cambridge, Cambridge University Press.

Polanyi, K. (1944 [2001]) *The Great Transformation*, Boston, Beacon Press.

Rifkin, J. (2014) *The Zero Marginal Cost Society*, New York, Palgrave Macmillan.

Robbins, P., Hintz, J. and Moore, S. (2010) *Environment and Society*, Oxford, Wiley-Blackwell.

Sayer, A. (2015) *Why We Can't Afford the Rich*, Bristol, Policy Press.

Skågeby, J. (2015) 'The changing shape of sharing: Digital materiality and moral economies', *Discover Society*, Vol.18 (March): http://discoversociety.org/2015/03/01/the-changing-shape-of-sharing-digital-materiality-and-moral-economies/ (accessed June 2015).

Tully, J. (1994) 'Rediscovering America: The *Two Treatises* and Aboriginal rights', in G.A. Rogers (ed.), *Locke's Philosophy: Content and Context*, Oxford, Clarendon, pp.165–196.

Tyfield, D. (2008) 'Enabling TRIPs: The pharma-biotech-university patent coalition', *Review of International Political Economy*, Vol.15, pp.535–566.

Vickers, J. and Yarrow, G. (1991) 'Economic perspectives on privatization', *The Journal of Economic Perspectives*, Vol.5, pp.111–132.

Weins, K. (2015) 'We can't let John Deere destroy the very idea of ownership', *Wired*, April: www.wired.com/2015/04/dmca-ownership-john-deere/ (accessed June 2015).

Wellen, R. (2013) 'Open access, mega-journals and MOOCs: On the political economy of academic unbundling', *SAGE Open*, Vol.3, pp.1–16.

Wood, E.M. (1998) 'The agrarian origins of capitalism', *Monthly Review*, Vol.50 (July–August): http://monthlyreview.org/1998/07/01/the-agrarian-origins-of-capitalism/ (accessed June 2015).

Index

2007–2008 global financial crisis (GFC),
    5–6, 74, 82, 102, 109, 143, 192, 205,
    225; public reaction to, 73

accumulation by dispossession, 274
Acemoglu, Daron, 124, 125
African Communities League (ACL), 233
agency costs, 60 63
agency theory, 57, 58, 59, 60
Ailenei, Oana, 266
Airbnb, 286
Akter, Kalpona, 231
Albert, Michael, 189
Alchian, Armen, 277
alienation, 181, 182
Amable, Bruno, 112
Amin, Ash, 263
Amin, Samir, 27, 32
anarchism, 187, 188, 223; evolutionary, 188
animal spirits, 185
Anthropocene, 133, 136
anti-austerity movements, 192
anti-trust laws, 202; *see also* Sherman
    Antitrust Act
Apple, 207
Apter, David, *The Politics of
    Modernization*, 30
Arctic Co-operatives Limited (ACL), 235–8
    passim
Argentina, 254, 270
Aristotle, 221
Arrighi, Giovanni, 27; *The Long Twentieth
    Century*, 126
asceticism, 21, 22
Ashoka Foundation, 261
Asiento contract, 34
Association for the Taxation of financial
    Transactions and Aid to Citizens
    (ATTAC), 248

Bakan, Joel, 95; *The Corporation*, 241
Bakunin, Mikhail, 188; *God and the State*,
    244

Ban Ki-moon, 110
Bangladesh, 235
Bangladesh Center for Worker Solidarity,
    231
Bangladesh Consensus, 232
Banker Ladies, 233
banks, 64, 65
Barbados, 34
Barkan, Joshua, 74, 81, 129
Barker, Drucilla, 185
Baxter, Lynne, 71
Beckles, Hilary, 37
Beder, Sharon, 96, 97
Benefit Corporation, 266
Bengal, 39; 1772 famine in, 39
Bentham, Jeremy, 165, 166, 168, 219
Berle, Adolf, 46, 59, 61, 74
Beveridge, William, 245
Big Data, 285
Bill & Melinda Gates Foundation, 79
biosphere, 134
Birch, Kean, 241, 263, 266, 278
Bishop, Matthew, 79
Black Star Line, 233
Blair, Margaret, 62
Blake, William, 26
boards of directors, 93, 94
Boatright, John, 219
Bobbitt, Philip, *Shield of Achilles*, 119
Bolivia, 270
bonuses, executive, 67
'bottom of the pyramid' theory, 229
Bouchard, Marie, 263, 266
bourgeoisie, 17, 180 *see also* class
Boutang, Yann Moulier, 284
Bowie, Norman, 215
Bowman, Scott, 5, 74, 87, 93, 94
Braithewaite, John, 128, 286, 287
branding, 53
Bratton, William, 49
Brazil, 106, 112, 113, 254, 270
Bretton Woods System (BWS), 108, 120,
    126

Columbus, Christopher, 28
Combination Act (1799) (Britain), 243
Commercial Code (2003) (Japan), 65
commodities, fictitious, 8, 141
Commoner, Barry, 134
Commons, John, 182, 190
commons, 136, 137, 189, 278, 281; anti-
    commons, 282; commons-based
    ownership, 284; commons-based
    production, 283, 284; commons-based
    property rights, 283; environmental,
    141; tragedy of, 137, 142, 189, 278, 280
Community Economies Research
    Network (CERN), 237
Companies Acts (Britain), 51
comparative advantage, 31
compensation, 196
competition, 89, 181, 218; limits to, 198;
    market competition, 155, 156
consumption, conspicuous, 182, 183
contracts, nexus of, 50, 51, 57, 58, 59, 62,
    277
control, conceptions of, 52
cooperation, 188
co-operatives, 259, 267
Copyleft licence, 284
corporate governance, 93, 98; internal,
    94, 95
corporate revolution, 5, 42, 45, 46, 48, 52,
    54, 88, 276
corporate social performance, 76
corporate social responsibility (CSR), 71,
    72, 76–84 passim, 128, 258, 261; social
    contract model of, 77; stakeholder
    model of, 77, 78; three-dimensional
    model of, 77; evolution of, 74, 75;
    explicit and implicit, 76
corporate social responsiveness, 76
corporations, 5, 6, 43–50 passim,
    53, 54, 57, 80; as moral agents,
    77; as moral environment, 77; as
    pathological institutions, 241; as
    social institutions, 52; as 'too-big-to-
    fail', 6, 205; as totalizing institutions,
    241; corporate citizenship, 77;
    corporate governance see governance,
    corporate; corporate personhood,
    43, 44, 48, 49, 54; Japanese, 66,
    67; legal definitions of, 50; legal

evolution of, 49; legal structure of, 48;
    multinational corporations (MNCs),
    81, 102, 109, 127, 128, 207, 231, 248,
    250; organizational structure of, 48;
    social service function of, 62; social
    structure of, 48; see also power,
    corporate
Coulthard, Glen, 190, 191
Cox, Robert, 92, 97, 98
Creative Commons licence, 284
Credit Default Swaps (CDSs), 83
credit unions, 235, 267
crowdsourcing, 285
Cuba, 151, 245, 270
Cumbers, Andrew, 278

Dartmouth College vs. Madison (1818)
    (USA), 51
Darwinism, Social, 188
De George, Richard, 215
de Soto, Hernando, *The Mystery of
    Capital*, 124
Deakins, David, 5
Dees, J. Gregory, 261
demesne land, 14
democracy, economic, 253
Demsetz, Harold, 277
Dene people, 236
dependency theory, 32, 33
Derber, Charles, 82, 95
deregulation, 128, 200
determinism, economic, 42, 48, 49, 52
developing countries, 105, 112, 127
development, 30, 31, 125, 228, 230;
    sustainable, 76, 135–6, 139
Devonshire Initiative, 78
Dicken, Peter, 107, 112, 113; *Global Shift*,
    106
Diggers, 243
disclosure, 203, 204
Discovery, Age of, 28
discovery procedure, 155
dispossession, 282, 287
Dodd, Merrick, 61
Donaldson, Thomas, *Corporations and
    Morality*, 77
Drahos, Peter, 286
Drayton, Bill, 261
Drucker, Peter, 245

Food and Drug Administration (FDA) (USA), 198
food labelling, 203
fossil fuels, 145
Foster, John Bellamy, 135
Foucault, Michel, 92
Fourier, Joseph, 263
France, 28, 38, 254, 263; 1848 revolution in, 244
Franklin, Benjamin, 20
Frase, Peter, 282
Fraser, Nancy, 185
free trade, 4, 31, 116, 124
freedom, 16, 160, 174
Freel, Mark, 5
Freeman, R. Edward, *Strategic Management*, 77
Friedman, Milton, 75, 76, 80, 89, 212, 216, 217, 228,
Friedman, Thomas, 26, 29, 104, 124; *The Lexus and the Olive Tree*, 104

Galbraith, John Kenneth, 175
Gap, The, 207
Garden City movement, 132
Garvey, Marcus, 233, 234
General Agreement on Tariffs and Trade (GATT), 108, 120, 123
General Electric, 53
General Motors, 201, 287
Genoa (Italy), 28, 126
geographical indications, protected, 279
Germany, 45, 64, 126; corporate governance system in, 65
Gesell, Silvio, *The Natural Economic Order*, 252
Gibney, Alex, *Enron: The Smartest Guys in the Room*, 98
Gibson-Graham, J. K., 247, 248, 262
Giddens, Anthony, 110
Global Crossing, 97
'Global Minotaur', 126
Global North, 104, 105, 127, 146
Global Reporting Initiative, 78
Global South, 33, 104, 105, 112, 127, 146, 225, 228, 229, 230, 232
globalization, 101–13 *passim*, 117, 128, 207, 248, 249; ages of, 108; alter-globalization movement, 189, 248;

anti-globalization movement, 248; financial, 102, 103
Glover, Jonathan, 79
GNU Public Licence, 284
gold standard, 120, 121
'golden straightjacket', 104, 124
Goldman, Emma, 187, 188
Goldman Sachs, 83, 205
good life, 270
Google, 222, 286
Gordon Nembhard, Jessica, *Collective Courage*, 234
governance, corporate, 49, 57, 61; in Germany, 64, 65, 76; in Japan, 64, 65; relational system of, 76; stakeholder models of, 62, 64, 65, 67; global, 110, 116–21 *passim*, 125–9 *passim*; private, 129
government: big government, 195; government failure, 199, 200, 201; role of labour force in, 64
Graeber, David, *Debt: The First 5000 Years*, 241
Graefe, Peter, 264
Grameen Bank, 232, 267
Great Recession (2009), 102
Greece, 192, 254; 2015 financial crisis in, 225
Green, Michael, 79
Green New Deal, 143
greenhouse gases, 144
Greenpeace, 116
greenwashing, 82, 207
Grenada, 34
Griffin, Keith, 125
gross domestic product (GDP), 106
growth, limits to, 132, 137; *see also* Club of Rome, *Limits to Growth*
guilds, 44
Guyana, 36

Haiti, 235
Hall, Peter, 112
Hardin, Garrett, 137, 142, 189, 278
Harriss, John, *Depoliticizing Development*, 230
Hart, Keith, 226
Harvey, David, 101, 274; *A Brief History of Neoliberalism*, 3

Keynesian National Welfare State
(KNWS), 111
Keynesianism, 111
Khurana, Rakesh, 214
Klein, Naomi, 254
knowledge, 92
Korea, North, 244
Kropotkin, Peter, 188; *Mutual Aid*, 269
Kuiper, Edith, 185

labour: division of, 29, 164 (internal,
159, 160, 161; manufacturing, 158;
social, 152, 155, 158, 159); domestic,
186, 187; labour market, 16, 17, 151;
unpaid, 8, 186; wage labour, 15, 17,
181
labour movement *see* trade unions
labour theory of value, 29, 181
laissez faire thought, 245
land: market for, 15
Latin America: social economy in, 270
Lay, Kenneth, 98
Leadbeater, Charles, 261
Lehman Brothers, 83, 228
Lenin, V. I., 27
Levellers, 243
Lewis, Avi, *The Take*, 254
liberation theory, 233
licensing, 203
limited liability, 49, 50, 54
Lincoln, Abraham, 36
Local Exchange Trading Systems (LETS),
251, 252
Locke, John, 220; *Two Treatises on
Government*, 276, 277
Lohmann, Larry, 145, 146
Long Depression, 74
loyal agent argument, 218
luck, 157
Lukes, Steven, 97; *Power: A Radical View*,
92
Luther, Martin, 21
Lynn, Barry, 89

Macey, Jonathan, 58
Mair, Johanna, 261
Malleson, Thomas, 253, 280
Malthus, Thomas, 135
management studies, 215

managerialism, 45, 46, 54, 75
managers, 51, 52, 57, 59, 60, 63, 76
mandates, 203
Marcos, Ferdinand, 230
marginalism, 169
Marginalist Revolution, 167, 169
market-dominant minorities (MDMs),
229
markets, 2, 5, 6, 46, 47, 88, 149, 232; as
self-correcting, 149, 151, 154; free
markets, 4, 282; labour market, 151;
market exchange, 169, 170; market
failure, 137, 138, 196–9 *passim*;
market forces, 42; political market,
200
Marti, Ignasi, 261
Martin, Roger, 74, 75, 77, 84
Marx, Karl, 13, 17, 18, 23, 24, 152, 158,
159, 180, 181, 182, 221, 241, 244, 274,
276, 277, 282; *A Contribution to the
Critique of Political Economy*, 23; *Das
Kapital*, 13; with Friedrich Engels, *The
Communist Manifesto*, 244
Marxism, 13, 17, 23, 24; 'vulgar' Marxists,
24
Mason, Paul, 245, 246
Mauritius, 36
May, Christopher, 117, 119, 120, 127, 129,
286
McGoey, Linsey, 79
McKay, Adam, *The Big Short*, 82
McKibben, Bill, 145
McLean, Murdith, 262
Means, Gardiner, 46, 59, 74, 89
Meckling, William, 50, 59, 277
Médecins sans Frontières, 4
Menger, Carl, 169
Mennonite Central Committee (USA),
250
mercantilism, 29
merchant companies *see* trading
companies
Métis people, 236
Micklethwait, John, 43, 44
microfinance, 232, 258, 267
Microsoft, 89
Milan (Italy), 28
Millennium Development Goals, 123
Miller, Ethan, 269

Prashad, Vijay, 98
predestination, 21
preference, 171, 172, 175; manipulation
    of, 175
privacy, 222
private interest theory, 201
privatization, 142, 278, 279, 280, 282
Proctor and Gamble, 53
production, 7; means of, 18
profit, 20
Progressive Movement, 199
proletariat, 180, 181
property, 274, 275, 285; as a human right,
    276; collective, 281; criticisms of, 28;
    intellectual *see* intellectual property
    rights (IPRs); legal definitions of, 275;
    personal, 275; private, 9, 151, 275, 276,
    277, 278, 280, 282, 287; 'property is
    theft', 9; real, 275
property rights, 220, 253, 276, 277, 279,
    280, 282, 283
prosumers, 286
Protestant work ethic, 22
Protestantism, 21, 22
Proudhon, Pierre-Joseph, 9, 188, 263
public choice theory, 199, 200, 201
public interest theory, 196–9 *passim*, 201

Rampton, Sheldon, 98
Rana Plaza, fire at, 231
Rankin, Katherine, 232
Rastafarianism, 233
rational choice theory, 204
rationality, 185; bounded, 176; rational
    economic man *see* homo economicus;
    rational ignorance, 200
Rawls, John, 245
Raynolds, Laura, 250
Reagan, Ronald, 200
Red de Trueque network, 252
red tape, 202
Reformation, 21
regulation, 81, 82, 127, 195, 196, 199–201
    passim, 206–8 *passim*; civic, 207,
    208; forms of, 202; of banks, 205;
    private, 128; regulatory arbitrage, 207;
    regulatory capture, 200
Reich, Robert, 82; *The Work of Nations*, 103
religion, 22

rentiership, 15, 282, 283, 286
resistance, logic of, 242
resource scarcity, 135, 145
responsibility, 79, 80, 83
restrictions, 202
Rethinking Economics movement, 163
revolving door, 96, 98, 200
Ricardo, David, 31, 283; *Principles of
    Political Economy and Taxation*, 32
Rifkin, Jeremy, 222, 245, 279
rights, 220, 221, 222; customary, 14, 15;
    human, 54; negative and positive, 220;
    see also intellectual property rights
    (IPRs) *and* property rights
Robber Barons, 74
Robbins, Paul, 144
Robins, Nick, 39
Robinson, James, 124, 125
Rockefeller, John D., 74
Rockefeller Foundation, 228
Rodney, Walter, 27, 36, 225; *How Europe
    Underdeveloped Africa*, 32
Rome, ancient, 43
Rostow, Walt Whitman, *Stages of
    Economic Growth*, 30
rotating savings and credit associations
    (ROSCAs), 235, 238
Rousselière, Damien, 263, 266
Roy, William, 46; *Socializing Capital*, 52
Royal Africa Company, 38
Ruggieri, Andrés, 254
Russia, 106, 112, 113, 244
Russia Company *see* Muscovy Company

Saint-Simon, Henri de, 263
Santa Clara vs. Southern Pacific (1886)
    (USA), 51
Sarbanes-Oxley Act (2002) (USA), 98, 202
Sayer, Andrew, 282
Schumpeterian Competition State (SCS),
    111
Seattle protests (1999) *see* World Trade
    Organization (WTO), 1999 protest
    against
Securities and Exchange Commission
    (SEC) (USA), 83
self-employment, 234, 235
self-interest, 165, 166, 173, 174, 204, 216
self-sufficiency, 14